CIRCULATING BOOK
NOT WITHDRAWN

POVERTY, U. S. A.

THE HISTORICAL RECORD

ADVISORY EDITOR: David J. Rothman
Professor of History, Columbia University

CATHOLIC CHARITIES IN THE UNITED STATES

JOHN O'GRADY

Arno Press & The New York Times
NEW YORK   1971

Reprint Edition 1971 by Arno Press Inc.

LC# 71—137180
ISBN 0—405—03118—1

POVERTY, U.S.A.: THE HISTORICAL RECORD
ISBN for complete set: 0-405-03090-8

Manufactured in the United States of America

CATHOLIC CHARITIES
in the
UNITED STATES

HISTORY AND PROBLEMS

Nihil Obstat

✠THOMAS J. SHAHAN,

Imprimatur

✠MICHAEL J. CURLEY,
Archbishop of Baltimore

BALTIMORE, MD.
July 6, 1931.

Catholic Charities in the United States

HISTORY AND PROBLEMS

John O'Grady, Ph.D., LL.D.

*Professor of Sociology at Catholic University of America
and Trinity College, Washington, D. C.
Secretary, National Conference of Catholic Charities*

With an introduction by
BISHOP SHAHAN

**NATIONAL CONFERENCE OF CATHOLIC CHARITIES
WASHINGTON, D. C.**

Copyright, 1930
JOHN O'GRADY

PRINTED IN U. S.
BY
RANSDELL, INC.

INTRODUCTION

The Magna Charta of Catholic charity was written on Mount Olivet, when Jesus Christ said to His disciples: "For I was hungry, and you gave me to eat; I was thirsty, and you gave me to drink; I was a stranger and you took me in; naked and you covered me; sick and you visited me; I was in prison, and you came to me. . . . Amen I say to you as long as you did it to one of these my least brethren, you did it to me." (Matt. XXV, 35-40.) In this brief but divine conspectus of the opportunities and duties of charity at the dawn of the Christian era, we read the first page, as it were, of that consuming love of our neighbor in Jesus Christ that transcended at once all human barriers and, despite whatever obstacles and sufferings, swept one day all the knowledge, power and culture of the Mediterranean world into the bosom of Holy Church. By His own life of universal beneficence (Acts X, 38) and by the exemplary parable of the Good Samaritan (Luke X, 33) Jesus Christ interpreted beyond cavil the practical import of His new social charter. It is this new thing in the history of mankind, the charity of Jesus Christ, that tided over the moribund ancient world into a haven of security, built up a firm religious and social framework for the rude and uncivilized men who inherited its immense site and its mighty wreckage, and breathed into their new political and social order the fire and vigor of Christian convictions as to the moral dignity and the social rights and obligations of all men.

Catholic charity in the United States, by whatever links of time and distance, is closely related to every large phase of Catholic religious and social life of the past, east and west. The men of Germany and Ireland, of Spain and France, and Italy and Poland, who brought the Catholic faith to these shores in the last century were deeply imbued with the belief and practice of their races as to the traditional character and responsibilities of the great Christian virtue that had raised their ancestry from the lowest moral levels to the fullness of Christian life and a rich multiplicity of its works. They were ready, therefore, to respond, whenever occasion offered, to the claims and suggestions, even to the ideals of Christian Charity. The evidence of this is spread on every page of this volume. But while they had nothing to learn as to the nature and gravity of their fraternal obligations in Jesus Christ, they were confronted by appalling obstacles in the way of their fulfillment. They had come to the United States in almost horde-like numbers, torn suddenly from their ancient seats in Europe, every human tie rudely broken, the experience and training of their humble class or strata no longer available, too often unhappy victims of religious and racial hatred or dislike that affected them seriously in a social and economic way. The integrity of their families, the faith of their children, their natural rights as parents in their offspring, loomed large in their thoughts and inspired their earliest efforts and sacrifices. Local associations, religious and racial, humble asylums and refuges, miscellaneous institutions, arose as if by magic, only to disappear and arise elsewhere as the restless multitude moved westward in search of better conditions, ever disintegrating along its endless trek.

After the Civil War the American Catholic eye took in a larger sweep of duties and opportunities in the domain of charity. Ecclesiastical concern and interest kept pace with the new growth of Catholic life both as to works of charity and their administration, until from ocean to ocean there spread a very creditable network of charitable institutional life administered with incomparable devotion by many religious communities of men and women.

For the first time this remarkable social phenomenon offers

INTRODUCTION

the broad lines of its history and its available statistics in these valuable pages that represent the patient toil and conscientious research of some years. It is a comprehensive work, and as such will no doubt encourage much special research in many quarters, documentary, biographical, and descriptive. Thus arise in due time those "Annals and Chronicles" of our American Catholic charities that are truly the sweet odor of the Gospel and a mirror of the best Christian life.

A really complete history of American Catholic charity ought to register, if it were possible, all personal works, the vast output of private charities. This, however, is not in keeping with the spirit or letter of the Gospel. On the other hand, such a history could very well incorporate a multitude of charities, national in extent, occasioned by public disasters and misfortunes, never long absent from the scene of life; the charities that war calls forth on such an enormous scale; the charities exercised by and through our missionaries in heathen lands. Were it possible to chronicle all this as an appendix to the history of organized and institutional charity, what an edifying page it would make in the lurid record of our daily life!

Let us be content meanwhile with this splendid record of a century of our organized charities, and let us not cease from their support and development! Only too often our Catholic faith does not register any higher than our devotion to the cause and the interest of Catholic charity.

✠Thomas J. Shahan.

Washington, D. C.
July 3, 1931.

AUTHOR'S PREFACE

For those who are engaged in social work the present is very real. Scores of problems crowd into every day demanding an immediate solution. So much attention is consumed by present situations that we have little time for the past. We are inclined to lose sight of the forces and circumstances that gave birth to our institutions and organizations.

It is very clear that we cannot understand the ideals, traditions and attitudes that find expression in charitable agencies without some appreciation of their genesis. Every one of them carries with it the impress of many conflicts, many personalities, many successes and failures. These have become a part of its very life. Unconsciously they color its outlook and influence its attitudes.

There would be a better understanding of the problems of Catholic charities in the United States today if more was known about their history. As a student and worker in Catholic charities for many years the writer has found a constant urge to delve deeper into the past. He has been amazed at times to find how little Catholic organizations and institutions know about their own history. He could not fail to notice a very striking connection between the lack of historical perspective and their outlook on present problems.

Our charities have been one of the most important points of contact with American life. They represent an effort on our part to meet the great social problems growing out of American life. They represent the struggles of the immigrants to work out their own problems in their own way. Catholic charities also express the immigrant's answer to the efforts of American Protestantism on his behalf. One can not appreciate the problems of Catholic charities without an understanding of the social problems and movements of the country.

A history of Catholic charities is a very component chapter in the history of American social work and thus far it has been a neglected chapter. Non-sectarian and Protestant social work has grown out of the conditions created by immigration. Catholic charitable institutions and organizations emerged from these same conditions. For many years Catholic and non-Catholic charities approached the immigrant from different angles. They were inspired by different philosophies. In recent years there has been a decided drift towards more cooperative relationships in dealing with concrete problems of poverty, neglect, delinquency, health, leisure time and social reform.

Our knowledge of the history of Catholic charities in the United States has been advanced very greatly by the publication of histories of religious communities and diocesan histories that have appeared in recent years. It is to be hoped that before many years every religious community and every diocese will have a history worthy of its traditions.

The writer would like to regard this book as the product of the cooperative thinking of hundreds of persons engaged in Catholic social and charitable work in the United States. Without the active cooperation of the various religious communities, lay organizations and diocesan agencies of Catholic charities it could never have been possible. Among those who have aided in the assembling of the material and the making of extensive bibliographical researches special thanks are due to my co-workers, Alice Padgett, Catherine O'Connor, Jane Gallagher and Miriam Cavanagh. I also wish to thank the students of St. Mary's Seminary, Baltimore, and Catherine McMahon for assistance in reading a number of Catholic periodicals. Appreciation is also due to Rev. Francis P. Havey of the Sulpician Seminary, Washington, D. C., for placing at my disposal his very valuable notes representing many years of patient effort and toil.

Bishop Thomas J. Shahan, Rector Emeritus of the Catholic University of America, and Doctor Richard J. Purcell, Professor of History at the same university, have very generously examined the entire manuscript. The volume owes so much to Bishop Shahan that he might well lay claim to joint authorship. Dr. Purcell is responsible for a number of important changes in the presentation of the material. He devoted weeks of patient effort to the editing of the manuscript. The author, however, assumes full and exclusive responsibility for the form and content of the volume. The only merit he claims for it is that it represents a pioneer effort in a new and uncultivated field. He hopes that the work may be an inspiration to others to cover the field more thoroughly.

JOHN O'GRADY.

Washington, D. C.
July 3, 1931.

CONTENTS

CHAPTER I

THE PIONEERS

Effects of Reformation on English Catholic Beneficence.—Opposition of American Colonists to Catholicism.—Catholic Population of Colonies After Revolution.—Catholic Population in Time of Bishop Carroll.—Society of St. Sulpice.—Visitation Convent at Georgetown.—Sisters of Charity.—Sisters of Loretto.—Sisters of Charity of Nazareth.—Sisters of St. Dominic.—Sisterhoods of the Colored.......pp. 1-17

CHAPTER II

THE FIRST FRUITS

The Ursuline Sisters.—Sisters of Charity of Emmitsburg, Maryland.—Sisters of Charity in Philadelphia.—St. John's Orphanage in Philadelphia.—Sisters of Charity in New York.—Sisters of Charity in Baltimore.—Sisters of Charity in St. Louis.—Sisters of Charity in Cincinnati.—Sisters of Charity in Boston.—Numerous Calls Made on Mother Seton's Daughters.—Other Religious Communities.—Recapitulation.................................pp. 18-33

CHAPTER III

THE OLD IMMIGRATION AND ITS PROBLEMS

National Origins in 1920.—Old and New Immigration Issues.—Irish Immigration, 1840-1860.—German Immigration After 1830.—Land Values in the Early Days.—Contribution of Early Irish Immigrants to Canal Building - Irish Immigrants as Unskilled Laborers.—Creation in 1847 of Board of Commissioners of Immigration.—Castle Garden—First Immigration Depot.—Regulation of Immigration Becomes Federal Concern..................pp. 34-49

CHAPTER IV
COLONIZATION AS A PANACEA

Free Land the Loadstone.—The Stages in Land Development.—Canals First Channels of Communication.—Irish Immigrant Becomes American Industrial Worker.—Irish Immigrants Not Purely Agricultural People.—McGee's Irish Colonization Scheme Suffers.—Maryland and Kentucky Catholic Settlements Become Patterns.—Father Demetrius Gallitzin's Pennsylvania Settlement.—Irish Immigrant Society Organized in New York.—Organized Catholic Colonies in Nebraska and Minnesota.—The Minnesota Irish Immigration Society.—Archbishop Ireland and Catholic Colonization in Minnesota.—Other Catholic Settlements.—Association Formed to Nationalize Catholic Colonization.—Immigrant Bureau at Castle Garden in 1883.—Weak and Strong Points of Catholic Colonization.pp. 50-70

CHAPTER V
CATHOLIC CHILD-CARE BEFORE THE CIVIL WAR

Early Child-Caring Institutions.—Diocesan Sees Established, 1840-1860—An Asylum in Rochester.—An Asylum in Albany.—The Orphan Asylum as a Unit of the Parish.—The Development of Orphan Asylums.—The Parish Still Active in the Development of Orphan Asylums.—An Orphan Asylum in Pittsburgh.—The Parish Orphan Asylum Now Almost Extinct.—Orphan Asylums Become City-Wide Responsibility.—The Irish and Orphan Asylums.—The Germans and Orphan Asylums.—German Catholic Orphan Associations.—Cincinnati the Pioneer City in Organized Care of German Children.—German Orphanage in St. Louis.—German Orphanage in Louisville.—Buffalo's Care of German Orphans.—Philadelphia and New York Organize German Asylums.—Baltimore and

Pittsburgh Care for German Orphans.—The Sisters of Charity of Emmitsburg and Child-Caring Institutions.—The Objectives of the Sisters of Charity of Emmitsburg.—The growing Autonomy of the Dioceses.—The Sisters of Charity of Emmitsburg Reluctant to Care for Boys.—The Bishops' Task of Providing for the Dependent Children of the Immigrants.—Care of Dependent Children in Chicago.—Early Efforts of the Dioceses of Buffalo, Cleveland, Milwaukee and St. Paul to Provide for Orphaned Children.—The Resources of the Church in Coping with the Problem of Child-Care.—Contrast Between Early Catholic Institutions and Those After 1840................pp. 71-88

CHAPTER VI

AFTER THE ALMSHOUSES

Catholic Population Increases After 1860.—Eighteen Dioceses Formed Between 1860 and 1880.—Older Dioceses Have Increased Problems After Civil War.—Beginnings of Catholic Lay Organizations.—Removal of Children From Almshouses First Step in Catholic Child-Care.—Almshouses in Ohio in 1867.—Massachusetts Has First State Board of Charities.—Monson Almshouse, Massachusetts.—Beginnings of a State System of Child-Placing in Massachusetts.—Ohio, Michigan and New York Plan Removal of Children From Almshouses.—Meeting of Various Boards of Charities in 1876.—Meeting Influences Six States to Make Separate Provision for Children.—American Philosophy of Child-Care Soon Determined.—Early State Policies of Child-Care Governed Later Programs.—Children are Placed in Free Western Homes.—Catholic Sisterhoods Look to Institutions for Immigrant Children.—Catholic Institutions a Preventive Against Protestantism.—Protestant Reaction Against Catholic Institutions.—Per Capita Payments to Catholic Institutions Attacked.—New York State Board of Charities Makes Reasonable Recommendations.—Protestant Agencies Continue Their Attack Against Per Capita Payments.—Drift Towards Public Child-Care...pp. 89-105

CHAPTER VII

A VOCATIONAL PROGRAM FOR THE CHILDREN OF THE IMMIGRANT

Proselytism of Early Protestant Child-Placing Organizations.—Barter of Irish Catholic Children.—Lack of Catholic Facilities for Children Over Twelve Years of Age.—First Provision for Catholic Children Over Twelve Years of Age.—Hospital Organized in Baltimore for Fever-Stricken Irish Immigrants.—Second Attempt to Provide for Boys Over Twelve Years of Age.—Boston Protectory for Catholic Boys.—New Era of Protection of Catholic Children.—Real Catholic Leadership Follows Civil War.—Dr. Ives Organizes Society for Protection of Destitute Catholic Children.—Beginnings of the New York Catholic Protectory.—New York Catholic Protectory Receives State and City Aid.—Early Policies of the New York Protectory.—Placing Program of Protectory Proves Unfeasible.—Lincolndale Agricultural School for Boys.—Larger Catholic Institutional Program Urged.—Archbishop Spalding Furthers Catholic Industrial School Movement.—St. Mary's Industrial School, Baltimore.—St. John's Protectory, Buffalo.—Industrial Schools Established in Seventies and Eighties.—Institutions Complementing the Industrial Schools.—Catholic Industrial School Movement Languishes After 1885.—Catholic Industrial Schools After 1900.—Problem of Personnel.—A Preventive Program for Juvenile Delinquency..............................pp. 106-128

CHAPTER VIII

MOTHERS AND INFANTS

Growing Need of Provision for Infants.—Buffalo Diocese First Recognizes Problem.—Bishop Timon Establishes First Infant Home.—St. Louis Diocese Has Second Infant

Home.—Infant Homes Established Between 1855 and 1870.—New York Foundling Hospital.—Recognition of Obligations to Mother as Well as Child.—Out-Door Department of New York Foundling Hospital.—System of Wet Nursing Dies Out.—Care of Infants and Mothers Recognized as Inseparable.—Infant Homes Evolve Plans for Permanent Care of Children.—New York Foundling Hospital Finds Free Homes in West.—Early Child-Placing Systems Break Down.—The New York Foundling Hospital Adopts Boarding Home Plan.—Infant and Maternity Homes a Part of Diocesan Programs After 1870.—Infant and Maternity Homes Established Between 1890 and 1910.—Infant and Maternity Homes Established After 1910.—Catholic Infant and Maternity Homes in United States.—Medical Standards of Infant and Maternity Homes.—Basic Objectives of Early Catholic Infant and Maternity Homes.—The Recent Modified Attitude of Catholic Infant and Maternity Homes.—Social Service in Infant and Maternity Homes.—Smaller Dioceses Use Homes of Larger Dioceses.—Casework Service in After-Care.....pp. 129-146

CHAPTER IX

CHILD-CARE AFTER THE CIVIL WAR

American Catholic Charities a Defense Against Protestantism.—Recognition of the Child's Religion in Child-Care Programs.—Public Child-Caring Agencies Remained Protestant in Character.—Catholic Children's Homes Established Between 1885 and 1900.—First Organized Movement to Protect Religious Life of Catholic Children Under Public Care.—Catholic Children's Homes Established Between 1900 and 1915.—Catholic Children's Homes Established Since 1915.—Number of Old Institutions Closed After 1915.—The Year 1915 Marks New Era in Child-Care.—Early Catholic Institutions Founded on Racial as Well as

Religious Basis.—Later Catholic Institutions Followed Same Trends.—French Canadians Have Own Institutions for Children.—Poles Have Own Institutions for Children.—Bohemian Catholics Have Own Institutions for Children.—Italians Develop Special Facilities for Their Children.—New Developments Will Rest on Fact Basis.—Negro Somewhat Overlooked by American Catholic Charities.—Catholic Institutions for Colored Children, pp. 147-162

CHAPTER X

PROTECTIVE CARE FOR GIRLS

Immigrant Women Find New Conditions.—Beginning of Protective Program for Women and Girls.—Two European Communities Responsible for Catholic Protective Program. —Sisters of Our Lady of Charity of Refuge.—Sisters of Our Lady of Charity of the Good Shepherd.—Good Shepherd Program Represents New Attitude in the United States.—Elements of Good Shepherd Program.—Sisters of Mercy.—New York Foundation.—Pittsburgh Foundation.— Sisters of Mercy Depart from Original Purpose.—The Good Shepherd Sisters Represent Single Objective.—Philadelphia Foundation of Sisters of the Good Shepherd.—St. Louis Foundation of Sisters of the Good Shepherd.—Good Shepherd Foundations Between 1850 and 1860.—Good Shepherd Foundations Between 1860 and 1870.—Good Shepherd Foundations Between 1870 and 1914.—Sisters of Our Lady of Charity of Refuge.—Admission Policies of Good Shepherd Homes.—System of Classification.—Religion as a Reformative Influence.—Health Programs in Good Shepherd Homes.—Health Program of Cleveland Home.—Mt. St. Mary's Training School, Cincinnati.—Educational Programs.—The Magdalen.—Early Good Shepherd Homes Largely Self-Supporting.—Recent Changes in Financial

Programs.—Good Shepherd Homes Part of Larger Program.—Other Religious Communities Interested in Delinquents..pp. 163-182

CHAPTER XI

CATHOLIC CARE OF THE SICK

The Sisters of Charity Enter the Hospital Field in the United States.—First Organized Catholic Hospital.—The Oldest Hospital in Michigan.—St. Mary's Hospital, Rochester, New York, Illustrates Early Difficulties in Hospital Work.—The Sisters of Mercy Take Up Hospital Work.—Sisters of St. Joseph of Carondelet Third Religious Community in Hospital Field.—Public Charities in the United States Before Civil War.—The Work of Catholic Sisterhoods in Hospitals an Inspiration.—The Catholic Sisterhoods in the Epidemics.—The Catholic Sisterhoods in the Civil War.—The Value of Nursing Done by the Sisterhoods.—Influence of War Activities in Evolution of Catholic Hospitals in the United States.—The Development of Catholic Hospitals After the Civil War.—Hospitals Follow the Pioneers in the Western States.—Industrial Hospitals After the Civil War.—Nature's Elements Play Part in Introduction of Sisters Into Hospital Work.—The German Sisterhoods An Important Factor in Hospital History.—An Italian Community Provides Hospitalization for Its Own People.—An Interpretation of the Rapid Rise of Hospitals Since 1870.—Schools of Nursing in Connection With Catholic Hospitals.—Higher Standards for the Nursing Profession.—The Evolution of the Catholic Hospital.—Some Deficiencies in the Social Service Programs of Catholic Hospitals.—Social Service Department in Relation to the Diocesan Charities.—The Convalescent Home as a Complement to the Modern Hospital.—Special Hospitals: Institutions for Mental and Nervous Cases.—Institutions for the Tubercular.—Institutions for Incurables.—Home Nursing..........pp. 183-212

CHAPTER XII

CATHOLIC CARE OF THE AGED

Almshouse Only Type of Institution in Early Nineteenth Century.—Almshouses Essentially Protestant Institutions.—Change in Attitude of Almshouse Officials After 1870.—Almshouses Resist Change.—Earliest Catholic Homes for Aged in the United States.—The Little Sisters of the Poor.—Brooklyn Cradle of the Little Sisters of the Poor in the United States.—Cincinnati Foundation.—New Orleans Foundation.— Baltimore Foundation.— St. Louis Foundation.—Philadelphia Foundation.—Louisville Foundation.—Boston, Cleveland and New York City Foundations.—Washington Foundation.—Albany Foundation.—The Year 1872 Sees Thirteen Homes of Little Sisters of the Poor.— Richmond Foundation.— Chicago Foundation.—Twenty-six Foundations Since 1881.—Story of the Little Sisters of the Poor.—Little Sisters Dedicated to the Destitute Poor.—Little Sisters Disregard Social Work Canons.—Aged Homes of Other Religious Communities.—Immigrant Groups Establish Aged Homes.—Difficulties of Financing Part Pay and No Pay Aged Homes.—St. Teresa's Home of Cincinnati Solves Financial Problem.—Catholic Home for Aged Ladies, Washington, D. C., Has Successful Program.—Diocesan Homes for Aged.—Institutional Programs Alone Can Not Solve Problem of Aged........pp. 213-234

CHAPTER XIII

THE SOCIETY OF ST. VINCENT DE PAUL AND THE DEVELOPMENT OF CATHOLIC CHARITIES

Early America Dominated by Protestant Spirit.—First Charities of Catholic Immigrant Racial in Origin.—Ozanam's Program of Practical Charity.—The Beginnings of the St. Vincent de Paul Society.—St. Vincent de Paul Society in United States First Brought Together Various Immigrant

Groups.—First American Conference of St. Vincent de Paul in St. Louis.—Elder Mullanphy National Figure in Catholic Work in United States.—Society of St. Vincent de Paul Made Rapid Progress in United States.—Sunday School and Secular School Work First Projects of Society.—Society Interests Itself in Destitute Immigrant Catholic Children.—Priests' Advent Has Marked Departure of Laity in Catechetical Work.—Society First Brings Consolation of Religion to Prisoners.—Society Devotes Attention to Relationship of Ill Health to Poverty.—Summer Outings Become an Absorbing Project.—Apostolate of the Sea.—Society Warns Against Catholic Child-Placing in West.—The Catholic Home Bureau of New York.—Society Undertakes Spiritual Care of Catholic Children in Houses of Refuge.—Organized Recreation Programs Undertaken by Society.—The Ozanam Association.—Relationship Between St. Vincent de Paul and Charity Organization Society.—Society Pioneering Group Since Civil War.—Society Adverse in Beginning to Paid Service.—Central Office Established by Society in Baltimore.—Adjustment of Society to Central Agencies Under Diocesan Auspices.—Society Has Aided Development of National Outlook in Catholic Charities.—Division of Organization of Society of St. Vincent de Paul in the United States.—The National Meetings of the Society of St. Vincent de Paul as a Stimulus to Catholic Charities in the United States.—Agitation for the Reorganization of the Society of St. Vincent de Paul in the United States.—The Society of St. Vincent de Paul Takes Initiative in Organizing Catholic Charities.—Organization of Catholic Women's Charitable Societies.—National Conference of Catholic Charities.—The Literature of the Catholic Charities Movement.—The Conference a Union of Catholic Viewpoints.—The Vincentians the Backbone of the National Conference.—A Catholic Charities Monthly Advocated.—The Vincentians' Part in Formulating Standards of American Philanthropy.—The Influence of the Vincentians Through the National Conference on Child Welfare.—A True Evaluation of the Society of St. Vincent de Paul...................................pp. 235-271

CHAPTER XIV

THE NEW IMMIGRATION AND ITS PROBLEMS

Industries Attract Immigrants After 1880.—Immigration from Southern and Eastern Europe.—Racial Differences Retard Leadership Development.—Catholic Church Feels Strain of New Immigration Tides.—Immigrants Form Insurance Associations.—The Immigrant's Contribution to American Industry.—Problems Facing the Immigrant.—Growing Opposition to the Immigrant.........pp. 272-286

CHAPTER XV

THE FRINGES OF PARISH LIFE

New Emphasis on Poverty in Relation to Home Conditions.—Settlement Movement Offers First-Hand Contact With Poor.—Settlement Movement an Awakener for Catholics.—First Catholic Settlement, Santa Maria Institute, Cincinnati.—Catholic Settlement Movement Gains Through Leadership of Converts.—St. Rose's Settlement, New York City.—Living Among Poor, the Basic Principle of Religious.—Settlements are Organized under Both Lay and Religious Auspices.—Brownson House, Los Angeles.—Settlement Program for Mexican Immigrants in Los Angeles Diocese.—Christ Child Society, Washington, D. C.—Merrick House, Cleveland.—Weinman Club, Detroit.—Margaret Barry Settlement, Minneapolis.—Madonna Center, Chicago.—Charles House. Rochester, New York.—World War Gives Impetus to Settlement Work.—The National Catholic War Council.—Settlements Aided by National Catholic War Council.—Mexican Problems in Southwest.—European Immigrant Problems in East and Middle West.—

Work of Sisters of Charity in Cincinnati Marks New Epoch in Catholic Charity.—Settlements of Servants of the Immaculate Heart of Mary and the Franciscan Sisters of the Atonement.—Settlements of Helpers of the Holy Souls.—Newly Established Religious Communities Have Important Part in Settlement Work.—Reduced Immigration Has Influenced Settlement Movement...............pp. 287-307

CHAPTER XVI
A SUPPORT FOR THE HOME

First Institutions a Safeguard of Religious Life of Children.—Recognition of Need for Complete Child Welfare Program.—The First Catholic Day Nursery.—Religious Apostolate and Day Nursery Development.—Rapid Spread of Day Nurseries in Nineties.—St. Joseph's Day Nursery, New York City.—St. Elizabeth's Day Nursery, Chicago.—Mission Helpers, Servants of the Sacred Heart, Make Departure in Nursery Programs.—Day Nurseries in Cincinnati and Cleveland.—Place of Day Nursery in Social Work Program.—Diocesan Charities Lend Hand to Day Nurseries.
pp. 308-317

CHAPTER XVII
THE CONTRIBUTION OF CATHOLIC WOMEN

Women the Pioneers in Parish Charitable Organizations.—Earliest Charitable Societies of Women.—Women's Organizations Local in Character.—The Ladies of Charity.—The Association of Catholic Charities of New York City.—The Broader Viewpoint of the Association of Catholic Charities of New York.—Development of the Ladies of Charity.—The Queen's Daughters.—St. Margaret's Daughters—Catholic Women as a Factor in the Financing of Charitable Institutions.—The New Era of Women's Organizations.—The Christ Child Society of Washington.—Branches of the Christ Child Society.—Beginning of a National Women's

Organization.—Travelers' Aid Program of the Catholic Woman's League of Chicago.—Catholic Women's Leagues of Brooklyn and Pittsburgh.—Guild of Catholic Women of St. Paul.—The League of Catholic Women in Detroit.—Further Expansion of Leagues of Catholic Women in the United States.—Protective Work for Girls Adopted by Women's Organizations.—The Big Sister Movement.—The Catholic Daughters of America.—Early German Benevolent Societies.—The Central Verein of America.—The Federation of German Catholic Women's Societies.—Post-War Developments in Catholic Social Work.—Catholic Women's Organizations in a Coordinated Program.—The Survival of the Fittest.—New Interests Inspired by National Council of Catholic Women.—The National Council of Catholic Women and the National Catholic Welfare Conference.—Origin of National Council of Catholic Women.—The National Council Subdivides Into Diocesan Councils.—The Program of the Diocesan Councils of Catholic Women.—Problems of the Diocesan Councils.—The National Catholic School of Social Service.—The Breadth of Interest of the National Council of Catholic Women..........pp. 318-342

CHAPTER XVIII

PRODUCTS OF THE SOIL

Early American Church Struggles to Meet Needs.—Communities of American Origin Arise.—Sisters of Charity of the Blessed Virgin Mary of Philadelphia.—Sisters of Charity of the Blessed Virgin Mary of Dubuque.—Oblate Sisters and Holy Family Sisters Undertake Work for Colored.—Sisters, Servants of the Immaculate Heart of Mary.—American Religious Communities Become Localized.—Sisters of Charity of Leavenworth.—Franciscan Sisters of Glen Riddle.—Franciscan Sisters of Buffalo.—Franciscan Sisters of Syracuse.—Sisters of St. Agnes.—New Religious

Communities Devoted to Catechetical Work.—Sisters of the Holy Family, San Francisco.—Missionary Servants of the Blessed Trinity.—Parish Visitors of the Immaculate Heart of Mary.—Society of Missionary Catechists.—Handmaids of the Most Pure Heart of Mary.—Sisters of the Blessed Sacrament for Indian and Colored People.—Mission Helpers, Servants of the Sacred Heart.—Home Nursing Communities are Formed.—Sisters of St. Mary.—Dominican Sisters of the Sick Poor.—Congregation of Dominican Sisters of St. Rose of Lima.—Foreign Mission Sisters of St. Dominic.—Franciscan Sisters of the Atonement.—Dominican Sisters of St. Catherine Di Ricci.—Religious Communities with a Racial Appeal.—Sisters of St. Casimir.—Sisters of SS. Cyril and Methodius.................pp. 343-368

CHAPTER XIX

THE CALL TO OTHER LANDS

The Immigrants and Early Religious Life of America.—The Sulpicians Lay Foundations of American Catholic Charities.—The Fruits of the Catholic Revival in France and Germany.—The American Church Welcomes European Assistance.—The New York Children's Aid Societies.—Child-Placing Program of New York Children's Aid Society.—The Children's Mission to Children.—The Association for Improving the Condition of the Poor.—Protestantism Fights for Self-Preservation.—Poverty of the Catholic Church in America.—Both Schools and Institutions of America Protestant in Character.—Religious Communities Active in Charitable Field Between 1830 and 1860.—Basic Principle of European Religious Communities of Women.—The Sisters of Mercy.—The Evolution of the Work of the Sisters of Mercy in the United States.—European Religious Communities Follow Plan of Pioneer American Communities.—The Sisters of St. Joseph of Carondelet.—The Brothers and Sisters of the Holy Cross.—The Sisters Marianites of the Holy Cross.—The Sisters of Providence of St. Mary-of-the-Woods.—The Franciscan Sisters of Oldenburg.—The Sisters of the Precious Blood.—The Benedictine Sisters.—Sisters of the Presentation of the Blessed Virgin Mary.—The Sisters of Charity of St. Augustine.—Programs of Newly Arrived European Communities Shaped by American Needs.—Some European Communities Adhere to Original Objectives.—Factors Making for Uniformity of Good Shepherd Sisters' Work.—The Sisters of the Poor of St. Francis.—French Communities Aid American Charities, the Grey Nuns.—The Grey Nuns of the Cross and the Grey Nuns of the Sacred Heart.—The Sisters of Charity of Providence.—Advantages and Disadvantages of a Diocesan Community.—The Sisters of the Holy Names of Jesus and Mary.—The Problem of Caring for Male Orphans Intensified by Withdrawal of Sisters of Charity.—The Brotherhoods Partially Solve the Problem of Boys' Asylums.—The Industrial School Movement Impeded by Limited Membership of the Brotherhoods.—Religious Communities of Women from Germany Concentrate on Hospital Organization.—The Poor Handmaids of Jesus Christ.—The Franciscan Sisters, Daughters of the Sacred Hearts of Jesus and Mary.—Sisters of the Third Order of St. Francis of the Holy Family.—Hospital Sisters of St. Francis of Springfield.—Poor Sisters of St. Francis Seraph of the Perpetual Adoration.—The Franciscan Sisters of the Sacred Heart.—The Sisters of Misericorde.—The Little Sisters of the Poor.—Diocesan Responsibility for Child-Care After the Civil War.—Religious Communities Entering the Charitable Field in the United States After the Civil War.—The Sisters of Charity of the Incarnate Word.—European Religious Communities Devoted to the Welfare of Their Own People.—The Felician Sisters.—The Sisters of the Holy Family of Nazareth.—The Missionary Sisters of the Sacred Heart.—The Missionary Sisters of the Third Order of St.

Francis.—The Home Missionary Service Attracts New Communities.—The Sisters of Bon Secours.—The Little Sisters of the Assumption.—The Society of the Helpers of the Holy Souls.—The Sisters of the Little Company of Mary and the Sisters of the Divine Saviour.—The Missionary Sisters, Servants of the Holy Ghost.—French Anti-Clericalism of Present Century Aids Catholic Charities of the United States.—Latest European Communities Coming to the United States for Social Service.—The Church in America Becomes of Age............................pp. 369-415

CHAPTER XX

TOWARDS A COORDINATED PROGRAM

The Orphanage as a Diocesan Responsibility.—A Broader Horizon for Charitable Organizations.—The Catholic Home Bureau of New York Marks New Era in Catholic Child-Care.—The Pioneers Recognize Trend Towards Home-Placing of Children.—The Catholic Charitable Bureau of Massachusetts.—The Program of the Catholic Charitable Bureau of Boston.—The Diocesan Commission of Hartford.—Juvenile Courts.—The Society of St. Vincent de Paul Sponsors Juvenile Courts.—The Personnel of the Juvenile Court.—The St. Vincent de Paul Society and its Relation to the Charity Organization Society.—Baltimore takes Initiative in City-Wide Catholic Family Welfare Program.—Baltimore Central Office Develops First Coordinated Program.—Leaders in the Movement for a Coordinated Program.—Steps Leading to the National Conference of Catholic Charities.—Charter Members of Original National Conference of Catholic Charities.—Original Objective of the First National Conference of Catholic Charities.—An Indication of Change in Catholic Charities Programs.—The Mission of the National Conference.—Training Courses for Social Workers.—Programs Based on Surveys.—The Trend from Institutional Care to Home

Care for Children.—The Need of Systematic Programs of Child-Placing.—Beginnings of City-Wide Service in Catholic Relief.—The St. Vincent de Paul Society the First Step in Coordinated Program.—Diocesan Directors Appointed.—Financial Support for the Coordinated Program.—The Influence of the Community Chest Movement on the Development of Diocesan Organizations of Charity.—Diocesan Financial Federations.—Dioceses Without Coordinated Programs.—Obstacles in the Way of Further Development of Diocesan Organizations.—Post-War Programs of Catholic Charities.—The Institution as a Basis of a Diocesan Program of Child-Care.—The Drift Towards Boarding Home Care.—Problems of a City-Wide Program of Family Relief.—Diocesan Agencies as a Guide for Parish Organizations.—Protective Care in the Programs of Diocesan Organizations.—Recreational and Character-Building Efforts of Diocesan Organizations.—The Place of the Catholic Hospital in the Diocesan Program.—The Mission of the Diocesan Organization of Catholic Charities to the Laity..pp. 416-449

Bibliography................................pp. 450-456

Index ....pp. 457-475

CHAPTER I
THE PIONEERS

Effects of Reformation on English Catholic Beneficence

The Reformation wiped out every vestige of Catholic beneficence in England. The monasteries, with their associated hospitals, asylums, alms houses, and schools, were confiscated for the benefit of the king, his retainers and favorites. The Catholic religion was outlawed; its practice was forbidden; and a price was placed upon the heads of its priests. Catholics were denied the right of holding property. The government extended to Ireland the same penal code that had been applied in Great Britain, but here the penal laws were applied even more ruthlessly. Under Cromwell thousands of English Puritans were planted in Ireland and given title to Irish lands. While the vast majority of the Irish and a small minority of the English adhered to the old faith, they did so at a desperate sacrifice.

Despoiled of their lands, Catholics were reduced to a condition of poverty. They could have access to the benefits of education only under conditions that were impossible for them. In the face of their situation one wonders how Catholics under English rule retained any vestige of culture; how they developed such splendid leaders to battle for their cause; and how in such a short period after their emancipation they were able to regain much of their old prestige.

English Catholics, generally speaking, belonged to the upper classes. Through their personal influence they were able to have their property retained in their own names or in the names of friends as trustees. With their property saved from confiscation, they were able to educate their children. What was true of the English Catholics in regard to the ownership of land was also true in a lesser degree of some of the Irish

Catholics. At any rate some of the prominent Irish families retained a portion of their land. Many Irishmen, moreover, were able to make considerable money through trade with continental countries.

Through the whole period of persecution Irish Catholics were compelled to depend for education on the hedge-school masters and on continental colleges. Seminaries for the education of Irish priests were organized in Paris, Rome, Salamanca and Louvain. Irish clerics also attended many of the regular continental colleges.

Opposition of American Colonists to Catholicism

The English colonists in North America were even more violently opposed to Catholics than the members of the established Church of England. They had sought a home in the new world in order that they might enjoy religious freedom, but this same freedom they denied to others.

In 1634 Lord Baltimore raised the standard of religious liberty in Maryland; members of all faiths were welcome to his colony and were given freedom to practice their religion, but as soon as the Protestants gained control of the colony they began to persecute the Catholics who had given them a haven not many years before. Like Lord Baltimore, William Penn believed in religious liberty. In 1682 he established his colony of Pennsylvania not only as a refuge for Quakers, but for all who believed in God and the Blessed Trinity. Pennsylvania was the only American colony in which the freedom of Catholics to practice their religion was never interrupted.[1]

Lieutenant Governor Logan of Pennsylvania, writing in 1729 in regard to "a ship from Dublin with 100 Catholics and convicts which had just arrived in Delaware," stated, "It looks as if Ireland is to send all her inhabitants hither, for last week not less than 6 ships arrived and every day 2 or

[1] R. J. Purcell, *The American Nation*, p. 110.

THE PIONEERS 3

3 also arrive.'' When he went on to say, ''The common fear is that if they continue to come they will make themselves masters of the province,'' he probably was not exaggerating.² During the first three quarters of the eighteenth century there was a steady stream of immigration from Ireland to the United States. Between the years 1767 and 1774 the total Irish immigration to the colonies was about 100,000. Two-thirds of this number were Catholics and one-third were descendants of the Protestant settlers in Ireland.³ A conservative estimate has placed the number of persons of Irish birth and descent in the United States in 1790 at 550,000.⁴ It may be assumed that between 100,000 and 150,000 of these were born of Catholic parents or descended from Catholic ancestors.⁵

A recognized historian has estimated that the minimum number of persons of German birth and extraction in this country at the outbreak of the Revolution was 225,000.⁶ To the German element must be added those people of Dutch birth and ancestry whose numbers had increased to a total of 240,000 in 1790. Of the combined German and Dutch elements in the United States in the year 1790 it is probable that not more than 100,000 were of Catholic stock.⁷ The total number of persons of French birth and extraction in the United States in 1790 has been variously estimated. Some historians place it at approximately 100,000. Of these about 75,000 were of Huguenot extraction and 25,000 were descendants of the Catholic Acadian exiles, who had been driven from their native home by the English governors. On account of their inhuman treatment, only about 2,000 of them had retained the faith.⁸

² M. J. O'Brien, *A Hidden Phase of American History*, p. 271.
³ *Ibid.*, p. 289.
⁴ Gerald Shaughnessy, *Has the Immigrant Kept the Faith?* p. 43.
⁵ *Ibid.*, p. 44.
⁶ A. B. Faust, *The German Element in the United States*, Vol. I, p. 285.
⁷ Shaughnessy, *op. cit.*, pp. 47-48.
⁸ *Ibid.*, pp. 50-51.

Catholic Population of Colonies After Revolution

When the colonies threw off the yoke of England their Catholic population was about 22,000 souls, out of a total of 3,000,000.[9] When we compare the estimated figures of Catholic population with the estimated number of persons of Catholic descent we find a wide discrepancy. The early Catholic settlers in the colonies were like the lost tribes of Israel: they faced the perils of an unknown land and found their way through trackless forests. They had not only to face the dangers of an unknown land, but they had also to encounter the most violent religious opposition. Scattered here and there through the wilderness, their names and traditions are preserved throughout the original states from Maine to Georgia. Take up the list of early land grants in Pennsylvania, Maryland, Virginia, North and South Carolina and Georgia and one finds thousands of Irish names. As the early Catholic settlers entered the wilderness there was no priest to follow them. In their native countries, the most extreme persecutions did not deprive them of the opportunity of practicing their religion. In fact, the more severe the persecution, the greater became the ardor of their religious faith. In their homeland even during persecutions, it is true, they lived among persons of the same faith and they had the continuous support and encouragement of their priests. In the new country they lived amidst a people who were violently opposed to their religion. Outside of Pennsylvania and, for a short time in Maryland, the exercise of their religion was not tolerated. While under such conditions the first generation might have persevered, the second and third generations naturally succumbed to the influence of their environment.

Catholic Population in Time of Bishop Carroll

When John Carroll was appointed in 1789 the first bishop of the Church in America he was confronted with the task

---

[9] Peter Guilday, *Life and Times of John Carroll*, Vol. I, p. 57.

of building up a church out of the scattered remnants of early Irish, English, German and French colonists. At most, he had only 30,000 Catholics. They were confined largely to Maryland and Pennsylvania. New York and New Jersey had few members of the faith, but in the other colonies Catholics were practically unknown. There were, however, Catholic settlements made by the French throughout the West in Detroit, Green Bay, Prairie du Chien, Peoria, Cohokia, Chartres, Kaskaskia, Vincennes, Natchez, New Orleans and Mobile.[10]

When Bishop Carroll took possession of the see of Baltimore there was no Catholic charitable institution or organization of any kind in the United States. There was no hospital, no institution for children, no home for the aged. This was naturally a matter of great concern to the bishop. He knew that the Church could not flourish without works of charity, the first fruits of the faith. Before he could think of aught else, however, he had to provide priests for his scattered flock. The French Revolution, which was the cause of so much suffering to the Church in France, proved a blessing in disguise for the infant Church of America. Well might a writer in *The Catholic Almanac or Laity's Directory of 1822* state:

"O, truly fortunate revolution in France! Every true Catholic in this country may exclaim, which has brought us so many edifying and enlightened instructors! There is no part of the United States that can not bear witness to their zeal, and should not be eternally grateful. Where is the youth of a liberal education, sincere piety and correct morals, who has not been formed by one or more of the clergy of France, emigrants to this country? Where is the College or Catholic establishment that has not been or is not now under their direction? They have taught our youth, they have instructed and enlightened our people, and directed thousands in the way

[10] *Ibid.*, p. 58; Shaughnessy, *op. cit.*, p. 36.

to heaven, they have enlarged and extended the kingdom of Christ on this side of the Atlantic, they have sown and watered a seed which will hereafter spring up and yield an amazing increase...."[11]

Society of St. Sulpice

The first fruits of the Revolution for the infant Church of the United States was the coming of members of the Society of St. Sulpice. Bishop Carroll wanted a seminary for the training of priests; and he gladly seized the opportunity presented by the Revolution to invite the Sulpicians to Baltimore. This community was an organization of secular priests founded by Abbé Olier in 1642 for the especial purpose of preparing young men for the priesthood. Bishop Carroll felt that he could not have been more fortunate in obtaining the right type of instructors for his future priests. As the new seminary in Baltimore did not develop as rapidly as had been expected, it was possible to use the Sulpician Fathers for missionary work in the scattered Catholic settlements. Thus they gave to the American Church the splendid missionary traditions of their native France. By virtue of their zeal, culture and tradition, they were qualified to build firmly and securely the foundations of the new Church. They gave expression to that spirit and tradition which has led to the development of some of our finest religious communities. In fact one of the first tasks to which they set themselves was the creation of religious communities which would be replicas of those that had been the glory of France.

Visitation Convent at Georgetown

Bishop Carroll was very much interested in securing for the United States religious communities of women for educational work. He tried to prevail on the Carmelite nuns of Hoogstraet, Belgium, who had settled in Port Tobacco,

[11] Page 103.

Maryland (1790), to open a school for the training of girls in religion and the domestic arts. The Carmelites, however, refused to deviate from their contemplative rule. In 1801 the Poor Clares from France opened an academy for girls in Georgetown, D. C., which was the first school conducted by sisters within the original boundaries of the United States. In 1799 Rev. Leonard Neale, at that time president of Georgetown College, endeavored to associate Miss Lawler and her companions who had recently come from Ireland with the Poor Clares. Failing to make the necessary arrangements, Father Neale secured a house nearby for his newly-found teachers. It was his hope to found an educational center for Catholic women. His hope was realized in part when the Poor Clares returned to France (1805) and he acquired their school for Miss Lawler and her companions. Later as Archbishop of Baltimore he succeeded in having Miss Lawler and her companions recognized as a community of Visitandines (1816)[12].

In establishing the Visitation Convent at Georgetown, Archbishop Neale was not thinking exclusively of those who were able to pay. His thoughts, like those of his predecessor, went out to the poor and the orphan. It is evident that he desired that the sisters should use the proceeds of their pay school as a means of supporting a number of orphans. In regard to the Visitation Convent, a contemporary writer stated: "This convent in George Town is composed of about 50 nuns whose object after paying due worship to God, by the recitation or singing of the divine office, at various hours in the day, and, sanctifying their souls by these and other religious duties, is to take care of the education of young persons of their sex, of the various classes of society. Thus besides a number of young ladies who are pensioners in the house, they educate also some helpless orphan girls whose merely necessary expenses are defrayed by charitable persons; and they have

[12] Guilday, *op. cit.*, Vol. II, pp. 492-495.

a day school for the poorer class where upwards of 100 girls receive instruction. . . ."[13]

The Georgetown Visitation Convent became the prototype of a large number of Catholic institutions that sprung up in the various cities of the United States during the second, third and fourth decades of the nineteenth century. Thus were laid the foundation stones of Catholic education and of Catholic charities in America; for the first American Catholic schools were also charitable institutions. They combined all the functions of our present boarding schools, parochial schools and homes for dependent and neglected children.

Sisters of Charity

Bishop Carroll's anxiety to develop teaching communities in the United States was very evident from his efforts to have the Carmelites start a boarding school at Port Tobacco. In subsequent years, it was his privilege to lay the foundations of a community which was to realize his fondest hopes. The story of the founding of the Sisters of Charity has been told so frequently that it need not be repeated in any detail. This community in its infancy represented the ideals of two converts, Samuel Cooper and Mrs. Elizabeth Seton, as well as of Father Du Bourg, a Sulpician, and Archbishop Carroll. The beginnings of the community bring us to a seemingly fortuitous meeting (1806) between Father Du Bourg and Mrs. Seton, who was seriously considering the religious life. She also had to give thought to her five orphaned children. Through the kindly interest of the Filicchi Brothers, business associates of her husband, she was relieved of the financial responsibility of educating her children.[14]

Before her meeting with Father Du Bourg Mrs. Seton had considered joining the Ursulines at Montreal, but he pleaded with her the cause of Catholic education in Maryland. He

---
[13] *Catholic Almanac, 1822*, p. 93.
[14] Sr. Mary Agnes McCann, *The History of Mother Seton's Daughters*, Vol. I, pp. 3-11.

would provide a lot on the grounds of St. Mary's Seminary on which her school might be erected. Bishop Carroll, Bishop Chèverus and other eminent educators joined with Du Bourg in pressing these claims: "They saw in her conversion and in her devotion to the training of the young the solution of the educational problem which dated back to the earliest Jesuit schools in Maryland."[15] In response to their pleadings, Elizabeth Ann Bayley Seton set out on a memorable journey to Baltimore, June, 1808,[16] and opened her school in that city September, 1808. Through the influence of Du Bourg and other professors in St. Mary's Seminary, her venture attracted a number of able workers: Cecilia O'Conway, "Philadelphia's first nun;" Maria Murphy, a niece of Matthew Carey, the Philadelphia publisher; Mary Ann Butler of Philadelphia, Susan Clossy of New York, Mrs. Rose White and Catherine Mullen, both of Baltimore.[17] In June, 1809, the embryonic community adopted a provisional rule drawn up by Father Du Bourg.

Mother Seton was not satisfied to remain in the little house on Paca Street which had been secured by Father Du Bourg. She visioned bigger and better things. As she was endeavoring to mature her plans for the future, there appeared a ministering angel to the first Sisters of Charity in the person of Samuel Cooper, a Virginian convert, who later entered the priesthood. He possessed considerable means which he was anxious to utilize for some work of religion. Fortunately for the Sisters of Charity he sought the advice of Father Du Bourg. Mr. Cooper finally decided to secure a foundation for the new community with the understanding that it should be located at Emmitsburg, Maryland.[18] In July, 1809, Mother Seton and her companions took possession of the "Stone

[15] Guilday, *op. cit.*, Vol. II, p. 497; sketch of Chèverus by R. J. Purcell in *Dictionary of American Biography*.
[16] McCann, *op. cit.*, Vol. I, p. 11.
[17] *Ibid.*, Vol. I, pp. 15-22.
[18] McCann, *op. cit.*, Vol. I, pp. 17-18.

House," their original home near Emmitsburg.[19] The valley and the school soon took their names from the sisterhood which was first dedicated under the protection of St. Joseph.[20]

The question of a permanent rule for the society was one that gave Mother Seton, Father David, who had succeeded Father Du Bourg as spiritual advisor, and Archbishop Carroll the most serious concern. Apparently, David was anxious to make the American foundation a part of the original organization of the Daughters of Charity of St. Vincent de Paul. In 1810 Bishop Flaget, who had just been appointed head of the newly created see of Bardstown, brought over with him a copy of the rules and regulations of the Daughters of Charity. These rules were studied carefully by Mother Seton, Archbishop Carroll, Father Du Bourg and Father David. There was a fear in Carroll's mind that the French community would not be suitable to conditions in the United States, where he held that emphasis should be on educational work. In a letter to Mother Seaton, he stated his views as follows: "In the meantime assure yourself and them of my utmost solicitude for your advancement in the service and favor of God; of my reliance on your prayers; of mine for your prosperity in the important duty of education, which will and must long be your principal, and will always be your partial employment. A century at least will pass before the exigencies and habits of this country will require and hardly admit of the charitable exercises towards the sick, sufficient to employ any number of the Sisters out of our largest cities; and therefore, they must consider the business of education as a laborious, charitable and permanent object of their religious duty."[21]

After careful study, Archbishop Carroll and Father Du Bourg decided to accept the rule of the Daughters of Charity of St. Vincent de Paul with the necessary modifications for

[19] *Ibid.*, Vol. I, p. 25.
[20] *Ibid.*, Vol. I, p. 21.
[21] *Ibid.*, Vol. I, p. 59.

American conditions. This Dr. Charles G. Herbermann emphasized: "The principal point on which the rules were changed in order to adapt them to American conditions concerned the activities of the Sisters in schools, for the Daughters of Charity of St. Vincent devoted themselves entirely to the service of children unable to pay for their education. This could be done in France because the nuns had an assured income from other sources. In the United States, on the contrary, Mother Seton's Sisterhood had no income whatever, and the Sisters must therefore earn their daily bread in part by their teaching activity. However, from the beginning, Mother Seton's community devoted themselves largely to the education of the poor, and in later years this has been their principal work." [22]

The religious community, whose foundation Mother Seton, with the advice and counsel of Bishop Carroll and the Sulpician Fathers, planted in Emmitsburg has grown and extended its manifold activities until it has reached all parts of the United States. The religious who now look to Mother Seton as their foundress number about 8,000, a great army whose lives are devoted to education and charity. True they are not all under one government, nor do they all look to one center for inspiration. The parent home of the community, together with the other homes that come under its jurisdiction, are a part of that world-wide community of the Daughters of Charity of St. Vincent de Paul. A few years ago the American province of the Sisters of Charity with headquarters at Emmitsburg, was divided and a new province established with headquarters at Marillac near St. Louis. Other branches of Mother Seton's community are the Sisters of Charity of Mt. St. Vincent-on-the-Hudson, the Sisters of Charity of Mt. St. Joseph-on-the-Ohio, the Sisters of Charity of Leavenworth, the Sisters of Charity of Convent Station,

[22] Herbermann, C. G., *The Sulpicians in the United States*, p. 224.

New Jersey, the Sisters of Charity of Greensburg, Pennsylvania, and the Sisters of Charity of Halifax in Nova Scotia.

Sisters of Loretto

In 1811 a French émigré and a member of the company of St. Sulpice journeyed from Baltimore to Kentucky to take charge of the newly established diocese of Bardstown. This new diocese was for the middle west what Baltimore had been for the entire east. On his trip west Bishop Flaget was accompanied by another French émigré and a son of St. Sulpice, Father David.[23] Bishop Flaget, endowed with the splendid religious traditions of his native France, gave first thought in the building up of the Church in his diocese to the development of zealous missionary priests. With this purpose in mind, he opened a diocesan seminary. But, he was well aware of the need of consecrated religious women in the ministry of education and of charity. Without their aid, he could not guarantee the young a religious education, nor could he bring to the poor the consolations of Christian charity.

Three years before the establishment of Mother Seton's Daughters, Father Nerinckx, "the Apostle of Kentucky," had made plans for the establishment of a religious community of women in that state.[24] He renewed his efforts again, in 1807, but without success. It was not until after the arrival of Flaget that he succeeded in realizing his objective. In 1812, this zealous missionary, Father Nerinckx, decided to establish a "little day school for the children of his congregation of St. Charles,"[25] and appealed to Mary Rhodes, recently come from Maryland, to take charge of the school. Miss Rhodes had received a convent education and was anxious to devote herself to a religious life. The story of the primitive beginning of this institute is graphically described by a

[23] See sketches of Flaget and David by R. J. Purcell in the *Dict. of Amer. Biography.*
[24] C. P. Maes, *Life of Rev. Charles Nerinckx*, p. 135.
[25] Ben. J. Webb, *The Centenary of Catholicity in Kentucky*, p. 234.

member of the Society of Loretto: "The arrangement was perfected, and the school was opened in a couple of abandoned cabins that stood on an eminence, on the opposite side of Hardin's creek from the residence of Mr. Rhodes (the brother of Mary Rhodes), and half-way between it and St. Charles' Church. They were wretchedly dilapidated, and without other flooring than the bare ground. They were roofed with rough boards that had shrunk so far apart as to afford but slight protection against the intrusion of wind and snow. The playground for the children was a diminutive affair, separated from the near forest by a few sections of rail fencing."[26] Miss Rhodes was soon joined by another teacher, Christine Stuart. The two teachers, with another young associate, Ann Hevern, decided to fit up a refuge for themselves in seclusion from the world.[27] Father Nerinckx saw in these women a realization of his cherished hope of a religious community. He obtained from Bishop Flaget the authority to receive them and others who might follow their example in his new community. On April 25, 1812, the three postulants were received by Nerinckx into an association which he named Friends of Mary at the Foot of the Cross.[28] "The convent consisted of a hollow square of log cabins; it was situated near the church of St. Charles and was called *Loretto*, after the famous asylum of the Holy Virgin in Italy."[29] The conditions of the original Sisters of Loretto were those of all western pioneers who built their cabins from logs hewn from the forest and lived on the products of the land cleared and cultivated by their own hands.

Father Nerinckx's new community was essentially a missionary enterprise. He knew that without religious education the children of Kentucky's Catholic pioneers could not be saved to the Church. He planned to accept in his first

[26] *Ibid.*, p. 234.
[27] *Ibid.*, p. 235.
[28] *Ibid.*, p. 235.
[29] M. J. Spalding, *Sketches of the Life, Times and Character of the Rt. Rev. Benedict Joseph Flaget*, p. 289.

school not only those who could pay but also orphans and the children of the poor. The regular tuition was $32 per year, but orphans were received gratis. As the sisters found that they were unable to support themselves and their school by tuition fees, they made up the deficit by spinning and weaving for their neighbors.[30]

Nerinckx had little hope of securing a sufficient number of local recruits or material resources to develop his community, so he turned his eyes to France in anticipation that the country which had sent so many pioneer missionaries to America would not fail him. In 1815, the Kentucky apostle journeyed to France, but, unfortunately for the Kentucky missions, France was then just recovering from the horrors of the Revolution and needed all its resources to reconstruct the church at home. Nerinckx, however, succeeded in securing material aid in his native Belgium. What encouraged the founder of *Loretto* most during his trip to Europe was the approval of the Holy See for this institute.[31]

Sisters of Charity of Nazareth

Father David, who accompanied Bishop Flaget to Kentucky, was destined to take a prominent part in laying the foundations of the Church west of the Alleghenies. Aside from his labors in the development of the diocesan seminary, David's outstanding contribution was the establishment of the Sisters of Charity of Nazareth. Bishop Flaget wanted a religious community to assist him in building up the Church in his diocese. Father Nerinckx's plans for a community were matured but one community was not sufficient. The bishop applied for assistance to the Sisters of Charity at Emmitsburg, but Mother Seton could not yet divide her forces. Thereupon he committed the task of organizing a

---
[30] J. A. Burns, *The Catholic School System in the United States*, pp. 228-229.
[31] Webb, *op. cit.*, p. 240.

The Pioneers

suitable community to Father David, his able lieutenant and later coadjutor bishop.³²

In November, 1812, two young women who had heard of Father David's project placed themselves under his spiritual direction. Within a few months they were joined by others. David's rules for the new community were in principle the same as those governing the Daughters of Charity of St. Vincent de Paul. In June of 1813, the community had its retreat and elected its first officers. The objects contemplated by the founder of the Sisters of Charity of Nazareth, besides the personal sanctification of the members, were: "First, the exercise of the corporal and spiritual works of mercy towards the poor, the sick and the ignorant; and, second, the promotion of *Christian* education among the young of the weaker sex.'"³³

The first residence of the new community consisted of a part of a log house on the farm lands of St. Thomas' Seminary, in Nelson County, Kentucky. Later the Sisters moved about a mile and a half distant to a new log cabin, which was built by the seminarians and consisted of two rooms with a half-story attic. In this primitive building the sisters opened their first school at Nazareth, August, 1814.³⁴ The erection of a new convent was begun May 26, 1826, and in December, 1829, the community was granted a charter by the legislature of Kentucky.³⁵

Sisters of St. Dominic

Ten years after the establishment of the Sisters of Charity of Nazareth another religious community, the Sisters of St. Dominic, made its appearance in Kentucky. Its inception was due to the superior of the Dominican Order, Thomas

---
³² *Ibid.*, p. 245; Spalding, *op. cit.*, pp. 291-293; Anna B. McGill, *The Sisters of Charity of Nazareth, Ky.*, pp. 19-44.
³³ Spalding, *op. cit.*, pp. 292-293.
³⁴ McGill, *op. cit.*, pp. 20-24.
³⁵ Spalding, *op. cit.*, p. 293.

Wilson, O. P. From his congregation of St. Rose, Father Wilson had no difficulty in obtaining suitable subjects for the new community. The first home of the neophites was a log cabin attached to St. Rose's Convent. After a year they were able to move into a home of their own on land secured by one of the members, Sister Angela Sansbury. This home had only three rooms, one for a chapel, another for a kitchen and refectory combined, and another for a general living room and dormitory. An old still-house on the farm was fitted up as a school where the sisters began their educational work. A year's provisions were given by the pupils' parents for tuition.[36] Like the Sisters of Loretto and the Sisters of Charity of Nazareth, the Sisters of the Third Order of St. Dominic in Kentucky had to suffer all the hardships of pioneers. When the first year's provisions brought by the pupils gave out, they suffered from the lack of sufficient food. They had to beg from door to door to secure funds for the building which was to replace their improvised school.[37]

While the Dominican Sisters of Kentucky have not exercised a large influence on Catholic charities in the United States, the branches that have grown from the original foundation have played an important role. There are in the United States, at the present time, some twenty communities of the Third Order of St. Dominic, of which five sprang directly or indirectly from the Kentucky foundation. Some of the Sisters of St. Dominic give themselves exclusively to educational work, while others devote their sole attention to charity work, or at least divide their efforts between teaching and charity.

Sisterhoods of the Colored

The missionary zeal of Father Nerinckx knew no bounds. In the colored population of the United States, he saw a

---
[36] V. F. O'Daniel, *The Father of the Church in Tennessee*, pp. 176-178; Webb, op. cit., p. 262.
[37] *Ibid.*, p. 263; A. C. Minogue, *Pages from a Hundred Years of Dominican History*, pp. 53-58.

THE PIONEERS 17

golden harvest for the missionary and the educator. In May, 1824, he took definite steps to organize a colored sisterhood, when he admitted three Negro girls to the religious life, having provided a special religious garb and a special rule for them. Unfortunately his death, three months later, ended a plan which might have accomplished much for the colored race. This work was taken up by another French émigré from St. Sulpice. In 1827, Father Joubert, who deserves the title of "Apostle of the Colored Catholics in America," took over the instruction of colored children, whose families had been exiled or immigrated from San Domingo some years before and were now dwelling in Baltimore.

The children to whom Father Joubert was called upon to impart the elements of Christian doctrine could not read and he, therefore, decided that little progress could be made without a school. While he was contemplating his project for a colored school, the priest came into contact with some women of Baltimore who had been conducting a free colored school for about a year: Elizabeth Lange, a Cuban, and Marie Rosine Boegue and Marie Frances Balais, natives of San Domingo. In these women he found not only the nucleus of his school but also of a colored religious community, the Oblate Sisters of Providence, which he finally established in 1829. Thus a Sulpician exile with true toleration and foresight became the pioneer of Catholic educational and charitable work among the colored people of the United States.[38]

[38] Herbermann, *op. cit.*, pp. 231-234.

CHAPTER II

THE FIRST FRUITS

Ursuline Sisters

The Ursuline Sisters in New Orleans established the first institution for dependent children in the territory now included within the United States. Governor Bienville endeavored to get the Jesuits to establish a school for the training of boys in Louisiana, but while they were prepared to engage in missionary work in the colony, they could not see their way to establish a school. However, they agreed to induce the Ursulines, then the foremost teaching community in France, to come over and establish a school. In February, 1727, ten Ursuline sisters selected from various convents of the order in France sailed for Louisiana, where they were probably the first professional elementary school teachers to set foot on American soil.[1]

Two years after the Ursulines landed in New Orleans, we find that their convent served the double purpose of a boarding school and an orphanage. The number of orphans under their care was greatly increased by the Indian massacre at Natchez in 1829. Writing in July, 1830, Father Le Petit of New Orleans described the work of the Ursulines as follows:

> The little girls, whom none of the inhabitants wished to adopt, have greatly enlarged the interesting company of orphans whom the nuns are bringing up. The great number of these children only serves to increase their charity and attentions. They have formed them into a separate class, and have appointed two special matrons for their care.
> There is not one of this holy sisterhood but is de-

[1] J. A. Burns, *The Catholic School System in the United States*, p. 68.

lighted at having crossed the ocean; nor do they seek here any other happiness than that of preserving these children in their innocency, and giving a polished and Christian education to these young French, who are in danger of being almost as degraded as the slaves. We may hope, with regard to these holy women, that before the end of the year they will occupy the new mansion which is destined for them, and which they have for so long a time desired.

When they shall once be settled there, to the instruction of the boarders, the orphans, and the girls who live without, and the negro women, they will add also *the care of the sick in the hospital*, and the house of refuge for women of questionable character. . . . [2]

The new convent of which Father Le Petit speaks was occupied on July 17, 1734, and still stands. Until recently it was used as a residence of the archbishop of New Orleans. It is one of the historic sights of New Orleans and is known as the "old Archbishopric."[3] The people were at first most indifferent to the educational advantages afforded by the nuns, but the capacity of the hospital was early overtaxed.

The orphans of New Orleans were cared for by the Ursuline Sisters from 1727 until 1834, when the children were removed by the city and placed in the Poydras Orphan Asylum. The Ursulines now passed to other shoulders a responsibility that they had carried for more than 100 years. Their pioneer efforts paved the way for Mother Seton's Daughters, who took charge of the New Orleans Female Orphan Asylum in 1830. The Sisters of Charity and their co-workers of later arrival, the Marianite Sisters of the Holy Cross, have perpetuated during the past century the same traditions of charity established by the Ursulines during the preceding century. New Orleans may, therefore, be said to have an unbroken history of Catholic charities for more than two centuries.

[2] Spalding, *op. cit.*, pp. 157-158.
[3] J. G. Shea, *History of the Catholic Church in the United States*, Vol. I, pp. 568-572.

Sisters of Charity of Emmitsburg, Maryland

Organized Catholic charities in the original territory of the United States began with the opening of St. Joseph's Academy at Emmitsburg July, 1809. This original institution of the Sisters of Charity in the United States was really a boarding school, day school and orphanage. The children of the poor were taught and cared for as well as the children of those who could afford to pay. In fact, the work of the sisters at Emmitsburg began with a free school for the poor children of the neighborhood. At the present time Emmitsburg continues the same traditions set up by its founders. In its college and academy, it always provides for a considerable number of girls who are selected from the various institutions for dependent and neglected children conducted by the community.

Mother Seton's sisterhood was not destined to be confined long to Emmitsburg. Calls for assistance naturally came from scattered Catholic settlements throughout the country for sisters to take charge of their schools, to care for their dependent and neglected children, and to organize hospitals for the care of the sick. Mother Seton's mission was to lay the foundation not only for Catholic education but for Catholic charities in the United States.

Sisters of Charity in Philadelphia

The first call for the service of the Sisters of Charity beyond the confines of Maryland came from Philadelphia in 1814. The yellow fever epidemic that had raged in that city in 1797 deprived many Catholic children of their parents. The members of the Catholic congregations decided to make plans for the care of these children. They secured a house near the German Catholic Church of the Holy Trinity and placed the children in charge of a matron. During the course of six or seven years the enthusiasm of the original promoters of the project waned and it began to look as if it were destined to fail. At this juncture Rev. Michael Hurley, pastor of St. Augustine's Church, became the leader in the cause of Philadelphia's Catholic dependent and neglected children. He was ably assisted by Cornelius Tiers, a man of means and influence, who in 1807 joined him in founding the "Society of St. Joseph for the maintaining and educating of Roman Catholic orphan children of both sexes." Three years later there were fifteen orphan children in its care. In 1814, the trustees of the society asked the Sisters of Charity to take charge of the institution. When the sisters arrived in October, 1814, they found "13 children in rags" and an institution loaded with a heavy debt.[4] The privations of the early days were extreme: "For three months Sisters and children ate no bread at their principal meal, using instead potatoes which were their chief article of food during the first year. They drank coffee made of corn without sugar, and procured fuel from the tanyards. By degrees their wants became known and friends came to their relief."[5]

Like other American cities along the Atlantic seaboard, Philadelphia began to have large accessions to its population in the twenties of the last century. To the Church was presented a new problem, which was to grow in vastness and complexity with each decade, and which was to tax its educational, charitable and religious resources to the limit. As strangers with few resources making their way in a new country, the immigrants were exposed to more hazards than the native population. As a result of the trying ordeals to which they were exposed in their journey over and after their arrival here, many of the immigrants died prematurely and left their children dependent on public charity. If the Church did not provide for the children, there was no recourse except the sectarian almshouse.

[4] *Records of the American Catholic Historical Society,* Vol. I, 1884-86, p. 176.
[5] McCann, *op. cit.,* Vol. I, p. 74.

St. John's Orphanage in Philadelphia

The circumstances which gave rise to the establishment of St. John's Orphanage in Philadelphia are typical of the foundation of many of the Catholic children's homes in the United States. It is the story of the children of immigrants deprived of their parents by premature death. In the hard winter of 1829 a number of children of immigrant parents were reduced to dire need: "Their parents, recently from Ireland, had died leaving them helpless. . . . There was no door of charity open to them except the almshouse. St. Joseph's Orphan Asylum was already full. Their first friends . . . were themselves poor."[6] Many of them were girls in service, but the charity of the poor Irish immigrants was not restrained by their poverty. They decided to organize a subscription list for the children of their deceased fellow immigrants. But they needed more than money, they needed an institution to take care of the children and to place their charity on a permanent basis. At this juncture John Hughes, pastor of St. John's Church and afterwards archbishop of New York, came to their assistance. A society was organized consisting chiefly of poor immigrants. The services of the Sisters of Charity were secured to take charge of the children. A house was rented in Prune Street at $400 per annum. Furniture was provided by a few charitably inclined women. The number of children at first was only eight, but it was very soon doubled.[7] Such was the beginning of St. John's Orphan Asylum in Philadelphia.

The methods of financing St. Joseph's and St. John's orphan asylums in Philadelphia are of particular interest, in view of subsequent developments in Catholic charities. The main source on which the promoters of the institutions relied for support was the dues paid by the members of these associations. The sisters also received certain returns from their

---

[6] J. G. Hassard, *Life of Most Rev. John Hughes, D.D.*, p. 88.
[7] *Ibid.*, pp. 88-89.

day schools. This income was supplemented by an annual charity sermon in the various churches.

Sisters of Charity in New York

In 1817 a call for assistance came to Emmitsburg from Mother Seton's native New York City, where Bishop John Connolly was anxious to have the Sisters of Charity establish a foundation for education and charity. Little did the bishop or Mother Seton realize what a large part the Sisters of Charity would play in the metropolis of America or the vast immigration problems which would be met in this gateway to America during the century to follow. In reply to Connolly's request, Father John Du Bois, spiritual director of the Sisters of Charity and later bishop of New York, specified in detail the conditions under which the sisters would be sent to New York. The trustees were to have entire charge of the financial affairs of the orphan asylum, and the sisters were to be left free to manage the internal affairs of the institution according to their own rules. An association of the Ladies of Charity was to be formed to assist the sisters in promoting the work of the institution. A certain sum of money (about $40 a year) was to be allotted annually to the sister superior in New York "for her and her Sisters' clothing." In the admission and removal of orphans the sister superior was to be consulted. The traveling expenses of the sisters between Emmitsburg and New York were to be paid by the trustees of the institution in all cases where it became necessary to recall the sisters for the good of the institution.[8]

The sisters left Emmitsburg June, 1817, and on their arrival in New York took possession of the small frame building in Prince Street, whose legal title was The New York Catholic Benevolent Society. During the first year only five orphans came under their care; but during the next year the little flock increased to twenty-eight, one-third of whom

[6] McCann, *op. cit.*, Vol. I, pp. 89-90.

were boys. In a short time a school was opened in connection with the orphanage.[9]

In 1830 a similar institution for children was opened in Brooklyn under the Sisters of Charity. The legal title of the institution was the Roman Catholic Orphan Asylum Society in the City of Brooklyn, County of Kings. In 1833 the community opened a special institution for half-orphans in New York City. In 1836 the Roman Catholic Benevolent Society of New York was changed to the Roman Catholic Orphan Asylum. In 1852 the Roman Catholic Orphan Asylum and the asylum for the relief of the children of poor widowers and widows united.[10]

Sisters of Charity in Baltimore

A few months after Mother Seton's death in 1821, her sisters were invited by Archbishop Maréchal to take charge of St. Mary's Orphan Asylum in Baltimore. Within a few years the free school operated in connection with the orphan asylum was providing education for 400 children. In 1825 the sisters opened St. John's Female Benevolent School at Frederick, Maryland, and in 1827 they organized a special department for orphans in connection with the school.[11] In 1825 the sisters went to Washington at the invitation of the Very Rev. William Matthews,[12] pastor of St. Patrick's Church, to take charge of St. Vincent's School and Orphan Asylum.[13]

Sisters of Charity in St. Louis

While he was bishop of New Orleans, Doctor Du Bourg, the first spiritual director and really the co-founder of the Sisters

[9] *Ibid.*, Vol. I, pp. 91-92; J. Shea, *op. cit.*, Vol. III, p. 180; J. R. Bayley, *A Brief Sketch of the History of the Catholic Church on the Island of New York*, pp. 77-78.
[10] In 1921 the Roman Catholic Orphan Asylum sold its property and buildings at Kingsbridge. The board of trustees thereupon decided that instead of building a new institution they would use their funds for the care of children in boarding homes.
[11] McCann, *op. cit.*, Vol. I, pp. 126-128.
[12] *Archives* of Mt. St. Joseph's College, Emmitsburg.
[13] From 1825 to 1900 St. Vincent's was located at Tenth and F Streets N. W., Washington, D. C. The school was discontinued in 1850. In 1900 the downtown property was sold and the institution moved to its present location in Edgewood. In 1827 the name was changed from St. Vincent's Orphan Asylum to St. Vincent's Home and School.

THE FIRST FRUITS 25

of Charity, brought over a number of Lazarist priests from France, who have filled the same role in building up the Church in St. Louis as the Sulpicians have in Baltimore. One of the members of this little band was Father Joseph Rosati, later first bishop of St. Louis. Bishop Du Bourg was, therefore, responsible for the beginning of the work of both the sons and daughters of St. Vincent de Paul in the United States. And it is an interesting coincidence that Bishop Rosati, one of the little band that Du Bourg invited to this country, should have been responsible for first associating the work of the sons and daughters of St. Vincent de Paul in the United States. In June, 1828, Bishop Rosati addressed a very significant communication to Father Bruté, president of St. Mary's College, Baltimore: "I come to obtain through your intervention three Sisters of Charity for a hospital in St. Louis. . . . Without having said one word, a very rich man offers me a very beautiful piece of ground with two houses in the city of St. Louis. He will give besides another lot with other houses that will bring a revenue of six hundred dollars a year. He will give one hundred and fifty dollars for the journey of the Sisters, three hundred and fifty to furnish the house. But, he will not leave it in the hands of mercenaries; if we do not get the Sisters of Emmitsburg this establishment will fail, for I see too many difficulties to obtain any from France, and those of Kentucky do not understand hospitals."[14]

Doctor Bruté, in common with the other advisers of the Sisters of Charity, thought that the time had not yet come for them to take up hospital work.[15] During the first two years of the community's existence Archbishop Carroll had always insisted that its fundamental objective was the school and that it was only after the school had been provided for that the sisters should devote themselves to other things. In-

[14] *Ibid.*
[15] McCann, *op. cit.*, Vol. I, p. 138.

deed, the infirmary of the medical school of the University of Maryland, which the community had taken over in 1821, was a severe drain on its resources.

The tradition of a few years could not stand in the way of this strong appeal. Here was a new field of labor from which they could not turn away their faces. This project was sponsored by one of the wealthiest and most devoted Catholic laymen of his time, John Mullanphy. Mullanphy had always been interested in works of beneficence. In 1827 he gave to the religious of the Sacred Heart a house, twenty-four acres of valuable land and a thousand dollars to assist in opening a seminary for young ladies with the express condition that the religious should continue to provide for twenty orphan girls.[16] He offered a similar bequest to the Jesuit Fathers of the University of St. Louis, but they were unable to accept it at the time.[17]

In November, 1828, the Sisters of Charity arrived in St. Louis. Their hospital at first consisted of "old and dilapidated houses of wood."[18] Mr. Mullanphy, aided by other citizens, soon provided a spacious hospital building on Spruce and Fourth Streets, which was opened in December, 1831. Within a few days he purchased an adjoining lot with two houses, one of which was to be used as an orphan asylum for boys. In 1834 Bishop Rosati gave the sisters a building for an orphan asylum for both boys and girls. A year later they had under care forty-six orphans and an equal number of

---

[16] Mr. Mullanphy feared very greatly lest the orphan girls cared for by the religious of the Sacred Heart be educated out of their surroundings. He therefore required that they should be obliged to go barefoot a large part of the year and that they should enjoy no beverages from overseas such as coffee. This condition in the Mullanphy bequest has since been liberalized by the courts of Missouri. In order to comply with the provisions of the Mullanphy bequest, the religious of the Sacred Heart in connection with their academy on Maryland Avenue, still continue to care for twenty dependent children who are selected by the senior surviving member of the Mullanphy family. The dependent children, however, are separated entirely from the students in the academy.

[17] Lawrence Kenny, S.J., "The Mullanphys of St. Louis," *Historical Records and Studies*, Vol. XIV, pp. 70-111.

[18] *Letters of Leopoldine Society*, Vol. I, p. 29.

day scholars from the city. This was the first Catholic orphanage in the west.[19]

Even as early as the third decade of the last century, the Catholic laity were not entirely inactive in charitable affairs. A number of Irish immigrants had laid the foundation of St. John's Orphan Asylum in Philadelphia. Unto this day John Mullanphy remains a towering figure in Catholic beneficence in the United States. Not merely a man of money, he was a man of ideas. His benefactions were not confined to St. Louis, but he gave generously when the first institutions of Catholic charities were established in Boston and Cincinnati. He seemed a sort of national philanthropist to whom Catholic organizations everywhere felt free to appeal. As in Philadelphia and in St. Louis, so also in Cincinnati, the laity took part in the development of Catholic charities.

Sisters of Charity in Cincinnati

Edward Fenwick, the first bishop of Cincinnati, like all the pioneer bishops of the United States, was burdened with a multitude of responsibilities. Between 1820 and 1830, immigrants in large numbers began to pour into Ohio. On all sides there was the cry for missionaries and more funds. Settlers as a whole were poor, and Catholics were the poorest of the poor. Bishop Fenwick wanted to build a college and seminary. To him these problems were more pressing than the care of the orphans, but some of the laity were intent on securing the services of the Sisters of Charity to organize an orphanage and charity school in the diocese. Writing to the Propagation of the Faith at Lyons, a representative of Bishop Fenwick made the following significant statement: "Two or three Catholics of the city (Cincinnati) wish to establish the Sisters of Charity here, and one of them has already gone to Emmittsburg to make arrangements with the superior

---

[19] John Rothensteiner, *History of the Archdiocese of St. Louis*, Vol. I, pp. 448-449.

of that institute. His Grace in order not to lose what these gentlemen are willing to devote to the good work has to cooperate with them, and notwithstanding their good will it is presumed that he will have to be responsible for a considerable portion of the expenses. The new seminary, the future college and the poor will derive great benefits from this institution of which the school will bring about numerous conversions. These considerations have induced His Grace to cooperate in this good work in spite of the expense."[20]

Soon after their arrival in Cincinnati, October, 1829, a Catholic layman, Mr. Cassilly, presumably one of those referred to in the letter to the Propagation of Faith, provided the sisters with a house in which to begin their work.[21] A few months after their arrival Bishop Fenwick wrote to the Propagation of the Faith: "I have brought from Baltimore 4 Sisters of Charity. Their establishment will prosper I hope. They have already 106 children in their school and 5 orphans in the asylum."[22] Subsequent reports show that with the coming of the immigrants, the number of orphans increased greatly within the next five years.

This institution, known as St. Peter's Orphan Asylum and Free School, was named after St. Peter's Cathedral, with which it was closely associated. It was supported from the proceeds of an annual charity sermon at the cathedral and by St. Peter's Benevolent Society, whose members contributed twenty-five cents a month and conducted a number of benefits throughout the year for the asylum and school.[23] As early as its second year, Father Frederick Résé, later bishop of Detroit, could describe its important work in a letter to the Society for the Propagation of the Faith:

> Our orphanage becomes every day more of a charge to us particularly since the cholera has ravaged the

[20] Letter from M. Clicteur, June 28, 1929. *Annals of Propagation of the Faith*, Vol. IV, pp. 514-516.
[21] McCann, *op. cit.*, Vol. I, p. 162.
[22] *Annals of the Propagation of the Faith*, Vol. IV, p. 533.
[23] McCann, *op. cit.*, Vol. I, pp. 203-206.

city, because the number of orphans has increased very greatly since the visit of this plague. Many of the children have been placed in Protestant homes where they are obliged to remain until they are eighteen years old and which they leave without religion or instruction.

The number of immigrants from the north of Germany, Alsace, and Lorraine, is greater than ever and most of these people have spent their last penny before reaching Cincinnati. We have taken care of poor young girls by placing them in the orphans' home directed by the Sisters of Charity, but we do not know how to place the boys who are likely to pass into the hands of Protestants among whom they almost always lose their faith. We are, therefore, thinking of founding a kind of infirmary or hospital where, while caring for the sick poor, we shall keep also these poor children and thus save them from perdition.[24]

When the orphanage was first opened, there evidently was not a large demand for its services; but as soon as the immigrants came in large numbers its resources were taxed. The immigrants were poor, they had no reserves against the strains of life in their new situation. A physique weakened by long and arduous travel, lack of economic resources and lack of adequate health facilities in American cities made the immigrant an easy victim of poverty and disease.

Sisters of Charity in Boston

The struggle for the establishment of the first orphan asylum in Boston is typical of the difficulties in the way of the early development of Catholic beneficence. The Catholics were in number few and largely Irish immigrants who had come from New Brunswick. Bishop Benedict J. Fenwick was anxious to secure the Sisters of Charity to conduct an orphan asylum and free school for girls. In response to his invitation, the sisters arrived in Boston in 1832. As there were no funds on hand to purchase a building for an orphanage,

[24] *Annals of the Propagation of the Faith*, Vol. VI, pp. 199-205.

they rented a house and opened a day school. Like the original Daughters of Charity of St. Vincent de Paul, they found that their work brought them into contact with a number of dependent children whom charity urged them to take into their own home.[25] The first orphan came from a poor family consisting of an insane mother with two children, who had been deserted by the husband and father. The bishop asked the sisters to care for the girl, while he received her little brother into his own home.

As the number of children increased, a special effort was made in 1833 to raise a building fund. A fair given at Concert Hall netted $2,000 as an endowment. A second fair held in 1839 netted a similar amount, while a third fair in 1841 netted about $3,000. A number of small legacies, including $1,000 from John Mullanphy of St. Louis, brought the total raised for the orphanage up to $9,000. With this amount on hand, Bishop Fenwick purchased a building which would serve both as an orghanage and a day school.[26] This gives a vivid picture of the struggles incident to the early development of Catholic charities in the United States—nine years to raise $9,000 for St. Vincent's Orphan Asylum, the first charitable institution of Boston.[27]

Numerous Calls Made on Mother Seton's Daughters

It was remarkable to what an extent Mother Seton's Sisters answered the numerous calls made on them between 1815 and 1840. Calls came to them not only from Philadelphia, New York, Baltimore, Washington, Cincinnati, St. Louis,

---

[25] James Fitton, *Sketches of the Establishment of the Church in New England,* pp. 136-139; J. B. Cullen, *The Story of the Irish in Boston,* p. 212; *Baltimore Catholic Mirror,* April 3, 1875.
[26] Fitton, *op. cit.,* pp. 136-139.
[27] By 1845 the building purchased in 1841 was insufficient to meet the needs. A new building was secured for the sum of $18,000. On account of inclement weather a fair organized to secure funds for the new building netted only $750. Another fair the following year brought $3,500. In 1855 a new site was acquired at Shawmut and Camden Streets for $21,000. The new building was completed in 1858. The total cost of the building, including the land, was $81,000. During the panic of 1857 great difficulty was experienced in raising money for the new building. Andrew Carney came to the rescue with a contribution of $12,000. (*Ibid.,* p. 139; Cullen, *op. cit.,* p. 213.)

Boston and New Orleans, but also from Albany, Harrisburg, Utica, Norfolk, Richmond and Pittsburgh. The sisters opened an orphan asylum and school in Albany (1828), in Harrisburg (1828), in Wilmington (1830), in New Orleans (1830), in Richmond (1834), in Utica (1834), in Pittsburgh (1835). What was there in the Church that could promote such a successful movement? In Maryland there was the original Catholic settlement. Many Maryland Catholics owned land which, in that day, was an important source of wealth. Many of the Maryland families, moreover, had retained their cultural and religious traditions. In Kentucky the Catholics were largely of Maryland stock but were generally very poor. In St. Louis many old Catholic settlers had made money in the fur trade. In Louisiana Catholics owned the land and other natural resources of the state. Outside of these few centers, the Catholic population was composed almost entirely of recent immigrants. The Church, moreover, was concerned not only with the works of charity, but also with providing the essentials of religion for the rapidly increasing population.

Other Religious Communities

While the Sisters of Charity of Emmitsburg occupied the center of the stage in Catholic charities, they were not alone in the field. From the beginning, the Sisters of Charity of Nazareth regarded the care of orphans and the needy as an important part of their program. The first superior of the community, Mother Catherine Spalding, anxiously looked forward to the time when "God would place in the hands of the Sisters the means to serve Him in the person of His forlorn ones."[28] The opportunity presented itself at the expiration of Mother Catherine's first term of office in 1831, when she went to Louisville to open the Presentation Academy near St. Louis' Church. Shortly after opening the academy, the sisters learned that there were two children on the city

[28] McGill, *op. cit.*, p. 51.

wharves whose parents had died on their way from New Orleans. The children they received into their school. Within a year four more children were given shelter. During the cholera epidemic of 1832 the number of children increased greatly. While the epidemic raged the sisters generously gave their services, not only for the care of the orphans but also for nursing the sick in their own homes. Such was the origin of St. Vincent's Orphan Asylum in Louisville, and such were the beginnings of the charity work of the Sisters of Charity of Nazareth.[29]

As a part of his program for education and charities in the diocese of Charleston, Bishop John England established a community of the Sisters of Mercy in 1829. Two years later this community opened a boarding and day school for girls in Charleston. Beside the boarders who were able to pay, the institution received a number of orphans.[30] In 1838 he essayed another venture in social welfare work. He organized a sort of mutual protective society for Catholic workmen known as the Brotherhood of San Marino. The brotherhood supported a small hospital in which its members might be nursed during epidemics then so prevalent in that city. The year in which the organization was perfected Charleston was visited by the cholera plague, and under the direction of the Sisters of Mercy a group of volunteer nurses labored night and day in the houses which the brotherhood converted into a temporary hospital.[31]

Recapitulation

The pioneers in Catholic charities in the United States did not recognize a clear line of demarcation between education and charities. The education of the young and the care of dependent and neglected children went hand in hand. In a country in which the Catholic population consisted of scattered settlements, in a country, moreover, in which there

[29] *Ibid.*, pp. 51-53.
[30] Peter Guilday, *Life and Times of John England*, Vol. II, pp. 134-136.
[31] *Ibid.*, Vol. II, pp. 160-162.

were few rich, and in which there were tremendous opportunities for all, it was to be expected that education rather than charity would be stressed. Catholics had scarcely any educational facilities. The number of homeless children to be cared for would not be large for some time to come. This attitude was borne out by the experience of the first Catholic free schools and orphanages. It was not at all uncommon to find an institution caring for five orphans and providing educational facilities for 100 or more children. It was with the rise of the immigration tide that an intense demand for Catholic charities appeared.

Financing was a serious problem for the first schools and orphanages. Returns from the pay pupils would not support the orphans, and hence the nuns devised various ways and means of supporting their institutions. Among the most popular methods was the annual charity sermon in the churches as followed in Baltimore, Philadelphia, New York and Cincinnati. An association with a large dues-paying membership was another popular means, as well as a way of acquainting the laity more fully with the work. This plan later reached its highest development in the German Catholic orphan asylums. The idea of giving people something for their money seemed to appeal to those charged with the destinies of the pioneer Catholic charitable institutions. That was a favorite method then, as now, for raising money for Catholic work.

Very little attention seems to have been given by the early institutions to the care of dependent boys. Probably the situation affecting the Catholic dependent boys was not such as to call for an organized program. The care of the boy away from his home did not demand serious thought and planning until considerably later in the immigrant rush. Then religious communities could no longer escape this problem; and, as will be pointed out later, the ways and means of dealing with it gave rise to serious differences of opinion both within and without the communities.

CHAPTER III

THE OLD IMMIGRATION AND ITS PROBLEMS

National Origins in 1920

Excluding immigrants and descendants of immigrants from Canada, Newfoundland, the twenty Latin-American Republics and the Canal Zone, the United States in 1920, had a white population of 89,332,158. Of these 53,532,345 were immigrants or descendants of immigrants who came to this country after 1790 and 41,288,570 were descendants of colonists who had arrived before 1790.[1] Between 1820 and 1910 a total of 25,421,929 Europeans migrated to the United States. Germany headed the list, having sent 5,351,746; next in the scale came Ireland with 4,212,169. The former Austro-Hungarian Empire and Italy contributed respectively 3,172,461 and 3,086,356.[2] These figures describe the largest and most significant movement of peoples in all history. During the past century the peoples of Europe who have been the victims of economic, political or religious oppression have turned to the United States as a haven of refuge.

Old and New Immigration Issues

Immigration, on the whole, has been regarded as an asset by the majority of students of the economic development of the United States. The immigrants as a general rule were men and women in the prime of life. Each and every one of them represented a capital asset of about $3,000. Immigration, and Catholic immigration particularly, did give rise to a number of issues of a non-economic character. From the beginning there was an acute racial feeling. The original settlers and their descendants who had given the country its

[1] Immigration Quotas on the Basis of National Origin. *Senate Document No. 65.* Seventieth Congress, 1st session, pp. 6-9.
[2] *Reports of the Immigration Commission. Abstracts,* Vol. I, p. 65.

political and cultural institutions were unwilling to make any concession to the political or cultural traditions of the immigrants. These were accentuated by differences in religious beliefs. In fact, it might be easily contended that religious differences were basic. Native Protestants were bitterly opposed to the incoming Catholics. Catholics regarded Protestants here as the last remnant of their persecutors. It is not easy for us, at this date, to get a true picture of the attitude of native Americans towards the immigrant in the first decades of the last century. Even in the late sixties children of Irish parents in New England schools had epithets of all kinds hurled at them by their fellow pupils. For many years Catholics were relegated to certain definite sections of New England towns, and, it was impossible for them to acquire property in other sections.

The greater part, by far, of contemporary literature deals with the coming of those peoples who have more recently sought refuge on our shores. The first immigrants, the English, the Germans and the Irish, it is said, were good material; but those who began to come in numbers after 1883, the Slavs and Italians, we are told, were not easily assimilated and their large numbers constituted a serious menace to American culture and standards of living. If we refresh our historical memories, we will find that the Germans and the Irish were considered just as objectionable in the thirties and fourties of the last century as the Italians and the Slavs in the first decade of the present century. When Irish and German immigration was at its high tide opposition to it found its most extreme form in the Native American and the Know-Nothing movements. When immigration from southern and eastern Europe reached a large volume its most extreme and outspoken opponents banded themselves together in what was known as the American Protective Association. It must not be assumed for a moment that opposition to immigration has been confined to the Native American, the Know-Nothing and the A. P. A. groups and their late brother, the K. K. K. The most powerful opposition to unrestricted immigration has not come from the extreme fomenters of religious hatred. In recent years an increasing number of persons have been allied against unrestricted immigration on purely economic grounds.[3]

From the economic standpoint there is good reason for believing that the ebb and flow of immigration were in rather close consonance with American industrial conditions: "A striking fact which first attracts the attention of one who examines the statistics since 1840 is the close sympathy between immigration and the industrial prosperity and depression of this country. Indeed, so close is the connection that many who comment on the matter have held that immigration during the past century has been strictly an industrial or economic phenomenon." [4] The great opposition to unrestricted immigration in this country came from those who believed that it was a serious menace to American institutions and ideals. When the immigrants began to come to the United States in the first decades of the nineteenth century they found a country whose institutions had assumed a fairly definite form. The immigrant himself brought some of his own institutions and his own peculiar outlook on life. A conflict was inevitable. The American was in possession, he held the fort; he would be satisfied with nothing less than the complete submission of the immigrant.

Reference has already been made to the line of demarcation usually drawn between the old and the new immigration. The old immigration came from the countries of northern Europe, principally Germany, Ireland, Great Britain, Norway and Sweden. This old immigration increased very gradually during the twenties and thirties of the last century. It reached mountain-like proportions during the forties and fifties. It

---

[3] There are some excellent sections on immigration and the various native movements in R. J. Purcell, *The American Nation*.
[4] J. R. Commons, *Races and Immigrants in America*, p. 63.

THE OLD IMMIGRATION 37

began to decline somewhat during the sixties and seventies. In the late eighties immigration from southern and eastern Europe assumed large proportions and continued its upward climb until the outbreak of the World War. The two countries, Germany and Ireland, which contributed the largest share of the older immigrants also contributed the largest number of Catholics. The greatest problem which confronted the Catholic Church in the United States from 1830 to 1880 was to provide for the religious needs of German and Irish immigrants. All its work during this long period is colored by the outlook and the needs of these two peoples. In studying the evolution of Catholic social work in the United States we must keep in mind the racial traditions of the Germans and the Irish and more particularly the Irish, because they constituted the largest element in the earlier immigration and because they congregated in cities to a much larger extent than did the Germans.

Irish Immigration, 1840-1860

The story of Irish immigration to the United States, particularly from 1840 to 1860, is a sad one. During those twenty years the total Irish immigration to this country was 1,734,-268. Between 1847 and 1854, inclusive, 1,186,928 Irish immigrants came to the United States. It is only in the light of the long train of circumstances preceding it that an exodus of such a proportion of the people of Ireland becomes intelligible. Under ordinary circumstances people do not leave their own homes and remove themselves forever from their native associations even at the beckoning of greater economic opportunities. But the situation in Ireland was far from ordinary during the seventeenth and eighteenth centuries. By a series of penal laws passed by the English Parliament in the decade 1690-1700 the people of Ireland saw the land turned over to English settlers and their trade brought to ruin.[5] Ire-

[5] George O'Brien, *Economic History of Ireland in the Eighteenth Century*, pp. 3-5.

land entered on the eighteenth century with a poor economic outlook: "The first eight years of the century were marked by no great economic progress in any direction and in many respects by economic retrogression. In the years 1779-1782 a great revolution took place. The restraints which fettered trade were loosened and the independence of Irish Parliament was reasserted. The twenty years that followed were conspicuous for continued progress towards prosperity. Rents rose rapidly, population increased, industry revived, trade flourished and the wealth of the country grew by leaps and bounds. Had not Ireland's independence been extinguished she would have developed into a rich and powerful nation. England, jealous of Ireland's new found prosperity, determined once more to assume control of Irish affairs." [6]

With their trade destroyed the Irish people had no other resource but to fall back on the land. The Irish peasant, of course, could not rent the best land. It had been turned into pasture by its alien owners. There was nothing left for the rank and file of the people except to crowd together on the poorest land. Keen competition for even the poorest soil drove rents to a maximum point. Subdividing of small holdings continued until in 1841, 44.9 per cent of all the land holders in Ireland occupied less than five acres.[7] The people on these small farms lived practically on the potato crop. They depended on public works and such other sources of day labor as the neighborhood provided in order to pay their rents. Wet seasons and the blight, year by year, made the potato crop ever more precarious as a main source of livelihood. The landlords, too, were opposed to further subdivisions of the land and commenced to promote consolidations. In many instances landlords encouraged emigration to the United States in order to have an opportunity of clearing their lands. The situation came to a climax in 1847. In that

[6] O'Brien, *op. cit.*, p. 7.
[7] M. J. Bonn, *Modern Ireland and Her Agrarian Problem*, p. 46.

year the potato crop was a total failure. The small land holders were left without a livelihood. Those who could obtain passage turned to America for relief. Some landlords even offered free transportation to their tenants, in order that they might be free to clear their estates. Many who could not pay their way found employment in English towns.

There was nothing planned or systematic about the great tide of Irish emigration. It was just a mad, headlong rush of a people from a dungeon in which they were exposed to slow and painful death. Where they were going they knew not. They were just seeking nature's first escape from suffering. The dangers of the new land and the journey thereto could not be any more real than those to which they had been exposed at home.

In 1847 Irish immigration to the United States doubled that of any previous year. In 1846 it totaled 51,752, in 1847 it had reached 105,536; but the end was not yet. The way was opened and the stream grew larger. In 1848, 112,934 Irish came to the United States; in 1849 the figure was 159,398; in 1850 it was 164,004; and in 1851 the tide of Irish immigration reached its crest with 221,253. In the years 1852, 1853 and 1854 there was a very gradual falling off in numbers with totals for the respective years of 159,548, 162,649, and 101,606. By 1855 the flow of Irish immigration had returned to its normal level of 49,627.[8]

Weakened as they had been by their sufferings at home the Irish immigrants of the late forties and early fifties were ill-prepared for the arduous journey to America. It is no wonder, therefore, that thousands of them died on the way to the land of their hopes. Disease stalked their path from the time they left home until they were settled in the new world. The difficulties of the famine-stricken immigrants almost beggar description. A report of a United States Senate Committee (1853), based on a careful study of sickness

[8] *Reports of the Immigration Commission. Abstracts*, Vol. I, pp. 74-77.

and mortality on board immigrant ships, gave an accurate picture of their sufferings. The following suggests the salient facts: "During the four last months of 1853, 312 vessels arrived at New York from European ports, with 96,950 passengers. Of these vessels 47 were visited by cholera, and 1,933 passengers died at sea, while 457 were sent to the hospitals on landing, there, in all probability, to terminate in a short time their miserable existence, making nearly 2 per cent of deaths among the whole number of persons who had embarked for the New World, and nearly 2½ per cent if those who were landed sick be included." [9] This report noted considerable difference between the sickness and mortality rates among passengers on ships sailing from English as compared with those sailing from German ports. Of 112 ships arriving from Liverpool in the last four months of 1853, 24 had cholera; of the 20 vessels arriving from London in the same period five had cholera; of the 52 vessels arriving from Bremen only three had cholera.[10]

The abnormally high mortality rate on British ships was due to overcrowding, to lack of proper sanitation, to insufficient food, to inadequate facilities for preparation of food, and to the weakened physical condition of the Irish passengers. In regard to the food allowance on British ships the report declared: "The object of providing the one pound of bread per diem for each passenger was to guard against utter destitution. It surely never could have been contemplated that an adult should rely upon so scanty a portion for necessary sustenance from the day of sailing to that of his landing. Yet to what an immense extent has this been practiced in voyages to Quebec, and occasionally in voyages to ports in the United States. The indigent Irish, unfortunately, avail of this pittance, and arrive out in a condition but little better

[9] *Report of the Select Committee of the Senate of the United States on the Sickness and Mortality on Board Emigrant Ships.* Washington, D. C., 1854, p. 9.
[10] *Ibid.*, pp. 9-10.

than that of starvelings, so emaciated and prostrate that they have to be conveyed forthwith to hospitals."[11]

The Germans were not compelled to go through the same ordeal as the Irish. They were not handicapped by a physique weakened by insufficient food. The Germans had a better understanding of the conditions which would confront them in the new world. The German ships were far better fitted for immigrant passenger service than the English ships.[12]

The stories of individual ships recount with more harrowing detail the sufferings of the Irish on their way to America. The ship, *Lucy Thompson,* after a passage of 29 days arrived in New York from Liverpool on September 11, 1853, with a loss of 40 out of 835 passengers due to cholera. The *Isaac Webb* arrived at New York from Liverpool in September of the same year after a passage of 29 days. Of the 773 passengers who had set sail, 77 had died of cholera. *The Washington* arrived at New York, October 23, 1853, after a passage of 41 days. It had 952 passengers on board, having lost 81 of cholera.[13]

Emigration from Ireland decreased from 101,606, in 1854, to 49,627, in 1855. In 1864 the number of immigrants again increased to 63,523; and, in 1867, it increased to 72,879. This increase was probably the result of the prosperity and increased demand for labor following the Civil War. In 1873 the number of Irish immigrants reached 77,344,[14] due to poor economic conditions in Ireland resulting from a general decline of agricultural prices. After 1873 Irish emigration to America shows marked variations depending on the economic situation in England and the United States. The people in Ireland who were intending to emigrate could secure fairly exact information regarding industrial conditions in the United States from their friends in this country.[15]

[11] *Ibid.,* p. 48.
[12] *Ibid.,* pp. 32-71.
[13] *Ibid.,* pp. 6-7.
[14] *Reports of the Immigration Commission. Abstracts,* Vol. I, pp. 77–83.
[15] *Ibid.,* pp. 84-96.

German Immigration After 1830

Beginning with 1830 there was a steady increase in German immigration to the United States. In the decade 1830-1840 over 152,000 German immigrants came to this country. The high point in German immigration came between the years 1846-1854 when from 57,500 in 1846, it mounted to 215,009 in 1854.[16] The revolutionary troubles in Germany in 1848 played a part in the exodus to America during the years immediately following. The opportunities presented by the United States, moreover, had been widely advertised in Germany. Particular stress was placed on the possibilities of acquiring good land at a nominal cost. There is probably no European people whom the cheap land of America so attract as the Germans.

Another high mark in German immigration came after the Civil War. From 1866 to 1873, the Germans came at the rate of 130,000 annually. Military duty and hard circumstances at home compared with the possibility of securing free land in America were largely responsible. German immigration, in fact, continued with fluctuations until it reached finally its lowest point in 1898. By this time the cheap land of America had disappeared and the development of the German Empire as an industrial nation had increased opportunities at home.[17]

Land Values in the Early Days

The United States offered unlimited opportunities to members of the old immigration to acquire on the same basis as natives cheap lands in the middle west. Beginning with 1820, land might be obtained from the Federal Government at a nominal charge of $1.25 an acre.[18] Furthermore in 1840 Congress gave settlers the right of preemption.[19] The land policy

---

[16] Faust, *op. cit.*, Vol. I, pp. 583-585.
[17] *Ibid.*, Vol. I, pp. 586-587.
[18] E. L. Bogart, *An Economic History of the United States*, p. 256.
[19] *Ibid.*, p. 261.

THE OLD IMMIGRATION 43

culminated in the famous Homestead Act of 1862 which made it easy and profitable for persons with little capital to acquire a farm home. This Act granted a free homestead not exceeding 160 acres to the actual settler. The title to the land passed to the settler after a five years' residence.[20]

The Germans availed themselves of the opportunities afforded by free land to a far greater extent than the Irish. A large number of the Germans came with free land as their definite objective. The Germans, moreover, emigrated in groups which made easier their settlement on distant lands. Most of the Irish immigrants of the forties and fifties knew little about the opportunities afforded by cheap land. They had left their own country under duress and they had no definite plans for their future. When they landed in New York, they were prepared to take the first work that was offered them. In regard to the work of the Irish immigrants in New England, a recent writer has stated: "They dug the canals, built the railroads, excavated for foundations, constructed the wharves and acted as laborers, stevedores and porters. Not many of them were mechanics and there were very few Americans who felt their competition. They performed the services the natives were unable or unwilling to do."[21] Only after the Yankees, in large numbers, had set out in quest of larger opportunities in the west were even the factories opened to the Irish.

Contribution of Early Irish Immigrants to Canal Building

The Irish immigrants of the twenties and thirties of the last century almost built the canals. The Erie Canal was built largely by Irish labor, and many of the Catholic settlements from Albany to Buffalo owe their origin to the Irish of the Canal Zone. After completing the canal, the Irish workers acquired title to or squatted on the adjoining land. Irish laborers and

[20] *Ibid.*, p. 299.
[21] "The Second Colonization of New England," by M. L. Hansen, *The New England Quarterly*, October, 1929.

contractors had an important part in building the Illinois and Michigan Canal extending from Chicago to LaSalle, a distance of about 100 miles. When the work on this canal was begun in 1836 large bodies of Irishmen were attracted from the eastern cities by the prospect of steady employment at good wages. Because of financial embarrassments, the state substituted "canal scrip" for cash, in payment of canal workers and contractors. The "scrip," however, soon reached a point at which it was no longer negotiable for cash. The only source of relief was in exchanging "scrip" for land in the neighborhood. Hence, it was that Irish settlements came to be formed along the canal from Chicago as far as Peoria.[22]

Before 1850 the steam boat passing over the canals, rivers and lakes was the chief means of transportation in the United States. The Erie Canal connected the west with New York City. Pennsylvania had built a canal connecting Philadelphia and Pittsburgh. The Ohio Canal connected Lake Erie with the Ohio River. The railroads which had been built before 1850 were regarded as feeders for waterways. By 1860 railroad transportation exceeded water transportation. It was estimated in that year that the railroads were carrying two-thirds of the total internal trade of the United States.[23] Large numbers of immigrants and particularly the Irish were employed in building railroads during the thirties, forties and fifties of the last century. Irish labor also played a very large part in building the transcontinental railroads after the Civil War.

Irish Immigrants as Unskilled Laborers

Such records as are available in regard to Irish immigration between 1830 and 1860 show that the Irish immigrants were compelled to take up menial and unskilled labor. When they could not find work in the cities they hired out to railroad and canal contractors. The contractors or subcontrac-

---
[22] "Irish Settlements in Illinois," *Catholic World;* Vol. XXXIII, May, 1881, p. 157.
[23] Bogart, *op. cit.,* p. 224,

tors took advantage of the immigrants by promoting rivalries and by absconding frequently with their wages. An article in the *Baltimore Catholic Mirror,* April 9, 1853, paints a vivid picture of the dangers of railroad work for Irish immigrants:

> On account of the difficulty of procuring employment in the cities many immigrant laborers are induced by the offer of liberal wages to engage on the railroads. This is, undoubtedly, the worst kind of work for the temporal and spiritual welfare of the laborer. The abominable conduct toward them by many contractors has rendered this kind of employment anything but agreeable to once well-conducted men. The contractor, or boss, as he is styled, when he sees labor can be had on cheaper terms, foments divisions between the different gangs so that one party will drive the other off the work and he then advertises for a dozen men or more offering good wages to all. When these arrive after a long journey they are sorely grieved to find that there is a superabundance of labor and consequently are obliged to take whatever wages are offered. Thus the contractor gets his work done on cheaper terms. Again the poor laborer is frequently defrauded of his hire by swindling contractors who pocket the money and abscond with their plunder to a remote part of the Union. The mode of living on the railroads is uncomfortable and demoralizing. Sometimes the laborers board with the contractor who generally keeps a grog-shop where their earnings are expended on the purchase of whiskey at an exorbitant price. At other times they are lodged in log houses, in which on account of poor construction, they are exposed to the inclemency of the seasons. Their wages vary from 75c to $1.25 a day, the former given in the North and Middle States, the latter in the Southern States, where the heat is oppressive and the climate unhealthy, and for this they are obliged to work from sunrise to sundown. Their condition is rendered more miserable by their own party feuds and factions. The contractors have fostered a provincial and hostile feeling in order that they might more readily carry into effect their fraud and injustice.... How different is

the conduct of the German laborer. When he arrives in America instead of loitering in lodging houses, gambling and drinking, he gets into the interior of the country, either in the northern or western states, where he loses no time in getting employment. He seldom goes to work on the railroads, but secures work on a farm and when he has saved some money by frugality and industry he purchases a plot of ground where he builds a house.

No people emigrated to America under more unfavorable conditions than the Irish, but even under the best conditions early immigrants were bound to undergo serious hardships in adjusting themselves to primitive American conditions. Other immigrants did not escape their share of trials. In a letter to the Leopoldine Society of Vienna, in 1841, Father John N. Neumann, later bishop of Philadelphia, pictured the hardships of German immigrants. He wrote that most of the German immigrants were either destitute or were heavily in debt. Their poverty-stricken condition compelled them to send their children to work. It happened that very often poor German parents gave their small children to wealthy Americans who brought them up as Protestants.[24] In a letter addressed to the same association, in 1835, Father Probst of Detroit said that the Germans in Rochester, New York, were mostly poor and also lacked spiritual care. Father Probst recalled that forty years previously a great number of German Catholics emigrated to America and fell away from the Church through the lack of a priest.[25]

Creation in 1847 of Board of Commissioners of Immigration

If the immigrant succeeded in escaping the perils of the sea and landed safely in America, he still had to run the gamut of the extortionate boarding-house keepers, ''bogus'' ticket agents, and dishonest forwarders. Some of the most

[24] *Letters of the Leopoldine Society,* Vol. II, 1841, pp. 56-62.
[25] *Ibid.,* Vol. I, 1835, pp. 64-65.

disgraceful tales are told in regard to overcharges made by boarding-house keepers and the misrepresentation of ticket agents. Before 1847 the immigrant was not given any legal protection. The vultures who desired to prey on his ignorance boarded the ship as soon as he landed. The health authorities tried to do what they could to see that the immigrant did not spread disease in the community. The poor laws officials endeavored to protect taxpayers against immigrant paupers.

Since about two-thirds of the immigrants to the United States came through the port of New York, immigration was a matter of vital concern to both the state and city authorities. There was a large amount of criticism in the early forties about the treatment of immigrants on landing in the city. A number of private organizations were establishing headquarters in order to protect the immigrant against fraud and to develop a systematic program of immigrant aid. It was felt, however, that these organizations were unequal to meet the situation. Finally the legislature passed a law in 1847, which created the Board of Commissioners of Immigration of the State of New York.[26] The commissioners were authorized to give relief and protection to immigrants arriving at New York. The law provided that the commissioners might require shipowners to deposit $300 for each immigrant to compensate the state in case he should become a dependent within five years. Instead of depositing this bond, shipowners might pay a per capita tax for each immigrant.

The work of the commissioners of immigration of New York State marked the beginnings of a systematic plan of public aid for immigrants. A number of buildings were erected on Ward's Island in which medical care and temporary housing were provided. Immigrants were assisted in establishing contact with their relatives, and they were also directed to employment opportunities. The efforts of the commission-

[26] *Report of New York State Commissioners of Immigration 1847*, p. 15.

ers, however, could not be entirely successful until they succeeded in securing a special landing place for all immigrants arriving at New York, for as long as immigrants were landed at any pier, sharpers who preyed upon weaknesses had every opportunity of practicing their frauds. They were able to neutralize the good work done by the representatives of the state. With a special landing place, it would be possible to exclude all those who sought to victimize the immigrants. At this central point might also be gathered bona fide representatives of transportation companies and private relief organizations who were interested in the immigrant's welfare.

Castle Garden, First Immigration Depot

After eight years of agitation the Commissioners of Immigration finally succeeded in establishing such a landing place at Castle Garden in 1855.[27] Here all the activities of the state, as well as of private immigrant welfare organizations centered.

Regulation of Immigration Becomes Federal Concern

By a decision of the United States Supreme Court (1876), the laws passed by New York State in 1847 and subsequent years were declared unconstitutional on the grounds that the regulation of immigration came distinctly within the province of the Federal Government. For the future the various states would have to look to Congress for all legislation affecting immigration, whereas heretofore Congress had given little attention to such legislation. By a law passed in 1819, masters of ships had been required to report the lists of their passengers and the ports from which they sailed. This statute set up standards which were designed to prevent overcrowding of ships and to provide a sufficient supply of food for the passengers.[28] By 1882 Congress took up the regulation

[27] J. T. Maguire, *The Irish in America*, p. 197.
[28] *Reports of the Immigration Commission*, Vol. XXXIX, p. 6.

of immigration in a systematic way when a law provided for a head tax of fifty cents on every immigrant entering the United States. It also excluded certain classes such as idiots, paupers, lunatics and convicts.[29]

In 1882 immigration legislation entered on a new era. Heretofore the immigrant was regarded as an important asset in developing the economic resources of the country. The western states no longer had great amounts of free land to offer. For the future, the immigrant was destined to become a city dweller. He must enter into competition with natives or with the older immigrant stocks. The immigrant who now sought admittance represented a different culture and spoke a different language from the immigrant that the country had known for nearly 100 years. This difference in language and culture gave racial and religious arguments against immigration a renewed force. There had always been opposition to immigration on these grounds, but the opposition had not been sufficiently strong to neutralize the economic advantages of immigration. In the eighties, the forces of race and religion began to join hands with organized labor in opposition to immigration.

[29] *Ibid.,* Vol. XXXIX, p. 32.

CHAPTER IV*

COLONIZATION AS A PANACEA

Free Land the Loadstone

Free land is frequently emphasized as the loadstone that attracted the immigrant to America. It certainly played a most prominent part in encouraging immigration and exercised a profound influence on the outlook of the American people for more than a century. Free land was held as a panacea for all the ills of the nation. Why should people suffer in cities as long as there was a vast continent that beckoned them and promised a reward from its seemingly inexhaustible resources?

The Stages in Land Development

The pioneers in the early westward development of the United States were interested in hunting and trapping, not in clearing the forest or bringing the land under cultivation. The hunters and trappers did not settle in any particular place. They were always seeking new fields in which game was more plentiful. On the trail of the hunters and trappers came the settlers who were attracted by the bounties offered by a rich soil. The first settlers had little thought of establishing permanent residences. As soon as their lands increased in value they took their profits and moved on to unsettled lands or possibly to the nearby cities. They were more land speculators than farmers. In the third state of development came farmers who were interested in a permanent home on the land. They were interested in improving the land, in rotation of crops, and in bringing to their work all that science and human experience had to offer.

* This Chapter appeared in *Studies*, Vol. XIX, No. 75 (Sept., 1930), under the title of "Irish Colonization in the United States."

Canals First Channels of Communication

For the Irish immigrants who came to this country during the years immediately following 1820, there were relatively few opportunities in the city. American industry was just entering the factory stage. The only communication between the eastern seaboard and the territory west of the Alleghenies was the stage coach. New Orleans was the natural outlet for trade between the middle west and foreign countries. One of the largest economic problems that confronted the American people was the opening of the channels of communication between the east and the middle west. Leaders of the nation regarded the canal as a means of linking the country, that had just been brought under cultivation, with the industrial centers. The development of American industry depended on ready access to the supply of raw materials, and the canal was the only means of this access. Hence the various states vied with one another in building canals. New York led the way with the Erie Canal which was begun in 1817. Pennsylvania, Maryland, Delaware, Ohio and Illinois followed suit. Between 1820 and 1830 over 800 miles of canals were opened to navigation. In 1830, 1,300 miles more were nearly completed.[1] As rivalry in canal building reached its height, there came the competition of the railroad. The first railroad was opened for traffic in 1830; but not until 1840 were railroads competing seriously with the rivers and canals.[2]

The digging of canals was the chief labor for Irish immigrants between 1820 and 1840. Indeed, it has been stated on reliable authority that practically all the canals constructed in America prior to the Civil War were dug by Irishmen.[3] Most of the railroads were also built by Irish labor. Their work on the canals and railroads gave Irish immigrants splen-

---
[1] Alvin Harlow, *Old Towpaths*, p. 73.
[2] Bogart, *op. cit.*, pp. 208, 210.
[3] Harlow, *op. cit.*, p. 4.

did opportunities of acquiring good land at nominal prices, but only the more enterprising availed themselves of this opportunity. Yet, Irish colonization began with the canal and railroad workers. Some of the more successful Irish colonies in New York State are found along the Erie Canal from Troy to Buffalo. Prosperous colonies are located along the Illinois Canal from Chicago to Peoria. The Irish in southern New York and northern Pennsylvania settled along the Erie and Lackawanna Railroad. If one studies the history of any Irish colony east of the Mississippi River, he will find that it traces its origin to the Irish railroad and canal workers.

Irish Immigrant Becomes American Industrial Worker

When Irish immigration reached its height in the forties and fifties, American industries held out increasing opportunities for employment to immigrants. Hence, the Irish tended to congregate more and more in the large industrial centers. They took the places of native workmen who had gone westward. Due to their lack of acquaintance with city life and their lack of organization, the Irish immigrants suffered unnecessary hardships. Those who were interested in their welfare continually bewailed the fact that they did not go to the land. How was it that a purely agricultural people entered industrial work when they might easily have secured rich land? This was the question continually before the minds of their advocates. An article in *Donahue's Magazine* expressed this tersely: "It has always seemed strange to every thinking person why the Irish who at home are the most purely agricultural people in Europe should be so fond of settling in the cities in America." This writer believing that the fact could be partially accounted for by the absence of ordered supervision in carrying out Irish immigration urged: "The British government was only too glad to get them out of Ireland and could hardly be expected to take much interest in their welfare in America, but it has always seemed strange that some organization was not put on foot either by intelligent laymen or by the Catholic Church to give shape to Irish immigration to America. This has been done for years by almost every European people except the Irish. Land is bought, plans are laid and sometimes the prairie broken up before the main body of immigrants leave Germany, England or Norway."[4] An editorial in the *Catholic Mirror*, of Baltimore, May 6, 1876, expressed the same thought. "Of the Irish immigrants who have come to the United States since 1840, about 60 per cent of the male adults were agriculturists in Ireland—farmers or laborers. The great majority of them have settled in the cities as day laborers or in some other menial employment. The present condition of this class according to Irish-American newspapers is one of great wretchedness and if we are to credit the said newspapers, the prisons and poor houses of the northern and eastern states have unfortunately too large a proportion of their inmates included from this population. Can nothing be done to influence the industrious and sober portion of them to seek homesteads in the country, where they at all events will have enough to eat and where their children will grow up independent farmers? The 'Do-Nothing' policy has existed long enough."

About a year afterwards Bishop John J. Hogan of St. Joseph stated: "We have suffered our Irish Catholic emigrants to drift solitary and isolated into the byways. These young people should have been kept in families with their parents and settled in neighborhoods and communities of their own. We have suffered them to become hirelings, to die in damp kitchens and cellars."[5] Addressing himself to the same subject Dean Byrne of Trenton said: "There is hardly a thinking mind which does not perceive how great a mistake our Irish people made by crowding into large Ameri-

---
[4] "Irish Immigration. Where to Found Irish Settlements in America." *Donahue's Magazine*, Vol. III (1880), pp. 527-528.
[5] *Baltimore Catholic Mirror*, April 7, 1877.

can cities. They have lost by it virtue, wealth and stability. It is an irreparable evil. . . ."[6] Thirty years before an Irish leader who had been prominent in the '48 movement in Ireland, raised his voice against the concentration of the Irish in the slums of American cities. D'Arcy McGee marvelled that a people who in Ireland hungered for land, when they reached America where a "day's wages would have purchased an acre of wild land in fee, wilfully concurred . . . to sink into the condition of a miserable town tenantry, to whose squalor even European seaports could hardly present a parallel." Never in the history of the world had a "purely agricultural population so suddenly and unpreparedly" been "converted into mere town laborers."[7] Mr. McGee dreamed of a back-to-the-land movement as the best means of saving the Irish in America. Seventy-five per cent of the Irish immigrants to the United States remained in the cities while in Canada the ratio was reversed. Seventy-five per cent of the Irish in Canada belonged to the settled, well-ordered country class. Why could not the same conditions prevail in the United States as in Canada? McGee painted most alluring pictures of Irish settlements in the United States with churches and schools as the center of their lives. In securing settlers for his model communities, he proposed to appeal especially to persons of means. His settlements scattered throughout the United States would enable the Irish to exercise a permanent influence on American life. Several Catholic leaders both in the United States and in Canada became interested in his project and met in a conference on Irish immigrant aid at Buffalo, February 12, 1856. Some eighty Catholic Irishmen, lay and clerical, were present; on all sides it was regarded as the most important meeting of Irishmen which so far had taken place in America.

The Buffalo Convention had two important objectives; first,

[6] *Ibid.*
[7] Isabel Skelton, *Life of Thomas D'Arcy McGee*, pp. 259-260.

COLONIZATION AS A PANACEA 55

to study the land available for settlement by Irish immigrants, and secondly, to secure the means necessary to settle the immigrants on the land. For McGee who was the central figure in the convention the problem was very simple: "We have the land; there exist the means by which it may be made accessible to the poorest; to apply the means to that end is our object."[8] He estimated that there were 100,000 Irish immigrants with means whose savings were deposited in the banks. On the other hand there were some 200,000 Irish immigrants without means. These would be anxious to settle in a farming community were a way opened for them. The men with means, he urged, should form joint-stock companies to take up land in selected sections of the United States and Canada. The poor men would settle the land and repay the money advanced in five, seven or ten years.

Irish Immigrants Not Purely Agricultural People

In this movement to get the Irish on the land, McGee encountered many difficulties. As the head of the movement he was more of an inspirational leader than a practical organizer. The Irish immigrants apparently were not enthusiastic about land which for 200 years had been so closely associated with their oppression. D'Arcy McGee, like others, assumed as a guiding principle that the Irish were an agricultural people. For centuries the Irish at home had lived off the land. Why, therefore, should the Irish in America take to city life? The tendency was to overlook a fundamental fact in the character of this immigration. In 1841 there were 310,436 from one to five acre farms in Ireland representing 44.9 of the total number of farms in the country; in 1851 the number of farms under five acres had fallen to 88,083, or 15.5 per cent of the farms of the country.[9] It may be assumed that every one of the 222,353 farms of less

[8] *Ibid.*, p. 272.
[9] Bonn, *Modern Ireland and her Agrarian Problem*, p. 46.

than five acres abandoned between 1841 and 1851 represented an immigrant family. These families did not live off their land. In fact, they gave little time to the cultivation of the land beyond raising a few patches of potatoes. In a sense, they were agricultural laborers. To the small tenants from rural Ireland, who should really be classed as agricultural laborers, must be added the town-laborers, who came over in large numbers in the forties and fifties. These facts should disabuse one of the idea that the Irish immigrants were purely agricultural and explain why they did not take so readily to American farms.

Settlement on land called for financial resources. Most of the Irish immigrants of the forties and fifties were a poor people fleeing from persecution and oppression. When they landed in New York, New Orleans or Montreal practically penniless, they were glad to avail themselves of any opportunity for earning a livelihood. It might have been possible for the Catholics of America to advance sufficient funds in order that their immigrant brethren might avail themselves of the land opportunities, but it is questionable whether the majority of the Irish immigrants would have become farmers under any conditions.

In America the Irish were faced by a hostile people. Opposition first reached an acute form in the eastern cities, the centers of the nativist and Know-Nothing movements of the forties and fifties, which were aimed directly at the Irish immigration. In the cities of the east, the Irish immigrant made his first stand for recognition, and here he first attained a recognized social and political status. Many Irish leaders did not look with favor on the movement to place them on the land because they were afraid that they might lose the influence they had already acquired in urban centers. The cities therefore came to be regarded as a sort of rampart that protected the spiritual as well as economic welfare of the immigrants. Removal of the Irish from the cities was viewed by many observers as depriving them of helpful safeguards of their faith.

McGee's Irish Colonization Scheme Suffers

McGee's controversy with Archbishop Hughes served to discredit him as a leader of an Irish Catholic movement. Hughes was entirely out of sympathy with the methods and program of the leaders of the Forty-eight Movement in Ireland. He was therefore loath to see one of these leaders in a position of leadership among Catholics in America. He had just taken a determined stand against the Young Ireland Movement in the *Freeman's Journal* in September, 1848, when McGee appeared in America to champion its cause. A bitter controversy with a bishop, whom Irish immigrants regarded as a champion, did not help the colonization scheme, and the poor immigrants lost confidence in McGee and his plans.[10]

McGee's program for the redemption of the Irish from American slum life could not die. Free land was in the air. Everybody was talking about it. Newspapers and magazine articles, high-powered salesmen for land companies and official agents of state governments sought the public ear in order to tell of the opportunities of the west. There was scarcely a family in the industrial centers that did not at some time think of settling in some middle western state. Recently the writer talked with a member of an original Nebraska colony concerning the circumstances that accounted for his going west. He said that the people around his neighborhood were all talking about the opportunities of the west. Persons from out of town who had already gone westward were writing continually to their relatives and friends trying to induce them to come out to "God's country." His parents finally caught the fever and set out one day for Illinois with these other families. For two years they farmed in Illinois

[10] H. A. Brann, *Most Reverend John Hughes*, p. 106.

until an opportunity presented itself of securing good, free land in Nebraska. The movement gripped the imagination of the American people. As people were made acquainted with the opportunities of free land, they planned their own westward movement. Catholic families were attracted by places in which other Catholic families had settled in the hope of practicing their religion.

Maryland and Kentucky Catholic Settlements Become Patterns

Many leaders interested in the welfare of Catholic immigrants were unwilling to see the settlement on the land by accident or individual planning. They were afraid lest the immigrants might drift into sections where they would have no opportunity of practicing their faith. They felt that for the urban Irish it was necessary to have an organized movement to get them out on the land. It was thought, moreover, that such a movement would assist immigrants with the capital necessary for a proper start. The funds, of course, would be advanced on a strictly business basis to be repaid over a period of years. Large numbers of Catholics who came to America before the Revolution or in the early days of the Republic, had lost their faith because they drifted into places where there was no church or priest. On the other hand, there was the example of the Catholic settlements in Maryland and Kentucky. Many pioneer leaders, who fashioned the Church in America, were products of Maryland and Kentucky. The settlements in these two states stood out as an example of what Catholic communities should be. It was felt that if other groups could be banded together in similar fashion, that there would be nothing to fear for their religious welfare, while if permitted to drift the immigrants might be lost forever to the faith. This was the thought of D'Arcy McGee, and through his zeal and enthusiasm he gave it a new color and a new appeal.

COLONIZATION AS A PANACEA 59

Father Demetrius Gallitzin's Pennsylvania Settlement

The settlement established by Father Gallitzin at Mount Loretto, Pennsylvania, materially emphasized the possibilities of Catholic colonization. Gallitzin was a Russian prince and a convert who decided to dedicate his fortune and his life to the spiritual welfare of American Catholics. During a missionary visit to the region of the Alleghenies (1796), he conceived the idea of forming a Catholic settlement. With his own means he purchased land adjoining the 400 acres that had been donated for a church by Captain McGuire, a Marylander who was an original settler in western Pennsylvania. He turned over the land to settlers at a nominal price on easy terms; he established at his own expense sawmills, grist mills and tanneries for the benefit of his people. This colony of Mount Loretto really became the cradle of Catholicity in western Pennsylvania, for his missionary field covered the entire region now included in the dioceses of Pittsburgh and Erie and a large part of Harrisburg. In his efforts to develop his colony Gallitzin mortgaged his own fortune. When the Russian government disinherited him for becoming a Catholic and a priest, he was reduced to serious financial straits and was compelled to appeal to the charitable public for assistance in meeting his financial obligations.[11]

Irish Immigrant Society Organized in New York

The Irish Immigrant Society organized in New York in 1841 did much to call the attention of the immigrants to the opportunities of American land. Indeed, the promoters assumed that one of its principal purposes was to turn immigrants from the city to the country, as was well noted in an article in the *New York Freeman's Journal:*

> The misfortune, the privations, the utter degradation to which multitudes of those who remain here are

[11] *Catholic Encyclopedia,* Vol. VI, pp. 367-369; see also sketch of Gallitzin by R. J. Purcell in the *Dict. of Amer. Biography.*

reduced from ignorance of the true advantages which the country presents to the laboring, sober and industrious immigrant are evils that call still more strongly upon the benevolent exertions of the philanthropic.

The way of gaining competency if not all the comforts is in the interior of the country. And yet in the city streets we find squalid poverty and wretchedness if not vice in underground hovels. Who can see this and know the remedy and not feel it his sacred duty to use his knowledge for the relief of sufferers.[2]

Industrial conditions in the eastern cities were then rather chaotic. The land of the west provided a universal panacea. When the industrial conditions in the cities became more stabilized, and when the Irish began again to find work in the cities, there was no longer such universal clamor for their transfer to the farms.

Organized Catholic Colonies in Nebraska and Minnesota

The first organized colonies that trace their organization to the agitation during the fifties to place the Irish on the land were those begun by Father John Trecy of Nebraska and General James Shields in Minnesota. It must not be assumed, however, that these colonies represent the total net result of the movement. Large numbers of families went west on their own initiative. In many instances lesser individuals induced families to settle on the land, which they bought and resold to settlers. The organized settlements, however, exercised a wide influence in attracting people to their vicinities. Families took it for granted that if they acquired land near a Catholic settlement, they would be provided with religious facilities.

Father Trecy, one time priest in the Diocese of Dubuque, conceived the idea of organizing a Catholic colony in Nebraska in 1853. In his efforts to recruit members for his colony Father Trecy encountered opposition from Catholic

[12] Jan. 16, 1841.

leaders in eastern cities and particularly from Archbishop Hughes of New York. A surviving member of Trecy's colony informed the writer that he had heard the priest himself tell how he had been ordered out of New York by Archbishop Hughes. But Father Trecy was not discouraged, for he was working under the inspiring leadership of Bishop Mathias Loras of Dubuque, who was intensely interested in Catholic colonization. In the early part of 1855 he secured land in Dakota county in northeastern Nebraska, and in the spring of the following year he assembled his prospective colonists at Dubuque, Iowa. Every family had sufficient food for two years and all the necessary equipment for the cultivation of virgin prairies. On June 1, 1856, the prospective colonists, with the blessing of Bishop Loras, set out from Garryowen near Dubuque on the long trail to Nebraska. Nearly every family had its own covered wagon in which it carried its food supply, household utensils and farm implements. A number of the families brought cows, sheep and chickens. Two men, who with their wives joined the colonists just before they reached the Des Moines River, did not have any covered wagon. They drove the cattle and the sheep. The journey from Dubuque to Sioux City, which can now be completed in 10 hours, required six weeks, for the country traversed was without bridges and roads. It was like tracing a path through the wilderness. When the party reached the Des Moines River they found it at high-water mark. Fording was out of the question. There seemed, therefore, to be no alternative except to wait until the waters receded. Father Trecy, however, was determined to get across immediately. With the aid of some of the more enterprising spirits of the party, he used one of the covered wagons as a flat boat. This enabled the colonists to get over the river without delay and bring all their provisions.

When the colonists reached their destination in Nebraska, just twelve miles from Sioux City, they found a finished log cabin, a second log cabin under construction and a dugout on the hillside. Miles and miles of prairie stretched out before them peopled by roving Indians. In this bleak country they must struggle against the aborigines as well as the unpropitious elements. There were, however, many redeeming features. They had sufficient food and the soil was rich. The settlers had to construct their log cabins and prepare the ground for crops. The first season was an ordeal. As the crops were ready for the harvest, swarms of locusts consumed everything within sight. Their first year's work had gone for naught. The succeeding years brought better luck. When Father Trecy established his colony, Nebraska land had not been surveyed. Settlers here and there along the Missouri River had merely acquired squatters' rights. No settler knew how far his farm extended. Only by agreement with his neighbors could there be any determination of property rights. By the terms of the later homestead act each settler's share was reduced to 160 acres, or a quarter of a section of land.

The headquarters of Father Trecy's original settlement was known as Old St. Johns. It was located on the west bank of the Missouri River, but because of changes in the course of the river the settlement was compelled to move its headquarters. Relocated it also changed its name to Franklin for St. Johns, later O'Gorman, after the first bishop. More recently the settlement has become known as Jackson.

The most striking evidence of its success was the extent to which the settlers persevered. During the first 10 years only two families left the settlement, and these were attracted by the discovery of gold in Colorado. The success was due largely to the leadership of Father Trecy. He worked with the pioneers in breaking the virgin prairie. He was with them in all their difficulties. He selected his settlers carefully. He was particularly fortunate in his selection of land. His understanding of conditions in the new west enabled him to give them the best advice in cultivating the soil.[13]

General Shields also exercised a marked influence on Catholic colonization in the west. On leaving the United States Senate in 1855, General Shields went to Minnesota to select some lands that had been awarded him for his service in the Mexican War. He was so favorably impressed with the state that he decided to go east and organize a large colony of Irish-Americans to settle on the fertile lands of Rice and Le Sueur counties. General Shields also encountered vigorous opposition in the east, especially from Archbishop Hughes. Under stress of this opposition, he saw his picture of Catholic colonization gradually fade. However, he secured some concrete results. The fruits of his labors as a colonizer are the townships of Shieldsville, Erin, Kilkenny and Montgomery in Rice and Le Sueur Counties, Minnesota, where still reside hundreds of industrious and prosperous farmers.[14]

The Minnesota Irish Immigration Society

The close of the Civil War marked the beginning of an era of industrial expansion. Through the building of the transcontinental railroads the fertile lands between the Mississippi and the Rocky Mountains were connected with the industrial centers of the nation. The settler on the virgin prairie was now provided with profitable market for his goods. He no longer depended on the covered wagon to reach his destination. It was possible for him to secure good land at a nominal price within easy access of a railroad. Land opportunities were greater than ever. Under the Homestead Act of 1862 it was possible for each settler to secure a title to 160 acres of arable land at a nominal charge of $15. The prospective settler might purchase railroad lands from $2 to

---

[13] The material in regard to Father Trecy's colony was supplied to the writer by Mrs. John Boler, 913 South Thirty-sixth Street, Omaha, Nebr., a member of the original group that traveled with Father Trecy.
[14] *Minnesota Historical Society Collections*, Vol. XV, p. 711.

$11 an acre with eleven years to pay. Catholic leaders, therefore, felt that the time had arrived to make a new effort to bring the Irish back to the land. The most important step in this direction was the organization of the Minnesota Irish Immigration Society in 1866. In explaining its purposes the promoters referred to the "tendency of the Germans and Norwegians emigrating to the United States to hasten to the northwest to build up homesteads and labor for themselves. The Irish crowded into large cities or flocked around public works to toil for others, the wealth of their labor giving neither to themselves nor their children but to the profit of shady speculators in whose eyes they are merely Irish."[15] Their conservative hopes were expressed in the preamble to the society's constitution: "In its infancy it cannot expect to be able to do more than afford information, advice and protection to the emigrant."

Archbishop Ireland and Catholic Colonization in Minnesota

The Minnesota Irish Immigration Society paved the way for the work of one of the greatest colonizers, John Ireland of St. Paul. From the beginning Bishop Ireland had given his hearty support to the work of the Minnesota Immigration Society. He believed, however, that a more definite plan of organization was needed. The Catholic colony promoted by a Catholic organization represented his ideal. In January, 1876, he secured from the St. Paul and Pacific Railroad twelve townships of railroad land, or seventy-two square miles, on the main line in Swift County, Minnesota. By the purchase of depreciated railroad bonds, which were exchangeable for land at par value, the archbishop found that he could place good land at the disposal of the settlers for $1.75 to $3.50 an acre.[16] In 1875 he purchased from the Sioux City and St. Paul Rail-

---

[15] *New York. Freeman's Journal,* July 30, 1864.
[16] An Invitation to the Land. Reasons and Figures. Published by the Catholic Colonization Bureau of St. Paul, Minn., 1877.

road 70,000 acres of land in Nobles County in the southwestern part of Minnesota, about 200 miles west of St. Paul.[17]

Archbishop Ireland planned to organize his colonies on a strictly business basis. For this purpose he organized the Catholic Colonization Bureau of St. Paul as distinct from the Minnesota Irish Immigration Society, of which he had been president (1876.) Settlers were given ten years to pay for their land. All prospective settlers were advised that they would need capital amounting to $400 to build a log house, buy implements and support themselves for the first year.[18] Archbishop Ireland's colonies made a strong appeal throughout the country. In the spring of 1876, eighty families settled in Swift County, Minnesota. By the spring of 1878 about four hundred Catholic families had settled in the county. All the land owned by the colonization society was quickly taken up. Large numbers of Catholic families, who were unable to buy railroad land in Swift County, acquired land in the adjoining Stevens County. And there sprang up such towns as Avoca, Clontarf, Croke, Graceville.

Other Catholic Settlements

While Archbishop Ireland was organizing his Minnesota colonies a number of Catholic colonization projects were developed in other sections of the country. The Irish Catholic Benevolent Associations of St. Louis and Philadelphia organized colonization societies and purchased land for the settlers, respectively, in Pottawattomie County, Kansas, and in Charlotte County, Virginia.[19] In 1873 General John O'Neil established a Catholic settlement at O'Neil, Nebraska. In 1877 Thomas Hynes established a Catholic settlement at O'Connor, Nebraska. With the aid of Bishops Ireland, O'Connor and

[17] Irish Immigration to the West in *Haverty's Irish American Illustrated Almanac*, 1878, pp. 97-99.
[18] *New York. Freeman's Journal*, April 29, 1876.
[19] *Baltimore Catholic Mirror*, March 30, 1878.

Spalding, this colony was more fully developed and the nearby colonies of Greeley and Spalding were established.

Among those who were influenced by the success of Archbishop Ireland's endeavors there is one to whom special reference should be made, John Sweetman, a wealthy landowner of County Meath, Ireland. Mr. Sweetman was one of those who regarded American land as a cure-all for the ills of the poverty-stricken Irish farmer. In 1880 he arrived in St. Paul and explained to Archbishop Ireland his desire to purchase land in Minnesota and turn it over to Irish settlers on easy terms. The archbishop encouraged him in his project, but advised him to secure first-hand knowledge of existing Catholic colonies. After studying the situation, he acquired 18,000 acres of land at Currie in Murray County from the Minnesota and St. Paul Railroad. In May, 1881, his first colonists arrived from Ireland. They were absolutely penniless. Mr. Sweetman was compelled to provide them with all the equipment necessary for farming. After two years of bitter experience this high-minded philanthropist learned that unless a settler had his own money invested in land the difficulties of pioneer life proved too great for him. He was inclined to use the proceeds of the first harvest on land for which he had paid nothing to go to the city and work for wages.[20]

Association Formed to Nationalize Catholic Colonization

Archbishop Ireland was deeply conscious of the fact that Catholic colonization could not be organized effectively on a local basis. While his Catholic Colonization Bureau at St. Paul had done good work, much more could be done if the work was nationally organized. Constant references to Minnesota and Archbishop Ireland gave rise to many rumblings. It was charged that colonization was being exploited entirely

---

[20] "The Sweetman Irish Colony," by Alice E. Smith, *Minnesota Historical Collections*, Vol. IX, p. 331.

as a means of developing the archdiocese of St. Paul and the state of Minnesota. In order to give Catholic colonization its proper national setting a general conference was called by St. Patrick's Society of Chicago March 17, 1879, with the following objects:

> (1) To counsel together as to the best and most efficient means to provide and encourage immigration to land, of and in localities where the blessings of religion and the advantages of education among those of the faith and kindred are present.
> (2) To effect organization under suitable auspices of a central bureau in each of the chief countries where the necessary information to immigrants and colonists will be furnished. This bureau will guide and assist in getting the immigrant to his destination.
> (3) To form if possible a national association to systematize and direct our countrymen through information and through resources, to make it practicable to bring within the reach of the poorer classes an opportunity to become landowners and cultivators of land.[21]

In the Chicago meeting Archbishop Ireland was able to lay the basis of a national program for Catholic colonization. In that meeting he had associated with him two other outstanding bishops, Spalding of Peoria and O'Connor of Omaha, and a prominent Catholic layman who henceforth was to take a position of leadership in the movement. At the Chicago conference a committee, appointed to reduce its discussions to a concrete program, met a few weeks later and organized the Irish Catholic Colonization Association of the United States. Among the members of the board of directors who signed their names to a statement outlining the functions of the association were: Archbishops Ireland, Gibbons of Baltimore, Williams of Boston, Bishops Ryan of Buffalo, O'Connor and Spalding, and Messrs John Lawler of Prairie Du Chien, Wisconsin, and W. J. Onahan of Chicago.[22]

[21] *New York Freeman's Journal*, Feb. 22, 1879.
[22] *Ibid.*, June 7, 1879

The Irish Catholic Colonization Association was a joint-stock company incorporated under the laws of Illinois. It proposed to take up colonization on a systematic basis. It would purchase land and sell it to prospective colonists. If those who desired land were unable to pay cash, they might buy the land on credit and have their payments extended over a number of years. Through its long-term payments the association expected to help those who desired to settle on land but did not have sufficient means. There was no intention of encouraging those who were absolutely destitute to go out on the land. It was thought every prospective settler should have $600 or $700. It was an almost universal experience that the settler who was provided with everything and did not have any stock in the land was apt to be a failure. In 1879 Ireland and Spalding made a tour of the eastern cities for the purpose of arousing interest in the colonization movement. In the same year Archbishop Ireland, through his agent in Liverpool, Father Nugent, succeeded in transferring 300 persons from one of the poorest districts in Ireland to Big Stone County, Minnesota.[23]

Immigrant Bureau at Castle Garden in 1883

One of the interesting by-products of the Irish Catholic Colonization Association was the establishment of an Immigrant Bureau for help and guidance at Castle Garden. The leaders of the colonization movement were convinced that even at this late date the Catholic immigrant aid was not properly organized. In describing the situation Mr. Onahan stated that: "Many Irish organizations on the seaboard are good on parade but not beneficial actually. The zeal of the managers and workers at Castle Garden is very fine but they have too much work on their hands and are likewise hampered by lack of resources. The work of the Immigrant Aid Society should begin where the work and functions of the

[23] Irish American Colonies, *Catholic World*, XXXII (Dec., 1880), p. 346.

Castle Garden authorities terminate."[24] It was a well-known fact that many of the abuses about which there had been complaint for thirty years still continued. Our immigrants were frequently charged more than first-class fare from New York to Chicago and given the worst possible accommodations. As a result of the recommendations of the colonization association Cardinal McCloskey appointed Rev. J. J. Riordan to take charge of the newly organized immigrant bureau at Castle Garden in October, 1883.[25]

During the eighties there was a gradual waning of interest in colonization. Year by year the supply of free land was becoming more limited. The great development of American industries provided a larger outlet and more immediate opportunities for gain. The Irish turned their attention to America's rapidly developing industries. During the eighties and nineties thousands of them attained greater success in these lines than they ever could have on the farm. In fact, many who were already settled on the farms were attracted by the larger opportunities of city life.

Weak and Strong Points of Catholic Colonization

Archbishop Ireland's work in Catholic colonization will ever be regarded as one of the finest contributions that has ever been made to immigrant welfare and hence to the building of the Catholic Church in the United States. The work undoubtedly had its weak points and its failures. One still hears many pathetic tales of colonists who had no experience in farming and who were ill prepared for the hardships of the pioneer's life. Some of the colonists from small towns in Ireland had no knowledge of farming. Even for those who had experience in tilling the soil in Ireland the breaking of the virgin prairie was a new experience. The methods of cultivating Minnesota and Nebraska land were far different from

[24] *New York Freeman's Journal*, Dec. 9, 1882.
[25] *Ibid.*, Oct. 27, 1888.

those used in Ireland. In view of the many difficulties, the work of Archbishop Ireland and his associates as a whole must be regarded as a striking success. While some of the colonists failed and drifted back to the city the greater number remained and have built up prosperous Catholic farming communities. The great publicity attracted to the work of the Catholic colonization movement undoubtedly attracted thousands of immigrants who were not a part of the organized colonies to avail themselves of the opportunities of free land. Colonization could never be regarded as a panacea for all the immigrants. It could scarcely be regarded as an alleviation cure for poverty. It was intended for persons with initiative and ability who already had some capital with which to begin.

CHAPTER V
CATHOLIC CHILD-CARE BEFORE THE CIVIL WAR
Early Child-Caring Institutions

Before 1840, sixteen Catholic institutions for dependent and neglected children had been established in the United States. The care of dependent and neglected children away from their own homes was only a part of the work of these institutions; in fact, in the beginning it was only a small part of their work. Each and every one of them operated day schools for poor children as well as for pay-pupils. A major part of their earnings was derived from their pay schools. Before 1840 the care of dependent and neglected children did not seem to be a problem outside of a few cities like Baltimore, St. Louis, Louisville, New York, Philadelphia and Boston. Due to the immigration tide there was naturally a very large increase in the number of dependent and neglected children during the next two decades.

Diocesan Sees Established, 1840-1860

During the decade 1840-1850, sixteen new dioceses were established, making a total of thirty-two dioceses, six of these archi-episcopal sees in 1850. Between 1850 and 1860, eleven new dioceses and three vicariates were established.[1]

An Asylum in Rochester

In a number of cities orphan asylums antedated the establishment of dioceses. In 1845 Rev. Bernard O'Reilly petitioned for the Sisters of Charity to conduct an asylum in Rochester. Four sisters were sent and assumed charge of an institution which had formerly been under lay managers. Father O'Reilly expressed the conviction that the sisters

[1] Shaughnessy, op. cit., pp. 132, 144.

should at once open a pay school. A sister who was the first to enter the home, April 10, 1845, related: "What a house! How poor we were at first! Even the beds we slept on were borrowed, but we did not know it until the fall, and they were sent for. . . ."[2]

An Asylum in Albany

In 1828 Bishop Du bois of New York successfully urged the Sisters of Charity of Emmitsburg to open an orphan asylum in Albany:

> The Sisters arrived in Albany October 17th. Father Smith rented a small house for the Sisters, but for their school he rented an old abandoned bake-house. It was a queer school-house, the chief ornament of the class room was an old rickety oven, a rendezvous for rats. Poverty and privations of all kinds were the portion of the Sisters who cast the first mustard seed in Albany. They were so poor that they could not buy a stove, and a wood fire in an open fireplace, was their greatest comfort through the rigors of that pitiless climate. On May 19, 1829, Father Smith wrote Mother Augustine at Emmitsburg: 'I am happy to tell you that the Sisters are successful in Albany. The pupils are numerous and every day increasing. I was aware that if I could get the good Sisters of Charity to Albany that a blessing would accompany them and my expectations have been realized. . . .'
>
> The Sisters had been two years in Albany when the scourge of Asiatic cholera devastated the land in 1831. Up to this time the establishment had existed only as a day school, but now the orphans were crying in the streets. The Sister Servant of the school sought means to succor them. An Asylum grew up adjoining the church and was opened the following May, 1832.[3]

The Orphan Asylum as a Unit of the Parish

Many of the orphan asylums established in the United States before 1860 were essentially parochial in character.

---

[2] *Archives* of Mt. St. Joseph's College, Emmitsburg.
Ibid.

This was due to the character of the parishes, which were really separate and autonomous entities. The people of the parish often represented a distinct immigrant settlement. Its members came from a certain county in the old country. In a hostile country they felt that they could not expect any assistance from the outside. They could not let their children go to the poor houses because it would be an eternal disgrace; they could not permit them to become beneficiaries of Protestant philanthropy because they would be lost to the faith. And just as the immigrants banded together for the preservation of their faith and natonal ideals so also did they associate together for the development of mutual assistance. Racial societies assisted persons in need. Some of the immigrant nationalities brought strong traditions of fraternalism. The Germans, particularly, had long experience with fraternal societies. They developed in America the same kind of parish societies that had been found useful in the old country. The Irish without much experience with fraternal organizations found expression largely through organizations that had been developed for the purpose of preserving their natural inheritance. The parish fraternal, or racial society, in the spirit of neighborly service might satisfy the normal charitable needs of an immigrant group under ordinary circumstances, but they were unable to bear up under the severe strains created by frequent epidemics.

The Development of Orphan Asylums

Cholera epidemics carried off large numbers of parents and left their orphan children dependent upon charity. This situation led to the establishment of orphanages both on a city-wide and diocesan-wide basis. The scourge of Asiatic cholera in Albany in 1831 had compelled the Sisters of Charity to open an orphan asylum for children. On June 3, 1848, a little band of six Sisters of Charity arrived in Buffalo on the invitation of Bishop John Timon to care for the orphans left parentless by the ravages of the cholera then epidemic. Three of the sisters were assigned to hospital duty and the other three set about establishing an orphan asylum. They first began work in a house adjoining old St. Patrick's Church on the corner of Broadway and Ellicott Streets. Soon afterwards the bishop bought the lot and building of the Buffalo Orphan Asylum and later old St. Patrick's Church was remodeled into an orphan asylum to meet the growing demands made upon the sisters.

In 1852, the revenue being very small, a select school was opened; but as the accommodations for it were limited on account of the large number of orphan children, the proceeds were insufficient and the sisters were obliged to seek provisions from the neighboring farmers. This means of support was kept up for many years. In 1862 the select school was closed. A small kitchen was fitted up in the basement of the church and soup and bread were furnished the poor. This custom was also followed during the severe winter months until the end of the Civil War.[4]

Since the Sisters of Charity were now confining their efforts to the care of girls, Bishop Timon made separate provision for the boys whose parents had been swept away by the cholera of 1848. At first it was necessary to care for the boys in private homes. A boys' asylum known as St. Joseph's was opened at Lancaster in 1850. Four years later the boys were removed to a building on Best Street, in Buffalo. In 1856 Bishop Timon gave the asylum a tract of sixty acres on Limestone Hill,[5] the present site of Our Lady of Victory Institute.[6]

---

[4] The above citation is taken from a report on the history and development of St. Vincent's Orphan Asylum, Buffalo, prepared for the writer by the sisters now in charge of the institution. It illustrates very graphically the difficulties encountered by the early Catholic orphan asylums.

[5] C. G. Deuther, *The Life and Times of the Rt. Rev. John Timon*, p. 170.

[6] In 1857 the new St. Joseph's Orphan Asylum at Lackawanna was placed in charge of the Sisters of St. Joseph.

The Parish Still Active in the Development of Orphan Asylums

While the dioceses played an increasingly important part in the development of orphan asylums after 1840, many parishes continued to take the initiative in their development. In 1850 Rev. Peter Havermans established orphan asylums for boys and girls at Troy, New York.[7] From the *Catholic Directory of 1855* we learn that the Roman Catholic Orphan Asylum and St. Vincent Home for Boys were originally attached to St. Patrick's parish church in San Francisco.[8] St. Joseph's Orphan Asylum, Washington, D. C., now known as St. Joseph's Home and School, was established by a group of prominent Catholic laymen in 1854 under the leadership of Rev. T. O'Toole, pastor of St. Patrick's Church. The report of St. Patrick's parish for 1904 states that for twenty-five years after its establishment all the food used by St. Joseph's was begged by the sisters at the Washington markets.[9] St. Joseph's, however, was not the first institution for dependent and neglected boys in Washington, for St. Matthew's Orphan Asylum was established in connection with St. Matthew's Church in 1843. It was in charge of the Sisters of Charity until 1846. Between 1846 and 1852 it was under the Christian Brothers. In 1852 the institution seems to have been discontinued. In this connection it may be repeated that the first Catholic orphan asylum established in Washington (1825), namely, St. Vincent's Orphan Asylum, now known as St. Vincent's Home and School, owed its existence to the Rev. William Matthews, pastor of St. Patrick's Church.[10] St. Joseph's Home and School and St. Vincent's Home and School have continued to maintain a close affiliation with St. Patrick's Church, whose pastor has always been chairman of the boards of both institutions.

[7] W. P. Letchworth, *Homes of Homeless Children, Annual Report, New York State Board of Charities, 1876*, pp. 473, 476.
[8] Page 209.
[9] *Archives* of St. Patrick's Church, Washington, D. C.
[10] *Archives* of Mt. St. Joseph's College, Emmitsburg; *cf.*, Chapter II.

An Orphan Asylum in Pittsburgh

Another good illustration of pastoral initiative in the development of orphan asylums is St. Paul's Orphan Asylum in Pittsburgh. The increase in the number of dependent children in Pittsbugh in the late 1830's aroused the sympathy of Rev. John O'Reilly, pastor of St. Paul's Church in that city. On July 6, 1838, Father O'Reilly organized St. Paul's Orphan Society. He selected twelve laymen to serve with him as the board of trustees of the institution. To avoid confusion with a Protestant organization the name of the agency was changed to St. Paul's Roman Catholic Orphan Society. A charter was obtained from the state legislature, April 3, 1840, legally authorizing the association "to receive, care for and dispose of any orphan child or children or such other children as may be deprived of one parent."[11] Shortly after its organization St. Paul's Roman Catholic Orphan Society proceeded to build an orphanage. The management of the institution was turned over to the Sisters of Charity. In 1845 the Sisters of Charity withdrew and were succeeded by the Sisters of Mercy in March, 1846; in the interim the girls were cared for by some lay women and the boys by the Presentation Brothers.

St. Paul's, like other institutions for children, was impressed very much by the possibility of placing the older boys out in good farm homes. The institution had received a bequest of a large farm near the city on condition that an orphan asylum be built for older boys. In 1849 a number of boys were placed on the farm for agricultural training under the direction of the Franciscan Brothers. However, the program, like many others of its type, did not work out successfully.[12] Ten years later another unsuccessful effort was made to work out a similar plan in a new location under the Franciscan

---

[11] A. A. Lambing, *A History of the Catholic Church in the Dioceses of Pittsburgh and Allegheny*, p. 504.
[12] *Ibid.*, pp. 504–505.

Brothers. In 1866 plans were completed to accommodate both boys and girls in a new St. Paul's Orphanage on Tannehill Street.[13] In 1898 the institution moved to its present location at Crafton Station.

The Parish Orphan Asylum Now Almost Extinct

The parish orphan asylum is now largely a thing of the past. Those originally organized on a parish basis have become city-wide and diocesan-wide institutions. The diocese has taken the place of the parish as the unit in Catholic child-caring work.

Orphan Asylums Become City-Wide Responsibility

The parish as a child welfare agency did not disappear without a struggle. When the orphan asylum endeavored to make a city-wide appeal many were inclined to say: "Well, that belongs to such and such a parish. Why should it appeal to outsiders for support?" In many places this attitude was a serious difficulty in the way of diocesan appeals. As late as September, 1864, Archbishop Spalding of Baltimore, in a letter addressed to the pastors of the diocese, laid special stress on the fact that the orphan asylums of Washington and Baltimore were not local or parochial in character: "We would wish to impress upon you that our charitable institutions and more particularly our orphan asylums, are not local but general or Catholic; and that the managers should feel bound, as far as they will be able, to receive Orphans without discrimination from all the parishes of the city in which they are established, so all the parishes of the city should feel equally bound in conscience to aid and support them. . . ."[14]

The Irish and Orphan Asylums

The question of nationality loomed large in Catholic child-care work in the United States. Since the Irish were

---
[13] *Ibid.*, pp. 505–507.
[14] *Baltimore Catholic Mirror*, Sept. 17, 1864.

the first Catholic immigrants to come to this country in large numbers the volume of dependency was greater among them than among the other nationalities in the forties and fifties. As the Irish congregated in the rising industrial centers, they were therefore more subject to the vicissitudes of industrial life and were exposed to social forces that broke up their communal traditions.

A knowledge of the English language gave the Irish immigrants, however, certain advantages in adjustment. They were glad to use the existing Catholic facilities for the care of their children. They worked with the original Catholic groups in making these facilities more adequate. In the development of many Catholic children's institutions, however, we can not fail to note both direct and indirect appeals to the pride of Irish immigrants. In the first appeal used by the board of directors of the New York Catholic Protectory in 1863 we have the following significant statement: "In the first place we address ourselves to Irishmen who constitute the great body of Catholics in this city while as we all know the children of the Irishmen make up by far the largest proportion of ruffians for whom we are called upon to provide."[15]

The Germans and Orphan Asylums

The Germans felt that the Irish were doing their best to provide for their own dependent and neglected children. They felt that it would be a reflection on their national honor to look to the Irish to take care of German children. The Irish have lead the way, the Germans must now follow their example. This attitude is expressed clearly in a letter of a German missionary, later Bishop Neumann of Philadelphia, to the Leopoldine Society of Vienna in October, 1841: "Very often poor German parents give their small children to Americans who accept them gladly in order to bring them up as

---

[15] *Annual Reports*, New York Catholic Protectory, May, 1863, to Sept. 30, 1875, p. 15.

Protestants. This happens most frequently with newcomers. The same situation developed in times past with the French and Irish families, but the Bishops recognizing the danger established orphanages under the care of the Sisters of Charity. These Sisters already number two hundred and have seventeen orphanages. Since these orphanages were established by French and Irish Bishops, children of these nationalities get the preference. There should be several orphanages for the German children in order to save them but the help for this work must come from Germany.''[16]

German Catholic Orphan Associations

In their orphan asylums the Germans were actuated by the same spirit that found expression in their various fraternal societies, whose purpose was to protect their members against sickness and premature death. The orphan asylum was a part of the same program. In line with their fraternal traditions the first step of the Germans in establishing orphan asylums was to develop sustaining associations. Every member of such an association felt that he was providing insurance against possible child dependency in his own family. He was assured in the event of premature death that his children would be provided for by the association.

The German Catholic Orphan Associations in different cities are governed most democratically. The affairs of each association are in the hands of a board of directors elected annually by a vote of the membership. The powers of the board of trustees are quite limited, as all important questions of policy are referred to a vote of the membership. As the membership dues are not sufficient, the usual method of supplementing the finances is an annual collection in the German Catholic churches of the city. This collection relieves the German churches from any appeal for other diocesan orphanages.

[16] *Letters of Leopoldine Society*, Vol. II, 1841, pp. 56-62.

Cincinnati the Pioneer City in Organized Care of German Children

Cincinnati was the first city in which the German Catholics provided organized care for their children. When the German immigrants came to Cincinnati in the 1830's, they were quite poor. When the epidemic of 1832 removed a large number of the bread-winners of the families, St. Peter's Orphan Asylum was forced to provide for their children. As the Germans became better established, this arrangement proved unsatisfactory and they organized a movement to establish their own orphan asylum. In 1837 they organized St. Aloysius Orphan Society. Father John M. Henni, a pastor in Cincinnati and later archbishop of Milwaukee, was the guiding spirit.

Since the care of dependent boys was a pressing problem the society decided to place them in family homes until a separate building could be provided. In order to assist in raising funds the society decided to publish a magazine known as the *Wahrheitsfreund* under the editorship of Father Henni. In 1839 the society acquired a building to house the orphans. The institution was operated by a lay personnel until 1842, when it was given over to the Sisters of Charity, who remained in charge until 1846. Since 1877 the administration of St. Aloysius Orphan Asylum has been in charge of a chaplain assisted by the Sisters of Notre Dame of Cleveland.[17]

German Orphanage in St. Louis

Between 1849 and 1860 orphan asylums for German Catholics were established in such centers as Buffalo, Louisville, St. Louis, Pittsburgh, New York City, Baltimore and Philadelphia. In 1849 the German Catholics of St. Louis decided to establish an orphan asylum. The epidemic of that year had left a great many children without parental care. The two existing Catholic institutions were over-crowded.

---

[17] J. H. Lamott, *History of the Archdiocese of Cincinnati, 1821–1921*, pp. 301–302.

Since half of the children were Germans, racial pride was stirred. In June, 1850, a committee of priests and laymen made a strong plea to the German Catholics of St. Louis to come to the rescue of their children: "For a long time the German Catholics of St. Louis have felt the need of a German Roman Catholic Orphan-Home, and the wish to found such an institution has often been expressed by the charitably disposed. . . . Now, as the means of a few are not sufficient to carry out the difficult project of satisfying this pressing demand, it seems advisable to organize a society. . . ."[18] In the same month the German St. Vincent's Orphan Society was established in St. Louis. A building was acquired, and within a year St. Vincent's Orphan Asylum was in full operation. The institution depended for support on membership dues, an annual festival and an annual collection in the German churches of the diocese.

Archbishop Peter R. Kenrick's pastoral letter giving approval to the establishment of the German St. Vincent's Orphan Asylum in St. Louis is quite significant: "Besides the two asylums already in existence we have deemed it advisable to approve the erection of a German Male and Female Asylum, as well to comply with the wishes of that portion of our flock who use the German language, as to diminish the burdens on the existing Asylums, and to obviate the necessity of making additions to them, which otherwise would soon be necessary. . . ."[19] In a very laudable way the archbishop was fostering the racial pride of the Germans.

German Orphanage in Louisville

In 1849 a number of men, parishioners of the Immaculate Conception Church at Louisville, organized St. Joseph's German Roman Catholic Orphan Society of that city. In 1850 the society opened St. Joseph's Orphanage.[20]

[18] Rothensteiner, op. cit., Vol. II, p. 21.
[19] Ibid., Vol. II, p. 22.
[20] Webb, op. cit., pp. 543–544.

Buffalo's Care of German Orphans

The German Roman Catholic Orphan Asylum of Buffalo, organized in 1852, was placed under the Sisters of Notre Dame. The asylum was necessitated by the cholera of 1849 which carried off the heads of a great many German immigrant families and left their children dependent on St. Mary's parish for support. The children were first cared for by the families of the congregation. In 1875 the asylum was placed under the direction of the Sisters of St. Francis.[21]

Philadelphia and New York Organize German Asylums

St. Vincent's Orphan Asylum in Philadelphia was founded by the German Roman Catholic School Society of Philadelphia and vicinity in 1855.[22] St. Joseph's German Orphan Asylum of New York City was founded by Father Joseph Helmproecht, C.SS.R., of the Church of the Holy Redeemer (1859),[23] when in his visitation of the hospitals he found a number of German children who had been orphaned.[24]

Baltimore and Pittsburgh Care for German Orphans

In 1849 a colony of the School Sisters of Notre Dame took charge of the girls' department of the school in connection with St. Philomena's Church in Pittsburgh. Since there was no orphanage for German children the sisters received a number of the female orphans into their convent. The building soon became over-crowded and it became necessary to build St. Joseph's German Orphan Asylum on Troy Hill. The institution was to be supported by an association and by collections in the German Catholic churches.[25] In 1854 Rev. Anthony Smith, C.SS.R., established St. Anthony's German Catholic Orphanage in Baltimore. This institution was organized on the same principles as the German Catholic institutions elsewhere.

[21] Letchworth, *op. cit.*, pp. 134, 135.
[22] P. A. Baart, *Orphans and Orphan Asylums*, p. 118.
[23] *Ibid.*, p. 96.
[24] *Catholic World*, Vol. XLIII (Aug., 1886), p. 681.
[25] Lambing, *op. cit.*, pp. 512–514.

The Sisters of Charity of Emmitsburg and Child-Caring Institutions

Before 1846 practically all the institutions for dependent and neglected Catholic children were conducted by the Sisters of Charity of Mount St. Joseph's, Emmitsburg. This was the great pioneering community in Catholic charities. The growth of this community has been remarkable. It has attracted ladies of old Catholic families as well as recruits from Europe in the service of sheltering, protecting and catering to the educational needs of dependent children of all classes of immigrants. While the Sisters of Charity at this time had homes in the more important cities, they were governed from a central motherhouse at Emmitsburg.

The Objectives of the Sisters of Charity of Emmitsburg

From the beginning the Sulpician Fathers had fairly definite ideas in regard to the program and objectives of the Sisters of Charity. They regarded the society as a means of extending to the United States the splendid work and traditions of the Daughters of Charity established by St. Vincent de Paul in France more than 200 years before. It was quite apparent that Archbishop Carroll was not in accord with the original plans of the Sulpicians in this respect. He regarded the Sisters of Charity primarily as an educational community. He felt that for a hundred years the American Church would not have to deal with the problems of charity that so occupied the religious communities in Europe. Although in the beginnings of the Sisters of Charity the Sulpician spiritual directors were willing to compromise with the archbishop in regard to the mission of the new community, this did not mean that the Sulpicians changed their fundamental views. They naturally set great store on the advantages that the sisters would reap from union with the world-wide community.

The Growing Autonomy of the Dioceses

While the Sisters of Charity were working out their future program with their spiritual directors at Emmitsburg, there were other forces at work in the American Church which threw difficulties in the way. There was the increasing consciousness on the part of new dioceses of their local autonomy and sufficiency. In the beginning they looked to Baltimore as their guide and inspiration. As they grew to maturity many of them felt more independent. Now the Sisters of Charity were regarded as a Baltimore diocesan community. New York was loath to entrust its major problems of education and charity to a community whose rules were formulated in Baltimore. In the mind of the diocesan authorities, New York, moreover, faced many problems in which the utmost flexibility was demanded. It, therefore, leaned towards a local community, governed locally, which would better understand local conditions.

The Sisters of Charity of Emmitsburg Reluctant to Care for Boys

The circumstance that finally brought the conflict between the Sisters of Charity of Emmitsburg and the bishop of New York was the general order issued by the superior at Emmitsburg that the sisters could no longer take care of boys over four years of age. This was in accordance with the constitution of the Daughters of Charity of St. Vincent de Paul which was being applied to the American Sisters of Charity. The rule had been enforced in other cities with the acquiescence of local authorities and the substitution of other communities in boys' institutions. In New Orleans the Brothers of the Holy Cross took over the care of male orphans; in St. Louis the Sisters of St. Joseph did not hesitate to take over this work.

From the beginning the Sisters of Charity seemed to be adverse to caring for boys. Most of their early institutions were intended for girls exclusively. In regard to Cincinnati, for instance, we find that: "The Sisters of Charity did not ... and would not in 1836 accept boys into an orphanage. The bishop's request to Emmitsburg for the Sisters to undertake a separate boys' orphanage for the German Catholics of Cincinnati was refused."[26] By reason of the disinclination of the Sisters of Charity to take care of older boys, the various dioceses were compelled to look to more flexible communities to assume this responsibility.

The Bishops' Task of Providing for the Dependent Children of the Immigrants

The bishops appointed to new dioceses established during 1840-1860 found that one of their first tasks was the care of the dependent children of the immigrants who succumbed in plagues or fatigue of American life. The immigrants recognized the fact that they were living in a hostile environment. They did not expect much from sectarian or public philanthropy. They were really thrown back on their own resources which were naturally slender. In view of this situation, the problem of the bishops was indeed complex.

Care of Dependent Children in Chicago

The situation in Chicago in 1850 may be regarded as typical. In the *Catholic Directory* of that year there is the following statement in regard to the care of the female orphans at St. Mary's Asylum:

"The deplorable conditions of many Catholic children whose parents had died of cholera and other diseases rendered it necessary to call upon the congregations of the city to alleviate the distress of these destitute orphans. A number of children of both sexes were at first boarded out and clothed at the expense of the Bishop till at last about the first of September a frame house of small dimensions was rented for the

[26] Lamott, *op. cit.*, p. 301.

female orphans who were placed under the maternal care of four Sisters of Mercy. Thirty-three girls have already been received and their number is daily increasing. We rely on Providence for the support of them. The Catholics of the city though scarcely any are in prosperous circumstances have generously responded to the call and our Protestant fellow-citizens have evinced great interest and liberality on the occasion." [27]

Then, in regard to the care of the male orphans at St. Joseph's Asylum we read that the bishop "has just ceded a small frame house, the residence of one of the priests of the Cathedral, to be used as a refuge for the male orphans. Thirteen were admitted at the opening and this number will be soon doubled. They are now under the care of two Sisters of Mercy. The scantiness of our means does not permit us to accommodate them as comfortably as we would wish, but we hope the good work will prosper and is only the beginning of more solid and extensive work of charity." [28]

Early Efforts of the Dioceses of Buffalo, Cleveland, Milwaukee and St. Paul to Provide for Orphaned Children

The bishops vied with one another in making provisions for orphans. No sooner had Bishop Timon arrived in Buffalo (1847), than he journeyed to Baltimore to secure the services of the Sisters of Charity to operate an orphan asylum in his new diocese. In 1851 Bishop Amadeus Rappé established St. Mary's Orphan Asylum for girls in Cleveland and in 1853 he opened St. Vincent's Orphan Asylum for boys. One of the first tasks of Bishop John M. Henni in the new diocese of Milwaukee was the establishment of St. Rose's and St. Joseph's Orphan Asylums for girls and St. Aemilian's Orphan Asylum for boys. All three institutions began their work about the year 1850.[29]

[27] Page 118.
[28] *Ibid.*
[29] *Archives* of Mt. St. Joseph's College, Emmitsburg.

From the moment of his arrival in the new diocese of St. Paul (1851) Bishop Joseph Cretin was anxious to provide for the sick and the orphans. In 1853 he began the erection of the St. Joseph's Hospital, the first institution of its kind in Minnesota. In the meantime a cholera epidemic broke out in the city. Temporary provision had to be made for the care of the sick and the orphan. The old log church in the city was converted into a hospital. When the new hospital was completed in 1854 it served the dual purpose of both a hospital and an orphan asylum.[30] Parishes in the leading industrial centers built their own orphanages, and the orphanage came to be recognized as a primary objective of every American diocese.

The Resources of the Church in Coping with the Problem of Child-Care

In providing for orphaned and half-orphaned children the Church had at its disposal only meagre resources. Most of its members were recent immigrants. They had difficulty in meeting their own requirements not to speak of contributing to works of charity. The Church, moreover, was experiencing serious difficulties in providing for the ordinary religious needs of the people. In assuming the care of the orphans, therefore, the sisters had to suffer many hardships. In the city of Boston it took nine years to secure sufficient funds to purchase a building for an orphan asylum.[31] When the Sisters of Charity first opened St. Patrick's Orphan Asylum, Rochester, New York, even the beds they slept on were borrowed.[32]

While between 1840 and 1860 the Church had limited financial resources it had a large number of men and women ready to dedicate their lives to the work. These were drawn

[30] Sr. M. Lucida Savage, *The Congregation of St. Joseph of Carondelet*, pp. 90–91.
[31] *Cf.*, Chapter II.
[32] *Archives* of Mt. St. Joseph's College, Emmitsburg.

in part from the old Catholic settlements in Maryland and Kentucky and in part from the various European countries. The brothers and sisters in charge of the orphanages were missionaries in the real sense. The orphanages were built on their labors and sacrifices. But the problems of child dependency between 1840 and 1860 were so great as to far outstrip all resources. No one could have forecast the vast immigrant tide. Both Church and State were ill-prepared to meet its problems.

Contrast Between Early Catholic Institutions and Those After 1840

The institutions for children established before 1840 were largely educational, with the care of the orphan as an incident in their work. After 1840 the care of orphaned and half-orphaned children loomed larger year by year. Public health and public welfare bureaus were practically unknown. For the sick, the dependent family, the orphaned child, and the insane, there was no form of public relief except a poorly administered and insufficient outdoor relief and the primitive poor house. Protestant philanthropy had not yet developed and therefore did not have the seductive attractions which it offered the immigrant after the Civil War. The immigrant in distress was therefore in a sorry plight. The adult met the situation somehow or other; at least his sufferings did not excite so much compassion but with the child it was a different story. A child here and there might be cared for by friends; but when parents were carried off in large numbers by prevailing epidemics, the care of their children became too much for private resources. Something had to be done. There is every evidence that the Church was alive to the situation and that it did everything possible to meet it. Established institutions were expanded. Many of them gave up educational work and devoted themselves entirely to the care of orphans.

CHAPTER VI
AFTER THE ALMSHOUSES
Catholic Population Increases After 1860

The continued immigration tide and the spread of the immigrants to new centers increased the problem of Catholic child-care in volume and extent after 1860. During the decade of the Civil War the Catholic population in the various eastern industrial centers increased greatly. In the factories Irish workmen took the places of Americans who had been called to the colors. The opening of the Mississippi Territory in the late sixties and the seventies also drew large numbers of American workers away from the east, thus leaving more places for the immigrant workers. Moreover, many immigrants, especially during the panic and depression of the seventies, began to heed the call of the new west. They reached out past the Mississippi River to Iowa, Nebraska, Kansas, Minnesota, Colorado, Montana and the Dakotas. The more enterprising of the immigrants were attracted by free land. After building the railroads they settled in the various towns that grew up along the way.

The Catholic Church in the United States followed the trail of the immigrant. His problems were its problems. New dioceses were developed in quick succession in the middle west in order to take care of the needs of the immigrants on the farms and the immigrant workers in the rising towns and cities. New dioceses were also established in the growing industrial cities of the east during the decades immediately following the Civil War.

Eighteen Dioceses Formed Between 1860 and 1880

Each new diocese that was established became a center of activity. The bishop was concerned not only with the construction of churches and the administration of the sacraments but also with the care of the orphans and a program of religious education for the children. Among the eighteen new dioceses organized between 1860 and 1880 in which the orphanage was one of the first objectives of the bishop were those of Scranton, Columbus, and Omaha. After his appointment as bishop of Scranton (1868), Rt. Rev. William O'Hara immediately turned his attention to the building of an orphanage for the diocese. By 1875 the St. Patrick's Orphanage in Scranton was in operation. The opening of St. Vincent's Orphanage, Columbus, Ohio, followed within seven years after the organization of the diocese. St. James' orphanage in Omaha followed immediately the appointment of a vicar-apostolic in that city.

Older Dioceses Have Increased Problems After Civil War

After the Civil War the continuous flow of immigration from European countries increased the population and multiplied the problems of the older dioceses in the east. During the previous decades the most serious problems for the immigrant were those of poverty and disease. The immigrant found it difficult to secure a position in the United States. Fathers and mothers were frequently carried off by epidemic diseases, leaving their children dependent on public charity. After the war the immigrant faced a new situation. The Civil War like all wars had an unsettling influence on the moral conduct of the people. It tended to pry the immigrant from his old moorings. Large numbers of them began to show open disregard for the moral standards of their ancestors. The new freedom of American life frequently spelled license to disregard fundamental ethical standards. Institutions for children, therefore, began to take on entirely new aspects. Their names even were affected. They became known as Homes for the Friendless, Homes for Homeless Children, and Homes for Wanderers. The basic principle upon which these institutions operated was not so much saving the child from poverty as rescuing him from vicious surroundings.

In discussing the development of Catholic protectories particular emphasis was placed on the activities of Protestant organizations in planning for Catholic children after the Civil War. The activities of Protestant organizations during this period gave a great impetus not only to the development of Catholic protectories but to homes for dependent and neglected children.

Beginnings of Catholic Lay Organizations

After the Civil War the economic and social status of Catholic immigrants was improved to a marked degree. Many of the children of the earlier immigrants had acquired wealth and social position. Through native ability many immigrants attained positions of prominence in the army. Their association in the army helped to bridge over the insuperable gulf between the immigrants and the native population. A new day dawned for Catholic lay organization. Catholic lay bodies came to rally the rank and file of Catholics in the defense of their rights and the promotion of their interests. Irish Catholics were no longer willing to accept insults without question. In the *German Central Verein* and the *Irish Catholic Benevolent Union* we have the beginnings of national Catholic organization and outlook.

Removal of Children From Almshouses First Step in Catholic Child-Care

One of the most important objectives of Catholic lay organizations was the care of the dependent and neglected children. Catholics were determined to do everything possible to save Catholic children from coming under the influence of Protestant organizations.

The first step in the development of Catholic and other forms of child-care in the United States was the removal of children from the almshouses. Before 1860 most of the children needing care away from their own homes were sent to almshouses where they were permitted to associate with a great variety of adult dependents. To those who are accustomed to the present high standards of child-care in American cities the accounts of conditions under which children were housed in these institutions in the fifties and sixties of the last century are almost revolting.

Almshouses in Ohio in 1867

In the report of the Ohio State Board of Charities for 1867 we have the following gruesome story of children in county infirmaries or almshouses in Ohio:

> There have been in thirteen infirmaries during the year as reported in the statistical table an aggregate of 220 children nearly all under ten years of age. Some of these are feeble-minded and they with the idiotic will soon be permitted to share in the provision made for such in the new State Idiotic Asylum. Some are blind and one at least deaf and dumb, many of them as pretty and as smart as little boys and girls can be.
>
> In no less than three infirmaries we found little boys confined for constraint or punishment with the insane. In one instance a little deaf and dumb boy was locked in a cell in the insane department opposite a cell in which a violently insane woman was confined. . . . He was crying bitterly and on being released made signs indicating that he was hungry.[1]

Massachusetts Has First State Board of Charities

It is a curious fact that until the Civil War the care of dependent and neglected children was untouched by any humanitarian movement. There had been a considerable amount of interest in providing separate treatment for the juvenile offender. A number of cities had developed juvenile reformatories but in regard to the dependent and neglected child

---

[1] *First Annual Report* of the Board of State Charities of Ohio, 1867, p. 35.

there seemed only indifference. This situation was not due so much to lack of sympathy as to lack of information. There was no agency to study the facts and set them before the public. The development of central state boards of charity, beginning with Massachusetts in 1863, brought about a new condition. These central state boards were primarily educational in character. In a short time they caught public interest and aroused public sympathy by their revelations in regard to the care of children in almshouses. In the various states there was a strong movement to do something about it. The picture of the child associating with adult dependents and frequently with depraved persons was repugnant to all human feelings and sympathies.

Monson Almshouse, Massachusetts

Massachusetts was the first state to make separate provision for the care of dependent and neglected children. The act of 1863 gave the board authority to make a suitable classification of public dependents. Pursuant to this authority the board decided to concentrate all the dependent and neglected children of the state at the Monson Almshouse in a sort of school for pauper children.[2] By this decision the institution at Monson practically lost its character as an almshouse. In 1866 the special section reserved for children received the title of State Primary School.[3] In 1872 all the adult dependents were removed from Monson and the institution was reserved exclusively for children.[4]

Beginnings of a State System of Child-Placing in Massachusetts

In Massachusetts as in other states, indenture was the accepted method of taking care of children brought up in the almshouses. These children were supposed to be placed out

---
[2] *Report* of Board of State Charities, Massachusetts, 1864, p. 277.
[3] *Third Annual Report* of Board of State Charities, Massachusetts, 1866, p. 45.
[4] Homer Folks, *The Care of Destitute, Neglected and Delinquent Children*, pp. 72-75.

in good families where they would acquire habits of useful work. Before the State Board of Charities of Massachusetts had been long in operation it found that the "good" families in which the children were placed were not always so desirable. Many times they mistreated the children under their care. The board felt that it was necessary to have some follow-up service for children discharged from Monson. It therefore employed a visiting agent who devoted his entire time to the after-care of the children discharged from the State Primary School.

The visiting service for the children discharged from Monson proved so satisfactory that the Massachusetts State Board of Charities was anxious to have it extended to all children who had become wards of the state. If such a service was necessary for dependent and neglected children, why should it not be necessary for the delinquent children discharged from the juvenile reformatories? The board, moreover, found that many parents were inclined to rid themselves of the responsibility of caring for their children by placing them in the various public institutions of the state. It also found that many of the children sent to institutions could have been cared for in foster homes. What the board had in mind was really the development of a central, state, child-caring agency to which wards would be committed and which would be authorized to provide for them according to their needs. On the recommendation of the State Board of Charities, the state legislature of Massachusetts provided the nucleus of such an agency in 1869.[5] In that year the legislature created a visiting agency under the State Board of Charities which would receive and provide suitable care for all child-wards of the state. Such were the beginnings of the state system of child-placing in Massachusetts.

[5] *Annual Report* of Board of State Charities, Massachusetts, 1869, p. 41.

Ohio, Michigan and New York Plan Removal of Children From Almshouses

In the decade of 1860 the movement for removal of children from almshouses and the making of special provision for them was well under way. In 1866 the state legislature of Ohio enacted a law empowering the county commissioners to establish children's homes.[6] In 1869 the governor of Michigan appointed a commissioner to make a complete study of plans for the care of dependent children in the state. The commissioner recommended three possible plans, any one of which might be applied in the state: first, the organization of a state child-placing agency through which children would be removed from the poor houses and placed in private homes; secondly, the placement of children in private orphan asylums to be supported there at public expense until placed out in families; thirdly, the establishment of a state children's home which would provide for all destitute children who were public wards. The legislature finally decided to establish a state children's home which was opened in 1874.[7] It was not the intention of the legislature that this home should care for all destitute children. The various counties were permitted to make arrangements with private institutions for the care of children on a per capita basis. In Michigan, therefore, public wards may be cared for in the state home or by arrangements with children's institutions or child-placing agencies.

In 1875 the state of New York passed a law directing the removal of the children from the poor houses. The various counties were authorized to make arrangements with private agencies for the care of children who became public wards.

Meeting of Various Boards of Charities in 1876

At a meeting of the various state boards of charities held in Detroit, in May, 1876, a resolution was passed favoring

[6] *Second Annual Report* of the Board of State Charities of Ohio, 1869, pp. 24.
[7] Folks, *op. cit.*, p. 75.

the removal of children from institutions intended for adult dependents. The following is the text of the resolution: "Resolved that this conference recommends that the various state Board of Charities use their influence to bring about such legislation in their respective states as shall cause dependent children to be removed from county poor houses, city almshouses and from all association with adult paupers and criminals and placed in family asylums, reformatories or other appropriate institutions."[8]

Meeting Influences Six States to Make Separate Provision for Children

In 1878 Wisconsin passed a law requiring the removal of children from almshouses but made no provision for them until seven years later when a state children's home was established. In 1883 Pennsylvania passed a law prohibiting the retention of children in poor homes for a period longer than sixty days. In Pennsylvania the counties were authorized to make arrangements with children's institutions and child-placing agencies for the care of children. In 1883 Connecticut passed a law directing the establishment of a temporary home for children in each county and prohibiting the retention of children over two years of age in almshouses. In 1885 Rhode Island established a state home for children and in 1892 made their removal from almshouses mandatory. In 1897 Indiana provided for the organization of a state placing-out agency to place children in private homes. New Jersey also created a state Board of Children's Guardians (1899) in order to place children in private homes.[9]

American Philosophy of Child-Care Soon Determined

It was during the period immediately following the removal of children from the almshouses that the attitudes and traditions of American states in regard to child-care were de-

[8] *Ibid.*, p. 28.
[9] *Ibid.*, pp. 78-79.

termined. Some states, like Massachusetts and New Jersey, decided to launch out into a program of child-placing. It was taken for granted that there were any number of good farm homes that were ready and willing to receive children if only given an opportunity to do so. All that was needed was a number of persons who would visit the homes frequently and thus guard the children against any possibility of mistreatment.

Moreover, it was much less expensive to place a child in a home than to care for him in an institution. This motive had a very far reaching influence in the development of the early systems of child-placing in this country. A number of states established central state schools for children. Among these states were Michigan, Minnesota, Wisconsin, Rhode Island, Kansas, Colorado, Nebraska, Montana, Nevada and Texas. From the beginning these state schools like all child-caring institutions had a child-placing program. In the early days, however, their child-placing was confined to the placement of older children in wage homes and the placing of very young children for adoption. In recent years, however, a number of the states, namely, Ohio, Connecticut, and Indiana established county homes for children. A number of states, including New York, Illinois, Pennsylvania, Maryland, and California, entered into arrangements with private institutions for the care of children. In some instances the institution was paid a certain definite sum for each public charge committed; in other cases the legislature appropriated a lump sum annually for institutions caring for public wards. In a few states both the lump sum and per capita plans of compensating institutions caring for state wards were in vogue.[10]

While the payment of public funds for the care of children in private institutions was inaugurated in the above mentioned states, it has not been confined to these states. In Michigan, with its state home, many counties, especially Wayne, the

[10] *Ibid.*, p. 82.

most populous in the state, depend on private institutions for the care of children and pay for them on a per capita basis. In Wisconsin and Iowa the same plan is in operation.

Early State Policies of Child-Care Governed Later Programs

The policies of the various states in regard to the care of children have been governed largely by the programs which they adopted after the removal of the children from the poor houses. The states that adopted public child-caring programs in the beginning have tended to follow their original programs. The states that decided to utilize private agencies have adhered to this plan. In some states, like Michigan and Wisconsin, the public program has not been developed sufficiently to meet all the needs of dependent children. They have, therefore, entered into a definite arrangement with the private agencies. No matter how large the public program of any state, it has not been sufficient to meet all the needs of children requiring special care. In every state, therefore, we find that private agencies play an important part in childcare. In states in which the public bodies charged with the care of children have entered into definite arrangements with private agencies, private child-care has assumed a much more important role.

Children Are Placed in Free Western Homes

From the report made by Commissioner William P. Letchworth of the New York State Board of Charities (1876), it is quite clear that the private child-caring facilities of the state were already taxed to capacity. If they decided to take over the children who were to be removed from the almshouses, they might enlarge their institutional facilities or place out in homes a certain number of the children. Of course it would be much less expensive to place children out in free homes in the middle west than to retain them in institutions. Large Protestant agencies, moreover, like the New

York Children's Aid Society, the Brooklyn Children's Aid Society, according to Letchworth's report, had been most successful in finding good homes for children. These agencies had established institutions for the care of children but they were looked upon more as temporary shelters. Home-placement was to be regarded as the only program of long-time care for children.

This report may be regarded as joining issues that had been developing for a number of years in the field of child-care. The large Protestant agencies wanted children placed out in good homes in the middle west. They seemed to have an unlimited number of good farm homes in the new territory that had just been opened up for settlement. The Yankee who had migrated from New England had a golden opportunity of doing a missionary work and at the same time advancing his own economic interests. For him of course, economic advancement was a part of a great religious program. The Catholic sisterhoods were rather adverse to the farm home idea. Somehow or other it smacked of Protestantism. They had heard of the thousands of children of Irish immigrants who had been picked up on the streets of New York City and sent to Protestant homes in the middle west. They were afraid lest the farmer, even the Catholic farmer, while he appeared to be influenced by high motives, might be thinking too much of the economic gains he would secure through the children placed in his home.

Catholic Sisterhoods Look to Institutions for Immigrant Children

The Catholic sisterhoods looked primarily to the religious faith and economic well-being of the children of the immigrants. They wanted to see the children strong in the faith and given every opportunity of lifting themselves out of economic distress. They wanted to retain the children in institutions until they had sufficient training to equip them for decent positions. They regarded the institution as an important agency for raising the immigrant above his present economic level. To the orphanage they would have added an industrial school. They would teach the children trades so that they might return to the community life, self-respecting and self-supporting. The religious felt that the children also needed a deep grounding in the truths of their faith in order to withstand the forces of an unfriendly environment. Moreover, in proportion to their number, the immigrants did not have many private homes that were suitable for the placement of children. The immigrant Catholic settlers in the middle west were having a hard struggle in providing for their own needs, not to speak of concerning themselves about the welfare of friendless children.

As a result of the arrangements entered into between the cities and counties in New York state and the various private agencies in regard to the care of children, the population of the Catholic institutions increased very rapidly. Soon there was a demand for new institutions. Between 1875 and 1885 seven new Catholic institutions for children were established in New York City.

Catholic Institutions a Preventive Against Protestantism

The great development of Catholic children's homes from 1870 to 1890 provided facilities for the care of most of the Catholic dependent and neglected children. These institutions went a long way towards establishing as a fundamental working principle that every child should be brought up in the faith in which he was born. Catholic institutions gradually reached out to the Catholic children that hitherto had been cared for by sectarian or public agencies.

The building of institutions for his own dependent children was a great victory for the immigrant. He had at his disposal ways and means of preventing Protestant inroads on the faith. The orphan asylums were pictured as a ladder by which thousands of children might climb out of the depths of poverty to the heights of prosperity.

Protestant Reaction Against Catholic Institutions

The program of the Catholic church in building orphan asylums for its own children made the Protestant agencies somewhat uneasy. They were particularly disturbed because Catholic institutions were assisted from the public funds. All kinds of wild statements were made: that America was returning to a union of Church and State; that Catholic institutions were growing rich at public expense. The attack on Catholic institutions was directed by the very people whose policies were the justification for these institutions. Moreover, with the building of Catholic institutions, the Protestant child-placing agencies had few children of the Irish for placement in Protestant homes in the middle west. They could no longer make the same proselytizing appeal to their supporters. They had to look around for new sources of strength. They had to discover a new rallying cry. Catholic institutions were developing rapidly in number and size. City after city, as a matter of practical economy, made arrangements to pay them on a per capita basis. The new Protestant attack was not aimed directly at Catholicism, but rather at the defenses which the immigrant had built to preserve his children's faith.

Per Capita Payments to Catholic Institutions Attacked

The attack on Catholic children's institutions in New York state was aired in the legislature in 1880. It was contended that per capita payments were made to children's institutions in an unsystematic manner. It was further contended by some members of the legislature that since the large expenditure of public funds for child-care imposed a heavy tax upon the city of New York, the amount should be limited within fixed bounds and definite rules and regulations should be made governing its distribution. Since it was impossible for the legislature to make the careful investigation that the subject demanded, it therefore directed the State Board of Charities "to examine the whole question of the appropriations aforesaid, their properties, the proper amount of distribution and . . . report the result of their investigation, with their recommendations upon the subject to the assembly of 1881."[11]

In the course of its investigation the State Board of Charities of New York found that, since 1850, there had been a rapid increase in the appropriations to private charitable institutions in New York City. In 1850 the amount appropriated was $9,863; in 1855 it increased to $83,150; and in 1860 there was a further increase to $128,850. The appropriations for 1865 brought a slight increase of approximately $8,000, the amount appropriated in that year being $136,650. In 1870 the appropriation was increased almost threefold. In 1875 it again increased almost threefold. The figures for 1870 were $334,828; for 1875, $825,905; and for 1880 the appropriations from the tax funds for the care of public wards through private agencies was $999,741.41. To this should be added the amount received from the excise fund. In 1870 an appropriation for private charities was made for the first time from the excise fund. The amount given in that year was $14,000. In 1880 the amount appropriated for private charities from the excise fund was $414,516.37.[12]

The investigation of the State Board of Charities showed that in some institutions there was a tendency to extend their charity unduly. It did not make much difference to them, so the investigators contended, how many children they received so long as their board was paid by the city. In fact the larger the number of children the smaller the per capita

---

[11] *Report* of New York State Board of Charities, 1881, p. 4.
[12] *Ibid.*, p. 5.

cost to the institution. The Board assumed throughout that the great increase in the number of institutions and the large increase of institutional population was due to public aid. What could have been done with the children in the absence of the institutions? Undoubtedly, there were some who could have been cared for in their own homes, but the number would not be large. In all likelihood, the great majority of the children would have to be cared for outside of their own homes. No doubt, it would have been cheaper to turn them over to Protestant children's aid societies for distribution in good Protestant homes in the west but this was the very thing against which the immigrants and the Catholic Church were struggling. They were determined that their dependent children should be brought up in the faith; and the institution was the available guarantee. The institution was a rescue mission through which the children would be saved to the faith.

New York State Board of Charities Makes Reasonable Recommendations

The board recommended a number of reasonable changes in the regime of the child-caring institutions of New York City. It urged that the institutions be required to make more detailed annual reports, that there should be a more definite understanding in regard to per capita rates and the types of children to be cared for by each institution. Some institutions for delinquents were receiving children under eight years of age, while some institutions for infants were retaining them until they reached eighteen years of age. It was recommended that such practices be discontinued.[13]

Protestant Agencies Continue Their Attack Against Per Capita Payments

The recommendations made by the New York State Board of Charities were not sufficient to change the attitude of many

[13] *Ibid.*, p. 18.

Protestant agencies towards the Catholic children's institutions. Their ultimate objective was to secure a constitutional amendment which would make it impossible for the cities and counties in New York State to make per capita payments for the care of children in private institutions. They were not satisfied with any changes in the institutional regime. All their criticisms were aimed towards their fundamental objective. Through the eighties and the early part of the nineties they conducted an organized campaign against the payment of public funds to private institutions. They wanted the state to care for its wards through public agencies. The problem of added cost was no concern to them. They contended that private institutions had been over-developed through public aid. They did not consider how far the total cost to the public would be increased by the development of public institutions. It was a question of fundamental principles rather than the detailed standards of child-care. The Catholics wanted to see their children cared for under Catholic auspices, and as taxpayers they felt that the state was fully justified in assisting them. They felt that there was no reason why the state should not assist them, for they were rendering a public service at a minimum cost. In fact, they were sharing in the double burden of supporting state as well as their own institutions. Protestant agencies, however, did not want to see the standards of child-care deviate from the pattern set by the majority.

Drift Towards Public Child-Care

The controversy in regard to public and private child-caring institutions in New York State did not change the status quo in that state very materially. The arrangements originally entered into in 1875 have remained with slight alterations. What has been true in New York has also been true in most other jurisdictions. The states have adhered quite generally to the basic policies developed when the children were removed from the almshouses. There are, however, a few notable exceptions. The District of Columbia for a long number of years depended on private institutions to care for its public wards. Beginning in 1892, however, it developed a system of public child-care. Within the past three years the counties in Wisconsin have begun to make payments to private institutions for the care of children. Taking the situation throughout the country as a whole the drift has been towards the development of public child-caring agencies. In most of the states there is a decided preference for public child-care rather than the making of arrangements with private agencies.

CHAPTER VII
A VOCATIONAL PROGRAM FOR THE CHILDREN OF THE IMMIGRANT

Proselytism of Early Protestant Child-Placing Organizations

Nothing made a stronger appeal to Protestant philanthrophy, between 1840 and 1860, than the placing of the children of Irish Catholic parents in Protestant homes. During this period in the development of social work many organizations that now command positions of leadership in social work were unscrupulous in regard to destroying the faith of the Catholic children placed under their care. The fundamental thought was to remove the children from the influence of the Church under the guise of removal from the slums and place them in the homes of transplanted New Englanders in the middle west. Many leaders with Celtic names, who are affiliated with the Methodist and Baptist Churches, can trace their Protestantism to the child-placing societies. For example, the writer recently met a prominent social worker in the middle west with an Irish Catholic name. During the course of conversation reference was made to her possible Catholic ancestry. She was well aware of it. She explained that her father was a Methodist minister, who, as a child, had been placed out by an agency in New York City. His parents were Irish Catholic immigrants.

In the files of the Catholic papers for the sixties and seventies there are innumerable references to the work of Protestant child-placing agencies proselytizing Catholic children. In January, 1876, it was announced at Peru, Illinois, through large posters, that on the ninth of the month a number of orphans from a New York institution would be brought there for distribution. On the appointed day a great crowd gathered to witness this new form of barter. A number of German and Irish Catholic families endeavored to make the necessary arrangements for receiving the children; but were informed by the agent of the institution that all the wards were to be placed in Methodist families and brought up Methodists. On inquiry a local priest found that nine of the fifteen children offered for placement were Catholics.[1]

Barter of Irish Catholic Children

A letter to the *New York Freeman's Journal*, May 26, 1866, called attention to the sale of forty or fifty children, principally of Irish Catholic parentage at Piqua, Missouri, two months previously. As bidders were scarce a Catholic priest, Rev. F. Donohue, secured five of the children at a stipulated price. The letter refers to another sale of children of Roman Catholic parents in Hudson, Michigan, about the same time. "What a howl," says the writer, "would be raised all over the country if these children were only blacks."

Lack of Catholic Facilities for Children Over Twelve Years of Age

Before 1860 all dioceses in the east had made some provision for the care of dependent and neglected Catholic children through their orphan asylums. These institutions, however, confined their efforts to children under twelve years of age. Dependent, neglected and delinquent children over twelve had to be sent to public and Protestant institutions and so far as Catholic children were concerned there was little choice between the two types of institutions. Catholics could expect as little from the public as from the Protestant institutions. The attitude of Catholic leaders is well expressed in the annual report of the New York Catholic Protectory for 1866: "Has the state succeeded in excluding from its institutions all distinctive religion and all sectarian teaching and influ-

[1] *Baltimore Catholic Mirror*, January 1, 1876.

ence? Inquire at the Juvenile Asylum, the Five Points House of Industry and the House of Refuge. Is not the Protestant religion inculcated in these institutions and only the Catholic religion excluded? Where among the managers of these institutions is a Catholic to be found? Where among their superintendents, their teachers, their preachers do you find a Catholic? Where among their acts of worship is a Catholic act tolerated?"[2]

First Provision for Catholic Children Over Twelve Years of Age

The first constructive effort to provide for Catholic children over twelve years of age was made by the Brothers of St. Joseph in connection with Notre Dame University, South Bend, Indiana, in 1846. The brothers established a manual labor school for orphans. It was their plan to receive boys between twelve and sixteen years of age and to teach them useful trades. They hoped to extend this work by establishing another school in one of the large cities of the east, but this plan did not mature.[3] At the same time that the Brothers of St. Joseph established their school at Notre Dame, the Sisters of the Holy Cross established a similar school for girls at Bertrand, Michigan.[4]

Hospital Organized in Baltimore for Fever-Stricken Irish Immigrants

With the great rise in the tide of Irish immigration in 1847, Rev. James Dolan, pastor of St. Patrick's Church at Fell's Point, Baltimore, became interested in making suitable provisions for the children of immigrants. On one occasion during that year he was summoned to minister to a shipload of sick and dying immigrants that had just reached the port of Baltimore. With the aid of the Sisters of Charity he or-

---
[2] *Annual Reports*, New York Catholic Protectory, May 1, 1863, to September 30, 1875, p. 104.
[3] *Catholic Directory*, 1847, p. 115.
[4] *Ibid.*, 1850, p. 110.

A Vocational Program

ganized a temporary hospital in which hundreds of fever-stricken passengers were attended. The children of those who died had to be provided for by some charitable agency. The orphanages were not in a position to care for older children. Father Dolan, thereupon, conceived the idea of establishing an institution for the care of boys over the age of twelve. Such an institution would receive not only children who could not be cared for by the orphanages but also those who were to be discharged from orphanages. The practice heretofore had been to remove the child from the institution after he had reached the age of twelve and place him out in a home with practically no investigation or supervision. Father Dolan had in mind an industrial school where the child would be given a sound vocational education and where he would remain until capable of earning his own living.

Second Attempt to Provide for Boys Over Twelve Years of Age

In the early part of 1848 Father Dolan purchased 116 acres of land on the York Road, about three miles from Baltimore as a site for his new institution for which he secured the Brothers of St. Patrick from Ireland.[5] Through lack of proper support Father Dolan was unable to carry out his original idea. He was forced to satisfy himself with two small institutions for dependent and neglected children respectively known as the Dolan Aid and St. Patrick's Orphanage. His plan may have been premature, but in the later years of his life he saw his idea carried out under the auspices of the Xaverian Brothers on a far more extensive scale.

Boston Protectory for Catholic Boys

One of the most important contributions to the protection of Catholic boys before 1860 was made by a zealous convert, Rev. Father Haskins of Boston. Haskins, as a Protestant,

[5] *U. S. Catholic Magazine*, Vol. VI (1847), pp. 447-448; Vol. VII (March, 1848), pp. 151-152.

had become disgusted with the methods employed in public institutions to win the children of Irish Catholics away from their faith. As soon as he entered the Church he decided that he would devote himself to counteracting this situation. About 1854 he established in Boston the House of the Angel Guardian for homeless and wayward Catholic boys. The institution was supported by an association known as the Society of the Angel Guardian.[6] In 1876 the Brothers of Charity, a Belgian religious community, took over this establishment.

New Era of Protection of Catholic Children

After the Civil War there was a new awakening on the part of Catholic leaders in regard to the care of wayward children. The war had increased the number of children who needed care away from their own homes. It had also given Catholics a new sense of importance in the life of the nation. As they had fought for the preservation of the Union and had discharged all the duties of citizenship, why should they be excluded from the rights of citizenship? The war, for the time being at least, dissipated many of the old anti-Catholic prejudices. It aided materially in bridging over the gulf between natives and immigrants.

Real Catholic Leadership Follows Civil War

After the war, moreover, there appeared a new type of Catholic leadership that was vitally interested in the welfare of the Church. This new leadership had been schooled in the activities of the various racial organizations and especially in the Conferences of the Society of St. Vincent de Paul. The latter society was the first lay organization in which Catholics of all races made common cause. Before the war the leaders that had been developed by the St. Vincent de Paul Society had found an outlet for their zeal in parish activities.

---

[6] *Baltimore Catholic Mirror*, May 28, 1859; Dec. 16, 1876.

They were now intent on developing a larger field and they found their enlarged opportunities in the care of homeless and delinquent children. The beacon lights of the new program were Dr. Levi Silliman Ives of New York and Archbishop Martin J. Spalding of Baltimore. It is interesting that the clarion call for lay service should have been sounded by Dr. Ives, a convert to the Church and formerly Protestant Bishop of North Carolina. It was most appropriate, moreover, that Dr. Ives should have selected New York as the theatre of his operations. There Protestant agencies were most active in winning Catholic children away from their faith. There the need for a Catholic program for the care of the children of immigrants was most urgent. Dr. Ives was fortunate in being able to associate with him a number of active St. Vincent de Paul men who had first-hand knowledge of the religious tragedies of Catholic childhood.

Dr. Ives Organizes Society for Protection of Destitute Catholic Children

Under the leadership and inspiration of Dr. Ives a society for the protection of destitute Catholic children was organized in New York in May, 1863. This new venture had the fullest support and approval of the Archbishop of New York. A lay board of twenty-six men and an advisory chaplain were selected to guide its destinies. Once organized, the board of the society made a special plea to Irishmen in New York City: "In the first place we address ourselves to Irishmen who constitute the great body of Catholics in this city while, as we all know, the children of Irishmen make up by far the largest proportion of sufferers for whom we are called upon to provide. Vast numbers of these defenseless young creatures are daily wandering over the face of this great city, exposed to all the horrors of hopeless poverty, to the allurements of vice and crime in every disgusting and debasing form, bringing ruin on themselves and disgrace and obloquy. Our object is to extend to these little sufferers a helping hand, to raise them from their state of degradation and misery and to place them in a condition in which they may have a fair chance to work out for themselves a better destiny."[7]

In a lecture given at the Cooper Institute in November, 1864, Dr. Ives stated that while the parish schools and the two Catholic orphanages were doing good work and were liberally supported, half of the Catholic dependent and neglected children of New York were left without protection and religious training. Through the Society for the Protection of Destitute Catholic Children Dr. Ives hoped to see Catholic children brought up in their own faith. The society had no desire to become a proselytizing agency; he would accord to Protestant children the same rights which he demanded for Catholic children.[8]

Beginnings of the New York Catholic Protectory

Within a few weeks after its organization the Society for the Protection of Destitute Catholic Children rented two houses connected by their yards on Thirty-sixth and Thirty-seventh Streets near Second Avenue. In these two houses the boys' department of the New York Catholic Protectory had its beginnings. This department was given over to the Christian Brothers, who have since retained charge.[9] A few months after the boys' department had been under way the board of directors of the Catholic Protectory was able to announce the opening of the girls' department in a rented building on the corner of Eighty-sixth Street and Second Avenue, known as the House of the Holy Angels, under the direction of the Sisters of Charity.

When it became apparent that, with its limited facilities in the city, the New York Catholic Protectory could not meet

[7] *Annual Reports*, New York Catholic Protectory, May 1, 1863, to September 30, 1875, p. 15; *New York Freeman's Journal*, June 13, 1863.
[8] *Ibid.*, Dec. 3, 1864.
[9] *Annual Reports*, New York Catholic Protectory, May 1, 1863, to September 30, 1875, p. 41.

the demands made upon it, the directors purchased a 114-acre farm near Westchester in 1865. On this site the board planned immediately to erect buildings for boys and girls.[10]

One of the greatest and most enthusiastic Catholic gatherings in the history of New York witnessed the laying of the corner stone of the new boys' building by Archbishop John McCloskey August 4, 1865. It was very evident that the Protectory made a strong appeal to the Catholics of New York.[11]

The financing of the Catholic Protectory was a challenge to the zeal and ingenuity of its board of directors. By order of the archbishop a collection was taken up in the Catholic churches of New York in 1864. This collection brought in a total of $8,053.46. In 1867, $6,324.36 was received in donations. It was not the intention of the board to depend on private benefactions exclusively. Protestant institutions were looking to the city and state for support. Why should not Catholic institutions receive a fair measure of compensation for the care of public wards?

New York Catholic Protectory Receives State and City Aid

In 1864 the Catholic Protectory received $15,000 from the city for the care of children and a $2,000 appropriation from the state. In 1865 it received $15,000 from the city and $1,838 from the state. In 1866 it received $21,318.38 from the city and $52,505.71 from the state. In 1870 the institution received a total of $133,830.09 from the public treasury, of which $122,220.27 represented payments from the city for the care of children and $11,610.72 its pro rata share of the state charity fund. In 1870 the Protectory also received a special grant of $50,000 from the legislature towards its building fund. In 1874 the state appropriation was discontinued and since that time the Catholic Protectory has de-

[10] "The Catholic Charities of New York," *Catholic World*, Vol. XLIII (August, 1886), p. 681.
[11] *Baltimore Catholic Mirror*. August 5, 1865.

pended for its support on per capita payments made by the city for the care of children and on private contributions.[12] This change of policy on the part of the state affected not only the Catholic Protectory but all private child-caring homes in New York State.

Early Policies of the New York Protectory

It was the original purpose of the Catholic Protectory to care for wayward and homeless children over twelve years of age. In this it was to supplement the work of the orphan asylums. Under pressure of increasing demands for child-care in New York City the institution found it impossible to adhere to this original objective. Due to insistent demands of parish priests and public officials, those in charge of the Protectory had to receive many children under twelve years of age for whom there was no room in other institutions. In the early years of the Catholic Protectory it must be remembered New York City did not have its present agencies for child-care; it had very few facilities for the specialized care of children. The care of children in their own homes was as yet in an embryonic state.

In the early days of the New York Catholic Protectory its officials were not very sanguine about the possibilities of finding good country homes for city children. "Some years previous to the establishment of the Protectory," said Dr. Ives in 1864, "I had been in the practice of securing good homes in the country for untrained and destitute Catholic children and although I succeeded in finding places for many I can call to mind only a single instance where the child did not abscond or prove utterly ungovernable and worthless. Our experience has been substantially the same since the commencement of our work in the institution. We have appren-

---

[12] *Annual Reports*, New York Catholic Protectory, May 1, 1863, to September 30, 1875, pp. 95–439; see also "State Aid to Public Institutions, New York City, as Compared with State Aid to Catholic Protectory," by Rev. I. T. Hecker, *Catholic World*, Vol. XXI (June, 1875), p. 289.

A Vocational Program 115

ticed a considerable number of orphans to good Catholic masters and we are pained to say that the majority of these orphans have proved to be wholly unmanageable. Now from these facts it seems to me quite manifest that the system which is flooding our western country with undisciplined, vicious children is much to be deprecated.'"[13]

Placing Program of Protectory Proves Unfeasible

Evidently the Protectory did not long adhere to this point of view, for in the report of 1867 there was a very vivid description of an 8,000-mile trip through the middle west taken by the brother rector and the president of the board for the purpose of making arrangements for the placement of children in farm homes. Possibly the officials of the institution believed that with more careful selection and supervision the farm-home would work out satisfactorily. The Protectory officials may also have been carried along on the general wave of enthusiasm for the transfer of the Irish from New York to western farms. It became apparent subsequently, however, that it was impossible for any institution, no matter how efficient, to select and supervise farm-homes in the vast territory between the Rocky Mountains and the Atlantic coast.

The founders of the New York Catholic Protectory regarded the institution as an agency for the spiritual salvation of the children of the streets. By proper religious instruction and the teaching of useful trades they expected to raise their wards above their slum environment. They thought that many of these products of the street would some day become tillers of the soil instead of returning to the dangers of city life. The idea of making a properous farmer out of the city boy played an important part in molding the policies of the Protectory, as of other Catholic institutions.

[13] *Annual Reports*, New York Catholic Protectory, May 1, 1863, to September 30, 1875, p. 81.

Facts would have taught them differently, but there were very few facts at hand. The boy without training placed in a carelessly selected farm home without any arrangement for supervision might not succeed, but the boy with the right degree of training who was placed in a carefully selected and supervised home had every hope of success.

Lincolndale Agricultural School for Boys

Even after the various programs for the placement of children on farms had proven unsuccessful the officials of the Protectory still believed that, with the application of the right formula, the farm home would largely meet their problem. Not until 1912 were they ready to try the new formula, when they gave their support to a new agricultural school for boys at Lincolndale, under the guiding genius of Brother Barnabas. This school planned to confine its efforts to carefully selected boys and to find homes for these boys not far from New York.

Larger Catholic Institutional Program Urged

Dr. Ives' work in the development of the New York Catholic Protectory really made him a leader in Catholic lay action. The Church was beginning to feel the pulse of a new life. The Catholic laity was coming into its own. The Church was less fearful of the laity. Laymen were becoming educated and ready for leadership. All they needed was a cause and a leader who could capture their imaginations. Both in a sense were supplied by Dr. Ives. He held up before Catholics of the country their failure to make proper provision for wayward and neglected children. Dr. Ives believed that what the Catholics of this country needed was a larger institutional program that would supplement existing orphanages. He believed that the Church needed industrial schools throughout the whole land. Industrial schools in every city would save the homeless Catholic youth to the Church and make them better citizens.

The Protectory satisfied a great and crying need, but it did not complete the program of Catholic child-care. In fact, no institutional program could constitute the sum total of the Church's contribution to the welfare of dependent, neglected and delinquent Catholic children. In 1868, when enthusiasm for the development of Catholic industrial schools had reached a high point all over the country, a writer in the *Catholic World* ventured to point out some of the limitations of the program: "We are told that our city contains no fewer than 40,000 vagrant and destitute children.... What are we doing for them? We have orphan asylums; but most of these children are not orphans and even if they were the asylums have not room for a tithe of them. We have the Protectory at Westchester, but that is only for young criminals. We spoke, in a former number of the *Catholic World,* of the noble mission-school which the zeal and perseverance of one good priest has founded in St. James Parish in this city. If almost every church in New York were able to build an institution of a similar kind we might rest satisfied."[14]

Archbishop Spalding Furthers Catholic Industrial School Movement

Archbishop Spalding of Baltimore may be regarded as a co-worker of Dr. Ives in popularizing the movement for Catholic industrial schools throughout the country. From his wide contacts throughout the country the archbishop was well aware of the great losses sustained by the Church through its failure to provide for the dependent, neglected and delinquent children. He regarded the industrial school as the most practicable means of meeting this problem. One of the first projects to which he directed his attention on his transfer from Louis-

[14] "The Charities of New York City," *Catholic World,* Vol. VIII (Nov., 1868), p. 279.

ville to Baltimore was the establishment of an industrial school.

In a letter addressed to the priests and laity of Baltimore regarding the proposed school he said: "For years we have been losing hundreds of our poor children, particularly orphan and indigent boys. They are taken up from the streets or from the haunts of poverty, and are placed in institutions where their faith is either entirely neglected or artfully undermined. Do we not find all over the country thousands of persons, who, from their names, should be Catholics, but who, unfortunately, have abandoned the church and who rear up their families in ignorance, sometimes in hatred of her sacred principles? Thus the evil is propagated and continually multiplied from generation to generation. Hundreds of thousands, if not millions, who should belong to the church in this country, are now, unhappily through the criminal neglect of parents and the agencies above referred to, estranged from her communion. . . . The only practical remedy is the establishment, on a large scale, of protectories or industrial schools, in which poor boys, exposed to the danger of losing their faith, may be religiously educated and trained up to pursuits which will fit them to become useful members of society and ornaments of the church."[15]

St. Mary's Industrial School, Baltimore

In May, 1866, Archbishop Spalding called a meeting of prominent Catholics of Baltimore at which he outlined his plans for an industrial school to be known as St. Mary's Industrial School for Boys. The archbishop stated that four Xaverian Brothers would arrive from Belgium about August 1 to take charge of the school. Articles of incorporation had already been secured. A tract of land, consisting of 100 acres on the Frederick Road within a short distance of Baltimore, had been donated to the archbishop by Mrs.

---

[15] J. L. Spalding, *The Life of the Most Rev. M. J. Spalding*, p. 289.

A Vocational Program

Emily McTavish, a granddaughter of Charles Carroll, as a site for the new institution and temporary buildings were in process of construction.[16] It was estimated that a permanent building capable of meeting the needs of the school would cost in the neighborhood of $50,000. At the close of the meeting subscriptions amounted to $18,000.

St. Mary's Industrial School opened its doors and received its first boy October 3, 1866. In a few months the number of boys increased to forty-five, the utmost capacity of the temporary structure. The new building was begun in April, 1867, and completed in a little more than a year.[17]

In 1868 the Maryland legislature recommended the appropriation of $25,000 for St. Mary's Industrial School for the two years 1868-1869.[18] In 1869 the institution received an appropriation of $3,000 from the city council of Baltimore. In its appeal, both for public funds and private donations, the board of trustees of St. Mary's expressed the hope that in a short time the institution would become self-supporting. They had under way plans for the development of various industries from which they expected to secure considerable profit. Large investments were made in machinery and equipment of various kinds. Before long the board learned that an industrial school can not compete successfully with outside plants. In this connection St. Mary's Industrial School went through the bitter experiences of many schools of its type. It was not the first or last school that made an effort to combine productive efficiency with vocational training.

Its large investment in machinery meant a serious setback for St. Mary's Industrial School. The institution suffered a still more serious blow in the death of Archbishop Spalding in 1872. After due consideration the board of trustees decided that there was only one way in which St. Mary's could be saved and that was by making it a semi-public institution.

---

[16] *Baltimore Catholic Mirror*, May 26, 1866.
[17] *Ibid.*, February 13, 1869.
[18] *Ibid.*, March 28, 1868.

In 1872 the board applied for a change in the charter so as to enable them to receive delinquent boys from the city and state. It was felt that so long as the institution was discharging a public function it could rightfully appeal for public appropriations. The move was successful, so far as St. Mary's was concerned, and everything went smoothly until 1876. In that year a number of citizens applied for an order restraining the city from granting public funds to St. Mary's on the ground that it was a sectarian institution. While the court upheld the basic argument of the objectors in regard to lump sum appropriations, it contended that there was nothing in the constitution to prevent the city from making per capita payments to St. Mary's for its public wards.

For St. Mary's Industrial School, as for other schools of its type, the after-care and placement of the boys was an important consideration. In the beginning the brothers apprenticed a large number of the boys to farms, but soon learned that this did not work successfully. They therefore adopted the policy of retaining boys until they reached a self-supporting age. It acquired a building downtown to be known as St. James' Home, where boys who had been discharged from the institution might board until such time as they could find work and adjust themselves.[19]

St. John's Protectory, Buffalo

In Bishop Timon of Buffalo, Dr. Ives had another active co-worker in developing a protective program for Catholic boys. In 1861 Bishop Timon began to make plans for the care of boys who could not be provided for in the diocesan orphanage. With this purpose in mind he purchased a large farm at Limestone Hill in the present city of Lackawanna, where he erected St. John's Protectory. In 1864 it was incorporated under the title of "Society for the Protection of Destitute Roman Catholic Children at the City of Buf-

[19] *Ibid.*, November 17, 1877; see also Brother Julian, *Men and Deeds*.

falo."[20] It was placed under the direction of Rev. Thomas Hines, who was assisted by the Sisters of St. Joseph and who himself had experience as director of St. Joseph's Orphan Asylum for Boys at Limestone Hill.[21]

When Father Baker assumed charge of the institution in 1882 the name of St. John's Protectory was changed to Our Lady of Victory Home. Father Baker upon assuming charge did more than merely change the name of the institution. He refashioned its whole program. Before his time St. John's Protectory had many of the aspects of an ordinary penal institution—high walls, barred windows and rigid discipline. Father Baker very quickly liberalized the old methods of discipline and restraint. Our Lady of Victory Home is now one of Father Baker's Lady of Victory charities. The other institutions that make up the group are: The Working Boys' Home, St. Joseph's Orphan Boys' Asylum, The Lady of Victory Infant Home—a maternity hospital and a general hospital.[22]

The movement for the building of Catholic industrial schools was especially commended by the Second Plenary Council of Baltimore in 1866. "We, therefore," urged the Council, "earnestly exhort the bishops to defend with every possible care and solicitude the tender lambs of the Christian fold from the wolves that hang around them. Let them establish industrial schools everywhere but especially in the great cities where the number of those in danger is larger."[23] This naturally gave impetus to the development of protectories. Here was further evidence that Catholics were becoming more and more conscious of the losses that the Church was sustaining through failure to make adequate provision for its neglected children. It must not be assumed, however, that

[20] T. A. Galvin, C.SS.R., *A Modern Apostle of Charity, Father Baker, and His Lady of Victory Charities*, p. 233.
[21] *Ibid.*, p. 211.
[22] *Ibid.*, pp. 16–17.
[23] *Con. Plen. Balto. Decret.*, p. 446.

the task of building these new institutions was an easy one. Catholics were, for the most part, still poor.

Industrial Schools Established in Seventies and Eighties

Among the dioceses that established industrial schools in the period of 1870-1890 were St. Louis, San Francisco, Philadelphia and St. Paul. In 1871 a Catholic protectorate was established at Glencoe, Missouri, in the archdiocese of St. Louis. Under the leadership of Rt. Rev. Patrick J. Ryan, later archbishop of Philadelphia, the protectory was at first successful, but later languished because of lack of support. The property was taken over later by the Christian Brothers who made it their novitiate under the title of La Salle Institute.[24]

About 1875 the city of San Francisco established a youth's directory for the purpose of diminishing juvenile delinquency in the city. At first the agency confined itself to securing employment for children. Later its facilities were enlarged so as to enable it to care temporarily for children without suitable homes.[25] In 1886 the Misses Drexel purchased 200 acres of land near Bristol in the archdiocese of Philadelphia for the purpose of providing a home and school for Catholic boys who could not be cared for in the ordinary orphan homes. The boys were to be prepared for the various trades and also for farming. The protectory was to be in charge of the Christian Brothers.[26] An industrial school for boys was established in Clontarf, Minnesota, in the archdiocese of St. Paul about 1880.

From a reading of the contemporary literature of Catholic child-care it is very evident that those who were interested or engaged in the work did not draw clear lines of demarcation between the different types of children. Such literature as there is on Catholic child-care during this period pictures thousands of homeless, abandoned, destitute children roaming

---

[24] Rothensteiner, *op. cit.*, Vol. II, p. 280.
[25] *Baltimore Catholic Mirror*, June 16, 1877.
[26] *New York Freeman's Journal*, February 6, 1886.

A VOCATIONAL PROGRAM 123

the streets and being grabbed up by Protestant agencies and sent to good Protestant homes in the middle west. The industrial schools represented a heroic effort to do something for these children. As was to be expected, the industrial school did not classify its charges. Its basic thought was to save them to the faith.

Institutions Complementing the Industrial Schools

Side by side with the industrial schools, there was another group of institutions providing temporary care for homeless boys. In these the boy was to be retained until a permanent foster home could be found for him. A good illustration of this type of home is the Mission of the Immaculate Virgin, now located on Staten Island. It had its beginnings in St. Vincent's Newsboys' Lodging Home opened by the St. Vincent de Paul Society on Warren Street, New York City, in 1870. While still a layman the Rev. John C. Drumgoole had become acquainted with the work of the St. Vincent de Paul Society. After ordination he asked Archbishop McCloskey of New York to permit him to dedicate his life to the care of homeless and destitute boys. In 1873 he took over St. Vincent's Newsboys' Lodging Home from the St. Vincent de Paul Society. Within a period of four years the demand on this institution became so great that Father Drumgoole was obliged to acquire a larger house on Lafayette Place.

Father Drumgoole was not long satisfied with the development of a working boys' home. He visioned a village community in which a large number of children of both sexes could be brought together under the care of sisters. As a part of his program he acquired a farm on Staten Island where he gradually developed his village community. As a means of supporting the project, he organized St. Joseph's Union, which very quickly drew a large membership from the entire country.[27]

[27] "The Great Monument at Mt. Loretto," by John Shea, *Catholic World*, Vol. LVIII (October, 1893), p. 19; "The Catholic Charities of New York," *Catholic World*, Vol. XLIII (August, 1886), p. 681.

In a letter addressed to Cardinal McCloskey in April, 1884, Father Drumgoole tells about the opening of the new buildings on Staten Island the previous Thanksgiving Day. On this occasion 700 children visited Mt. Loretto. In the evening 400 larger boys returned to the house on Lafayette Place, leaving 300 in the new institution. Father Drumgoole stated that plans were under way for the care of homeless boys on Staten Island in accordance with the original purpose of his foundation. At the mission in Lafayette Place fifty people daily received free meals. Relief was also given to families in their homes.[28]

The example set by the St. Vincent de Paul Society and Father Drumgoole in New York inspired Catholics in a number of other cities. In 1871 Rev. Maurice Hickey established St. Vincent's Home for Newsboys in Brooklyn. The home, however, did not confine its efforts to newsboys. It received any boy who was in want. While it was intended primarily for working boys, it also received a number of boys under working age. It was Father Hickey's plan to provide permanent foster homes for homeless boys as soon as possible.[29]

A lodging house for Catholic boys, known as St. Vincent's Home, was established in Newark in 1882. The establishment of the Newark institution was due to the activities of the "Boys' Lodging House and Children's Aid Society" in winning Catholic boys away from the Church."[30] Fully one-half of the boys cared for by this agency were children of Irish Catholics. All the children were compelled to attend Protestant services. In 1883 a Catholic working boys' home was opened in Boston.[31]

---

[28] *New York Freeman's Journal*, April 19, 1884.
[29] *Ibid.*, February 15, 1879.
[30] *Ibid.*, October 21, 1882.
[31] "Catholic Life of Boston," by A. A. McGinley, *Catholic World*, Vol. LXVII (April, 1898), p. 21.

Catholic Industrial School Movement Languishes After 1885

After 1885 the movement for the organization of Catholic industrial schools and working boys' homes began to languish. This was probably due in part to the difficulties that had arisen in maintaining the existing institutions. It was also due in part to the difficulty of finding the necessary personnel. Catholic leaders were beginning to understand more clearly that the institution was only a partial solution of the problem. They began to realize more and more that institutions alone could not save Catholic children, but that the children had to be reached primarily through their homes and through the parochial schools.

The Church had barely learned to deal with the older immigration, when it was called upon to deal with the tide of the new immigration. Hundreds of thousands of immigrants from the Catholic countries of southern and eastern Europe were poured into this country every year. A large part of the energy and resources of the Church were consumed in providing religious instruction and worship for these new immigrants.

Catholic Industrial Schools After 1900

Since 1900 a number of new industrial schools have been established. In 1909 the State Council, Knights of Columbus of Indiana, opened an industrial school for boys in Indianapolis. In 1917 Father Flanagan began a home for boys under his name in Omaha. In 1916 Bishop Hoban of Scranton established St. Michael's Industrial School at Hoban Heights, Pennsylvania. In 1920 the St. Vincent de Paul Society founded an industrial school for boys in Milwaukee. In 1921 Father Wynhoven opened his new institution, Hope Haven, at Marrero, Louisiana. The institutions at Indianapolis and Milwaukee were intended primarily for delinquent boys. Hope Haven is a vocational school for boys who have graduated from the orphanages in New Orleans. It is planned eventually to expand the institution so as to care for all the children requiring special attention in the archdiocese of New Orleans. St. Michael's Industrial School at Hoban Heights, Pennsylvania, is for problem boys. It does not accept boys who have been seriously delinquent. The institutions that have been established since 1900 have grown out of peculiar local situations. They do not represent a national movement like the protectories of the earlier period. In fact, there is no longer the old interest in protectories that was manifested forty or fifty years ago.

Problem of Personnel

During the past few years the problem of personnel for Catholic institutions for older boys has become acute. There is a question as to whether or not we can depend on the sisters to take care of older boys. The various brotherhoods who did such splendid pioneer work in developing Catholic industrial schools, are diverting their attention to the educational field. We have, therefore, been finding it difficult to supply the proper personnel for some of our welfare institutions. It is quite apparent that the various dioceses can not look to the brotherhoods to take charge of their children's institutions. So far as the ordinary institution for dependent children is concerned, the problem is not so serious. The sisterhoods have been willing to take over the institutions of this type which the brothers were compelled to leave. The new demands on the brotherhoods have, however, made the problem of operating Catholic homes for older boys exceedingly acute, as a lay personnel is going to be quite expensive.

The problem of personnel has given rise to the question as to whether or not the various dioceses should proceed further with the development of industrial schools. In fact, there has been a serious question as to whether the existing institutions should be continued. An increasing number of persons believe that it is not practicable for the Church in the ordinary American diocese to provide an institutional program for the care of delinquent children. They believe that as a matter of practical policy the Church must surrender this field to the state.

The question has been raised by many students of juvenile delinquency as to whether or not the resources of the Church would not be more effective in developing a preventive program for juvenile delinquency rather than in developing an institutional program for delinquent. From everyday experience one finds that the children who come before the juvenile courts have had no religious training. Would it not be better to see that such children have religious training rather than try to care for them after their delinquency?

A Preventive Program for Juvenile Delinquency

In order to prevent juvenile delinquency one must reach its sources which are generally found in the home life. The juvenile delinquent usually has no religious training, as he ordinarily comes from a home without religious standards. For the children who can not be reached by a preventive program it would seem that in most dioceses, as a matter of practical policy, one must look to the public institutions. These institutions, it must be noted, have changed their attitude entirely towards religious training since the days when the first protectories were established. They now seek Catholic cooperation. They welcome any program of religious training, and we have only ourselves to blame if delinquent and semi-delinquent Catholic children in public institutions do not receive some measure of religious training.

Homes for working boys no longer fill the same need as forty years ago. The newsboy and the bootblack are either in their own homes or in school. Very few homes for working boys have, therefore, been established in recent years. The only two of recent origin are Father Dunne's Newsboys'

Home in St. Louis and St. Anthony's Home for Boys in Cleveland. Father Dunne's Home was originally intended for newsboys, but has really become an ordinary institution for dependent children. St. Anthony's Home cares for boys who have been discharged from the diocesan orphanage until such time as they are able to adjust themselves. It provides a center to which the boys can return when they are out of work or when various difficulties arise. In this way the home serves a useful purpose. Many of the older working boys' homes have followed the same drift as Father Dunne's Newsboys' Home.

CHAPTER VIII
MOTHERS AND INFANTS
Growing Need of Provision for Infants

With the immigration tide of the forties and fifties of the last century, Catholic leaders recognized the need of making special provision for infants and smaller children. Abandoned infants were frequently picked up by the police and placed in the almshouses, from which they were generally placed out in Protestant families. Many of these children were born of immigrant Catholic parents; they had been baptized in the Church and it was the duty of the Church to see that they were brought up in the faith. The existing children's institutions did not lend themselves very readily to the care of infants. The general hospital provided the only available asylum under Catholic auspices for the care of foundlings and abandoned infants.

Buffalo Diocese First Recognizes Problem

Buffalo was the first diocese in the United States to make separate provision for the care of infants: "In traveling through his diocese the much-loved Bishop Timon encountered many homeless widows and forsaken infants. Recognizing their need, he formed the idea of providing an asylum for these two most helpless classes of society at the opposite extremes on the road of life. This idea took permanent form as a result of the frightful cholera epidemic of 1848 which left in its wake many helpless victims who were in immediate need of care and shelter. The only provision that could be made for them at that time was at the sisters' hospital, but this proving neither convenient nor suitable for the best interest of children or patients, steps were taken to procure separate shelter. Providence furnished a means through the generosity and charity of Mr. Louis Stephen Le Couteulx, who in 1852 donated a large piece of land for just this purpose. Ready money was not then available for building, so a small wooden cottage was moved to the premises and the land fenced in. With this to begin with four sisters left the sisters' hospital with their charges to commence life in the new home."[1]

From the care of infants grew another very important part of the work of St. Mary's in the care of unmarried mothers. Shortly after its establishment the institution began to provide shelter and care for pregnant unmarried women.[2]

Bishop Timon Establishes First Infant Home

It is an interesting coincidence that the work for foundlings and abandoned infants in the United States should have been started by Bishop Timon, a member of the Lazarist community established by St. Vincent de Paul. Bishop Timon laid the ground work for the first conference of the Society of St. Vincent de Paul in the United States established in St. Louis in 1844. When he came to Buffalo in 1847 there was not a single institution of charity in the city or its environs. When he died (1867) Buffalo had two institutions for orphans, an infant home, a widows' home, a hospital and an industrial school. There was, however, no work that was closer to Bishop Timon's heart than the infant asylum. It has been told of him that many times he carried children in his own arms to St. Mary's. He became first president of the board and gave his services as secretary for some time.[3]

The original title of St. Mary's, namely, St. Mary's Lying-In Hospital and the Buffalo Widows' and Infants' Asylum indicates a rather curious combination. One can understand why the care of infants should be associated with the care of

---
[1] *Archives* of St. Mary's Infant Asylum and Maternity Hospital, Buffalo, N. Y.
[2] *Ibid.*
[3] *Ibid.;* Deuther, *op. cit.*, pp. 208–209.

unmarried mothers, but one can not appreciate so readily the association of infants with dependent widows in the same institution. In all probability the association represented an effort to meet two problems, namely, the care of infants and the care of the aged through one agency. They were the most vital and most pressing problems and it was not possible to have two institutions. As in all the early developments, a single institution had to satisfy a multitude of purposes. The day of specialization had not yet arrived.

In the 1890's St. Mary's, like a great many other Catholic institutions of its type, concluded that by adding a maternity department for pay patients it could increase its income and lighten its responsibilities very considerably. St. Mary's was already doing maternity work for unmarried mothers. There seemed to be no good reason why it should not be able to extend the same service to married women who could pay. In October, 1897, the institution was incorporated under its present title, St. Mary's Infant Asylum and Maternity Hospital.[4] It is probably now the largest maternity hospital in Buffalo.

St. Louis Diocese Has Second Infant Home

The second Catholic institution for the care of infants established in the United States was St. Ann's Widows' Home, Lying-In Hospital and Foundling Asylum of St. Louis. The institution was opened in May, 1853. St. Ann's owed its foundation to the zeal and vision of Archbishop Kenrick and Mrs. Ann Biddle, a daughter of John Mullanphy, the great benefactor of Catholic charities in St. Louis. She donated a plot of ground and Archbishop Kenrick provided for the building. Some years before the establishment of St. Ann's, John Mullanphy left a bequest for the care of ten widows. What he probably had in mind was the beginning of a home for the aged. The problem of old age as it affected

[4] *Archives* of St. Mary's Infant Asylum and Maternity Hospital, Buffalo, N. Y.

women was undoubtedly beginning to make a strong appeal. In planning the building of St. Ann's it was decided that it would be a simple matter to include a section for widows to satisfy the purposes of the Mullanphy bequest.[5] The care of infants was, therefore, associated with the care of orphans in this pioneer St. Louis Catholic charity.

From the very beginning St. Ann's Infant Asylum recognized that the care of foundlings was inseparably bound up with the care of unmarried mothers. Many infants were abandoned because the mothers did not have any place to go. One of the best means, therefore, of protecting the baby was by offering shelter and protection to the mother. St. Ann's, therefore, from the first offered shelter and protection to unmarried mothers as well as to dependent and neglected children.

Infant Homes Established Between 1855 and 1870

Between 1855 and 1870 seven Catholic infant and maternity homes were established: St. Vincent's Infant Asylum and Maternity Hospital, New Orleans (1855); St. Vincent's Infant Asylum, Baltimore (1856); St. Vincent's Infant Home and Maternity Hospital, Philadelphia (1858); St. Anne's Infant Asylum, Washington (1860); New York Foundling Hospital (1869); House of Providence, Detroit (1869); and St. Anne's Maternity Hospital, New York City (1869).

New York Foundling Hospital

The most significant Catholic work for mothers and infants established between 1856 and 1870 was the New York Foundling Hospital. The primary purpose of the foundling hospital was the prevention of infanticide. If the conditions attached to the care of their children were exacting it was feared that many mothers would make away with them. Every inducement was therefore offered to the mother to turn over her child to the institution for care. A reception crib

---
[5] Rothensteiner, *op. cit.*, Vol. II, p. 286.

was placed on the outside, where the mother might leave her baby without revealing her own identity. When the mother revealed her identity, she was not required to give any information in regard to her family.[6]

Recognition of Obligations to Mother as Well as Child

It early became apparent that the policies first adopted by the New York Foundling Hospital induced many mothers to rid themselves entirely of the obligation of supporting their children. The foundling authorities therefore decided that, while they had an obligation to the child, they also had an obligation to the mother. If the mother could be induced to avail herself of the shelter of the institution, if she could be induced to live under its restraint for a certain period, if she could only avail herself of the training opportunities that it offered, she would come out with an entirely different attitude towards life's obligations. In describing this new development, Commissioner Letchworth, in his report for the State Board of Charities in 1876, declared: "In this new outgrowth from the original and more immediate object of the Foundling Asylum, the hapless unwedded mother sees the institution expand from a mere ark of safety to her child into a protector and savior to herself."[7] As far as practicable the New York Foundling Hospital induced unmarried mothers to remain in the institution in order to nurse their children.

Out-Door Department of New York Foundling Hospital

One of the most interesting features of the New York Foundling Hospital was the out-door department. The department is significant because of the volume of work it undertook and because of its influence on other Catholic institutions in the United States caring for infants. The out-door department of the Foundling Hospital was not the result

[6] Letchworth, *op. cit.*, p. 240.
[7] *Ibid.*, p. 241.

of any definite plans, it was the product of necessity. In a very short time after the institution was opened it found itself taxed to capacity. The sisters felt that, in view of the conditions to which infants were exposed, something should be done to save them. Accordingly a plan was worked out to secure mothers who had lost their own children and to employ them as wet nurses. It was arranged to have these women take the children and nurse them in their own homes on a per diem basis.

The out-door department of the Foundling Hospital of New York grew very rapidly. In October, 1875, there were 500 children in the institution and 1,000 were being cared for through the out-door department. More than $11,000 a month was expended for the care of children with wet nurses. The standards of the nurses were guaranteed by a certificate from a physician. An officer employed by the institution also made regular visits to the homes in which infants were nursed. The members of the parish conferences of the Society of St. Vincent de Paul assisted the representatives of the Foundling Hospital in the work of home visitation.[8] Beginning in 1897 wet nurses were required to have Board of Health permits.

System of Wet Nursing Dies Out

The system of wet nurses instituted by the New York Foundling Hospital became a model for other Catholic institutions. Catholic infant and maternity homes in all the large cities came to regard wet nursing as an excellent means of relieving over-crowding. They were convinced moreover that the use of the wet nurse would mean a far lower mortality rate than their imperfect systems of feeding. Wet nursing followed the same course in the other institutions as in the New York Foundling Hospital. For several years it was most popular. Then the difficulties of supervising and securing

[8] *Report* of New York Foundling Hospital, 1890–1891.

the right type of wet nurses increased. In the meantime the methods of artificial feeding had improved; science now could offer a fair substitute for mother's milk. The foundling hospitals therefore decided to discontinue the use of wet nurses. Children not nursed by their own mothers were placed on artificial diet. Many of the Catholic institutions that had followed the leadership of the New York institution in the use of breast-feeding had already discontinued the practice. Soon all abandoned it.

Care of Infants and Mothers Recognized as Inseparable

The care of infants and the care of mothers became inseparably bound together in the New York Foundling Hospital and other like Catholic institutions throughout the country. It was really impossible to take care of the child without also extending a helping hand to the mother. In order to care for the mother the institution would have to give her care before as well as after the birth of her child. Very soon the institution caring for mothers and infants felt that its work would not be complete without a maternity department for the mothers under its care. When the New York Foundling Hospital built St. Ann's Protectory in 1880 it was simply following the established practice of similar Catholic institutions in other cities. When the Foundling Hospital decided to admit outside patients to St. Ann's Maternity Hospital in 1914, it was following institutions like St. Mary's Infant Asylum and Maternity Hospital of Buffalo, St. Ann's Widows' Home, Infant Asylum and Maternity Hospital of St. Louis, and St. Joseph's Maternity Hospital, Infant Asylum and Home for Little Children of Cincinnati.

Infant Homes Evolve Plans for Permanent Care of Children

From the very beginning the New York Foundling Hospital, as well as other Catholic institutions of its type, had to devise ways and means of making permanent plans for the children under their care. The directors of the institutions did not recognize that the plans presented any serious difficulties. In a new and developing country it was assumed that there were any number of Catholic homes ready and willing to open their doors to homeless children. The infants' homes in Washington, Baltimore, Philadelphia, Buffalo and Boston found all the homes they needed in their own immediate territory. All that was necessary was to have the pastors make an appeal from their pulpits to the generosity of the people. As a result of the appeal large numbers of applications for children began to pour into the church rectories. Each application was endorsed by the pastor and forwarded to the institution which immediately furnished the family with a child without any further question.

New York Foundling Hospital Finds Free Homes in West

The New York Foundling Hospital was in a different position from any other Catholic institution in the country. In point of numbers it dealt with more children than all the Catholic institutions of like character on the Atlantic seaboard. It was located in a highly congested urban center in which it was impossible to find homes for all the children in its charge. Therefore its officials turned their attention to the west, which was then regarded as the panacea for the Irish immigrant. Many of the immigrants who settled in the west became quite prosperous. If the west held out high hopes for the adult, why should not the same be true of the child? Why should not the immigrant settlers in the prairies be willing to provide homes for the children of their less fortunately situated brethren from New York? The immigrant settlers in the new states, it was argued, were persons with deep faith. They would certainly be influenced by an appeal in the name of Christian charity. Again had not the Protestant organizations placed large numbers of children in homes in the middle west? If such organizations had succeeded, why should not a Catholic organization be equally successful?

The early methods of child-placing adopted by the New York Foundling Hospital and other Catholic institutions look rather primitive today, but they must be appraised by the standards of their time. In the seventies all children's institutions and agencies regarded the placing of a child in a foster home as an easy matter. It was assumed that there were large numbers of families who were ready and willing to receive homeless children, if only they were appealed to in the proper way. If in response to an appeal, they applied for a child, there was no reason to suspect their integrity. It was only a matter of sending the child and depending upon them to give proper care and protection.

Early Child-Placing Systems Break Down

Only by experience was the wholesale placement of children without careful investigation found unworkable. Mrs. Jones, who is impelled by a strong appeal from her pastor to apply for a homeless child, is not always able to give the child proper care; she may not have the patience or understanding necessary to deal with another person's child. Mrs. Jones may be advanced in years and may never have had any experience with children, or she may have made a failure of her own children. Again, the child that the Jones family receives may not turn out as well as was expected. The child may have some inherited weakness of which she was unaware. The real parents, too, may come along some day and claim the child that they have never surrendered legally. One can therefore appreciate that the placement of children for adoption is bristling with difficulties.

The New York Foundling Hospital, like other pioneer agencies engaged in the placement of children, naturally ran into many of these difficulties. Very little was said about its successes. It was the failures that returned to plague its officials. Complaints were heard throughout the middle west about the poor placements made by the New York Foundling Hospital. Two of the sisters went out on a tour of inspection to canvass the situation first hand. Finally the whole system was remodeled. Agents were employed to visit prospective homes and supervise the children who had been placed. Even with a well-developed organization the Foundling Hospital found that it could not spread its efforts over a large territory. Without prohibitive expenditures of money, no one organization could maintain close contact with children placed in various states. The foundling authorities therefore decided to follow the only logical course that was open to them, namely, to limit their placement area. The area to which they decided to limit their placements included New York, New Jersey, Pennsylvania, Connecticut and Massachusetts.

The New York Foundling Hospital Adopts Boarding Home Plan

Even with its large institutional facilities, its use of wet nurses and its placement of children with persons who were willing to offer them a home with or without a view to adoption, the New York Foundling Hospital could not begin to provide for all the children committed to its charge. The institutional authorities were therefore compelled to have recourse to another method of care, namely, the boarding home. This plan called for the payment of a definite monthly allowance to mothers who were able and willing to give children the proper care. In this phase of its work the New York institution is unique among Catholic institutions in the country. Other institutions have depended very largely on their own institutional equipment and on homes that accepted the children free of charge. A number of them followed the Foundling Hospital of New York in the use of wet nurses but abandoned the plan some fifteen to twenty years ago. No other Catholic infant home has adopted boarding out of children as a part of its own program.

Infant and Maternity Homes a Part of Diocesan Programs After 1870

The infant home and maternity hospital became a part of the Catholic Charities program of all the larger dioceses in the country after 1870. The infant home cared for children from birth to five years of age, and the maternity hospital provided shelter and care for obstetrical service for unmarried mothers. Between 1870 and 1890 six Catholic infant homes and maternity hospitals were established: St. Ann's Asylum and Maternity Hospital, Cleveland, in charge of the Sisters of St. Augustine (1873); St. Joseph Maternity and Infant Asylum, Norwood, Ohio, in charge of Sisters of Charity of Cincinnati, (1873); St. Mary's Infant Asylum and Maternity Hospital, Dorchester, Mass., in charge of the Daughters of Charity of St. Vincent de Paul (1874); St. Vincent's Infant Asylum and Maternity Hospital, Milwaukee, Wis., in charge of the Daughters of Charity of St. Vincent de Paul (1877); St. Vincent's Infant Asylum and Maternity Hospital, Chicago, in charge of the Daughters of Charity of St. Vincent de Paul (1882), and St. Joseph's Children and Maternity Hospital, Scranton, in charge of the Sisters of the Immaculate Heart of Mary (1890).

Infant and Maternity Homes Established Between 1890 and 1910

Between 1890 and 1910, fifteen Catholic infant and maternity homes were established: Rosalia Foundling Asylum and Maternity Hospital, Pittsburgh, in charge of the Sisters of Charity of Greensburgh (1891); St. Vincent de Paul Infant Asylum, Providence, R. I., in charge of the Sisters of Divine

Providence (1892); St. Joseph's Infant Home, Utica, N. Y., in charge of the Daughters of Charity of St. Vincent de Paul (1893); St. Vincent's Maternity Hospital and St. Anthony's Home for Infants, Kansas City, Mo., in charge of the Daughters of Charity of St. Vincent de Paul (1899); Infant Asylum of Our Lady of Perpetual Help and Maternity Hospital, Manchester, N. H., in charge of Sisters of Mercy (1899); St. Vincent's Nursery and Babies Hospital, Montclair, N. J., in charge of Sisters of Charity of Convent Station (1899); Bethlehem Infant Asylum, Brightside, Holyoke, Mass., in charge of Sisters of Divine Providence (1900); St. Mary's Maternity Hospital and Infant Asylum, Syracuse, N. Y., in charge of Daughters of Charity of St. Vincent de Paul (1900); St. Mary's Mothers and Infants Home, Green Bay, Wis., in charge of Sisters of Misericorde (1900); St. Agnes Baby Home, Park Place, Oreg., in charge of Sisters of Mercy (1901); Our Lady of Victory Infant Home and Maternity Hospital, Lackawanna, N. Y., in charge of Sisters of St. Joseph of Buffalo (1906); Holy Innocents Infant Home. Portland, Me., in charge of Sisters of Mercy (1907); Bethlehem Home for Infants, Taunton, Mass., in charge of Sisters of Mercy (1909); St. Joseph's Infant Home, Troy, N. Y., in charge of Sisters of St. Joseph (1909); and St. Monica's Foundling Home, Sioux City, Iowa, in charge of the Benedictine Sisters (1910).

Infant and Maternity Homes Established After 1910

Fourteen Catholic infant and maternity homes have been established since 1910: Alabama Maternity and Infant Home, Mobile, Ala., in charge of Daughters of Charity of St. Vincent de Paul (1911); St. Agnes Infant Asylum and Maternity Hospital, West Hartford, Conn., in charge of Sisters of Mercy (1914); A. N. Brady Maternity Hospital and Infant Home, Albany, Daughters of Charity (1914); St. Rita's Home for

Infants, Pittsburgh, Sisters of III Order of St. Francis (1917); St. Joseph's Infant Home, Ebensburg, Pa., Sisters of St. Joseph (1921); St. Elizabeth's Infant Home, San Francisco, Daughters of Charity of St. Vincent de Paul (1921); Misericordia Hospital and Maternity Home, Chicago, Sisters of Mercy (1921); Catholic Infant Home, St. Paul, Sisters of St. Joseph of Carondelet (1923); St. Agnes Foundling Home, Kalamazoo, Mich., Sisters of St. Joseph (1925); Holy Infancy Home, Austin, Texas, Sisters of Charity of St. Vincent de Paul (1927); St. Elizabeth's Home for Infants, Indianapolis (1927); Catholic Infant Home, Los Angeles (1928); Our Lady's Home for Infants, Louisville (1928)[9]; and Corpus Christi Carmel, Duluth (1928), Sisters of Mt. Carmel.

Catholic Infant and Maternity Homes in United States

There are in all some forty-four Catholic infant homes and maternity hospitals in the United States. Practically all of these institutions care not only for infants but for unmarried mothers. A number of them without maternity departments depend on the general hospitals for their maternity work. The institutions with maternity departments generally receive private patients as well as unmarried mothers as a means of supporting the free work they do for unmarried mothers and infants.

Medical Standards of Infant and Maternity Homes

The medical standards of Catholic infant and maternity homes have improved greatly in recent years. When they were first organized they were far ahead of any other program in the country for the care of mothers and infants. Lack of resources, a sense of self-sufficiency and isolation from current movements has tended to retard their development. It must be remembered, moreover, that when Catholic infant and maternity homes were first started child welfare move-

---

[9] The infant homes in Indianapolis, Los Angeles and Louisville are under lay auspices.

ments outside the Church were distinctly Protestant and usually hostile to Catholics.

Most Catholic infant and maternity homes now have staffs of specialists in charge of their medical work. The preparation of diet for artificially fed children is under the supervision of a trained dietitian. The children are cared for by trained nurses. All babies born in the institutions are given a Wassermann test immediately after birth. Children who are received from outside are given a careful medical examination and a Wassermann test. All children are weighed and measured at regular intervals. In order to improve their nursery standards a number of Catholic infant and maternity homes have entered into special arrangements with the general hospitals in regard to nursery training. Nurses in training in the hospitals spend three months of their last year in the infant and maternity homes.

Basic Objectives of Early Catholic Infant and Maternity Homes

In the beginning the Catholic infant and maternity homes had as a basic objective the care of foundlings and abandoned children and the prevention of infanticide. When they extended their service to unmarried mothers, they thought not only of the mother but especially of the child. Mother and child were to them a part of the same problem. They wanted the mother to come to them freely. They were convinced that if they made conditions too rigid she might abandon or possibly do something worse to her child. They felt that in making the surrender of the child easy they were doing a service both to the mother and the child; to the mother in that she had come under the influence of the sisters for a certain period and to the child in that he was protected against possible harm and assured of a good foster home.

The institution did everything possible to protect the mother against public knowledge of her offense. If the facts should become known to her relatives, friends or associates, she could never face them again, and would therefore find it exceedingly difficult to readjust herself to a normal life. While if permitted to enter the institution quietly without questioning and investigation, and allowed to remain under an assumed name until her child was born and then permitted to surrender her child, she might return to the world without any fear for her future. She had learned her lesson, and it was hoped would never fall again.

The Recent Modified Attitude of Catholic Infant and Maternity Homes

In recent years Catholic infant and maternity homes have modified their attitude toward the problem of the unmarried mother very considerably. It would scarcely be true to say that they had changed their fundamental philosophy. They have still just as much interest in shielding the mother against publicity and in planning for the welfare of the child. They have, however, come to temper their gentleness towards the mother with a more careful inquiry into her case. They have learned from experience that some member of the family usually knows about the girl's condition, and the counsel of this person is valuable in conference.

The institutions have found that the immediate separation of the mother and the child was not a good plan from the standpoint of the child. No matter how well artificial feeding may have been perfected, infant mortality remained abnormally high. The physicians of the staffs were constantly insisting that the best means of reducing infant mortality was through breast-feeding. As a result of the pressure of their medical staffs, the institutions induced an increasing number of mothers to breast-feed their children. Breast-feeding meant that the mothers remained with their babies for a considerable period; it meant the development of attachment between the mothers and the children. The mothers, therefore, began to seek other plans for their children besides surrender. They talked the matter over with the sisters. As a result of their deliberations the mothers frequently decided to board the children in the institutions. In the meantime various plans for the children's future began to appear on the horizon. There were relatives who wanted the children for adoption or perhaps the girls married and were able to take the children into their own homes. At any rate, breast-feeding has become the accepted thing in Catholic institutions. The sisters everywhere speak most favorably of the results both from the standpoint of the mother and the child. They tell of the wholesome and stabilizing influence that it has had on the mothers, of the fifty per cent solution of their medical problems and the reduction to a minimum of the mortality rate.

Social Service in Infant and Maternity Homes

The sisters no longer depend on their own resources in dealing with unmarried mothers. They have found that they need a new type of service in order to deal effectively with the problems presented by this type of work; that is, case workers to study each case sympathetically as a basis for the formulation of plans adapted to the needs of the particular case. The general tendency seems to be to have this case work service supplied by the diocesan Catholic Charities, although a few institutions supply their own case workers.

Smaller Dioceses Use Homes of Larger Dioceses

Since there is a total of only forty-five Catholic infant and maternity homes in this country, it means that over half of the dioceses have no special provision for the care of unmarried mothers and infants. In the past many of the smaller dioceses have depended upon the larger dioceses for this work. In many instances mothers and infants were sent to institutions in the larger centers without any definite and formal arrangement on the part of the dioceses in which they had a legal residence. In the last few years the larger dioceses have taken cognizance of this situation. Since they began to make a more careful study of the admissions to their institutions, they have been taking up with the resident dioceses of mothers and children the question of financial responsibility. As a result of the discussions of particular cases many of the smaller dioceses have recently entered into specific arrangements with the institutions in the larger dioceses for the care of unmarried mothers and their children.

Casework Service in After-Care

A number of the smaller dioceses have been making use of the facilities afforded by their general hospitals for the care of unmarried mothers. A number af the general hospitals have special departments for the care of unmarried mothers who are awaiting the birth of children. Nearly all the hospitals with such an arrangement do not have any provision for the care of the mother and child after birth. The general plan is to have the child surrendered immediately and sent to the diocesan orphanage which endeavors to find a free home for the child. In at least one diocese an effort has been made to deal with this problem through casework service. The caseworker establishes contact with the mother immediately after she is received in the hospital. She talks with the mother about the plans for the care of her child. She makes known to her the arrangements that can be made for mothers who desire to nurse their children. When it becomes necessary to separate the mother and the child the caseworker frequently arranges to have the child cared for in a boarding home. In some instances arrangements are made with relatives to take care of the child. It is expected that under this plan the number of surrenders will decrease greatly.

About a year ago one diocese gave serious thought to the desirability of building a new infant and maternity home. After studying the matter carefully, the bishop decided that the institution was not necessary; that the maternity work incidental to the care of unmarried mothers could be cared for in the general hospitals and that the care of the mothers and infants could be provided for through the use of boarding homes.

CHAPTER IX
CHILD-CARE AFTER THE CIVIL WAR
American Catholic Charities a Defense Against Protestantism

The history of Catholic charities in the United States is almost a history of the struggle of the immigrant for the preservation of the faith of his children. The immigrant entered into a civilization essentially Protestant. The whole life and outlook of the country was Protestant. Many people honestly believed that a great favor was conferred on the child of the immigrant when he was rescued from his poor home in the slums and brought up in the ideals and virtues of Protestantism. Many others were governed only by sectarian or anti-Catholic prosleytzing agencies. Before the Civil War the immigrant who needed assistance had to look to Protestant sources. In fact, the public institutions were just as Protestant in character as those operated by the individual denominations. Their agents were often ministers or ex-ministers, or women who were aggressively evangelistic. The Protestant religion was a part of their life and their spirit. When the friendless children of the Irish were brought to them their only thought was to preserve them from the errors of "Romanism."

After the Civil War the immigrant found himself in a new order. In the battles for the preservation of the American nation the immigrant developed a leadership—a lay leadership—that was deeply conscious of his rights and possibilities. For centuries he had struggled for the preservation of his faith. He was not going to submit to the inroads of American Protestantism. Again, Protestantism was growing weaker and was less sure of itself as rationalism increased.

The struggle of the immigrant to save the faith of his children was long and arduous. No matter how many institutions he might build, it would be difficult to care for all the children of the faith. Large numbers of children would be cared for in the poor homes. In a number of states the children who were removed from the poor homes would be cared for by public institutions. There was, therefore, not only the question of building Catholic institutions but also of getting public institutions to recognize the child's right to be brought up in the faith of its parents.

Recognition of the Child's Religion in Child-Care Programs

In 1875 it became a recognized principle in New York State that a child should be brought up by an institution or organization of its own faith. It was not until 1894 that the child's right to be brought up in its own faith was recognized in the state of Connecticut, where incidentally the Irish had become a controlling political factor. Numbers obviously counted far more than arguments. Before 1894 the county institutions in Connecticut had been placing children out in Protestant homes without very much question. In that year the *Connecticut Catholic* began to call the attention of its readers to the situation. It was charged that the county institutions had been "diverted from their original purpose to well directed channels of religious proselytism."[1]

The case of a Catholic child placed in a Methodist family by the County Children's Home in New Haven in 1892 brought the Connecticut policy to a definite issue. Was a public institution in Connecticut free to place a Catholic child in such a home? Catholics appealed to the courts against the action of the New Haven Home; but the Supreme Court of the state contended since the institution was the child's legal guardian that it was not necessary for it to reckon with the parents in planning for him. The court decision only added further fuel to the fire. The agitation carried on by

[1] April 3, 1886.

the *Connecticut Catholic* moved the Catholics of the state from their stupor. No longer were they satisfied to let the majority deal with the children of the immigrant as they pleased. The time had come when the rights of the immigrant must be given consideration. The following incident describes in a very realistic way the rising power of the immigrant in Connecticut at the time. There was an agitation for the building of a new school in a certain district in Hartford. The Yankees needed the support of the Irish immigrants in order to have the school built. One day a Yankee leader approached one of the Irish immigrant leaders to secure support for the project. The Irishman, however, very promptly reminded him that while the Yankees in the district might still have the money that the Irish had the votes. When any large group of people exercises the right of suffrage its power must be reckoned with sooner or later. The agitation for the recognition of the rights of parents in the religious up-bringing of their children came to a climax in 1893. In that year the legislature passed a law providing that children should be placed in homes of the same religious faith as the parents. Commenting on this law, the *Connecticut Catholic* stated that under the new law the practice of proselytism in the county home was made virtually impossible.[2]

What the editor overlooked was that laws do not operate automatically. Their enforcement calls for continued vigilance on the part of the people whose interests they express. In Connecticut as in other states Catholics lulled themselves into a false security after obtaining legislation for the safeguarding of the religious faith of dependent children. As late as 1913 it was found that the county children's homes were not respecting the religious faith of the children in their home placements. At that time Bishop John Nilan estab-

[2] March 24, 1894.

lished a belated diocesan commission to follow up the Catholic children who had been placed in private homes.

Public Child-Caring Agencies Remained Protestant in Character

In the last two decades of the nineteenth century there was just as much need for the development of a Catholic child-caring program as during the previous decades. Public child-caring agencies were still evangelical in spirit and when possible in deed. They still continued to place Catholic children in Protestant homes. The Children's Aid Societies by and large still retained their sectarian character. There was, however, a marked advance on the part of Catholics to regain lost territory. With more adequate resources the Church was able to build more institutions. The organization of new dioceses had an important effect on the charitable work of the Church. Every new diocese meant a new center of Catholic charitable activity. The new immigration from southern and eastern Europe, moreover, created new problems for the Church, which was itself becoming "naturalized."

Catholic Children's Homes Established Between 1885 and 1900

Between 1885 and 1900 some fifty Catholic children's homes were established: Diocesan Orphanage and Home for the Aged, Ogdensburg, N. Y. (1885); St. Agatha's Home for Children, Nanuet, N. Y. (1885); St. Vincent's Home, Fall River, Mass. (1885); St. Vincent's Orphan Asylum, Fort Wayne, Ind. (1886); St. Mary's Home and Orphanage, Jacksonville, Fla. (1886); St. Michael's Orphanage, Jersey City, N. J. (1886); St. Peter's Orphanage, Memphis, Tenn. (1886); St. Joseph's Boys' Home, Manchester, N. H. (1887); St. Joseph's Home, Jersey City, N. J. (1887); St. Francis Orphan Asylum for Colored Girls, Normandy, Mo. (1887); St. John's Home for Boys, Wheeling, W. Va. (1887); St. Vincent's Technical School, Buffalo, N. Y. (1888); St. Mary's

Orphanage and Aged Home, Manitowac, Wis. (1888); House of the Angel Guardian for Boys, Leavenworth, Kans. (1888); Catholic Orphanage, Nazareth, N. C. (1889); St. Francis Home for Orphan Boys, Detroit (1889); St. Catherine's Orphanage, Anaheim, Calif. (1889); St. John's Orphanage, Grand Rapids, Mich. (1889); St. Joseph's Orphanage, Tucson, Ariz. (1890); St. Clara's Orphanage, Denver (1890); Sacred Heart Orphan Asylum, West Park-on-the-Hudson, N. Y. (1890); St. Joseph's Orphanage (French) Fall River, Mass. (1890); St. Joseph's Orphanage, Spokane, Wash. (1890); St. Peter's Diocesan Orphanage, San Antonio, Tex. (1890); St. Joseph's Home, Englewood, N. J. (1891); St. Mary's Home, St. Mary, Ore. (1891); St. Anne's French Canadian Orphanage, Worcester, Mass. (1891); St. Ann's Orphan Asylum, Salt Lake City, Utah (1891); St. Joseph's Home for Colored Orphan Boys, Wilmington, Del. (1892); Sacred Heart Orphan Asylum (Italian) New Orleans (1892); St. Vincent's Orphanage, Manchester, N. H. (1892); St. Francis Convent and Orphanage, Nevada, Mo. (1892); Home for Destitute Children, Newburyport, Mass. (1892); St. Vincent's Orphan Asylum, Roanoke, Va. (1893); St. Anne's Orphanage and Industrial School for Girls, Belmont, N. C. (1894); Institution of Mercy, Tarrytown, N. Y. (1894); St. Mary of Angels Home, Syosset, L. I. (1894); St. Mary's Orphanage, Mission San Jose, Calif. (1894); St. Francis Home, Oswego, N. Y. (1895); St. Otto's Orphanage, Little Falls, Minn. (1895); St. John's Protectory, Hicksville, N. Y. (1896); St. Benedict's Home for Colored Children, Rye, N. Y. (1896); St. Vincent's Orphan Asylum, Freeport, Ill. (1896); Guardian Angel Home for Children, Joliet, Ill. (1897); St. Dominic's Home, Hyde Park, N. Y. (1897); St. Ann's Institute, Bristow, Va. (1897); St. Vincent's Home, Davenport, Ia. (1898); St. Michael's Orphan Asylum and Industrial School, Hopewell, N. J. (1898); St. Peter's Orphan Asylum, Newark, N. J. (1898); St. Francis Orphan Asylum, Reading, Pa. (1898);

St. Joseph's Female Orphan Asylum and Gonzaga Memorial, Germantown, Pa. (1898); Angel Guardian Home, Brooklyn, N. Y. (1899).

First Organized Movement to Protect Religious Life of Catholic Children Under Public Care

Since the Civil War Catholics had not only organized a program for the care of Catholic children but they also tried to liberalize the attitude of public institutions towards the religious upbringing of Catholic children. Catholics strove for the recognition of the tolerant principle that children should be brought up in the religious faith of their parents. This was a long and uphill battle in which expediency won toleration or religious liberty. By 1900 the principle was generally recognized as a part of the public policy of the various states. But in the struggle for the recognition of the principle it was apparently overlooked that there was a distinction between policy and practice, that it was one thing to have a law inscribed in the statute books of the states and another thing to have it carried out in practice. Catholic organizations, therefore, came to recognize that if the letter and spirit of the law regarding the religious upbringing of children were to be effective, they must establish close working relations with the public agencies. The first organized movement in this direction was the establishment of the Catholic Charitable Bureau in Boston in 1902 as a guardian of the religious care of Catholic children who were wards of the state. The organization was indicative of a new trend in Catholic child care. It was a frank recognition on the part of Catholic authorities that in certain states a large part of the work of caring for Catholic children was to be carried on by the public authorities and that the best policy for Catholics was to recognize this fact and make the best arrangements possible for the religious care of the children. This did not mean any abatement on the part of Catholics to develop further their own program. It was quite clear, however, that the Catholic program or for that matter any other private child-caring program could not make the same progress in states committed to a public child-caring program as in states where the policy was to enter into arrangements with private institutions for the care of children.

Catholic Children's Homes Established Between 1900 and 1915

The development of Catholic child-caring work proceeded at a rapid pace between 1900 and 1915. A total of fifty-one new children's institutions were established during this fifteen year period. If we add the child-placing agencies to which reference is made in another chapter we will find that the development during this period was far more rapid than during the preceding period. The following is a list of the institutions established between 1900 and 1915, with the dates of their establishment:

Stanford Lathrop Memorial Home, Sacramento, Calif. (1900); St. Joseph's Institute for Boys, Marshall, Tex. (1900); St. Clara's Orphan Asylum, Polonia, Wis. (1900); St. John's Catholic Orphanage, Belleville, Ill. (1901); St. Joseph's Orphanage, Nashua, N. H. (1901); Sacred Heart Orphanage, Kearny, N. J. (1901); St. Anthony's Orphan Asylum, West Arlington, N. J. (1901); Sylvan Heights Home for Orphan Girls, Harrisburg, Pa. (1901); Our Lady of Grace Orphanage, Hoboken, N. J. (1902); St. John's Institute, Wichita, Kans. (1902); Sacred Heart Orphanage, Pueblo, Colo. (1902); The Albertinum, Ukiah, Calif. (1903); Atheneum Orphan's Home, East Lake, Birmingham, Ala. (1903); Sacred Heart Orphanage, Seattle, Wash. (1903); Queen of Heaven Orphanage, Denver, Colo. (1905); Regina Coeli Orphanage, Los Angeles, Calif. (1905); Hessoun Bohemian Catholic Orphanage, St. Louis, Mo. (1905); Sisters of Mercy Orphan Asylum, Worcester, Mass. (1906); St. Vincent's Home for Boys, Cincinnati, O.

(1906); Dunne Home for Boys, Dallas, Tex. (1906); St. Joseph's Orphanage, Dallas, Tex. (1906); Orphans' Home, Laredo, Tex. (1907); St. Joseph's Orphanage, Levy, Ark. (1908); St. Thomas Orphanage, Lincoln, Nebr. (1908); Mt. St. Joseph's Orphanage for Boys, Paterson, N. J. (1908); Orphelinat Franco-American, Lowell, Mass. (1908); St. John's School, Deep River, Conn. (1908); St. Joseph's Orphan Asylum, Milwaukee, Wis. (1908); St. John's Orphan Asylum for Boys, Summit, Pa. (1909); St. Basil's Orphanage, Philadelphia, Pa. (1910); Felician Sisters' Home for Boys, Jackson, Mich. (1910); St. Anthony Home, Sioux City, Ia. (1910); St. Mary's Orphan Asylum, West Conshohocken, Pa. (1911); Mt. St. Michael's Eastern Maine Orphan Home, Bangor, Me. (1911); Immaculate Conception Slovak Home, Middletown, Pa. (1911); St. Joseph's Orphanage and Home for Aged, Oklahoma City, Okla. (1911); St. James Orphanage, Duluth, Minn. (1911); Sacred Heart Orphan Asylum, Philadelphia, Pa. (1911); St. Raphael's Industrial Home and School, Providence, R. I. (1911); Orphanage of Carmelite Sisters of Divine Heart of Jesus, Milwaukee, Wis. (1912); Holy Family Orphanage, Pueblo, Colo. (1912); St. Joseph's Orphanage and Home for Aged, Oklahoma City, Okla. (1912); St. Joseph's Home for Homeless Children, East Chicago, Ind. (1913); St. Joseph's Home of Divine Child, Hammond, Ind. (1913); St. Leo's Italian Orphan Asylum and Day Nursery, Baltimore, Md. (1913); St. Charles Orphanage, Rochester, N. H. (1913); St. Anthony's Orphanage, Albuquerque, N. M. (1913); Briscoe Home for Orphan Boys, Kent, Wash. (1914); Guardian Angel Industrial and Training School, Peoria, Ill. (now listed as Orphanage) (1915); St. Joseph's Orphanage, Abilene, Kans. (1915); and Mercy Home and School, Newport, R. I. (1915).

Catholic Children's Homes Established Since 1915

By 1915 the movement for the building of Catholic orphanages had reached its crest. The next fifteen years witnessed a very marked decline in institution building, only twenty-four institutions having been built as compared with fifty-one during the preceding period: St. Michael's Industrial School, Falls, Pa., now at Hoban Heights, Pa. (1916); Bishop Quarter's School for Motherless Boys, Oak Park, Ill. (1917); Father Flanagan's Boys' Home, Omaha, Nebr. (1917); St. Mary's Home for Girls, Cresson, Pa. (1917); St. Joseph's Home, Wauwatosa, Wis. (1917); St. Joseph's Orphan Home, Superior, Wis. (1917); St. Stanislaus Orphanage, Nanticoke, Pa. (1918); St. Vincent's Children's Home, Pocatella, Idaho (1919) (closed 1928); St. Margaret's Orphan Home, El Paso, Tex. (1919); San Diego's Orphan Home, now Nazareth House Orphanage, San Diego, Calif. (1920); St. Louis Home and School for Boys, West Scarboro, Me. (1920); Sacred Heart Orphans' Home, El Paso, Tex. (1920); Maryknoll in Seattle, Wash. (1920); Morris Institute (for boys), Armstrong Springs, Ark. (1921); Maryknoll Home for Japanese Children, Los Angeles, Calif. (1921); St. Francis Orphan Asylum, Orwigsburg, Pa. (1921); St. Mary's Villa, Elmhurst, Pa. (1923); Little Flower Home for Care of Orphans and Destitute Children, Turton, S. D. (1924); St. Mary's Home, Lafayette, La. (1924); Christ Child Home, Des Moines, Ia. (1925); St. Joseph's Orphanage and Marcotte Home, Lewiston, Me. (1927); St. Monica's Institute (for colored), Kansas City, Mo. (1927); St. Paul Home for Infant Boys, Seattle, Wash. (1927); Sacred Heart Convent and Children's Home, Clarksburg, W. Va. (1928).

Number of Old Institutions Closed After 1915

Every new diocese that was established in the early days regarded it a sacred duty to build an orphans' home. A number of those dioceses that were established before 1915 and had caught up with their building programs became interested later in establishing institutions for special types of children. They were not the ordinary orphan homes. While progress was made in the building of new institutions after 1915, a number of old institutions eventually were closed. The Roman Catholic Orphan Asylum Society of New York disposed of its large institution at Kingsbridge and used the proceeds for the boarding out of children. In the Archdiocese of Cincinnati, two institutions have been closed; in Boston, one institution has been closed; and in Cleveland, two institutions have been combined. A movement is now under way for the combining of two institutions in Milwaukee.

The Year 1915 Marks New Era in Child-Care

In 1915 a new era in Catholic child-care in the United States was entered upon. Catholics began to look beyond the institution to the child's home, to recognize the need of other forms of care, at least for certain types of children who had been removed from their own homes, to look more and more to the facts, to take a more realistic view of our own limitations. In many local communities the Church could not provide for all the Catholic children needing care away from their own homes. In some states public agencies were well developed, and in a few cities non-sectarian agencies were endeavoring to cater to the needs of Catholic children. The Church authorities had to take a practical view of the situation. In many instances they made arrangements in regard to a division of labor with public and non-sectarian agencies. They had, moreover, to arrange programs of religious care for the Catholic children under the public and non-sectarian agencies.

Early Catholic Institutions Founded on Racial as Well as Religious Basis

Race has played an important part in the care of Catholic children. Most of the institutions established between 1850 and 1875 were intended for the children of Irish immigrants. Appeals for these institutions were made to the Irish on the basis of both religion and race. As the German Catholics naturally regarded existing Catholic institutions as Irish, they said to themselves in as many words "the Irish bishops and priests have provided for the children of their own people, it is our duty now to provide for our children." The German Catholics, therefore, went ahead and built their own institutions in all the large industrial centers. The Catholic authorities were not at all adverse to this program. In fact they rather encouraged it. The bishops felt that it relieved them of responsibility.

Later Catholic Institutions Followed Same Trends

The later immigrants likewise appealed to their own racial traditions to provide care for their children just as did the Irish and Germans. The Church, burdened as it was with a multitude of problems, naturally encouraged the later immigrants to provide ways and means of caring for their own children. From a practical standpoint it was recognized that the new immigrants would be more generous in working for and supporting their own institutions than they would be in supporting those already established by other nationalities. How often is it said of the newer immigrants that they will not support existing Catholic institutions because they regard them as Irish or German!

French Canadians Have Own Institutions for Children

The French Canadians who came to the New England mill towns in such large numbers in the seventies and eighties of the last century brought with them their own traditions in regard to charity. They did not want to depend on existing institutions. There was no reason why the same charity which had sprung up so naturally among the French on Canadian soil should not find its proper place in their new settlements. The Grey Nuns would surely follow the immigrants to the United States. This community had first come to the United States to take charge of St. Vincent's Orphanage, Toledo, Ohio (1855).[3] In 1890 they received their first call for service from the members of their own race in this country. In that year Father Prévost invited the Grey Nuns of Quebec to take charge of an orphan asylum which he had established for the children of French Canadians in Fall River, Mass.[4] Following the example of Fall River, institutions for the children of French Canadians were established in a number of other cities: St. Anne's French Canadian Orphanage was established in Worcester in 1891; St. Joseph's Orphanage, at Nashua, N. H., in 1901; and the Orphelinat Franco-American, at Lowell, in 1908.

Poles Have Own Institutions for Children

The Polish immigrants established institutions for dependent children in many of the cities in which they settled in large numbers. There is a large institution for Polish children, the Holy Family Orphan Asylum, with a present population of 310, in Pittsburgh. It was organized in 1900 by a group of Catholic laymen who felt that the children of Polish extraction in the diocese were not being cared for adequately.[5] In 1910 St. Hedwig's Industrial School at Niles, Illinois, was organized by the Rt. Rev. Paul P. Rhode, under the direction of Archbishop Edward J. Quigley. The building fund was raised by the Polish parishes of the Chicago archdiocese.[6]

A fairly typical situation leading to the development of an institution for Polish children is found in the diocese of Scran-

[3] Elinor T. Dehey, *Religious Orders of Women in the U. S.*, Rev., pp. 556-557.
[4] From manuscript prepared for the writer by Congregation of the Sisters of Charity of Quebec.
[5] From manuscript prepared for the writer by Miss Grace Buxton, St. Paul's Orphan Asylum, Pittsburgh.
[6] *The Archdiocese of Chicago*, published by St. Mary's Training School Press of Des Plaines, Ill., 1920, p. 762.

ton. For a number of years Bishop Michael J. Hoban had been urging the priests of the diocese to establish such an institution. The diocesan homes were already overtaxed. The Polish parishes, moreover, did not feel any special obligation to support the diocesan orphans' collection. The bishop felt that they would be more interested in an institution built and operated by their own people for the benefit of the children of their own race. A site was secured at Nanticoke, Pa., and a home under the name of St. Stanislaus Orphanage was opened, February, 1919. St. Stanislaus Orphanage is controlled by a society known as the Society of St. Stanislaus Orphanage, composed of the pastor and two lay persons from each Polish parish in the diocese of Scranton. The operation of the institution is vested in a board of nineteen directors, lay and clerical, elected by the members of the society.[7]

In addition to those already referred to, there are institutions for children of Polish extraction in the dioceses of Hartford, Buffalo, Cleveland, Detroit and Milwaukee.

Bohemian Catholics Have Own Institutions for Children

The Bohemian Catholics in the United States have two institutions for the dependent and neglected children of their race, St. Joseph's Bohemian Orphanage, Lisle, Ill., in the archdiocese of Chicago, founded in 1898, and the Hessoun at Fenton, Mo., in the archdiocese of St. Louis, established in 1905. St. Joseph's Bohemian Orphanage at Lisle receives children of Slovak and Croatian as well as those of Bohemian origin.[8]

Italians Develop Special Facilities for Their Children

The development of special facilities for the care of children of Italian parents was given a powerful impetus by the coming of the Missionary Sisters of the Sacred Heart to this

---
[7] A Study of St. Stanislaus Orphanage made by the writer, 1928.
[8] *The Archdiocese of Chicago*, p. 762.

country about the year 1890. This community was founded by Mother Cabrini at Codogno, Italy, in 1880. At the suggestion of Pope Leo XIII, Mother Cabrini and her associates set out for the United States for the purpose of undertaking missionary work among the Italians in this country.[9] In 1890 the community opened its first institution in this country, Sacred Heart Orphan Asylum, West Park-on-the-Hudson, New York. Two years later it established the Sacred Heart Orphanage at New Orleans. Thereafter institutions for children of Italian parents were established in rapid succession in the dioceses of Newark, Seattle, Denver, Los Angeles and Baltimore.

New Developments Will Rest on Fact Basis

Were it not for the restriction of immigration there probably would be more institutions of a racial character. As the older immigrants ascended in the economic scale, there were naturally fewer dependents among them. The ordinary diocesan child-caring homes are therefore in a much better position to save the children of the newer immigrants than they were thirty or forty years ago. Organized programs for Catholic charities, moreover, have been emphasizing the necessity of a fact basis for all new developments. It is becoming more and more difficult to build institutions without convincing the rank and file of the people that there is a real need for them. Most people are convinced that we have all the institutions for ordinary dependent and neglected children that are now required. Future developments in Catholic charities probably will be seen in an effort to reach the child more and more in his own home.

Negro Somewhat Overlooked by American Catholic Charities

Catholic charities has been so occupied with saving the children of the immigrants that it has given comparatively little

---

[9] "An Apostle of the Italians," by James J. Walsh, *Catholic World*, Vol. CVII, (April, 1918), p. 64.

attention to the welfare of the Negro. However, one must not be unmindful of the great sacrifices made by a number of religious communities for the development of charity work among the Negroes. They are the communities of colored women like the Oblate Sisters of Providence, founded in 1829, and the Sisters of the Holy Family of New Orleans, founded in 1842; and communities of white women like the Franciscan Sisters from England introduced into Baltimore in 1881, the Sisters of the Blessed Sacrament, founded by Mother Catharine Drexel in 1891, and the Servants of the Holy Ghost founded at San Antonio, Texas, in 1888.[10]

Catholic Institutions for Colored Children

One of the first Catholic institutions for dependent and neglected children of the colored race was the Lafon Boy Asylum at New Orleans established in 1872 by a wealthy colored gentleman, Anthony Lafon. Since its foundation the institution has been in charge of the Sisters of the Holy Family of New Orleans.[11] In 1877 a home for colored children was started by a colored woman in an alley in Baltimore. It grew and prospered until a large home was donated by a wealthy Catholic woman. This is the present St. Elizabeth's Home of Baltimore. The institution was taken over by the Franciscan Sisters from Mill Hill, England, in 1881. In addition to the aforementioned, there are the following Catholic institutions for dependent and neglected colored children: St. Francis Asylum, Baltimore, Md. (1867); Guardian Angel Home for Boys, Leavenworth, Kans. (1888); St. Joseph's Industrial School for Colored Boys, Clayton, Del. (1892); St. Peter Claver's Industrial School for Colored Girls, Baltimore, Md. (1893); St. Benedict's Home for Destitute Colored Children, Rye, N. Y. (1896); St. Francis Home, Savannah, Ga. (1898); Zimmer Memorial Institute, Mobile, Ala.; St. Francis

---

[10] "The Negro Race: Their Condition, Present and Future," *Catholic World*, Vol. LXIII (November, 1893) p. 219.
[11] J. T. Gillard, S.S.J., *The Catholic Church and the American Negro*, p. 199.

Colored Orphan Asylum, Normandy, Mo.; Mission Helpers' Day Nursery, Baltimore, Md., and St. Benedict's Nursery, New York City.

In dealing with the Negroes as in dealing with the children of the white race, the institution is no longer the only measure of our progress. In a Catholic social program for the Negroes, the children's institution properly administered must play its part; but without a program that reaches out into the home, and provides religious education for Negro Catholic children, without a program that develops a wholesome community life for the Negro, it can achieve little.

CHAPTER X
PROTECTIVE CARE FOR GIRLS
Immigrant Women Find New Conditions

One of the most far-reaching consequences of immigration was the rending of the home ties of a large number of persons. They were cut adrift in the American cities without the disciplinary aid of the ordinary sanctions of home or neighborhood. While the United States held out greater economic opportunities for them, it also presented greater hazards. A very large proportion of the immigrants came as individuals. They could not depend on family and friends as in the old country. Many who proferred friendship here were really persons who desired to exploit them. The situation was particularly difficult for women who had even less experience than foreign men. In America the immigrant woman had her first experience outside the home. Therefore it was that Catholic leaders of the forties and fifties of the last century gave or should have given special thought to the protection of women immigrants. Closely allied with this problem was the saving of children who were exposed to unwholesome parental influence. It was just as important to save the young girl from debasing influences as it was to save the adult woman from the moral dangers of city life.

Beginning of Protective Program for Women and Girls

In their efforts to protect the moral standards of women both within and without the homes, Catholic leaders did not forget those who had already fallen. They would not have been true to the best traditions of the Church if they had overlooked its great mercy towards repenting sinners. The protective program for women and girls that the pioneer leaders in Catholic Charities in this country envisaged reached out in three directions; to the single women away from home, to the child in its own home, to the women who had fallen from purity.

Two European Communities Responsible for Catholic Protective Program

In developing a Catholic protective program, the bishops looked for assistance to two European communities, the Sisters of Mercy and the Sisters of the Good Shepherd. The Sisters of Mercy were established by Miss Catherine McCauley in Dublin, Ireland, in 1827 for the visitation of the sick and the poor in their own homes, the care of orphans and the housing of homeless women. They were introduced into this country by Bishop Michael O'Connor of Pittsburgh in 1843. In 1866 the Pittsburgh sisters opened a home in Chicago. In 1846 Bishop Hughes of New York secured a band of the Sisters of Mercy from Dublin to open a home in New York.

Sisters of Our Lady of Charity of Refuge

The religious community popularly known as the Sisters of the Good Shepherd includes two communities, the Sisters of "Our Lady of Charity of the Good Shepherd" and the Sisters of "Our Lady of Charity of Refuge." The latter, the parent community, was established by the Blessed John Eudes at Caen, France, in 1641. The constitution of the original community provided that each house should be separate and independent.[1] During the first quarter of the nineteenth century there was a strong movement for bringing together the various Good Shepherd convents under one central motherhouse. This movement found expression through Mother Euphrasia Pelletier, superior of the convent at Angers. She pictured the Sisters of the Good Shepherd as a world-wide community but she was convinced that only by a strong central government could this objective be realized. She

[1] *Catholic Encyclopedia*, Vol. VI, p. 647.

aimed to make the house at Angers the center of the worldwide community. Her project was approved by the Holy See in a brief issued April 3, 1835. That her picture of a worldwide community was not idle thought was demonstrated by the fact that at her death (1868), 110 convents had been founded and sixteen provinces established in France, Belgium, Holland, Italy, Germany, Austria, England, Scotland, Ireland, Asia Africa, the United States and Chili.[2]

The reforms effected by Mother Euphrasia Pelletier in the Sisters of the Good Shepherd were of a purely administrative character. In its basic purposes the community was to remain the same as that founded by the Blessed John Eudes. In addition to the regular vows of poverty, chastity and obedience, all the Sisters of the Good Shepherd took a fourth vow, namely, to work for the conversion and instruction of penitents.

Sisters of Our Lady of Charity of the Good Shepherd

The Sisters of Our Lady of Charity of the Good Shepherd owe their beginning in the United States to Bishop B. J. Flaget of Bardstown. During a visit to his native home in France (1835), he became acquainted with the work of the sisters at their motherhouse in Angers. He expressed an earnest desire to have the community in his diocese. When the wish of the bishop became known many members from various homes signified their willingness to come to America. Finally it was decided that the first band of sisters to come to this country should consist of representatives from the different nations of Europe, France, Germany, Italy, Belgium and Ireland. The Sisters of the Good Shepherd arrived in Louisville in December, 1842. Their coming at this particular time was evidently somewhat unexpected. Bishop Flaget was busy with his new cathedral and had very little time to plan for them. In fact he would have much preferred to

[2] *Ibid.*, Vol. VI, p. 648.

see them postpone their coming for a few years. However, they were here and there was nothing to do except to make the best of it. For several months the new community had to accept the hospitality of the Sisters of Loretto. At the expense of the diocese a building was finally secured for them and they began their work in September, 1843.[3]

Good Shepherd Program Represents New Attitude in the United States

The work of the Good Shepherd Sisters was something entirely new in the United States. It represented an idea utterly at variance with the Puritan tradition which hardly extended aid to the woman who had become a victim of sex vice. No matter how depraved a woman might have been they did not give up hope for her. They were inspired by the thought that with the assistance of divine grace she might one day become another Magdalen. In fact they opened in their homes a special department for those whom they called Magdalens. After a woman had been in the penitent class for a certain number of years and had shown evidence of perseverance she was eligible to become a Magdalen. As a Magdalen she was permitted to take vows and to live under the rule of St. Theresa. It was not the intention of the Good Shepherd Sisters to confine their efforts entirely to women who had already become offenders. They made special arrangements in their homes for girls who were exposed to temptations of wrong-doing.

Elements of Good Shepherd Program

The program of the Sisters of the Good Shepherd includes three basic elements, religion, work and education. Every person admitted to the homes is to receive the advantages of religious instruction and practice. Their girls are en-

---

[3] Webb, *The Centenary of Catholicity in Kentucky*, p. 407; Spalding, *op. cit.*, pp. 336-339.

couraged to receive the sacraments frequently. A second very important element in the Good Shepherd rule is careful and systematic work. It is the aim of the sisters to keep their charges busy throughout the entire day with manual labor, school work and recreation. Again, there is a great advantage in dealing with delinquent girls by close personal contact. The Good Shepherd Sisters are with the girls all the time; they never lose sight of them. Without restraining them unduly, they are in touch with every movement they make. This is the reason why one does not hear of mutinies in Good Shepherd homes. They are practically unknown. It is remarkable to see what an influence the gentle sisters exercise over women who have descended to low depths of vice.

Sisters of Mercy

It is interesting to contrast the work of the Good Shepherd Sisters and that of the Sisters of Mercy in their beginnings in the United States. At the outset the work of one was intended to supplement the work of the other. The Sisters of Mercy aimed to provide protection and shelter for women away from home. The primary purpose of the Good Shepherd Sisters was the reformation of delinquents. In the course of their work the Sisters of Mercy were not always able to draw a clear line of demarcation between those who needed protection and those who needed reformation. In some instances the Sisters of Mercy were compelled to accept delinquent girls into their homes. Occasionally they established special institutions for delinquent girls. In Pittsburgh, they operated a home for such girls for a few years until it was taken over by the Good Shepherd Sisters in 1877.[4] In the development of their protective program in San Francisco the Sisters of Mercy were compelled to open an institution for delinquent girls (juvenile) which is still continued.

[4] *Lambing, op. cit.,* p. 517.

New York Foundation

Writing of the "House of Protection for Virtuous Destitute Female Domestics," about to be established by the Sisters of Mercy in New York in 1847, a correspondent of the *New York Freeman's Journal* observed:

> Such an institution is needed to save those without home, employment, friends and money from the calamities to which they are exposed. Such a House is conducted admirably by the Sisters of Mercy in Dublin.
>
> It is not only a necessity about to arise even while we write, some of these are obliged, to our own knowledge, to wander during the darkness of the night in the streets of this metropolis, to seek shelter from the cold blasts under some desolate sheds, having neither money in their purse nor parental roof, nor friends.[5]

Several years later the sisters opened the House of Protection for which they had been striving. The institution according to a contemporary description was to be a home and school for girls who went out to service or to the trades. Those who had no home or could not find employment were welcomed. All branches of house work such as sewing, cooking, washing and ironing were taught. No girls or women about whose character there was any question were admitted to the home. The same writer who describes the work of the home tells us that it owes its foundation to the generous charity of one lady.[6]

Pittsburgh Foundation

Referring to the work of the Sisters of Mercy in Pittsburgh shortly after their arrival in that city in 1842, a contemporary wrote: "The only House in the United States of the Order of Our Lady of Mercy is in Pittsburgh. Its object is the performance of the corporal and spiritual works of mercy. Its aim is to visit the sick and the poor, give aid and con-

---
[5] April 24, 1847.
[6] *Baltimore Catholic Mirror*, March 23, 1855.

solation to the afflicted and instruction to the ignorant and to give protection to distressed women of good character. . . . The House in Pittsburgh is the only one in the United States. It was founded in the beginning of this present year.'"[7]

Sisters of Mercy Depart from Original Purpose

Like so many other communities in the United States, the Sisters of Mercy have been unable to adhere to their original purpose. They have had to surrender to the irresistible demands made by Catholic education, which became the paramount question for the Church in America. It likewise became the paramount matter for most of the religious communities, who were compelled to assign most of their resources and the largest part of their membership to the schools. The Sisters of Mercy were no exception.

The Sisters of Mercy, however, continued to devote some attention to the works of charity. Like other communities they feel that they will not be blessed if they fail to carry out some of the original purposes of their foundation. The Sisters of Mercy at present operate a considerable number of homes for dependent children and devote a fair portion of their energy to hospitals. The nearest approach to the original protective program of the Sisters of Mercy are their boarding homes for women wage earners. The sisters operate such homes in Washington, Pittsburgh and St. Louis. To a certain extent these homes offer needed protection and shelter to young women.

The Good Shepherd Sisters Represent Single Objective

After their arrival in the United States the bishops came to regard the Good Shepherd Sisters as the great means through which the Church could carry on its mission for delinquent girls. In the Good Shepherd Sisters the Church found

[7] *Catholic Herald*, July 18, 1842.

a community with a singleness of purpose. By their constitution the sisters were dedicated to one objective, and from this purpose they were not to be deflected by any considerations or pressure.

Philadelphia Foundation of Sisters of the Good Shepherd

In a very short time the work of the Good Shepherd Sisters at Louisville became known throughout the land. Appeals, therefore, began to pour into the Louisville house from various bishops who were desirous of establishing the community in their dioceses. At the request of Bishop Francis P. Kenrick, Mother Marie des Anges, the superior of the Louisville house, proceeded to Philadelphia to establish a convent in that city (1847). Mother Marie remained in Philadelphia for eight years until the new home was on a firm basis.[8]

St. Louis Foundation of Sisters of the Good Shepherd

The second invitation to establish a home outside of Louisville came from Bishop Peter Richard Kenrick of St. Louis, a brother of the bishop of Philadelphia. The St. Louis house was opened in 1849. Bishop Kenrick turned over to the sisters a house left by a Father Cellini for aged priests. Mrs. Anne Lucas Hunt donated ground for a sisters' convent separate from the penitents' building. Funds were raised by the bishop for the erection of the convent. In a few years, the original Good Shepherd convent in St. Louis was completely surrounded by the business district. Mr. Adolphus Busch then came to the rescue of the sisters by donating their present property on Gravois Road. With the proceeds of the sale of their old property, $75,000 from Mrs. Winifred Patterson, and other donations, the sisters erected their present building which was ready for occupancy November 25, 1895.[9]

[8] Webb, *op. cit.*, p. 409.
[9] Rothensteiner, *op. cit.*, Vol. II, pp. 26–30.

In a pastoral letter issued February, 1849, Archbishop Peter R. Kenrick wrote as follows in regard to the Sisters of the Good Shepherd: "We have great satisfaction in being able to state to you, that we have added to the number of religious houses already established in this diocese, a small community of Our Lady of Charity, or Sisters of the Good Shepherd, who have lately arrived in this city from Louisville, Kentucky. The object of this institute is to afford an asylum, and means of restoration to those, who after having followed in the steps, may feel inclined to imitate the repentance of Magdalen. In this Asylum, in a house separate and apart from the residence of these admirable and devoted ladies, who consecrate their lives, under the solemnity of the religious engagement, to this most Divine work of imitating the Good Shepherd and bringing back to the fold the strayed sheep, such persons will be trained to habits of virtue and industry, until they can return to the world, with greater security among its dangers."[10]

Good Shepherd Foundations Between 1850 and 1860

Between 1850 and 1860 convents of Our Lady of Charity of the Good Shepherd were established in New York, Chicago, Cincinnati, and New Orleans. The sisters went to New York in 1857 at the invitation of Archbishop Hughes. According to an observer, the New York convent had attained considerable proportions since 1857. A total of 640 girls had been cared for in the penitent class; 400 had been cared for in the preservative class and a special department for Magdalens had been opened.[11] Between 1857 and 1877, the New York convent cared for a total of 7,241 persons.[12] The Chicago convent was founded by four sisters who came from St. Louis at the invitation of Bishop James Duggan (May, 1859). The

[10] *Ibid.*, Vol. II, p. 28.
[11] *New York Freeman's Journal*, March 11, 1859.
[12] *Catholic World*, Vol. XLIII (Sept., 1886), p. 809.

Sisters of Mercy turned over to them a home for delinquent girls. A larger home was rented in 1860. Bishop Duggan gave the sisters a piece of land on which a permanent building could be erected, and the priests of the diocese assisted in raising a building fund. No sooner had the building been finished than it burned to the ground. This misfortune aroused a new interest in the work of the Good Shepherd Sisters and funds were raised for a new building which was occupied until 1905. At that time a portion of the present home on Grace Street was occupied.[13]

Good Shepherd Foundations Between 1860 and 1870

Between 1860 and 1870 Good Shepherd convents were opened in Baltimore, Columbus, Cleveland, Boston, Brooklyn and St. Paul. The Baltimore convent was founded in 1864 by Mrs. McTavish who contributed $120,000 for the purpose.[14] In the first annual report to the board of directors of the Baltimore house (1865), the sisters stated: "The very day after our arrival, we received the first applicant for shelter. In the course of twelve months, we have admitted eighty-eight unfortunates, of these thirty-one have been restored to their friends, four have gone to our House of Louisville to become Magdalens and two have died. Forty-eight remain under our care. Considerable as is the number, we have already had to entertain, we venture to assert it would have been doubled if our home had been commodious enough to give them shelter."[15] The House of the Good Shepherd in Boston was the first new work of charity undertaken by Archbishop John J. Williams. In 1867 he obtained sisters of the order from New York, whom he established in a rented house on Allen Street provided with the equipment necessary for their work.[16] In 1865 the Sisters of the Good Shepherd opened their house

[13] *The Archdiocese of Chicago*, p. 747.
[14] *Baltimore Catholic Mirror*, March 4, 1872.
[15] *Ibid.*, April 26, 1865.
[16] W. F. Kenny, *Centenary of See of Boston*, p. 104.

in Columbus and in 1868 they opened their houses in Brooklyn and St. Paul.

Good Shepherd Foundations Between 1870 and 1914

In the decade following 1870, the Sisters of Our Lady of Charity of the Good Shepherd established houses in Indianapolis (1873), Newark (1875), Milwaukee (1877), and a second house in Philadelphia (1878). From 1880 to 1890, the sisters established houses in Detroit (1883), Washington (1883), Albany (1884), Troy (1884), Denver (1885), Kansas City (1877), and Trenton (1889). Between 1890 and 1900, they opened houses in Seattle (1890), Peoria (1891), Omaha (1894), a second house (for colored girls) in Baltimore (1892), and a house in Springfield, Massachusetts (1897). Since 1900 Good Shepherd houses have been established in Hartford (1902), Portland (1902), Sioux City (1903), Providence (1904), Dubuque (1904), Los Angeles (1904), Spokane (1905), Toledo (1906), Dallas (1909), and Houston (1914). At the present time the Sisters of Our Lady of Charity have forty-four houses administered in six provinces with headquarters respectively at Baltimore, Philadelphia, New York City, Cincinnati, St. Louis, and St. Paul.

Sisters of Our Lady of Charity of Refuge

The sisters who adopted Mother Pelletier's plan of central government were known as the Sisters of Our Lady of Charity of the Good Shepherd of Angers, but many houses desired to maintain their autonomy and adhere to the original plan of Blessed John Eudes in 1641. The sisters who adhered to the decentralized form of government are known as the Sisters of our Lady of Charity of Refuge. They were introduced into America by Bishop Timon of Buffalo in 1855. Since that time the community has opened the houses in Buffalo (1855), Pittsburgh (1872), Green Bay (1882), San Antonio (1897), Wheeling, W. Va. (1900), Pittsburgh (second house) (1906),

Buffalo (second house) (1907), Hot Springs, Ark. (1906), Rochester, N. Y. (1930), and Erie (1930). Hence with the forty-four homes operated by the Sisters of Our Lady of Charity of the Good Shepherd, the two branches of the community have a total of fifty-five homes in the United States.

Admission Policies of Good Shepherd Homes

The Good Shepherd Sisters planned to receive their penitents and the children in their preservation class from courts, social agencies, from parents, and relatives. They did not draw any hard and fast line as to the territory from which penitents and children would be received; in fact, the ordinary Good Shepherd home draws its clientele from a rather wide area.

As a result of their contacts with community chests and diocesan organizations of Catholic Charities, an increasing number of Good Shepherd homes have definitely limited the territory from which they will accept cases. A number of the homes are also availing themselves of the services provided by diocesan charities in investigating applications for admission. This provides them with a more effective method of determining whether or not the person for whom application is made should be removed from her own home. It also provides them with the facts necessary for proper classification of those under their care. Without a careful investigation of the applications for admission, the Good Shepherd home is liable to receive many children who should be cared for in their own homes or in the ordinary homes for dependent children.

System of Classification

Good Shepherd homes ordinarily divide their charges into the delinquent and predelinquent groups. Within these two classes, they have smaller classes of ten or fifteen girls. The sisters use the Magdalens quite extensively in supervising the smaller groups. They are also quite apt in developing leadership and organization among the girls, who on proving themselves reliable are given certain responsibilities.

Religion as a Reformative Influence

The Sisters of the Good Shepherd rely largely on the influence of religion in changing the lives of their penitents. Recently, the writer asked the mother superior of a Good Shepherd house how she succeeded in controlling the large number of delinquent girls committed to the home by the city courts. "Well," she said, "we depend more than anything else on frequent confession and communion. Once a girl begins to go to confession and communion frequently our battle with her is practically won. We have confession once a week. We do not force any girl to go to confession. We depend on our ability to convince her that it is the right thing. We encourage daily communion as far as possible. When a girl is first received, it frequently takes two or three weeks to talk her into going to confession and receiving Holy Communion. Practically every girl in the house at present goes to confession weekly and fully sixty per cent of the girls are daily communicants."

Health Programs in Good Shepherd Homes

Health is a large problem in the Good Shepherd home. The habits of the girls have naturally contributed to the undermining of their physical and mental health. A large number of the girls received have positive venereal infections. It is really impossible to develop a constructive program for these girls without reckoning with their physical and mental health. In dealing with health, the Good Shepherd Sisters have gone through the same experience as other agencies in dealing with delinquent girls. As the science of health has made rapid strides in the past half century, the houses of the Good

Shepherd like other social agencies have far more adequate health facilities at their disposal now than fifty or even twenty-five years ago. Nearly all the Good Shepherd homes have facilities for making thorough physical examinations and also mental examinations. They have either their own clinical equipment for examination or use of the local public clinical facilities.

Health Program of Cleveland Home

In the Cleveland Good Shepherd Home: "All girls committed by the juvenile court receive a complete physical examination before entering. Those received through other courts or privately are examined immediately upon entrance. All girls pass through the special clinic which is held twice a week at the school. The Wassermann and Neisser tests are part of the examination requirements. Dental examinations take place in the weekly dental clinic. Extractions and fillings are taken care of at once. Eye, ear, nose and throat specialists make routine examinations three or four times a year. Tonsil and adenoid operations are performed at the school."[17]

Mt. St. Mary's Training School, Cincinnati

The following is a brief description of the health program of Mt. St. Mary's Training School, conducted by the Sisters of the Good Shepherd in Cincinnati:

> Children received through the court or other social agency usually have general physical examinations before admission. In cases where this has not been done general physical examinations are made within a day or two after admission, and the findings are recorded on a record form prepared by the central clinic of the Com-

[17] "Health Program of Sacred Heart Training School for Delinquent Girls in the Convent of the Good Shepherd, Cleveland," by Anne E. King, *The Catholic Charities Review*, Vol. IX (Mar., 1925), pp. 106–107.

munity Chest and Council of Social Agencies of Cincinnati.

The dental findings are reported to the dental clinic.

Specific examinations are made on all delinquent girls for venereal infections in a special clinic which is under the jurisdiction of the local Board of Health. All positive cases are immediately placed on prescribed treatment.

Recommendations for discharge from the school are withheld until negative reports on microscopic examinations and Wassermann tests are obtained. All recommendations made after physical examinations are summarized and followed up.

Quarantine is not used for all new-comers. Each child is given a superficial examination by the resident nurse and if there is any evidence of communicable disease, admission is denied until a favorable report is given. The only exception to this is the venereal diseases, a special dormitory being provided for these cases.[18]

Educational Programs

The educational problems of the Good Shepherd homes are quite complicated as predelinquent and delinquent girls are usually retarded in their school work. The sisters provide an eighth grade education for all girls under eighteen years of age who have not finished the eighth grade. For the girls in the delinquent group, suitable vocational training is given. The educational courses in the Sacred Heart Training School for Girls, Convent of the Good Shepherd, Cleveland and Mt. St. Mary's Training School, Cincinnati, are illustrative of the educational program of the Good Shepherd Sisters. In the Cleveland institution:

> All girls under eighteen years of age are placed in classes. Often those over age who desire further training are allowed to take work in continuation classes.
> The girls are taken through the eighth grade. For

[18] "Health Program of Mt. St. Mary's Training School for Girls, Cincinnati," by Rose K. Golden, *Catholic Charities Review*, Vol. IX (Mar., 1925), pp. 107–108.

those of more advanced educational qualifications, a commercial school is provided. . . .

The more advanced pupils of the school take the commercial course, which includes business English, grammar, writing, penmanship, spelling, typewriting and dictaphone operation. . . .

Retarded pupils are placed in the "Opportunity Classes," so called because special care and attention are given to those whose opportunities have been few. Subnormals are carefully and painstakingly taken through the work suited to their ability. Those handicapped by a lack of English, . . . are greatly benefited by the extra help given in this division.

The girls are taught sewing, laundry work, housekeeping and kitchen work. In the laundry the girls manage the packing and ironing. The washing is done by men, paid employees of the institution. . . . Since the average period of training is of a year's duration the aim is to have each girl learn one occupation well. If a girl does not do well at the type of occupation at which she is first placed, she is changed, until a happier occupation is found for her. . . .[19]

The Magdalen

The Sisters of the Good Shepherd receive into their Magdalen group those penitents who express a desire to become members of the group and have all necessary qualifications. The principal qualification on which the sisters insist is the ability to persevere as evidenced by their good behaviour in the penitent class over a period of three years. Candidates for the Magdalen group must express a desire to remain in the home for the remainder of their lives. After a year's probation they take simple vows. The Magdalens represent the finest ideal of the Good Shepherd Sisters in dealing with their penitents. A group of women who have tasted the dregs of sin and wrong-doing give themselves to missionary

[19] "Educational and Training for Employment of Sacred Heart Training School for Girls, Convent of the Good Shepherd, Cleveland, Ohio," by Anne E. King, *Catholic Charities Review*, Vol. IX (April, 1925), pp. 144–145.

Early Good Shepherd Homes Largely Self-Supporting

In the beginning the convents of the Good Shepherd were established on the assumption that they would become largely self-supporting. Shortly after its establishment, the Louisville House of the Good Shepherd was self-supporting. During the first ten years of its maintenance the cost of operating the Baltimore house was $74,000 of which $57,000 was derived from the industry of its inmates. [20] According to a report in 1877, the annual expense of operating the New York house was $80,000. Of this amount $8,946.47 was received from the city. Nearly all of the remaining amount came from the labor of inmates.

Many of the Good Shepherd homes entered into arrangements with the cities for the care of delinquent girls on a per capita basis. The Indianapolis house made such arrangements after its establishment in 1873. Houses in Baltimore, New York City, Philadelphia, Chicago and Brooklyn made similar arrangements with their respective cities. The per capita amount paid by the cities was usually insufficient to meet the cost of care. The remainder had to be made up very largely from the work done by the sisters and those under their care. In a number of cities the courts committed children to the Good Shepherd homes without making any provision for their support. In these cities, the sisters had to secure the funds necessary to operate their institutions from private donations and from their earnings.

After the various Good Shepherd homes had been under way, few dioceses recognized a definite responsibility for their support. Many dioceses assisted in building the homes, but once they had been built the sisters were left to figure out

---

[20] *Baltimore Catholic Mirror*, March 4, 1874.

their own finances. This meant that for a number of years, the homes were dependent largely on their own earnings.

Recent Changes in Financial Programs

In recent years the financial programs of the Good Shepherd homes have changed considerably. The sisters found that it was exceedingly difficult to develop an up-to-date program for the care of those in their charge if they depended to so large an extent on their own earnings. They have come therefore to depend more and more on the contributions of the charitable public. In cities in which they participate in the Community Chest, the houses of the Good Shepherd have been able to secure a large part of their support from the chest. The same is true in cities with a Catholic Financial Federation. The superiors with whom the writer has talked have voiced the opinion that the Community Chest and the Catholic Financial Federation have been a great boon to the work of the community.

Good Shepherd Homes Part of Larger Program

The Good Shepherd home is gradually becoming part of a larger program for the care of Catholic delinquent girls. It has come to be recognized that without a casework program the home can not fully attain its purposes. It is assumed as a general principle today that a girl should not be received except after a careful investigation if she is to be dealt with intelligently. It also assists in determining how far the institution is in a position to meet the girl's needs. If she is an ordinary dependent child she should be sent to an institution for such children. If she is a feebleminded child she should be sent to an instiution for the feebleminded. Many times, moreover, it will be found that the girl can be left in her own home under careful supervision.

Besides the preadmission investigation, another function

of casework is the after-care of children discharged from the Good Shepherd Homes. The delinquent girl very naturally does not find it easy to adjust herself in the outside world. She needs some person to whom she can go for advice in moments of discouragement. She needs assistance in finding employment. There is a third important function of case work which is even more vital than either of the foregoing. In dealing with delinquency, prevention is more desirable than care. The social caseworker through her contact with schools and juvenile courts has an opportunity of establishing contact with young girls before they become seriously delinquent. The girls may be begging to get away from the control of their parents; they may not have the right type of companionship; they may not be acquainted with wholesome social opportunities. It is the duty of the social worker to act as a guide and counselor to such girls.

Other Religious Communities Interested in Delinquents

While the major part of the Catholic institutional work for delinquent and semi-delinquent girls is done by the Sisters of the Good Shepherd, reference must be made to three institutions conducted by other communities. The oldest of these institutions is the House of Mercy, San Francisco, established in 1862 and conducted by the Sister of Mercy. The second in point of time is the House of the Holy Family in New York City conducted by the Sisters of Divine Compassion under the auspices of the Association for Befriending Children and Young Girls, an association which grew out of classes for neglected children organized in 1869 by a number of Catholic women in connection with St. Bernard's Church in New York City. These women established an organization to which they first gave the name "The Association for Befriending Children,"[21] but which, in 1871, was

---

[21] "The Association for Befriending Children," *Catholic World*, Vol. XI (May, 1870), p. 250; *ibid.*, Vol. XLIII (Aug., 1886), p. 681.

changed to "The Association for Befriending Children and Young Girls."

When this association was organized, it proposed a rather broad program for women and young girls. It aimed to provide instruction for spiritually neglected children, to supply food and clothing for children in need, and to afford shelter and protection to predelinquent and delinquent girls. In 1870 the association opened its House of the Holy Family for the training of predelinquent and delinquent girls. In line with the general trend of the times it looked to the institution rather than to guidance and instruction in her own home as the most practical method of saving the girl from delinquency. So much so that in a short time the House of the Holy Family became the main objective of the Association. It did not abandon entirely its work for children outside the institution. In 1885 it opened two weekly industrial schools for Italian children in the basement of the Chuch of the Transfiguration of St. James, which were later merged into a single day school.

One of the most recent training schools for semi-delinquent and delinquent Catholic girls is the Corpus Christi House, Duluth, Minnesota, established by the Sisters of the Third Order of St. Dominic in 1920. The members of this community came over from England to undertake missionary work in the diocese of Duluth. Corpus Christi House was really a part of their larger program. Within the past three years this group of Dominican Sisters has adopted a Carmelite rule.

CHAPTER XI
CATHOLIC CARE OF THE SICK
The Sisters of Charity Enter the Hospital Field in the United States

The Catholic hospital in the United States owes its beginnings to the Sisters of Charity. The Ursuline Sisters in New Orleans are generally credited with the establishment of a hospital during the latter years of the eighteenth century, but this was scarcely more than an emergency arrangement. While the first work of the Sisters of Charity was the care of dependent children, not many years passed before the little community at Emmitsburg received appeals on behalf of the sick. The first call came from the authorities of the University of Maryland. They wanted sisters to take charge of the infirmary connected with the medical department of the university.[1] In 1827 seven or eight sisters came to Baltimore and took charge of the Marine Hospital for several years.[2]

First Organized Catholic Hospital

The first permanent venture of the Emmitsburg community into hospital work was in the Mullanphy Hospital at St. Louis. In 1814 as president of Mt. St. Mary's College, Baltimore, Dr. Simon G. Bruté received and entertained the first sons of St. Vincent de Paul who came to America. Among them was Father Joseph Rosati, destined to be the first bishop of St. Louis. Fourteen years later (June, 1828) Bishop Rosati sought the assistance of Bishop Bruté in obtaining the services of the Sisters of Charity for his proposed hospital in St. Louis, writing as follows: "I come again

[1] Madame De Barberey, *Elizabeth Seton*, p. 461.
[2] *Archives* of Mt. St. Joseph's College, Emmitsburg.

to obtain through your intervention three Sisters of Charity for a hospital in St. Louis. When I wrote to you for the first time, I had no certain information on which to build hopes of seeing an establishment of that kind in the city. I felt its necessity, and I desired to find some means to execute that which I wished to undertake. How admirable is Providence! Without having said one word, a very rich man offers me a beautiful piece of ground, with two houses in the city of St. Louis. He will give besides another lot with other houses that will bring revenue of six hundred dollars a year; he will give one hundred and fifty dollars for the journey of the sisters.''[3] In response to Bishop Rosati's call the sisters set out from Emmitsburg across the Alleghenies and down the Ohio. The institution, which they opened on their arrival, remained one of the landmarks of St. Louis for over a hundred years. Only last year (1930) the Mullanphy Hospital was replaced by the ultra-modern De Paul Hospital.

The Oldest Hospital in Michigan

In 1844 the Sisters of Charity went to Detroit, then a small town of 11,000, for the purpose of conducting two free schools. Their first quarters were three dilapidated log buildings on Larned Street. The next year, in spite of meager resources, the sisters fitted up a temporary hospital for the sick poor. This was the beginning of St. Mary's Hospital, the oldest in Michigan.[4]

St. Mary's Hospital, Rochester, New York, Illustrates Early Difficulties in Hospital Work

The difficulties that the Sisters of Charity encountered in their early hospitals are illustrated very clearly in the records of St. Mary's Hospital, Rochester, New York, which was opened in 1857. ''When the sisters came to Rochester, it

[3] *Ibid.*
[4] *Archives* of St. Mary's Hospital, Detroit.

The Care of the Sick

was with the intention of commencing a hospital. They had no funds, but something more reliable, a firm reliance upon the goodness of God. It was on Genesee Street that two small stables were secured, which with prompt energy were fitted up to receive the suffering poor. At this time the sisters met with the most disheartening discouragement—those who heard of the attempt of founding a hospital in the old stables laughed at the idea. The poor sisters had no funds and knew not where to look for aid, but they were not disheartened and persevered. The difficulties which they encountered were apparently insurmountable, but with ever-renewing courage and energy of faith, they succeeded in erecting a building which connected the two stables.''[5] This is a typical illustration of the difficulties of building up Catholic charitable institutions prior to the Civil War. All institutions of charity were greatly handicapped by lack of resources and personnel. The people on whom the sisters had to depend for support were mostly newly arrived immigrants, who were hard pressed in obtaining even the necessities of life. When one thinks of the difficulties which the sisters faced, their progress in early hospital work is truly remarkable. Between 1828 and 1860 the Sisters of Charity opened eighteen hospitals. Their work during this period may be regarded as an organized crusade for more enlightened care of the sick.

The Sisters of Mercy Take Up Hospital Work

In this crusade the Sisters of Charity were joined by other religious communities. The first of these, the Sisters of Mercy, made their initial departure in hospital work with the opening of Mercy Hospital, Pittsburgh, in 1847. From the moment of their arrival from Ireland in 1843 they had been active in visiting the sick in their homes and in protective work for girls. For them the hospital was a new but a very necessary venture. Thousands of immigrants, emaciated after

[5] *Archives* of Mt. St. Joseph's College, Emmitsburg.

a long and perilous journey in the coffin ships, were struggling overland to Pittsburgh. The Sisters of Mercy felt called upon to minister to the sick and the dying. They asked Bishop O'Connor for permission to turn the old ballroom of their residence, formerly known as "Concert Hall," into a hospital.[6]

Four years after the opening of Mercy Hospital in Pittsburgh Bishop William Quarter of Chicago invited the Sisters of Mercy to undertake a similar work in Chicago. Their first establishment in that city was the Illinois General Hospital, formerly the "Old Lake House." The sisters found practically the same situation in Chicago as in Pittsburgh. The poor were suffering from typhus fever, for Chicago like other cities, passed through severe epidemics in 1849 and 1854.[7]

In 1854 Bishop Joseph S. Alemany of San Francisco appealed to the motherhouse of the Sisters of Mercy in Kinsale, Ireland, for aid in caring for the immigrants in his diocese.[8] After their arrival in San Francisco the sisters placed themselves at the disposal of the city in caring for the victims of the cholera epidemic. Their experience in the cholera plagues in their own country had given them an excellent preparation for this task. The work of the sisters in the county hospital caring for the victims of cholera won the admiration of all who were interested in the alleviation of human suffering. A description of their work given by an eyewitness speaks eloquently of their zeal and self-sacrifice: "We visited yesterday the patients in the hospital; a more ghastly sight we have seldom witnessed. In the midst of this scene of anguish, sorrow, pain, and danger were ministering angels who disregarded everything to aid their distressed fellow creatures. The Sisters of Mercy, rightly named, whose convent is opposite the hospital, as soon as they learned the state

[6] Herron, *op. cit.*, p. 8.
[7] "Catholic Women of Illinois," by Margaret Madden. *Illinois Catholic Historical Review*, Vol. I (July, 1928), pp. 286-293; *The Archdiocese of Chicago*, p. 721.
[8] See sketch of Hugh Gallagher by R. J. Purcell in *Dict. of Amer. Biography*.

of things hurried to offer their services. They did not stop to inquire whether the poor sufferers were Protestants or Catholics, Americans or foreigners, but with the noblest devotion applied themselves to their relief. One sister might be seen bathing the limbs of the sufferer, another chafing the extremities, a third applying the remedies; while others with pitying faces were calming the fears of those supposed to be dying. The idea of danger never seems to have occurred to these noble women; self was lost sight of. If the lives of any of the unfortunates be saved, they will owe their preservation to these noble ladies."[9] For some time after the epidemic had subsided the sisters remained in charge of the county hospital. The public officials were deeply appreciative of their services, but their deeds of sacrifice were soon forgotten by many citizens in a wave of religious bigotry. The sisters therefore decided that if they were to carry on their mission of mercy for the sick they must have their own institution and in 1857 they opened St. Mary's Hospital, the first Catholic hospital in San Francisco.[10]

Sisters of St. Joseph of Carondelet Third Religious Community in Hospital Field

The Sisters of St. Joseph of Carondelet was the third religious community in the United States to make hospital work a part of their program. In 1847 they had come to Philadelphia from St. Louis at the instance of Bishop Francis Patrick Kenrick to take charge of St. John's Orphan Asylum in his diocese. One year after their arrival a Jesuit priest, Father Barbelin, prevailed upon them to open a hospital for Irish immigrants who were coming to Philadelphia in large numbers, many of them suffering from fever.[11] This was the beginning of St. Joseph's Hospital, the first hospital opened by the Sisters of St. Joseph in this country. It remained in

---
[9] Matthew Russell, S.J., *Life of Mother M. Baptist Russell*, p. 48.
[10] Herron, *op. cit.*, p. 158.
[11] Sr. M. Lucida Savage, *Sisters of St. Joseph of Carondelet*, p. 72.

their charge for ten years, when it was taken over by the Daughters of Charity of St. Vincent de Paul.

Early in 1850 the Sisters from Carondelet complied with a request of Bishop Richard Whelan of Wheeling to open a hospital in his episcopal city. The bishop rented a home for the purpose which was soon put in readiness. When the owner of the home learned that it was to be used by Catholic sisters, he refused to grant the necessary permission. The bishop then secured another temporary building in which the Wheeling Hospital had its beginning.[12] Like many other early institutions of its kind, it had to serve the double purpose of hospital and orphan asylum.

When the Sisters of St. Joseph arrived in St. Paul in 1851 they found that there was no provision for the care of the sick in the city or surrounding territory. As an important trading post it was attracting foreigners who did not have any institution to succor them in sickness and in need. Like other cities, St. Paul also suffered from the scourges of the cholera epidemics. There was need of a Catholic institution to care for both the sick and the orphan. Bishop Joseph Cretin, however, pushed his plans for the hospital. He secured a site from a philanthropic citizen and lumber from the forests of a Sioux chieftain. In 1853 work was begun on the building. While it was in process of erection a cholera epidemic practically laid the city waste. The old log church was turned into a temporary hospital and the sisters commandeered as nurses. The bishop, priests and seminarians joined hands with the workmen in rushing the new hospital towards completion. It was opened in the fall of 1854.[13]

Public Charities in the United States Before Civil War

The years between 1830 and the Civil War were years of struggle in Catholic work. The Church was not ready and

[12] *Ibid*, p. 74.
[13] *Ibid*, p. 90.

the country was not ready to care for the thousands of the destitute, the sick and the orphan. Public charities in America were in a primitive condition. They were the charities of a pioneering people who expected each man to take care of himself as well as he was able. The handicapped and the weak received but scant consideration. From its English antecedents and traditions the United States had inherited a hard and rigid attitude towards the poor. It had a dread of multiplying poverty by dealing with it in a kindly way. It had two accepted methods of caring for the poor—outdoor relief and the almshouse. The reaction against outdoor relief as expressed in the report of the British Poor Law Commission of 1834 made itself felt very deeply in the United States. American Protestant leaders were advancing the opinion with increasing confidence, that the care of the poor in their own homes should be left to private charities. It was the attitude of the leaders that gave birth to the Association for Improving the Condition of the Poor in New York in 1843. The other method of caring for the poor in the United States was a kind of catch-all. In the almshouse were placed all kinds of dependents—the sick, the insane, the feeble minded, adult delinquents and dependent and neglected children. The standards of these institutions were the lowest imaginable. One can readily appreciate how the sick fared under such conditions. A committee investigating Bellevue Hospital in 1837 painted a repulsive picture "of filth, no ventilation, no clothing, patients with high fever lying naked in bed with only coarse blankets to cover them, wards overcrowded, jail fever rife, no supplies, putrefaction, vermin." Only three physicians were assigned to the whole institution caring for about 2,000 persons, both sick and well.[14]

A report of Blockley, the municipal almshouse of Philadelphia, made in 1856, described conditions that were just as pitiful: "The institution now comprised small-pox wards,

---

[14] M. A. Nutting and L. L. Dock, *A History of Nursing*, Vol. II, pp. 329-330.

departments for the insane, an asylum for children, a lying-in department, a nursery, a hospital, and almshouses wherein were congregated the blind, the lame, and the incurables. All these departments were overcrowded, without proper classification, and entirely under the care of the pauper inmates, or paid attendants taken from the same class. The physical conditions of the place . . . . were in a shameful state. There was no gas; only small hand-lamps were in use. There was no laundry; the clothing was given out to a small army of washerwomen. In the hospital departments there was not a water-closet, and only one bath tub, that one being on the men's side.''[15]

The Work of Catholic Sisterhoods in Hospitals an Inspiration

We must keep in mind the conditions at Bellevue and Blockley and the other almshouses throughout the country in studying the hospital work of the Catholic sisterhoods between 1830 and the Civil War. The work of the sisters is the brightest page in hospital history during this period. When they opened their first hospitals, the sisters had little special preparation for the work, but they had zeal, self-sacrifice and sympathy for the suffering that made them an inspiring challenge to Protestant institutions. Just as the work of the Sisters of Charity among the French troops in the Crimea was a challenge to England to make decent provision for its sick and wounded in the hospital at Scutari and paved the way for the great contribution of Florence Nightingale and her followers, so was the pioneer hospital work of the Catholic sisters a challenge to America.

The Catholic Sisterhoods in the Epidemics

It was during the periodically recurring cholera epidemics between 1830 and 1860 that the work of the sisters shone

[15] *Ibid*, Vol. II, p. 335.

brightly. There is hardly a large city in the United States in which the sisters did not render heroic services in the cholera days. Reference has already been made to the services of the Sisters of Mercy in San Francisco and the Sisters of St. Joseph in St. Paul. Several of the Sisters of Charity sacrificed their lives during the cholera epidemic in St. Louis in 1832. Some of them arose from their own sick beds in order to minister unto the suffering poor. They did not confine themselves to their own hospital, but went from house to house nursing the sick.[16] So much were the municipal authorities impressed by the work of the sisters at this time that the city government decided to use Mullanphy Hospital for all the hospitalization of public wards. When the city opened its own public hospital in 1845, the sisters were placed in charge.[17] During the same epidemic, on August 25, 1832, the Sisters of Charity took charge of cholera hospitals Nos. 2 and 3 in Baltimore. Two of them contracted the disease and died.[18] Conditions in Blockley almshouse in Philadelphia reached such a pass during the cholera epidemic of 1832 that the city officials decided to appeal to Bishop Kenrick for Sisters of Charity from Emmitsburg to take over the management of the institution. The call was answered immediately by the superiors of the community, the sisters leaving Emmitsburg two hours after they had been summoned. So successfully did the sisters manage the almshouse that the officials of the city requested that they remain in charge of it permanently. Rev. John F. Hickey, then spiritual director of the community, was compelled to deny this request. He did not consider Blockley a department of charity in which the services of the sisters could be employed most usefully.[19] After the ravages of the epidemic had ceased the city council paid a glowing tribute to the labor

---

[16] *Archives* of Mt. St. Joseph's College, Emmitsburg.
[17] "The Mullanphys of St. Louis," *U. S. Catholic Historical Society*, Records, Vol. XIV, 1920.
[18] *Archives* of Mt. St. Joseph's College, Emmitsburg.
[19] *Ibid.*

of the sisters: "*Resolved* that the citizens of Philadelphia entertain an adequate sense of the courageous devotedness, assiduity and zeal of those women, and especially of the Sisters of Charity, who risked their lives and exerted all their energies to restore the sick to health, and to give comfort to the dying, and to protect the bereaved orphan."[20]

The Catholic Sisterhoods in the Civil War

Before the Civil War there were only three Catholic communities with extensive programs of hospital work. Another community, the Sisters of the Third Order of St. Francis of Assisi had just been called into the field in Philadelphia through the smallpox epidemic of 1858. During the course of the epidemic the sisters had taken poor girls into their convent to nurse them. This experience of the sisters in nursing led to the opening of St. Mary's Hospital in Philadelphia.[21] Thus we see that the hospitals begun by the Catholic sisterhoods before the war were opened to meet acute needs. As the sisters had risen to previous emergencies, it was quite natural that they should rise to the emergency created by the war between the states. In addition to the communities already engaged in hospital work many other communities placed all their resources and their personnel at the disposal of their country in the care of its sick and wounded. Among the communities entering the field of hospital and nursing work for the first time during the war were the Sisters of the Holy Cross, the Sisters of Charity of Nazareth, the Sisters of Charity of New York, the Sisters of Charity of Cincinnati, the Sisters of St. Dominic, Springfield, Ky., Sisters of St. Dominic, Memphis, Tenn., Sisters of St. Dominic, Springfield, Ill., Sisters of the Poor of St. Francis, Cincinnati, Ohio, the Sisters of Our Lady of Mercy, Charleston, S. C., Sisters of Our Lady of Mount Carmel, New

[20] *Records* of the American Catholic Historical Society, Vol. I, 1884–1886, p. 191.
[21] *Catholic Charities and Social Welfare Activities of the Archdiocese of Philadelphia, Year Book*, 1926, p. 17.

THE CARE OF THE SICK 193

Orleans, La., Sisters of Providence, St. Mary-of-the-Woods, Ind., Sisters of St. Ursula, Galveston, Tex.

In her book, *Nuns of the Battlefield,* Mrs. Ellen Ryan Jolly has dedicated a lasting monument to the services of sisterhoods during the Civil War. Its pages are replete with accounts of the heroism and self-sacrifice of the sisters who served their country during the great conflict between the states. In all sections of the country, they were in charge of the nursing at military hospitals. The Sisters of the Poor of St. Francis were in the Marine Hospital at Cincinnati and later at Columbus, Ohio; and the Sisters of Charity of Emmitsburg were in charge of the Lincoln General Hospital in Washington; and the Sisters of Mercy were in charge of the Stanton Hospital in the same city.[22] The Sisters of the Holy Cross took charge of military hospitals in Washington, Memphis, Paducah, Louisville, Cairo, and Mound City, Illinois.[23] These are just a few illustrations of the manifold services of the sisters during the Civil War.

The Value of Nursing Done by the Sisterhoods

The sisters were naturally a great asset in a crisis like the Civil War. According to a report of the American Medical Association, as late as 1869, they were the only organized group in the United States that realized the importance of nursing.[24] Most of the nursing in American hospitals was done by persons of inferior caliber and training. In the public hospitals a large share of the nursing was done by the inmates. While all the sisters who took up the nursing of the poor did not have any special experience or preparation, their general training and their willingness to work and to sacrifice for others raised their services to a high order. Moreover, the Civil War undoubtedly gave the sisters a new

---

[22] Pages 69–71; 115–116; 184–187.
[23] *A Story of Fifty Years,* from *Annals of Congregation of Sisters of Holy Cross,* 1855–1905, Notre Dame, Ind., p. 95.
[24] Nutting and Dock, *op. cit.,* Vol. II, page 366.

appreciation of the spiritual values of hospital service. Heretofore their largest field of activity had been the care of neglected children. After the war they had an opportunity of returning to one of their fundamental purposes, namely, the nursing of the sick.

Influence of War Activities in Evolution of Catholic Hospitals in the United States

Contacts with the sisters during the war gave the medical profession in different sections of the country an opportunity of appreciating their worth in hospital administration. Hence it was that physicians were anxious to see them extend their activities in the hospital field. As a result of their work at the Douglas Military Hospital in Washington during the war, the Sisters of Mercy were asked to take charge of the Baltimore City Hospital, the name of which was later changed to Mercy Hospital.[25] In the city of Alton, Illinois, a prison hospital housing about 4,000 Confederates and 1,000 Union soldiers was taken over by the Daughters of Charity in 1864. So much was the local community influenced by the work of the sisters in the military hospital that they were petitioned to open a private hospital in the city after the war. The petition was granted by the superiors of the community and the hospital of the Sisters of Charity growing out of their war work continues to serve the people of Alton.[26] Another Daughters of Charity institution that grew out of their war work was Providence Hospital in Washington. This hospital was opened in 1861 in the old homestead of the Daniel Carroll family on Capitol Hill. A frame building with some hospital facilities was later erected on the site of the present main building. Here the sick and wounded soldiers were cared for after the Battle of Bull Run. With the coming of

---

[25] Herron, *op. cit.*, p. 134.
[26] James A. Griffin (ed.), *Diocese of Springfield in Illinois Diamond Jubilee History*, pp. 545-547.

peace the facilities of the hospital were enlarged.[27] In another instance, the citizens of Cairo, Illinois, begged the Sisters of the Holy Cross to continue in peacetime the services which they had rendered so creditably during the war. With the aid of Dr. Horace Wardner, who had been associated with the community during the war, a temporary location was secured. Thus commenced St. Mary's Infirmary, the first of a long line of hospitals operated by the Sisters of the Holy Cross.[28]

Even during the conflict the opening of new Catholic hospitals did not cease. The pressing of large numbers of sisters into service imposed a severe drain on the communities, but they were nevertheless laying part of the foundations for the large superstructures that were to grow out of this war experience. Another of the war developments in Catholic hospitals was St. Vincent's Charity Hospital in Cleveland. In 1863 Cleveland with a population of 50,000 had only one city infirmary. Bishop Rappé immediately organized a movement for the building of a Catholic institution for the care of the sick and in 1865 Cleveland saw its first private hospital. St. Vincent's Charity Hospital has been in charge of the Sisters of Charity of St. Augustine from the beginning.[29] Another hospital founded during the war was St. Francis Hospital, New York City, opened in 1864 under the direction of the Sisters of the Poor of St. Francis.[30]

The Development of Catholic Hospitals After the Civil War

The development of Catholic hospitals since the Civil War is one of the most interesting chapters in the history of the Catholic Church. Between 1866 and 1876 thirty-eight hospitals were opened; between 1876 and 1886 forty-seven hospitals were opened; between 1886 and 1896, 102 were founded. Between 1896 and 1906, 123 hospitals were opened; from 1906

---
[27] *Archives* of Providence Hospital, Washington, D. C.
[28] J. M. Lansden, *History of Cairo, Illinois*, pp. 155–156.
[29] *Souvenir of the Golden Jubilee of St. Vincent's Charity Hospital*, Cleveland, pp. 10–16.
[30] *Catholic World*, Vol. XLIII (Sept., 1886), p. 809.

to 1916, 102 hospitals were added; and between 1916 and 1926 eighty-four hospitals were added to the long list of these institutions.

As has been emphasized before, the religious communities acquired valuable experience in hospital work during the Civil War, which was a splendid preparation for hospital service during the great period of expansion on which the country entered after the war. As every new diocese was established the bishop came to regard the hospital and orphan asylum as one of the most essential parts of his diocesan establishment. In fact, he many times combined the hospital and orphanage in one institution. He felt as much bound to make some provision for the sick as for the orphan. In the cities in which diocesan sees were established there were usually no hospitals except the almshouses. Severe epidemics of cholera, typhoid fever and other virulent diseases were still quite prevalent. In reference to Mercy Hospital, Davenport, Iowa, the first Catholic and first private hospital in Iowa, the *Catholic Directory of 1874* had the following interesting statement: "Mercy Hospital, Davenport, Iowa, conducted by the Sisters of Mercy. This institution founded 1869 by Rt. Rev. Bishop Hennessy, who with Rev. Father Palmourgnes had secured the property some years before for hospital purposes. It is the only institution of its kind in Iowa. . . . There are accommodations for fifty patients. . . . It is surrounded by twenty acres of land, ten of which is the gift of a truly Catholic and charitable lady, Mrs. Judy Mitchel, one of the oldest settlers in Davenport."[31] Before the hospital in Davenport had been in operation many years, the public officials were compelled to call upon the sisters to nurse the victims of epidemic diseases. Thus the Catholic Directory of 1878 stated: "The Hospital of St. John of God is located in a remote part of the grounds and is intended for the accommodation of cholera and smallpox patients. The building

[31] Page 186.

The Care of the Sick

was erected at the expense of the city of Davenport and for the special use of that class of patients and was turned over under special contract to the charge of the Sisters of Mercy with the understanding that such patients would be cared for by them."[32] Bishop Hennessy was responsible for bringing the Sisters of Mercy from Davenport to his diocesan see at Dubuque in 1879. Their first institution at Dubuque according to a current description, "comprises three departments, an infirmary for the sick and aged; an orphanage for the education of destitute children and a house of Providence where homeless and unemployed girls are provided with all the comforts of a boarding house,"[33]

Hospitals Follow the Pioneers in the Western States

Just as Mercy Hospital, Davenport, was the pioneer institution of its kind in the state of Iowa, so was Mercy Hospital, Omaha, the pioneer institute of its type in Nebraska. It was opened by the Sisters of Mercy under the leadership of the Vicar-Apostolic, O'Gorman, in 1871.[34] Many of the western cities in which Catholic hospitals were established were glad to entrust them with public responsibility for the care of the sick. Thus the Sisters of Charity were given charge of the sick poor in many counties in Montana in the early seventies. In 1873 two Sisters of Charity from the house at Helena, "crossed the mountains and founded a hospital in Deerlodge in a building that had previously been used as a Methodist Church and then known as Dr. Mitchell's Hospital." Pending their arrival, Dr. Mitchell attended to the county hospital, as he had done for years before, and on their arrival they were placed in charge of the sick poor of the county."[35] Three years previously the Sisters of Charity of Leavenworth had

---
[32] Page 248.
[33] *Ibid*, 1880, p. 249.
[34] *Ibid*., 1871, p. 314.
[35] *History of Montana, 1739-1885*, published by Warner, Beers and Co., Chicago, p. 564.

opened St. John's Hospital in Helena[36] and shortly afterwards were asked to take over the management of the territorial asylum for the insane.[37] Thus it was that the Catholic hospital became the pioneer in health and hospitalization in many of the frontier states. It followed the trail of the immigrant into the first industrial and trading centers of the middle and far west, where public authorities looked to it as a means of discharging their responsibilities towards the sick.

Industrial Hospitals After the Civil War

In the mining and railroad centers the Catholic hospital was particularly in demand during the decades following the Civil War. It was for the purpose of assisting miners disabled by accidents that St. John's Hospital, Helena, Montana, was organized by the Sisters of Charity of Leavenworth in 1870. In response to urgent appeals in 1879 the Sisters of Charity of Leavenworth went to Leadville, Colorado, to provide hospital care for the miners in that city.[38] In the early seventies there was no provision for hospital care for the men injured in the northeastern part of the lower peninsula of Michigan. In 1874, therefore, the citizens of Saginaw united in asking the Sisters of Charity of Emmitsburg to open a hospital in this lumbering center. As a means of financing the hospital a plan was worked out according to which tickets entitling the holder to one year's hospital treatment were sold to the mill employees at $5.00 each.[39]

Many of the railroads of the west and southwest were anxious to have the sisters take charge of hospitals established for the care of their injured employees. The Sisters of Charity of the Incarnate word were placed in charge of the Texas and Pacific Hospital at Marshall, Texas, and the

---

[36] L. B. Palladino, S.J., *Indian and White in the Northwest*, pp. 334–335, 434.
[37] *History of Montana*, p. 730.
[38] *History of the Sisters of Charity of Leavenworth, Kansas*, by a Member of the Community, pp. 135, 341.
[39] *Yearly Report of St. Mary's Hospital*, Saginaw, 1928, pp. 12–13.

THE CARE OF THE SICK   199

Missouri, Kansas and Texas Railroad Hospital at Sedalia, Missouri. The Franciscan Sisters had charge of St. Patrick's Wabash Railway Hospital at Moberly, Missouri, the St. Lucas Wabash Association Hospital at Decatur, Illinois, and St. Francis Wabash Railway Hospital, at Peru, Indiana.

Nature's Elements Play Part in Introduction of Sisters Into Hospital Work

An instance of the circumstances under which the sisters were introduced into hospital work is illustrated by St. Mary's Hospital of Rochester, Minnesota. This hospital, now familiarly known as the Mayo Brothers Institution, owed its origin to a terrible tornado which partially destroyed the city of Rochester in 1883, leaving many killed and injured in its wake. As there was no hospital nearer than St. Paul, about ninety miles distant, many of the injured were conveyed to the academy of the Franciscan Sisters. After a few days, a hall was temporarily fitted up for a hospital and the sisters came at the request of the elder Dr. W. W. Mayo who was in charge of the work. This incident showed the need of a hospital and plans were soon begun, thanks to the efforts of Dr. Mayo and Mother Alfred of the Franciscans, with the approval of Archbishop Ireland. Dr. Mayo personally supervised the work of construction, and the first operation was performed by his more distinguished sons, Drs. Charles H. Mayo and William J. Mayo in 1889. While the building was still under construction one of the sons, Dr. C. H. Mayo, made the prediction that the hospital would be a decided advantage to the community and would soon attract patients from the surrounding cities. His words have been amply justified by the subsequent history of the institution which today is known the world over as a surgical and clinical center.[40]

---
[40] *Souvenir of St. Mary's Hospital*, Rochester, Minnesota, 1922, pp. 14-21.

The German Sisterhoods An Important Factor in Hospital History

Many of the new Catholic hospitals established during the seventies and eighties owed their origin to German sisterhoods coming to the United States after 1870. The Franciscan Sisters of the Province of St. Clara founded the Pius Hospital, St. Louis (1874), St. Joseph's Hospital, Milwaukee (1879) and St. Mary's Hospital, Racine, Wisconsin (1882).[41] The congregation known as the Poor Sisters of St. Francis Seraph of the Perpetual Adoration founded St. Joseph's Hospital (Creighton Memorial in Omaha (1880), St. Mary's Hospital, Columbus, Nebr. (1881), St. Mary's Hospital, Emporia, Kans. (1882), St. Anthony's Hospital, Terre Haute, Ind. (1882), St. Francis Hospital, Colorado Springs, Colo. (1887), St. Francis Hospital, Grand Island, Nebr. (1887), St. Francis Hospital, La Crosse, Wis. (1887) and St. Elizabeth's Hospital, Lincoln, Nebr. (1889). One can readily appreciate why Bismarck's Kulturkampf which drove many religious communities out of Germany was the source of untold blessings to the American Catholic Church. These communities became a most important factor in the progress of Catholic social and charitable work in this country.

An Italian Community Provides Hospitalization for Its Own People

As has been emphasized so frequently throughout this volume each immigrant group coming to the United States brought its own missionaries and its own traditions and institutions of charity. A very good illustration of missionary work among their own people is found in the Italian Missionary Sisters of the Sacred Heart. This community has founded a number of hospitals and other charitable institutions in this country designed especially for work among

[41] Rothensteiner *op. cit.*, Vol. II, pp. 345–346.

Italian immigrants. Among the hospitals operated by this community are Columbus Hospital, New York City (1892), Mother Cabrini Memorial Hospital, Chicago (1911), and Cristoforo Columbo Hospital, Philadelphia (1924).

An Interpretation of the Rapid Rise of Hospitals Since 1870

The reasons given in the foregoing paragraphs are not sufficient in themselves to account for the rapid and continuous growth of Catholic hospitals since 1870. Why did hospitals grow at such a rapid rate when the growth of other forms of charitable work has been comparatively slow? In recent years the Catholic hospital has become largely a self-supporting institution. A religious community is invited to open a hospital in a city. It is given a small sum of money, possibly from $20,000 to $30,000 and a site with which to begin an enormous undertaking. In order to build the hospital the religious community borrows from $200,000 to $600,000 on its own credit. It must pay interest on a staggering debt to meet the ordinary operating costs which the proceeds of the hospital do not meet. The amount of money which it is able to secure through charitable bequests is negligible. The sisters must struggle as best they can to meet their heavy obligations with the hope that their hospital may some day be free of debt. It may be that when this long-awaited hour arrives the hospital will be able to carry part of the mortgage of some other hospital. This has been the course followed by most of the Catholic hospitals in the United States. It represents the strength and, at the same time, the weakness of the ordinary Catholic hospital. This plan has been a source of strength in that the hospital otherwise could not have progressed at least at such a rapid rate. It is easy to say that it should not have been so. Why should the various dioceses not have had organized programs for hospital extension? Why should they not have been able to secure capital for hospital building without compelling the sisters to incur such a debt? The bishops were hard pressed for funds for their orphan asylums and the education of their priests. They were at their wits' end to find money for their churches and schools. The sisters were willing to assume responsibility for the hospital. They knew their business so why not let them try their hand?

It should be remembered, moreover, that it is only within recent years that the technique of raising money for charitable activities has been developed. Catholic dioceses have learned to apply this technique in raising funds for the Catholic hospital. In the past few years diocesan-wide campaigns for hospitals have been conducted with notable success in Cleveland, Brooklyn and Syracuse.

Its financial methods have been a great source of weakness to the Catholic hospital. They have prevented it from doing many things that the sisters were most anxious to do. They have prevented it from developing the social policies that are an essential part of its mission to the sick and the poor and which only well endowed institutions can conduct.

Schools of Nursing in Connection With Catholic Hospitals

As we have seen, the Civil War revealed a woeful lack of good nursing in the United States. According to a report of the American Medical Association, made at its New Orleans meeting in 1869 the Catholic orders were the only ones to realize the importance of nursing.[42] The defects brought to light during the war led to an organized movement for nursing training during the seventies. In 1873 schools for the training of nurses were opened in Bellevue Hospital, New York, the New Haven Hospital in Connecticut, and the Massachusetts General Hospital at Boston.[43] The movement for systematic training of nurses was bound to influence Catholic

---

[42] Nutting and Dock, *op. cit.*, Vol. II, p. 366.
[43] *Ibid.*, Vol. II, p. 371.

hospitals. The sisters already had their own methods of training their members, but now the large hospitals were offering training opportunities for lay women. It was very evident that in time nursing would become a recognized profession and one of the most important avenues of opportunity open to women. The Catholic hospitals could not afford to disregard the signs of the times. Slowly, but none the less surely, they decided to open their own training schools. At the present time two-thirds of the 641 Catholic hospitals in the United States have training schools for nurses. Of the 429 schools for nurses in Catholic hospitals only 61 were in existence prior to 1900. The two oldest nursing schools, namely, those at St. Mary's Hospital, Kansas City, Missouri, and St. Vincent's Hospital, Erie, Pennsylvania, were established in 1874 and 1875 respectively.[44]

Higher Standards for the Nursing Profession

In recent years there has been an insistent demand for higher standards in training nurses. The pupil nurse is required to give more time to study and less time to the actual work of the hospital. In this regard nursing is passing through the same evolution as the older professions. There was first the apprenticeship system. Formal instruction was added gradually until it has become the most important part of the training. The great increase in the number of nurses in recent years has intensified the demand for higher training standards. Leaders in the field believe that higher educational and training standards are the most effective means of keeping the number of nurses within the requirements of the profession as well as increasing the skill and standing of the profession.

[44] "*A Survey of the Catholic Hospital of the United States and Canada*"—Reprinted from *Hospital Progress*, March, 1930, pp. 27, 28, 61, 64.

The Evolution of the Catholic Hospital

Up to about 1870 the Catholic hospital was entirely an institution of charity. Only the poor thought about using its facilities. The wealthy and middle class were filled with a deep prejudice against it. With the rapid improvement of standards and equipment in recent years, the hospital has become exceedingly popular with persons in all walks of life. Catholic institutions for the sick, on the whole, have kept pace with the general standards of hospital work. "The approval of the American College of Surgeons," says a recent survey of Catholic hospitals, "has always been regarded as a special badge of merit among hospitals. . . . It is significant of the progress of the Catholic hospital that of the 641 Catholic hospitals, 364 or 56.7 per cent have merited this distinction. The significance of this statement becomes still more apparent when it is realized that while the Catholic hospitals represent only one-tenth of the total number of hospitals, they represent almost one-fifth (18.4) of the total number of 'approved' hospitals."[45]

Some Deficiencies in the Social Service Programs of Catholic Hospitals

The fact remains that there is much that is still to be desired in the social service department of the Catholic hospital. It should be prepared to provide gratuitous care for the poor, to give reduced rates to the wage-earner who can not pay in full. It should be able to reach out into the homes of its wards and clinic patients in order that they may be relieved of the worries and anxieties that play such an important part in ill-health and recovery therefrom. It should be able to set the mind of the sick mother at rest in regard to the care of her children. By understanding the homes, conditions and habits of life of its patients, the hospital is in

[45] *Hospital Progress*, March, 1930, p. 111.

a much better position to diagnose and treat their illnesses. Industrial medicine has emphasized for us the close connection between disease and occupation. The hospital must have on hand the information about its patients that is necessary to evaluate this connection. It is of very little use for the physicians in the hospital to prescribe a program of treatment for their patients, if their suggestions are not carried out. How can they be assured that the poor person with diabetes will have the prescribed diet, that the cardiac patient will be able to secure the necessary change of occupation or that the anaemic child will be able to secure a sufficient supply of milk? The only way in which the physician can be assured that the details of his program will be carried out is through a medical social service department. This also is the only means of securing the information necessary for intelligent treatment of his patients. It is the only means, moreover, through which the hospital can reach out to the homes of the poor and relieve them of unnecessary worries during the period of their hospitalization. And how many Catholic hospitals are equipped with medical social service departments? Only seventeen, and of these eleven have been organized since 1919. If the hospitals only had the necessary financial backing, undoubtedly a very large number of them would have medical social service departments. This at present must remain a hoped-for ideal.

Social Service Department in Relation to the Diocesan Charities

There is another aspect of the medical social service department that must receive increasing consideration in Catholic Charities. The diocesan charities should be able to call on the Catholic hospital in providing medical and hospital care for Catholic families receiving service or relief. It should be able to look to the hospital for aid in formulating and carrying out a program of medical care for the children in Catholic institutions. Now it is a matter of common knowledge that the hospital can not give its best service to the diocesan charities without a medical social service department. Without the aid of a social service department, the workers in the diocesan charities find it practically impossible to establish close contact with the physicians in the hospital. In order to secure medical service for their clients, they must spend a large part of their time in the hospital. They must take upon themselves functions that really belong to hospital administration.

The Convalescent Home as a Complement to the Modern Hospital

The care of the sick can not be assumed entirely by the general hospital. The convalescent home, therefore, occupies a very large place in hospital work. It is a well-known fact that patients are only about eighty per cent cured when they leave the institution. The permanence of this eighty per cent cure will depend on how the remaining twenty per cent of the work is done. Many times everything that the hospital has done is lost because the mother returns to her home and takes up her household responsibilities before she is fully recovered. A two weeks' rest may mean the difference between success and failure in the medical program. The general hospital is not the place for the person who is recovering from a long illness. It is a place for the treatment of the acutely ill. It endeavors to turn over its beds as rapidly as possible, so that it may be able to reach an increasing number of those for whom its services are especially designed. In order to get the best results the hospital must be supplemented by the convalescent home.

One can not fail to note the disproportion between Catholic general hospitals and Catholic convalscent homes in the United States. There are some 640 Catholic general hospitals and only about twenty-five convalescent homes. Possibly, the disproportion may be accounted for by the relative difficulties of building and maintaining a general hospital as compared with a convalescent home. A hospital can be built and maintained without any considerable expense to the local community. It is different with a convalescent home. The people who need convalescent care, generally speaking, are least able to pay.

Catholic convalescent homes are of comparatively recent origin. The first of these homes, the Greylock unit in charge of the Sisters of Providence at Adams, Massachusetts, was organized in 1903. The second Catholic convalescent home in the United States, St. Elizabeth's Convalescent Home at Spring Valley, New York, grew out of the summer work of the Particular Council of the Society of St. Vincent de Paul of New York. St. Elizabeth's Home, according to its first report, was intended "for the building up physically of persons who are convalescing after an illness of which they have been cured, or those whose health has been impaired by overwork and lack of nourishment."[46]

One of the most interesting developments in Catholic convalescent work in this country was the opening of St. Francis' Country Home for Convalescents at Darby, Pennsylvania (1913). This home was due in great measure to the leadership of Monsignor Francis X. Wastl, who for a number of years had been chaplain at Blockley Hospital, where he secured first-hand information on the need of special institutions for convalescents. He saw large numbers of patients returning to their own homes only to break down or those whose health has been impaired by overwork and lack of nourishment."[46]

Although the number of Catholic convalescent homes is small, yet over one-half of them have been organized since

---

[46] Society of St. Vincent de Paul, *Report of Superior Council of New York to Council General at Paris*, 1906, p. 14.
[47] St. Francis Country Home for Convalescents, Darby, Pa. *Report*, 1913-1919, p. 7.

1927. This is a hopeful sign that a long-felt need in Catholic charities is beginning to make itself felt. It inspires hope for progress in the future.

Special Hospitals: Institutions for Mental and Nervous Cases

The earliest type of special hospital conducted under Catholic auspices is that designed for the care of mental and nervous cases. A number of the states called on the sisters to manage their hospitals for the insane. The State of Maryland requested the Sisters of Charity of Emmitsburg to take charge of the Maryland Hospital for the Insane in 1833. In 1840 the sisters withdrew from the Maryland Hospital and immediately opened their own institution which was known as Mount St. Vincent's. In 1844 they purchased Mount Hope College in which they laid the foundations of Mount Hope Retreat.[48] The experience they acquired in the Maryland Hospital in Baltimore and in their own institution prepared the Sisters of Charity to conduct similar institutions in other cities. In 1858 they founded St. Vincent's Sanitarium for nervous and mental diseases at Normandy, Missouri. This was followed by St. Joseph's Retreat, Dearborn, Michigan, the Providence Retreat at Buffalo in 1860 and the Louisiana Retreat, New Orleans in 1862. Besides these five sanitariums there are ten other hospitals for nervous and mental diseases in the United States: St. Vincent's Retreat, Harrison, N. Y. (1879), conducted by the Sisters of Charity of St. Vincent de Paul; the Alexian Brothers Hospital, Oshkosh, Wis. (1879); St. Bernard's Hospital, Council Bluffs, Iowa (1887), conducted by the Sisters of Mercy; St. Joseph's Sanitarium, Dubuque, Iowa (1895), conducted by the Sisters of Mercy; the Kneipp Sanitarium, Rome City, Ind. (1901), conducted by the Sisters of the Most Precious Blood; the St. Mary's Hill Sanitarium, Milwaukee, Wis.

---

[48] *Archives* of Mt. St. Joseph's College, Emittsburg.

(1912), conducted by the School Sisters of St. Francis; the Mt. St. Agnes Sanitarium, Louisville, Ky. (1913), conducted by the Sisters of Charity of Nazareth; the Mercyville Sanitarium, Aurora, Ill. (1915), the Mercywood Sanitarium, Ann Arbor, Mich. (1924), and the Mt. Mercy Sanitarium, Hammond, Ind. (1928), the last three conducted by the Sisters of Mercy.

The sisters showed a greater tendency to engage in work for the insane in the pioneer days than in recent years. The tendency recently has been to regard work for the insane as a public function. With the improvement in the standards of public hospitals there is very little inclination to open private institutions of any kind for the insane. The sisters feel, and probably rightly, that their limited resources can be applied more effectively in other fields.

Institutions for the Tubercular

Catholic hospitals for tubercular patients seem to be confined to those sections of the country in which climatic conditions lend themselves to the arrest of the disease. Some of these institutions are general hospitals with special departments for the treatment of tuberculosis, while others confine their care solely and only to tubercular cases. There are three Catholic hospitals of the general type, with special facilities for tubercular patients in New Mexico, two in Colorado and one in Arizona. The first Catholic tuberculosis hospital in the United States was St. Vincent's Sanitarium, Santa Fe, New Mexico, founded in 1865 by the Sisters of Charity of Cincinnati. This is now a general hospital and sanitarium combined for the treatment of tuberculosis. Other general hospitals in the United States with special departments for the treatment of tuberculosis are: St. Francis Hospital, Colorado Springs, Colo. (1887), conducted by the Poor Sisters of St. Francis Seraph of Perpetual Adoration; St.

Mary's Hospital and Sanitarium, Tucson, Ariz. (1888), conducted by the Sisters of St. Joseph; Glockner Sanitarium, Colorado Springs, Colo. (1889), conducted by the Sisters of Charity; St. Joseph's Hospital and Sanitarium, Albuquerque, N. Mex. (1901), conducted by the Sisters of Charity; St. Mary's Hospital, Roswell, N Mex., conducted by the Sisters of the Sorrowful Mother.

The institutions which deal entirely with various types of tubercular treatment are: St. Joseph's Sanitarium, New York City (1882), conducted by the Sisters of the Poor of St. Francis; Seton Hospital for Men, New York City (1892 or 1894) and the Nazareth Branch for Women, New York City, both conducted by the Sisters of Charity; Sanitarium Gabriels, Gabriels, N. Y. (1897), conducted by the Sisters of Mercy; Mt. St. Rose Sanitarium, St. Louis, Mo. (1900), conducted by the Sisters of St. Mary, Third Order of St. Francis; St. Joseph's Sanitarium, Asheville, N. C. (1900), conducted by the Sisters of Mercy; St. Joseph's Sanitarium, Hillsgrove, R. I. (1904), conducted by the Franciscan Sisters; St. Mary of the Lake, Saranac Lake, N. Y. (1910), conducted by the Sisters of Mercy; St. Anthony's, Woodhaven, N. Y. (1914), conducted by the Sisters of the Poor of St. Francis; St. John's Sanitarium, Springfield, Ill. (1918), conducted by the Hospital Sisters of St. Francis; St. Joseph's Sanitarium, St. Cloud, Minn. (1919), conducted by the Benedictine Sisters; Holy Cross Sanitarium, Deming, N. Mex. (1923), conducted by the Sisters of the Holy Cross; St. Joseph's Sanitarium, El Paso, Tex. (1927), conducted by the Sisters of St. Joseph.

Institutions for Incurables

There are in all ten Catholic hospitals for incurables in the United States: St. Francis Home for Incurables, Cincinnati, Ohio (1888), conducted by the Sisters of the Poor of St. Francis; Holy Ghost Hospital, Cambridge, Mass. (1893), conducted by the Grey Nuns; St. Francis Home for Incurables and Aged, New York City (1906), conducted by the Sisters of the Poor of St. Francis; St. Francis Hall for Incurables, Darby, Pa. (1913), conducted by the Sisters of Bon Secours; St. Camillus Hospital for Men, Milwaukee, Wis. (1924), conducted by the Camillian Fathers; Jenkins Memorial Hospital, Baltimore, Md. (1926), conducted by the Sisters of Bon Secours; Mother of Good Counsel Home for Incurables and Sanitarium for Convalescents, Normandy, Mo., conducted by the Sisters of the Poor of St. Francis. The following three are reserved exclusively for cancer patients: House of Calvary, New York City (1899), conducted by the Women of Calvary and the Dominican Sisters of Blauvelt, N. Y.; St. Rose's Free Home, New York City (1896), and Rosary Hill Convalescent Home, Hawthorne, N. Y. (1901), the last two conducted by the Sisters of St. Dominic of the Congregation of St. Rose of Lima, incorporated as the Servants of Relief for Incurable Cancer. It should be added that nearly all the hospitals in charge of the Sisters of the Poor of St. Francis care for a certain number of incurable patients.

Home Nursing

There is another activity which is closely related to the Catholic hospital and which constitutes an important part of any program of Catholic Charities, namely, the nursing of the sick poor in their own homes. There are many cases in which for obvious reasons the sick cannot be removed from their own homes. There are many cases in which the sick mother of a family will need not only nursing care, but also the assistance of some person who will help prepare the food and attend to other household responsibilities. We have a number of religious communities in the United States dedicated to this very important work of nursing the sick poor in their own homes. They are the Sisters of Bon Secours, the

Dominican Sisters of the Sick Poor, the Sisters of the Holy Ghost, Sisters of the Little Company of Mary, Little Sisters of the Infant Jesus, Poor Handmaids of Jesus Christ, Sisters of the Poor Handmaids of the Sacred Heart, Sisters Servants of Mary, Society of Helpers of the Holy Souls. Their history and work are described in the chapter dealing with European religious communities of women.[49] It is sufficient to say that they are rendering a service that is most essential in the care of the poor and a service that is not rendered by any other agency. They make themselves a part of the home and they give more attention to the details of family life than any other agency. Their continued presence in the home from morning until evening gives them a very far-reaching influence with the family. They teach homemaking by actual demonstration.

[49] Chapter XIX.

CHAPTER XII

CATHOLIC CARE OF THE AGED

Almshouse Only Type of Institution in Early 19th Century

Throughout the entire first half of the nineteenth century the almshouse was the accepted method of taking care of persons needing institutional relief in the United States. In this unclassified institution were herded together the aged and infirm, the insane, the feebleminded, the sick, and dependent and neglected children. In 1834 the Boston House of Industry, established thirteen years before, "to house the ablebodied poor and provide them with employment, contained 61 persons who were either insane or idiotic; 134 who were sick or infirm; 104 boys and girls of school age; 28 children at nurse; and an unclassified remainder among whom were 64 men who worked at picking oakum.[1] As late as 1856, Blockley, the Philadelphia almshouse, cared for smallpox patients, the insane, children, maternity cases, cases of acute illness, the blind, the lame, incurables.[2]

Conditions were much the same in similar institutions throughout the country. One cannot be surprised if the aged poor with any degree of self-respect were loath to enter such institutions. To go over the hill to the poorhouse was life's last resort. For the Irish immigrants the almshouse recalled many unpleasant memories; in Ireland the almshouse was only for the poorest of the poor and carried an indelible stigma. There inmates were ordinarily persons whose poverty was due to mental and moral handicaps rather than to economic causes.

[1] R. W. Kelso, *The Science of Public Welfare*, p. 200.
[2] Nutting and Dock, *op. cit.*, Vol. II, p. 335; A. A. Bliss, *Blockley Days*, 1883-1884; *Memories and Impressions of a Resident Physician*, p. 9.

Almshouses Essentially Protestant Institutions

For the immigrants, going to the almshouse meant that they considered themselves practically isolated from society forever. It meant moreover depriving themselves of every opportunity of practicing their religion, for no provision was made for any other form of religion except the semi-established Protestantism. Protestant authorities in these institutions saw no reason, or cared to see none, why the Catholic poor should not conform. It was only after 1870 when the Society of St. Vincent de Paul made systematic provision for Catholics in the various public institutions that the poor in the Albany almshouse were given any opportunity of practicing their religion. It has been pointed out that the almshouses in Connecticut placed Catholic children in Protestant homes as late as 1890. These are good indices of the religious outlook.

In regard to the teaching of religion in public institutions in the early days we have this interesting statement from the report of the acting President of the Superior Council of the Society of St. Vincent de Paul of New York to the Council General at Paris in 1873: "In such institutions in this country, which are supported entirely or in part by the public Treasury, the only religious exercises or institutions which the managers or other persons in charge have permitted or established have been very generally of the so-called 'non-sectarian' character. This system has been, as it is claimed, the outgrowth of a desire to do equal justice to persons of all creeds without extending special privileges to any. With this desire has been mingled a spirit of hostility to the Catholic Church, rendered more intense by an unreasoning fear of its purposes and ignorance of its doctrines." [3]

[3] Pp. 14-15.

Change in Attitude of Almshouse Officials After 1870

If there was lack of systematic care of the religious needs of the inmates in at least the eastern almshouses after 1870, it was due in most instances not to the authorities in these institutions but to apathy on the part of Catholics. The Report of the Particular Council of the Society of St. Vincent de Paul of Jersey City for 1882 made special reference to the religious work done by the Society in the public almshouse of that city: "Some few years ago since permission was obtained for a priest to visit the institution and say Mass on Sundays at an early hour the remainder of the day was taken up by the services of the city missionary and visiting bands of young men and women from the various Protestant Churches." The report then maintained that the failure to make more adequate provision for the needs of the Catholic inmates of the almshouse was due to the apathy of Catholics themselves.[4]

Almshouses Resist Change

The removal of the children from the almshouses in the seventies and eighties meant some improvement in their standards. The removal of the feebleminded and the sick at a later date was bound to bring further improvement. The making of special provision for the various groups that heretofore had been huddled together in the almshouse, supposedly gave the latter institution an opportunity to make special provision for the aged and infirm. However, the almshouse has resisted the process of change more stubbornly than any other American institution. The present almshouses are, in theory, at best special institutions for the care of the aged. A visit to these institutions in the rural sections of the United States would transplant one back to the days of fifty years ago. One finds there many persons who should be in other institutions; for if other institutions are crowded, the alms-

[4] *Ibid.*, 1833, p. 20

house or county infirmary takes all the leftovers. While some almshouses are prepared to give humane care for the aged, in most instances they are institutions to which the aged have recourse only as a last resort.

Development of Catholic Care of the Aged

Catholic charitable institutions have all grown out of the emergencies that confronted the Church in the United States. They meant the assumption of responsibilities that could not be escaped. The circumstances attending the development of Catholic institutions for the aged are entirely different from those associated with the child-caring institutions and hospitals. The penniless aged in the almshouses, undoubtedly, made an appeal, but their appeal was not so vital as provision for emergent sick or the children or the providing of religious worship for the masses of the people. In view of all the other needs that were pressing upon the Church, it is interesting to note that the care of the aged was hardly undertaken until the year 1868. It was due largely to the Little Sisters of the Poor, who unassumingly and independently have carried the burden of the care of the aged in this country. The growth of these institutions between 1868, the date of their arrival, and 1879 reads like a romance. The work of the Little Sisters of the Poor has expressed, in dramatic form the lesson of all Catholic charities that more depends upon sacrifice than on resources.

Earliest Catholic Homes for Aged in the United States

Before telling the story of the Little Sisters of the Poor, it might be well to note some of the earlier homes for the aged poor in the United States. The oldest Catholic institution for the aged is the Lafon Asylum of the Holy Family in New Orleans which was opened by the Sisters of the Holy Family in 1842 for the care of aged colored women. It now admits both men and women.[5] St. Ann's Widows' Asylum of Philadelphia was established by the Sisters of the Good Shepherd in 1849 and still carries on its original work under the Sisters of St. Joseph of Chestnut Hill.[6] Another pioneer Catholic institution for the aged was St. Francis Asylum in Buffalo, New York, opened by the Sisters of the Third Order of St. Francis in 1855. For a number of years previously the sisters had been engaged in visiting the sick and the aged in their own homes. After many difficulties they were able to purchase a lot on Pine Street for $800, where a two-story frame house was built in 1862. Here the old people and the sisters lived in great poverty. When the original building became too small for the increasing number of inmates, the sisters decided to erect a large building on the adjoining lot. The institution has gradually been enlarged until today it has become a commanding structure with a frontage of 263 feet on Pine Street.[7]

The Little Sisters of the Poor

In the early part of 1868 a general chapter of the Little Sisters of the Poor held at La Tour St. Joseph, France, decided to extend the work of the community to the United States. Although the community had been in existence only thirty years it had already opened 107 houses with 1,750 sisters caring for 13,000 aged persons.[8] This remarkable expansion was an evidence of the vitality and usefulness of the community. Their first thought was to begin in New Orleans, because of its large French population. After mature consideration of the whole question of the first foundation, Abbé

---

[5] *A Brief Sketch of the Congregation of the Sisters of the Holy Family of New Orleans,* manuscript prepared for the writer, 1930.
[6] *Catholic Charities and Social Welfare Activities of the Archdiocese of Philadelphia.* Year Book, 1926, p. 93.
[7] *History and Development of the Work of the Sisters of St. Francis,* manuscript prepared for the writer, 1929.
[8] A. Leroy, *The Little Sisters of the Poor in America from History of the Little Sisters of the Poor,* a translation from French under direction of the author, p. 238.

Ernest Lelièvre, the spiritual director who had been commissioned to pave the way for its mission to the United States, decided in favor of the north.[9]

Brooklyn Cradle of the Little Sisters of the Poor in the United States

He discussed with the archbishop of New York the possibility of a foundation in that archdiocese, but the archbishop was unready to give an immediate decision, due to the fact that the Sisters of Charity were about to open a home for the aged in the archdiocese. Thereupon the emissary of the Little Sisters approached Bishop John Loughlin of Brooklyn, who gave his consent to the immediate erection of a home of the Little Sisters in his diocese.[10] The first band of sisters arrived September 13, 1868, and within a week opened their house to the first aged person. It is an interesting coincidence that they received their first financial aid from Father Isaac Hecker, the founder of the Paulist community, who later rendered such yeoman service in the Catholic charities of New York.[11]

Cincinnati Foundation

Within a month, October 8, 1868, another band of sisters arrived in New York, under the direction of the assistant-general, Sister Marie de la Conception, who, by reason of her aptitude for spreading the work, was afterwards known as "Good Mother Foundation." With her little band she set out for Cincinnati where she immediately opened a home in an old school building near the cathedral.[12] After a short time the sisters moved to a more suitable location on Lock Street adjoining the old Samaritan Hospital.[13] Cincinnati,

---

[9] *Ibid.*, p. 239.
[10] *Ibid.*, pp. 239-240.
[11] *Ibid.*, pp. 242-243.
[12] *Ibid.*, p. 243.
[13] Lamott, *op. cit.*, p. 266.

therefore, ranks second in the long list of foundations of the Little Sisters of the Poor in the United States.

New Orleans Foundation

On December 19, 1868, we find "Good Mother Foundation" in New Orleans, the city on which the community had set its first hopes. A number of Catholic women in that city had already opened a home for widows and old people, but had not been very successful in its management. The Little Sisters were asked to take over the home and conduct it according to their rules. The city council contributed its part by voting $1,000 for repairs and improvements on the property.

Baltimore Foundation

Baltimore, a city with such long traditions of charity, the city that had been the birthplace of Catholic Charities in the United States, next received the Little Sisters with open arms. The *Baltimore Catholic Mirror* undoubtedly expressed the general sentiment of the people when it stated in its issue of April 12, 1869: "We have at last our Little Sisters." Evidently the Little Sisters must have been sought from the date of their arrival in the United States. Before their arrival, April 6, 1869, preliminary arrangements had been made for them to take over the work of the Widows' Asylum, an institution established by a legacy for the benefit of the widows of the city. The Abbé Lelièvre had entered into a contract with the board of trustees of this institution according to which its title was to be assigned to the Little Sisters with the understanding that they should always care for at least twenty-five widows or indigent women, free of charge.[14]

Evidently difficulties prevented the immediate execution of this plan because the sisters were compelled to begin their work in a rented house on Calvert Street. In the issue of

---

[14] *Baltimore Catholic Mirror*, February 20, 1869.

April 12, 1869, the *Catholic Mirror* issued an appeal to the people of the city to come to their assistance: "Any kind of a donation is welcome—old clothing, meat, vegetables, bread and remains after meals will be thankfully received by the sisters, and turned into some use for themselves, as well as for their charges." It is recorded that St. Mary's Seminary was among the first to come to their assistance, giving its left-overs from the table.[15]

St. Louis Foundation

The month following their arrival in Baltimore found the Little Sisters beginning their work in another Catholic center, St. Louis. Responding to the invitation of Archbishop Kenrick, a band of six sisters from the motherhouse in Brittany, France, arrived in St. Louis, May 1, 1869. The archbishop arranged accommodations for them at the convent of the Ladies of the Sacred Heart until in a few days they took possession of four small houses. They did not have a single piece of furniture for the houses. "'What would they do with an empty house,' they were asked? 'It is always in holy poverty that we begin; Divine Providence will provide,' answered the Sisters."[16] As usual the people came to their rescue. One person brought a stove, another a temporary altar, others brought beds, kitchen equipment, chairs and other articles of household furniture. One thoughtful person sent a horse and buggy to be used by the sisters on their begging expeditions. The second day after opening the house the sisters received their first aged person and within two months they had fifty inmates.[17] Within two decades the original house of the Little Sisters in St. Louis was enlarged three times and a new home built. This is just another illustration of the striking appeal of the Little Sisters of the Poor.

---

[15] Leroy, *op. cit.*, p. 246.
[16] Rothensteiner, *op cit.*, Vol. II, p. 333.
[17] *Ibid.*, Vol. II, p. 334.

THE CARE OF THE AGED   221

Philadelphia Foundation

Within three months after the beginning of their foundation in St. Louis the Little Sisters of the Poor opened an institution in Philadelphia in three rented buildings.[18] These limited quarters, however, soon proved insufficient, and the following year a site for a new building was acquired. Before the end of 1871 they had accommodations for 125 aged persons. An addition to the building, three years later, increased its capacity to 160.[19] Today there are three homes in Philadelphia each accommodating about 250 old folks.[20]

Louisville Foundation

Scarcely a month elapsed between the establishment of the first home of the Little Sisters of the Poor in Philadelphia and the foundation in Louisville. The *Baltimore Catholic Mirror* of October 30, 1869, stated: "The Little Sisters of the Poor arrived in Louisville some four weeks ago. The bishop turned over to them a house he bought for the purpose of establishing a seminary. The Sisters were to be allowed to use this building until they could erect one of their own."

Boston, Cleveland and New York City Foundations

Throughout the year 1870 the Little Sisters of the Poor continued to make steady progress in the United States. Foundations were made in Boston, Cleveland and New York City. In Boston they began in characteristic fashion—two rented houses without a stick of furniture constituted all their assets. Some good women collected a few dollars to meet their initial expenses. Public charity aroused by the clergy and the press, did the rest.[21]

---
[18] Leroy, *op. cit.*, p. 249.
[19] *Baltimore Catholic Mirror*, June 30, 1877.
[20] *Official Catholic Directory*, 1931, p. 167.
[21] Leroy, *op. cit.*, pp. 241-252.

Closely following the home of the Little Sisters of the Poor in Boston came the first home of the community in Cleveland. As has been noted in other chapters, Bishop Rappé was most solicitous for the care of the sick and the orphans of his diocese. This same solicitude he extended to the aged poor. In 1870 he invited the Little Sisters of the Poor to his diocese and provided them with a small house with accommodations for twelve aged persons. This was merely a temporary arrangement. Plans were made immediately to secure property and erect a suitable building for the care of the aged.[22]

According to the historian of the Little Sisters of the Poor in the United States the ceremony incidental to the blessing of their new home in Brooklyn created a strong incentive for the building of a similar institution in the neighboring diocese of New York. Many Catholics in New York expressed a desire to have the Little Sisters, and on September 29, 1870, a foundation was established.[23]

Washington Foundation

In 1871 the Little Sisters of the Poor opened a house in Washington. To Father Walter, the pastor of St. Patrick's Church, the sisters owed their coming to Washington. The Society of St. Vincent de Paul made preparations for their arrival, so that they found everything in readiness. Their home had been fitted up, and a number of ladies were busy preparing to serve them their first meal in the new home.[24] As the house was capable of accommodating only six aged persons, they were not long satisfied with their limited quarters. Within a year they acquired a new site in what was then the suburbs of Washington. Less than two years later a suitable building was opened and in a year it was free of debt. No charity in the city of Washington made a wider

---

[22] E. McK. Avery, *History of Cleveland and Its Environs*, Vol. I, p. 610; Leroy, *op. cit.*, pp. 252–253.
[23] *Ibid.*, p. 254.
[24] *Archives* of Little Sisters of the Poor, Washington, D. C.

appeal to all classes than the Little Sisters of the Poor. In 1874 Congress appropriated $25,000 to assist in their building program. In 1880 Congress added another $20,000 to aid in extending the work to aged colored persons.

The popularity of the Little Sisters of the Poor in Washington is not confined to any social class or group. As an evidence of their appeal to high society, the following statement from the *Baltimore Catholic Mirror* will serve: "A fancy ball took place on Saturday evening for the benefit of the Little Sisters of the Poor. The diplomatic corps was largely represented and society turned out en masse."[25] The Feast of St. Joseph has always been an event in the Little Sisters' home in Washington. Some of the most prominent people in the city visit the home on that date bearing their gifts and serving dinner to the old folks.[26] In 1874 the sisters made an appeal for assistance in grading their grounds. Several hundred men with wagons and teams volunteered and as a result an unsightly plot was turned into a beautiful garden.[27]

Albany Foundation

The Albany home of the Little Sisters of the Poor, opened in 1871, began in a small house capable of accommodating fifteen old folks. In a year, they moved into larger quarters.[28]

In the early part of 1872 Bishop O'Connor invited the Little Sisters of the Poor to Pittsburgh. They arrived in the city on April 24th of that year and were located temporarily in a home provided by the diocese. Before the end of the year they had secured larger quarters. By reason of increased demands made upon them they found it necessary to secure an additional building in 1873.[29]

---

[25] February 2, 1878.
[26] *Archives* of Little Sisters of the Poor, Washington, D. C.
[27] *Ibid.*
[28] Leroy, *op. cit.*, pp. 255-258.
[29] Lambing, *op. cit.*, pp. 499-501.

The Year 1872 Sees Thirteen Homes of Little Sisters of the Poor

In the summer of 1872 Abbé Lelièvre and Sister Marie de la Conception returned to Europe. Within a short space of four years they had succeeded in opening thirteen homes for the aged in the United States. They had planted their work firmly in the minds and hearts of American Catholics. What they had sown under such favorable auspices was bound to keep on producing fruit. The work would now take care of itself without any artificial stimulus. Most of the large centers were provided with homes for the aged. Demands would continue to pour in from other cities as rapidly as they could be satisfied. Within a year after their departure, foundations were made in Indianapolis, Detroit and Troy. The home in Troy was due entirely to the intiative of the Society of St. Vincent de Paul. With the assistance of the society, the sisters secured a building valued at $12,000 and within one year were caring for 100 aged persons.[30]

Richmond Foundation

In 1874 Mr. Shakespeare Caldwell purchased a home for the Little Sisters in Richmond. The *Official Catholic Directory for 1875* carried the following statement in regard to the home of the Little Sisters in Richmond: "The Sisters have recently arrived in Richmond and occupy an elegant house at the corner of Ninth and Marshall Streets, which was donated for a home for aged by the late Wm. Shakespeare Caldwell, Esq. Six Sisters have already charge of thirty inmates."[31]

Chicago Foundation

After the Chicago fire in 1871 the care of the aged poor in that city became a serious problem. The only institution

---

[30] *Report of Superior Council of New York to Council General*, at Paris, 1873.
[31] Page 308.

The Care of the Aged

for the aged was the county infirmary. The members of the Particular Council of the Society of St. Vincent de Paul accordingly petitioned Bishop Thomas Foley to invite the Little Sisters of the Poor to open a home in Chicago. The Little Sisters arrived July 15, 1876, and with the assistance of the society opened a home at Polk and Halsted Streets.

This home soon proved too small and in February, 1880, a new home was opened. Two years later a second home was opened.[32] In 1894 the Little Sisters established a third home for the aged in Chicago. The same year in which the Little Sisters began their work in Chicago, 1876, they opened a home in Milwaukee. As in other cities they began in Milwaukee with a small house with accommodations for only sixteen aged persons. In two years they had a building capable of accommodating 100 inmates.[33] In 1878 a home was opened at Newark, N. J., and in the same year a second home was provided for Brooklyn.

Twenty-six Foundations Since 1881

Between 1881 and 1900 the Little Sisters of the Poor made foundations in Providence (1881), New York City (second home 1881), Kansas City (1882), New Orleans (second home 1882), Evansville, Ind. (1882), Chicago (second home 1882), St. Paul (1883), Grand Rapids, Mich. (1884), Toledo (1885), Pittsburgh (second home 1885), Cincinnati (second home 1889), Minneapolis (1889), Somerville, Mass. (1889), Savannah (1890), Chicago (third home 1894), and St. Louis (second home 1896). Since 1900 the Little Sisters have made foundations in Mobile (1901), San Francisco (1901), New Haven (1901), Paterson (1902), Wilmington (1903), Nashville (1903), New York City (third home 1903), Los Angeles (1905), and Scranton (Maloney Memorial Home, 1908). In 1917 the Little Sisters of the Poor were presented with

---

[32] *The Archdiocese of Chicago*, pp. 752-753, 786-787.
[33] *History of Milwaukee*, published by the Western Historical Company, Chicago, p. 992.

a substantial and costly building equipped to provide every comfort for the care of the aged in Denver by Mr. John K. Mullen, the noted philanthropist.[34]

Story of the Little Sisters of the Poor

The story of the Little Sisters of the Poor in the United States is one of the most interesting chapters in American Catholic history. The rapid development of their work can not be explained except as a reward for heroic and sanctified sacrifices. From a human standpoint it is an appealing service. The Little Sisters work and toil for the most neglected members of human society. The aged poor have had few friends until recent years. Public provision for them was scanty. From morning until night, the Little Sisters passed from one store to another and from one office to another to plead in their behalf. They kept up an incessant pleading. Their simplicity appealed even to the stoniest hearts. They progressed quietly but nevertheless surely. The temporary building in which they first lodged the aged was soon replaced by a stately structure and before many years passed the building would be free of debt. Moving forward at such a rapid pace and yet adhering so firmly to their old traditions the Little Sisters of the Poor are one of the great enigmas of Catholic charities. Scarcely any community has made more progress and yet changed so little.

Since they entered this country, many devices have been invented that add very greatly to human comfort and convenience. Among other things there is the telephone and the radio that have become a part of the equipment of every household. The Little Sisters will have none of them in their homes and they claim that their old folks are perfectly happy and contented without them. They seemed to have mastered the art of bringing contentment and peace to the aged. The

---

[34] *Second Annual Report of the Catholic Charities of the Diocese of Denver, Inc.*, 1928, p. 65.

spirit of sacrifice and devotion they exemplify compensates for many things that the critical observer might regard as defects.

Little Sisters Dedicated to the Destitute Poor

The Little Sisters of the Poor are dedicated to the care of the aged poor. They have no desire to care for those who have saved in whole or in part for their old age. That may be the function of others. It is not theirs. If they find that an aged person has saved some money, they will not accept him until he has expended it. They do not object to an aged person having sufficient to take care of his burial. What then is to become of persons who have saved some money but insufficient for their last years and who can not or will not be taken care of in the homes of relatives. Catholic charities must provide for them in some way. It must create special institutions for the aged who are partially self-supporting in order to supplement the work of the Little Sisters of the Poor.

Charitable institutions, like individuals, relish a sense of security. One of their basic quests is a steady income and after they are assured a steady income they work on their endowment program. This is the way of business and charity copies increasingly from business. This, however, is not the way of the Little Sisters of the Poor. They do not relish a steady and secure income. Organized financing of social work and community chests have come, but the Little Sisters are still carrying out their old rule of soliciting alms. Some people have expressed the fear that they might suffer as a result of the community chest movement but they have actually prospered.

Their large French membership undoubtedly has something to do with the retention of the traditional spirit by the Little Sisters of the Poor. A community with an American membership could not resist the tide of the times so successfully.

The Little Sisters are a most useful element in American charities. Their sacrifice, their patience, their indomitable perseverance, and even their very simplicity are an inspiration. They talk little; they work steadily. They never advertise; yet, they are always before the people. They seem to disregard the future and yet they always have sufficient for their needs.

Little Sisters Disregard Social Work Canons

It is one of the canons of modern social work that a person should not be permitted to have access to free service except on the basis of a careful study. This inquiry into a person's needs assumes that it is desirable and honest for a person to pay for service when he can do so. It assumes moreover that an agency can render more intelligent service if it has on hand fairly complete knowledge of its clients. This fundamental canon of social work applies equally to homes for the aged as well as to other social agencies. The Little Sisters of the Poor again are different. They ask very few questions. They depend on their personal contacts with and observation of the aged and their friends to secure all the information which they need.

The Little Sisters of the Poor now have fifty homes caring for 9,316 aged persons in the United States. They cover a very large sector of Catholic work for the aged, but a wide area must be cultivated by other hands.

Aged Homes of Other Religious Communities

As the Little Sisters do not take care of the aged who are wholly or partially self-supporting, this necessary service has been undertaken by other communities, that have already established some ninety Catholic homes with over 7,000 aged persons. These homes usually care for aged persons of three classes: those who can afford to pay in full; those who can afford to pay part; and those who are unable to pay. Two institutions already referred to in this chapter, namely, St. Ann's Widows' Asylum of Philadelphia and St. Francis' Asylum of Buffalo, care for aged persons who are able to pay in whole or in part as well as for those who are unable to pay. A number of institutions of the same type were established during the decades following the Civil War. In 1868 the Sisters of Charity of Mt. St. Vincent-on-the-Hudson established St. Joseph's Home for the Aged through the generosity of Miss Elizabeth Kelly, who had, in 1866, deeded them some pieces of property for this purpose. Until her death in 1883, Miss Kelly was a constant benefactress of this home, which was also given public support from the excise fund of New York City.[35]

Another illustration of the pay home for the aged is that conducted by the Sisters of Mercy in Hartford. In 1880 Mother Angela Fitzgerald, the superior of the Hartford community, began to turn her attention to the care of the aged. She began at first on a small scale, but it soon became evident that she would need a larger building with more accommodations in order to meet the needs of the city and of the diocese. The new building was dedicated April 8, 1896.[36]

Immigrant Groups Establish Aged Homes

Racial bonds have played an important part in the development of the various Catholic charities including homes for the aged. In a few places immigrant groups have built institutions for the aged for their own members. Thus the House of Divine Providence in New York City was established for the care of destitute and aged French women (1906). In Chicago, St. Joseph's Home for the Aged was founded by the Franciscan Sisters of St. Kunegunda (1895).

[35] *Catholic World*, Vol. XLIII (Sept., 1886), p. 809.
[36] J. H. O'Donnell, *History of the Diocese of Hartford*, p. 459.

Difficulties of Financing Part Pay and No Pay Aged Homes

Working out a satisfactory financial program for homes for the aged intended for those who are unable to pay as well as for those who are able to pay in full or in part, has not been an easy task. The Little Sisters of the Poor have taken care of the aged under their charge without imposing any responsibility on the different dioceses. The homes for the aged that received full or part payment somehow or other have not felt that they had any right to appeal to the public. At least, they have not mastered the technique of public appeal. "The people pay those sisters. They say Mrs. Jones gave them a thousand dollars. Why should they not be self-supporting?" The public attitude and, very frequently, the attitude of the institutions themselves was based on an illusion. Mrs. Jones gave them a thousand dollars, but she has now been in the institution fully ten years. Mrs. Smith who gave them $500 has been there as long. The span of life of those from whom they received money seems to be abnormally long. In a short time, the institution found that all its money was going out and that none was coming in. This has been the fate of a number of pay institutions for the aged. One aged person had only $300, another $400 and another $500. The institutions were willing to accept them without further question and to assume the responsibility of caring for them for the remainder of their days. In the absence of other means of support such a policy was bound to be ruinous and short-sighted. But what, one may ask, has been the way out?

Other religious communities have associated the care of the aged with some other form of work. A usual combination has been that of the hospital and home for the aged. If sufficient funds were not on hand to care for the aged the hospital came to the rescue. Examples of the combination hospital and home for the aged are, St. Joseph's Hospital and

Home for the Aged at Fort Wayne, Indiana, opened in 1869 by the Poor Handmaids of Jesus Christ, and St. Joseph's Hospital and Home for the Aged in San Francisco, conducted since 1869, by the Sisters of St. Francis of the Sacred Heart. Another type of combination is found in St. Elizabeth's Home at Glen Riddle, Pennsylvania. This home was founded in 1874 by the Sisters of the Third Order of St. Francis and has been associated with their motherhouse ever since.[37]

St. Teresa's Home of Cincinnati Solves Financial Problem

A few Catholic institutions for the aged have solved their financial problem by charging sufficient to meet all their obligations. A good illustration of this plan is St. Teresa's Home in Cincinnati. For a number of years after its opening in 1910, St. Teresa's Home was operated like a great many other Catholic homes for the aged. It received from the old people lump sums from $200 to $500. In a few years it was in financial difficulties. About 1920 it instituted a new program. It decided that in the future it would charge all its patients according to their life expectancy. A person entering at sixty-two years of age has a life expectancy of ten years. The institution figured out exactly how much it would cost to maintain this person for ten years.[38]

Catholic Home for Aged Ladies, Washington, D. C., Has Successful Program

In a few places homes for the aged through the instrumentality of carefully selected and well-organized boards of directors have succeeded in working out successful financial programs. An illustration of this type of institution is the Catholic Home for Aged Ladies in Washington, which was founded in 1911 by Monsignor Edward L. Buckey. Origi-

---

[37] *Catholic Charities and Social Welfare Activities of the Archdiocese of Philadelphia, Year Book,* 1926, p. 95.
[38] *Brochure of St. Teresa's Home,* Cincinnati, Ohio.

nally the home was financed by the contributions of its board, by the proceeds of an annual entertainment and by donations received at an annual reception of its friends. The institution has now built up a considerable endowment, the return from which is sufficient to meet the deficit on payments for those under care.[39]

Diocesan Homes for Aged

In recent years there has been a tendency in certain dioceses to regard the care of the aged as a definite diocesan responsibility. These dioceses have found that they could not depend entirely on religious communities to shoulder this burden. In Erie the Sisters of St. Joseph have been operating a home for the aged since 1884. Three years ago the institution was destroyed by fire. The bishop then decided to assume responsibility for developing a modern institution. In the latter part of 1930 the new St. Mary's Home for the Aged in Erie, one of the finest of its kind in the country, was dedicated. No feature of comfort or convenience has been overlooked in creating a homelike atmosphere. Private rooms, some with private baths, adjoining rooms for aged couples, sun parlors, a dining room with tables for four, are some of the features that make St. Mary's a true home.[40] A careful study is made of all applicants for admission.

When Bishop Daniel J. Curley of Syracuse organized his first diocesan Catholic Charities campaign in 1924 he announced that part of the funds would be used for the care of the aged. Immediately after the campaign plans were made for a new home, which would embody the best experience of the country. After careful study the Loretto Rest was built at a cost of $850,000. Every reasonable comfort and convenience was made available. Competent medical and nursing care was provided. A separate section of the

---

[39] *Brochure of Catholic Home for Aged Ladies, Washington, D. C.,* 1929, pp. 1–7.
[40] *The Lake Shore Visitor,* December 12, 1930.

building was reserved for aged couples. Applicants for admission are studied by the diocesan charities. The home is open alike to those who are entirely penniless as well as to those who can pay in whole or in part.[41] A third example of a diocesan home for the aged is the McCormick Memorial Home at Green Bay, Wisconsin. This home is operated on the same plan as the Loretto Rest. Plans are under way, at present, for the building of a diocesan home for the aged in Omaha with part of the funds raised in the recent diocesan charities campaign.

Institutional Programs Alone Can Not Solve Problem of Aged

It is recognized very clearly that the problem of old age can not be dealt with by an institutional program alone. Under modern industrial conditions, there is an increasingly large number of persons who have been unable to save sufficient for the last years of their lives. The workman has to reckon with many hazards before he comes to old age. He has the eternal problem of sickness, both for himself and his family. Unemployment is always a threat. If he and his family are fortunate enough to enjoy continuous good health, and if he holds a steady job throughout his working life, he may be able to save something for his last days. But most workmen are not so blessed. According to reliable evidence fully one-third of the American wage-earners are unable to save for old age. A problem of such proportions evidently can not be met by private initiative. A sufficient number of institutions can not be built to care for all the aged persons that need assistance.

The majority of them do not need institutional care. With proper assistance, they can be cared for in their own homes. This is what the old age pension movement is seeking to accomplish. It assumes that there are a very large number

[41] *Campaigning for Christ. The Bishop's House of Charity Campaign.* Diocese of Syracuse, 1929.

of persons who through no fault of their own are unable to provide for old age, and that it is the duty of the state to make reasonable provision for their last years. It represents a new and more humane attitude on the part of the state towards the aged. Heretofore, the only evidence of public responsibility for the aged was the almshouse. Now a number of states including New York, Massachusetts, Wisconsin, Montana, provide a public pension for persons over seventy years of age who have no means of support. The chances are that in time other states will follow. As yet some states have left the matter entirely in the hands of the different counties. Critics regard the New York law as admirably suited to the purpose. It regards the granting of the old age pension as basically a county responsibility, but the county funds are supplemented by state appropriations, which virtually gives the state authorities the power of enforcing a uniform program throughout the entire state. Old age pensions do not mean that institutions will be displaced. There will still be a place for them; for even with the aid of the pension, there will be many persons who can not be cared for in their own homes or in the homes of relatives or friends.

CHAPTER XIII

THE SOCIETY OF ST. VINCENT DE PAUL AND THE DEVELOPMENT OF CATHOLIC CHARITIES

Early America Dominated by Protestant Spirit

From the very beginning the Irish and German Catholic immigrants to this country found themselves in a hostile environment. And as they increased in numbers America became all the more hostile to them. When want and hardships overtook them there was nobody to hold out the hand of fellowship. The Yankee regarded them as contenders for the undeveloped riches of his native land. He had grown up to despise and to fear the Church to which they professed allegiance. The native New Englander, and those he had made over according to his pattern, did not look on this country as a haven for the oppressed of many lands and many creeds. He wanted here only one cultural pattern, only one religion.

Any charitable assistance rendered to immigrants was a part of the missionary or proselytizing program of Protestantism. All charity in America was dominated by a sectarian spirit and under Protestant leadership. This was quite as true of public as of private institutions. Before the Civil War Protestantism was the only religion that the inmates of almshouses were permitted to practice. Catholic services in any form were religiously excluded from these institutions. Priests were not even admitted in case of sickness and death. The Catholic religion was regarded as a foreign religion. As a matter of course almshouses placed out all children in Protestant homes. Regardless of law they continued to do so in many institutions up to the end of the century.

All public and private charity was planned with a view to

winning the immigrant, and especially his children, to Protestantism. The immigrants really found themselves isolated in a strange land. The lot of the Irish immigrants, especially during the forties and fifties, was particularly unhappy. Arriving in an unknown land they had to struggle against fearful odds. Thousands of them were so emaciated by sickness that they did not have the strength to begin an unequal struggle, and other thousands were victimized by those who are ever ready to prey on the weak and the ignorant. The fact that they were thrown back on their own resources aided the immigrants in developing a system of mutual aid.

First Charities of Catholic Immigrant Racial in Origin

In the beginning the charities of the Catholic immigrant were closely intertwined with his efforts in behalf of his native land. There were St. Patrick's and St. Boniface's beneficial societies which made strong national appeals. They grew out of a well-developed racial consciousness. They not only helped the members of the race itself but they maintained ties of love for the homeland. In some of the immigrant societies mutual assistance was the basic objective while in others the preservation of racial ideals was fundamental. Yet while raising funds for Irish political and social relief or helping to perpetuate Irish or German traditions in America, they did not overlook the needs of their American racial brethren in distress.

Ozanam's Program of Practical Charity

In May 1833, Frederick Ozanam interested a number of his fellow students at the Sorbonne in works of practical charity. For some time past this little group of kindred spirits had been trying to work out ways and means of reviving Christian teaching and Christian fervor among the people. They finally decided that the best means of doing so was by actual demonstration. Ozanam was a deep student of early Church history which taught him that the chief explanation for the success of the Church in times past was charity and the willingness of its members to sacrifice themselves in the interest of their fellow beings. Such was the genesis of the idea of the St. Vincent de Paul Society.

The Beginnings of the St. Vincent de Paul Society

Ozanam regarded his little group as a leven that would gradually permeate the whole mass of society. Example for him was more influential than teaching or writing. He visioned the practice of charity spreading from one man to another until the world was reorganized on the basis of Christian love—utopian. visionary, if you will. It was characteristic of an age in which all thinkers were talking in terms of revolutionary ideas. Ozanam's ideal was a heavenly one which can not be realized fully in this imperfect world, but, like all great ideals, it was offered as an eternal challenge to mankind. It is an ideal for which a large body of men have striven under the auspices of the St. Vincent de Paul Society.

Ozanam supplied a practical method of developing the apostolate of Christian charity. The St. Vincent de Paul Society attunes itself readily to the exercise of charity in parish life. It is a practical means of raising the whole spiritual level of the parish. Every parish needs men that it can point to as inspiring guides and exemplars. This is a role that the St. Vincent de Paul men fill admirably. They form a kind of lay priesthood in the parish. Their work is closely associated with the pastoral ministry.

In instituting the St. Vincent de Paul Society, Ozanam satisfied a great need in the Church. This explains why the St. Vincent de Paul Society has made such an appeal in every modern civilized country. It is the one active lay society that is truly international in character. There is no

Catholic organization that has been so closely identified with Catholic lay effort during the past hundred years.

St. Vincent de Paul Society in United States First Brought Together Various Immigrant Groups

The story of the St. Vincent de Paul Society in the United States is most fascinating. It was the first lay organization to bring together the various Catholic immigrant groups. When the immigrants began to organize they united along racial and national lines; but as their difficulties continued to press more heavily upon them, they came to realize how much they had in common. They had to face nativist opposition to their religion and their foreign birth. They found themselves in a hostile environment quite out of accord with the Catholic traditions in which they had been nurtured. In America the whole atmosphere was intolerant of anything that was not Protestant. American Protestant leaders honestly believed that the great hope for the immigrant was to Americanize him after their own pattern. To do this in the case of the adult would be exceedingly difficult, therefore their hope rested with the children. Hence it was that Protestant philanthropy became so much interested in "saving the children of the immigrant."

It was through the medium of philanthropic effort that the most damaging attacks were made on the Catholic faith of the poor immigrants. The whole children's aid movement represented an organized effort to win immigrant dependent children from the faith. It was an interesting coincidence that in the field of Catholic charity the immigrants should have found an organization that brought them all together and enabled them to forget racial hostilities and language differences in a common cause. The St. Vincent de Paul Society became one of the fundamental agencies through which Catholics of all races gave expression to their traditional charities.

It served as a bond of union in their struggle for the preservation of the faith of their children.

First American Conference of St. Vincent de Paul in St. Louis

The first conference of the Society of St. Vincent de Paul in this country was established in St. Louis in 1845, just twelve years after the foundation of the society in Paris. The St. Louis Conference owed its existence to Bryan J. Mullanphy who had become acquainted with the work of the St. Vincent de Paul Society during his sojourn in the French capital. Mr. Mullanphy, a son of John Mullanphy, the philanthropist, had been identified with a wide range of charitable efforts in St. Louis, a city which in his time was the gateway of the middle west. Thousands of immigrants on their way westward in quest of free land found themselves in St. Louis with their funds exhausted. It was also a haven of refuge for those who could not survive the hardships of pioneer life on the prairies and in the Rockies. St. Louis was, therefore, confronted with a very serious immigrant aid problem. The plight of the Irish immigrants made a particular appeal to Mr. Mullanphy. It was with the thought of aiding immigrants, and especially Irish immigrants in distress in St. Louis, that he set up the Mullanphy Fund. Since the immigrants have disappeared the fund has been used for travelers' aid. It is now used to support the Mullanphy Travelers' Aid Society. The courts have sustained this policy as a part of the original intent of the founder.[1]

Elder Mullanphy National Figure in Catholic Work in United States

In his charitable work Bryan Mullanphy carried on the splendid traditions established by his father, John Mullanphy. The elder Mullanphy was the great pioneer leader in the de-

---

[1] Laurence Kenny, S.J., "The Mullanphys of St. Louis," *U. S. Catholic Historical Society*, Vol. XIV, pp. 70-111.

velopment of Catholic charities in St. Louis. His name and his generosity are inextricably bound up with all the early Catholic charitable institutions of the city. His benefactions in St. Louis made the elder Mullanphy a national figure in Catholic work in the United States. When the Sisters of Charity were building their first charitable institution they appealed to Mr. Mullanphy to come to their rescue and he became their largest single benefactor.

Society of St. Vincent de Paul Made Rapid Progress in United States

During the fifteen years following its organization in St. Louis the Society of St. Vincent de Paul made rapid progress in the United States. In 1847 the society was organized in Albany; in 1848 in New York City; in 1852 in New Orleans; in 1853 in Providence; in 1855 in Brooklyn; in 1856 in St. Paul; in 1857 in Chicago and Washington; and in 1858 in Philadelphia and Louisville.[2]

What contributed more than anything else to the success of the St. Vincent de Paul Society is that it became the medium through which the immigrants struggled for the spiritual salvation of the dependent and neglected children of their race. During the first dozen or so years of its existence, the St. Vincent de Paul Society was satisfied to remain in the position of a little parish relief-giving society. In this capacity it stood, side by side, with a number of other parish and racial societies. About 1860 the Society threw off its swaddling clothes and launched out into a larger program which caught the imagination of the Catholic people. The first general project that popularized the work of the Society

[2] NOTE: The Cathedral Conference, the original conference in St. Louis, was the only branch of the Society west of the Allegheny Mountains from its establishment in 1845 until 1858. In that year Dr. L. Silliman Ives, the distinguished convert, delivered a lecture in St. Louis on the work of the Society. Such enthusiasm was aroused by his words that eleven additional conferences were organized within the next two years. In 1860, the Particular Council of St. Louis was organized. ["Organization and Development of the Society in St. Louis," *St. Vincent de Paul Quarterly*, Vol. IX, No. 4 (Nov., 1904), pp. 325-332.]

was its Sunday school work. Catholic children in the almshouses were growing up without any instruction in their faith, which was proscribed in these institutions. Catholic parishes were as yet insufficiently developed to provide religious instruction for children, and as a result thousands of these children in the poorer section of our cities were being gathered into Protestant Sunday schools.

Sunday School and Secular School Work First Projects of Society

A paper read by E. J. Hussey, president of the Particular Council of Albany, New York. at the golden jubilee celebration of the Immaculate Conception Conference of Albany gave a vivid picture of the situation in that city in the late fifties. The conference he said had been sending one of its members to the almshouse on Sundays to teach catechism. This venture was doomed to failure because the bigotry caused by Know-Nothingism brought about the request that the Society discontinue such visits. Likewise, this same spirit was behind the movement to ensnare Catholic children into the "ragged schools" or establishments opened in the poorer sections of the city for proselytizing purposes. One of these schools was in Lower Hamilton Street, Albany. Here, in 1857, the Conference of the Immaculate Conception succeeded in rescuing some twenty children from the clutches of the enemies of the faith. After providing clothing they placed the children in parochial schools. As a means of effectively combating this evil the conference decided to open a Sunday school in the rear of 22 Van Zandt Street. Immediately afterwards a night school was established at which the members of the conference with great self-sacrifice devoted their energies to instructing the children, not only in the mysteries of faith, but also in secular subjects. On February 7, 1861, another Sunday school was opened in the extreme southern section of the parish of the Immaculate Conception, Albany. The attendance here was about forty children. By this time the spirit of intolerance had exhausted itself under political pressure and religious exercises were again permitted in the almshouse. Mass was celebrated by Bishop Wadhams at which sixty-seven inmates received Holy Communion. On November 2, 1865, a Sunday school was established in the western end of the parish in a section then known as Paigeville. This locality was then so far removed from any Catholic church that the people were quite neglected. It was found that the majority of the children were attending a Protestant school. The Sunday school established here by the Society proved to be the nucleus of the Church of St. Vincent de Paul.[3]

An article in the *Baltimore Catholic Mirror*, July 2, 1859, refers to the Sunday schools conducted by the St. Vincent de Paul Society in Chicago: "Since the first of May the attention of the Conferences has been more especially directed to teaching in Sunday schools in the different parts of the city. A Sunday school has been opened in connection with the members of the Confraternity of the School of St. Francis. St. Patrick's has an attendance of 160 boys. Another has been opened in a house especially rented for that purpose and 140 boys attend regularly. The Conference has also opened a day school under the direction of lay teachers. The members do more than teach. They go out into the streets and bring the Catholic boys in."

During the sixties and seventies the Society of St. Vincent de Paul in New York, Baltimore and Washington also assisted in the teaching of Sunday schools. Teaching of Sunday schools was one of the topics considered at the second national meeting of the Society held in New York in 1865. In an address on this topic, Very Rev. William Starrs, vicar-general of New York diocese stated: "We understand from the reports given to the New York Council during the year that more could be done—that there are members in Con-

[3] *St. Vincent de Paul Quarterly*, Vol. VIII, No. 4 (Nov., 1903), pp. 273-274.

ferences throughout the country who are not actively employed and they could give their time very profitably for that purpose."[4]

Society Interests Itself in Destitute Immigrant Catholic Children

About 1862 the attention of the St. Vincent de Paul Society was turned to another problem which was destined to consume a large part of its energies during succeeding decades. A number of Protestant children's aid societies in the eastern cities were engaged in placing children, often Catholics, from eastern cities in Protestant farm homes in the middle west. The members of the Society of St. Vincent de Paul were the first to call attention to this situation. They sounded a clarion call for action. In New York City, where the children's aid societies were most active, the Society of St. Vincent de Paul assumed the leadership in organizing the association for destitute Catholic children. Through the efforts of the St. Vincent de Paul Society an industrial school for boys[5] in charge of the Christian Brothers was established in Chicago in 1863.[6]

The first special work of the Particular Council of the Society of St. Vincent de Paul of New Orleans was the foundation of St. Vincent's Home for Destitute Boys in 1866.[7] In 1870 the Particular Council of the St. Vincent de Paul Society of New York opened a home for boys in an old warehouse on Warren Street. The purpose of the home was to neutralize the influence of the sectarian homes that had been established throughout the city. In 1871 Rev. John C. Drumgoole was appointed superintendent of the home on Warren Street, and later made it the foundation stone of a whole

---

[4] *Report of the Proceedings of the Second General Assembly of the Society of St. Vincent de Paul in the United States,* 1866, p. 23.
[5] This institution is now the St. Mary's Training School for Boys at Des Plaines, Illinois.
[6] *The Archdiocese of Chicago,* p. 786.
[7] *St. Vincent de Paul Quarterly,* Vol. XV, No. 1 (Feb., 1910), p. 22.

network of institutions on Staten Island under the auspices of the Immaculate Virgin.[8]

In their efforts to save dependent children to the faith, the members of the Society of St. Vincent de Paul did not confine themselves to the establishment of Catholic institutions. In the late fifties they made an effort to reach the Catholic children in almshouses and houses of refuge. After the Civil War the barriers in many localities that prevented their entrance to these institutions had been removed. In the early seventies a number of the local Societies were very active in providing instruction for Catholic children in public institutions. At the Third General Assembly of the Society held in Philadelphia in 1876 Mr. James Lynch, president of the Superior Council of New York, reported that a number of the members from that city visited Randall's Island regularly "and taught the children their catechism and prepared them for the Sacraments." At the same meeting Mr. Thomas Hynes of the Upper Council of Brooklyn reported: "To the Truant Home we have recently been allowed entrance for the purpose of teaching the poor Catholic children confined there."[9]

A number of other local branches of the Society of St. Vincent de Paul followed the example of the New York and Brooklyn units in providing religious instruction for Catholic children in public institutions. At the Fourth General Assembly of the Society held in Washington, in 1886, Mr. Nicholas M. Williams of Boston referred to the religious work done by the Society in his city for the Catholic children in a public child-caring home.[10] Beginning in 1890 the Society of St. Vincent de Paul of Providence sent a committee every Sunday afternoon to teach catechism to the boys in the state

---

[8] *Ibid.*, Vol. VI, No. 2 (May, 1901), pp. 97–103; *Report of Proceedings of the Third General Assembly of the Society of St. Vincent de Paul in the United States*, 1876, p. 26.
[9] *Ibid.*
[10] *Report of Proceedings of the Fourth General Assembly of the Society of St. Vincent de Paul in the United States and Canada*, 1886, p. 80.

school.[11] About the same time members of the St. Vincent de Paul Society of Washington began teaching catechism to the Catholic boys in the National Training School for Boys.

Priests' Advent Has Marked Departure of Laity in Catechetical Work

One may wonder why the Society of St. Vincent de Paul has not maintained its catechetical work for Catholic children under public care with the same enthusiasm that characterized its beginnings. In practically all places priests have been appointed to take charge of the spiritual welfare of Catholic children in public institutions. The laity have, therefore, assumed or been forced to assume that their work was done. Before the members of the St. Vincent de Paul Society first began to teach catechism in the public institutions, there was no provision for the religious welfare of the Catholic children in these institutions. The Vincentian catechists recognized the limitations of their own efforts. They were convinced that they could not organize a religious program except under the leadership of a priest. Their one great desire was to have Catholic chaplains appointed to public institutions. In very few places has a cooperative program been worked out between the chaplains and the lay catechists. In most places the coming of the priest has meant the departure of the layman.

Society First Brings Consolation of Religion to Prisoners

From the very beginning the St. Vincent de Paul Society seems to have had a peculiar penchant for reaching out into the most spiritually neglected groups in the fold. The members of the Society were the first to bring the consolations of religion to Catholic prisoners. On account of the prevailing attitude towards their religion they first experienced difficulty in securing admission to the prisons, but some time after

[11] *St. Vincent de Paul Quarterly*, Vol. IX, No. 1 (February, 1904), p. 9.

the Civil War this difficulty disappeared almost entirely. At the Third General Assembly of the Society held in Philadelphia in 1876 Mr. E. J. Hussey, president of the Particular Council of Albany, reported: "Until very recently a priest was allowed entrance only in cases of extreme emergency. For fifteen years we prayed that the door of the prison would be opened to us and that we would be allowed to visit the inmates. For some time recently we have been allowed admission and regularly a number of our members accompany the priest and assist him in his instructions."[12] At the same meeting President Lynch of the Superior Council of New York spoke of the "visiting by members of the Society of persons and especially youths in the city prison (The Tombs) and other places where prisoners were temporarily confined" and of the "supplying of Catholic prisoners in the state prisons with Catholic reading matter."[13] After it had established a home for boys, the next work to which the society in New Orleans devoted its attention was that in connection with prisons begun in 1871. In 1879 this work was enlarged to include the visiting of the parish prison and the police jail.[14] Prison work was given a prominent place in the program of the Fourth General Assembly of the St. Vincent de Paul Society in the United States held in Washington in 1886. The society was now making fair headway towards its goal to have Catholic chaplains in penal institutions. A number of them were present at the Washington assembly. A paper by one of the chaplains aroused great interest and enthusiasm. After the 1886 meeting prison visitation seemed to have made a powerful appeal to the local Vincentians in Washington. It developed some of the most outstanding and consecrated leadership of the Society. It was an object of very special concern to President Thomas E. Waggaman of the Wash-

[12] *Report of the Proceedings of the Third General Assembly of the Society of St. Vincent de Paul in the United States*, 1876, p. 26.
[13] *Ibid.*, p. 25.
[14] *St. Vincent de Paul Quarterly*, Vol. XV, No. 1 (Feb., 1910), p. 22.

ington Society from 1885 to 1886. It brought out such apostles as William F. Downey whom President Roosevelt characterized as "a model citizen and a man of whom Washington may well be proud," Rev. Joseph L. McGuire, the chaplain of the special works committee, an influential civic leader between 1900 and 1908, and Joseph Colton, "the prisoners' friend."

Society Devotes Attention to Relationship of Ill Health to Poverty

Between 1890 and 1900 the Society of St. Vincent de Paul, like other organizations dealing with families in need of special care, began to devote special attention to the relationship of ill health to poverty. During that decade various tuberculosis societies were organized to combat the great ravages of tuberculosis among the children of the poor. This naturally developed an emphasis on health programs and particularly on preventive health work. It gave a great impetus to the development of more adequate health facilities. As part of their general health programs, agencies dealing with families in need of relief became interested in providing summer outings for mothers and children. It was recognized that if mothers and children could get away from their cramped quarters in the city and enjoy the wholesome, invigorating air of the country, even for one week in the summer, it would not only improve their health, but also their whole outlook on life.

The St. Vincent de Paul Society was quick to catch the spirit of the new movement. In March, 1899, the Particular Council of the Society in New York decided to organize summer outings for mothers and children. In the beginning the program consisted merely of excursions to Belden Point.[15] In the early part of 1903 the society purchased the site and buildings for a Fresh Air Home at Spring Valley.[16]

[15] *Ibid.*, Vol. IV, No. 2 (May, 1899), pp. 151–153.
[16] *Ibid.*, Vol. VIII, No. 1 (February, 1903), p. 142.

Summer Outings Become an Absorbing Project

In 1901 the Particular Council of the Society of St. Vincent de Paul of Philadelphia took up the problem of summer outings as a matter of pressing necessity. A number of non-Catholic societies were taking children to the country every summer and, of course, they were taking a number of Catholic children. The members of the St. Vincent de Paul Society became concerned about the faith of the children provided for by non-Catholic agencies. The only alternative seemed to be the organization of a Catholic summer outings program. A committee, therefore, was appointed to make the necessary plans. A permanent site and permanent buildings were things that required careful planning and large expenditures. During the first five years the committee had to be satisfied with temporary locations. The work continued to grow from year to year; the number of children cared for increased from about 200 in 1901 to approximately 700 in 1907. In 1906 the Society, through the assistance of Archbishop Ryan, secured a farm of twelve acres with a fourteen-room house at Port Kennedy, Pennsylvania, about eighteen miles from Philadelphia. It was called the "Brice Home" after the name of the non-Catholic family who presented it to the archbishop. The Society planned to use its summer outing home as a convalescent home during the remainder of the year.[17]

In January 1905, Thomas M. Mulry and Edmond J. Butler of the Superior Council of the St. Vincent de Paul Society in the United States addressed a largely attended meeting of the Particular Council of Baltimore. In the course of his address Mr. Mulry stressed the fresh air work of the New York Vincentians and its place in a Catholic charities program; but the Society in Baltimore had set its mind on other projects from which it could not be diverted. Summer out-

---

[17] *Ibid.*, Vol. XI, No. 3 (August, 1906), pp. 253, 254, 297–299.

Society of St. Vincent de Paul 249

ings might be very necessary in New York but other things were more necessary in Baltimore.

There was, however, one member of the Baltimore Society, Mr. Joseph Brooks, who was deeply impressed by Mr. Mulry's talk. He was convinced that Baltimore needed such a program and was determined that Baltimore should have it. He finally won over the members of the Society with the rather distinct understanding that he would assume the leadership and the major share of the responsibility for the project. The aid of the Sulpician Fathers was enlisted. They agreed to let the Vincentians use, rent free, a fine estate near Catonsville. Such were the beginnings of summer outings for poor mothers and children under Catholic auspices in Baltimore.[18]

The Vincentians of Brooklyn were unwilling to be outdone by those in neighboring Manhattan. No sooner was the program under way in Manhattan than a similar movement was undertaken in Brooklyn. Lack of funds, however, preevnted the consummation of their program until 1906. In that year the Daughters of Wisdom, a community of exiled French Nuns, offered their property and volunteered to take charge of the children. Since that time the work has proceeded at an accelerated pace.[19]

Apostolate of the Sea

There is another special work of the Society of St. Vincent de Paul which has become a part of its international traditions, namely, the Apostolate of the Sea. The spiritual and material welfare of seamen away from home has made a strong appeal to Vincentians in seaboard cities. In 1903 the Particular Council of New Orleans felt obligated to do something for the welfare of seamen coming into port. With the approval and promise of support of all the conferences the council leased a building on the water front for the comfort

[18] *Ibid.*, pp. 250–252.
[19] *Ibid.*, pp. 252–253.

and convenience of seafaring men.[20]   A similar work for seafarers has been organized by the St. Vincent de Paul Society in Philadelphia, Boston, Brooklyn and Los Angeles.

Society Warns Against Catholic Child-Placing in West

One always notices in the St. Vincent de Paul Society a certain freshness of viewpoint. The Society is not satisfied with stereotyped solutions of social problems. There always appear in its ranks healthy differences of viewpoint as new ideas are contributed by the rank and file of its membership. Immediately after the Civil War when placement in the country homes in the middle west was regarded as a Utopia for dependent and neglected Catholic children, we have a note of warning coming from the ranks of the St. Vincent de Paul Society. At the Second General Assembly of the Society held in New York in 1866, Dr. Ives, President of the Association for the Protection of Destitute Catholic Children, and an active Vincentian, stated that the care of destitute children was primarily a matter of proper care and direction in their own homes. ''I have been employed for the last three years,'' he continued, ''in attending poor children, destitute children, a large part of whom are presented to me as truants, as children who are not governed by their mothers and in most cases their fathers are either dead or useless. . . . It struck me that this was an important work for the members of the St. Vincent de Paul Society who ought to know all these facts by experience because most of these children are within their reach and if proper influence were exercised over them so that they could be controlled through the kind rules of Sunday Schools or other modes of patronage they would not only be brought to do their duty towards their parents but become good and useful members of society. Let it be remembered that these children in many instances are not presented to us for want of means of support but simply for want of

[20] *Ibid.*, Vol. IX, No. 2 (May, 1904), p. 189.

obedience. . . . They can be reached by the Society of St. Vincent de Paul, and be brought to a state of obedience." This doctrine may be regarded as fundamental today but it was not so considered in 1866. Dr. Ives may be regarded rightly as the prophet of a new era in child care.[21]

The Catholic Home Bureau of New York

After 1870 the members of the Society of St. Vincent de Paul joined wholeheartedly in the movement to find homes for children in the overcrowded Catholic institutions. The question was discussed very fully and very freely at the Third General Assembly of the Society held in Philadelphia in 1876. The Vincentians from the east looked to their brothers in the west to aid in the matter. Protestant Children's Aid Societies had been able to find homes for children in the middle west. Why should Catholic institutions not be able to do likewise? Various plans were proposed. Western conferences might inform eastern councils and conferences of opportunities for placing children. Institutions might be established in the middle west that would accept children from the east. There was no unanimity of opinion on any plan. Many of the Vincentians were skeptical about any plan for the placement of children from the east in middle western homes. They felt that the middle west had sufficient problems of its own. The Superior Council of New York was finally delegated to address a letter to the bishops placing the Society at their disposal to carry out any plan they might adopt.[22]

Between 1890 and 1898 there was considerable discussion of institutional methods of placing children. It was charged that by reason of faulty methods of placement, many of the children found their way into the almshouses. Criticism of

---

[21] *Report of the Proceedings of the Second General Assembly of the Society of St. Vincent de Paul in the United States,* 1866, p. 74.
[22] *Report of the Proceedings of the Third General Assembly of the Society of St. Vincent de Paul,* 1876, p. 33.

the institutions which they had promoted found the leaders of the St. Vincent de Paul Society particularly sensitive. They were convinced that something should be done to meet it. There was no use in arguing that the institution alone could satisfy all the requirements of a child-caring program. The old methods of placing children out from institutions were now discredited. The St. Vincent de Paul leaders in New York, including Thomas Mulry and Edmond J. Butler, felt that the time had come for a new Catholic placing program. This was the thought underlying the organization of the Catholic Home Bureau of New York in the latter part of 1898. It had the wholehearted approval of Archbishop Corrigan. "The project of establishing a Catholic Home Bureau impresses me favorably and seems likely to accomplish good results. In the first place it will prevent over-crowding of our institutions and relieve us of the care of many children who are now dependent on charity and will enable them to become self-reliant." [23] A letter sent to the clergy by Mr. Mulry, who was its prime mover, explained in detail the functions of the Bureau:

> To place destitute, dependent, or neglected children in family homes in accordance with the laws of the State of New York, and for that purpose to receive such children by surrender, commitment or otherwise and to do such other work as may tend to improve the condition of the children.
> Experience has shown us that in the city of New York alone hundreds of children of Catholic parentage are every year placed in non-Catholic institutions, or families where their faith must almost inevitably be lost.
> We realize, too, that our Catholic institutions are in danger of becoming over-crowded, and their highest usefulness in a measure at least impaired by the necessity of retaining and properly caring for children long after the age when they might safely be placed in private families.

[23] *St. Vincent de Paul Quarterly*, Vol. IV, No. 1 (February, 1899), pp. 49–50.

'Tis true our well equipped institutions are doing a grand work for these children, but that work should be supplemented by an earnest effort on the part of the people to open up to these children, already trained and instructed, the avenues that lead to employment and self-support.[24]

The Catholic Home Bureau of New York was the forerunner of a number of similar projects in Catholic child care in the United States. In 1909 the Particular Council of the Society of St. Vincent de Paul in Washington established a Catholic Home Bureau modelled after the New York plan. In 1913 the Detroit Society opened a child-caring department which has become one of the largest and best equipped placing organizations in the United States.

Society Undertakes Spiritual Care of Catholic Children in Houses of Refuge

One of the first works of the Society of St. Vincent de Paul was the spiritual care of Catholic children in the houses of refuge. Contact with these children naturally led the more far-seeing members of the society back to the court procedure that brought the children to the institutions. A number of Vincentians were therefore very much interested in removing children from the ordinary criminal courts and developing a special procedure for them. Among the outstanding Vincentian leaders in this movement was Judge Timothy D. Hurley, an active member of the St. Vincent de Paul Society of Chicago. In the early eighties Judge Hurley organized the Catholic Visitation and Aid Society in Chicago for the purposes of visiting Catholics in the various public institutions and especially boys in the reform school. By reason of his interest in the care and treatment of juvenile delinquents Judge Hurley was appointed a member of the committee that formulated the first juvenile court law for Illinois

[24] *Ibid.*, Vol. IV, No. 2 (May, 1899), pp. 146–147.

which the legislature passed in 1899. The juvenile courts were supposed to deal with the presented cases on an individual basis. In order to do this the courts had to know the special considerations in each case, such as the home conditions surrounding the children, their progress in school and the manner in which their leisure was spent. In the past, courts had no machinery for securing information of this kind, and little interest in it. They depended upon such facts as could be secured from the plaintiff, the defendant, and the police. When the laws creating juvenile courts were first enacted no new officers were added to care for these added responsibilities. They were just given the personnel of the ordinary courts. In order that they might be able to do this work they were compelled to call upon private agencies including the St. Vincent de Paul Society. In a paper read at the International Convention of the St. Vincent de Paul Society in St. Louis in 1904, Mr. Patrick Mallon of Brooklyn described the work of the Brooklyn Society in connection with the children's court of that city. It employed a full-time woman worker as a probation officer for young women and girls in the Juvenile Court. This worker was given charge of the Catholic girls placed on probation. The members of the parish conferences cooperated with the probation officer in supervising the children under care.[25]

Organized Recreation Programs Undertaken by Society

In 1896 the Society of St. Vincent de Paul of New York began to think seriously of the possibilities of organized recreation for the boy on the city streets. Protestant agencies had been successful in organizing clubs and athletic programs for boys. Why could the Catholic parishes not do likewise? The Society, therefore, began to organize boys' clubs in the different parishes. A report of one of the clubs, in 1897, shows the progress of one year's work. Beginning with

[25] *Ibid.*, Vol. X, No. 3 (August, 1905), pp. 268-273.

only a small club room and a rather crude gymnasium, there had been added a library of over 400 books, a recreation room, a loft for drills and the practice of the newly organized fife and drum corps and a classroom where instruction was given in catechism, bookkeeping, and debating. The varied types of amusement and diversion appealed to the boys, and the club promised to be a real success.[26]

The Ozanam Association

In 1908 it was decided that it would be no longer desirable to carry on the boys' club movement as a special work of the St. Vincent de Paul Society in New York. The Ozanam Association was, therefore, established and assigned the four clubs which had heretofore been administered by the St. Vincent de Paul Society.[27]

Relationship Between St. Vincent de Paul and Charity Organization Society

The relations between the St. Vincent de Paul Society and the Charity Organization Society form one of the most interesting chapters in Catholic charities in the United States. In the early nineties the Vincentians of New York under the leadership of Mr. Mulry decided to affiliate themselves more closely with the Charity Organization Society. A number of them accepted membership on the district committees of the Society. A paper written by Mr. Thomas M. Mulry on the "Cooperation of United Charities" emphasized the new relations between Catholic and non-Catholic charities. He endeavored to show that the old spirit of proselytism was on the wane. The establishment of the Charity Organization Society, a non-sectarian clearing house, had done much to dissipate the old prejudice and to stress the mutual advantages

---

[26] *Ibid.*, Vol. II, No. 4 (November, 1897), pp. 316–317.
[27] *Ibid.*, Vol. XIII, No. 4, pp. 364–365.

of cooperation.[28] The situation which he described did not come about without a long struggle.

The writer had the privilege of hearing Mr. Mulry tell about his early contacts with the Charity Organization Society. It was like an excursion into another world. In the late eighties Mr. Mulry was an active member of a St. Vincent de Paul Conference in lower Manhattan, New York City. As a conference visitor he came into contact with many Catholic families in which the Charity Organization Society was active and from which they had received children and placed them in Protestant homes. He thought that if he could only join the district conference of the latter Society he could change its attitude and policies. He took up the matter with his pastor who timidly felt he could not advise him without communicating with the archbishop. From the archbishop word came later that the young man might affiliate with the Charity Organization Conference as an individual but not as an official representative of the St. Vincent de Paul Society. When Mr. Mulry affiliated with the district conference he found it thoroughly Protestant in all its attitudes and policies. A visitor would come before the conference and say the great difficulty with such and such a family is that it is dominated too much by the influence of the Roman Church, or it is too superstitious; the greatest service that can be conferred on the children of this family is to have them removed from Roman influence.

The same working relationship that existed between the St. Vincent de Paul Society and the Charity Organization Society in New York was also found in Baltimore. This without doubt marked the beginning of a new era in American charities. It made the Charity Organization Society a non-sectarian organization in reality as it always had been in name. It opened to the members of the St. Vincent de Paul Society an exceptionally rich field of experience. It gave

[28] *Ibid.*, Vol. III, No. 4 (November, 1898), pp. 314–315.

them a clearer understanding of their limitations and their possibilities. As a result of their contact with the Charity Organization Society they began to recognize that charity work was a cooperative work and that the individual agency could no longer work in isolation. Another idea that the Vincentians gathered from their contact with the Charity Organization Society was the need of full-time workers in order to make the work of the volunteers truly effective. In those days the line of demarcation between the volunteer and the paid worker was not so marked as at present. Many times the volunteer surpassed the full-time worker both in training and experience. The Vincentians, moreover, learned much from the Charity Organization Society in regard to the value of a central coördinating agency for charity. Later, they did much to popularize this plan in Catholic charities. Their contact with the Charity Organization Society was bound to have a far-reaching influence on the outlook of St. Vincent de Paul visitors. It opened up to them the channels of communication with a large fund of experience in social work and contacts with some of the best minds in the country.

Society Pioneering Group Since Civil War

Ever since the Civil War the Society of St. Vincent de Paul had been the pioneering group in Catholic charities in the United States. It was always looking ahead to new and unfilled needs in Catholic work. Its contact with the Charity Organization Society aided the Society of St. Vincent de Paul in further pioneering in Catholic charities. There were two elements in the program of the Charity Organization Society that especially impressed the Vincentian visitors. The Charity Organization Society set up a central clearing house for all the charities of the community. Why could not the St. Vincent de Paul Society do the same for Catholic charities with its various allied units? Why could it not establish a clearing house for its own parish conferences? A central clearing house would provide information on families moving from one parish to another. It would provide a central point of contact with the other social agencies of the city. It could aid families in parishes in which there was no St. Vincent de Paul conference.

Society Adverse in Beginning to Paid Service

At first the members of the Society of St. Vincent de Paul were not much impressed by the possibilities of paid service. They were inclined to place themselves on a pedestal above those who were compelled to accept pay for their work. One Vincentian of high standing whose experience has extended over forty years attributes the attitude of Vincentians towards paid workers to racial traditions. In the mind of the immigrant charity meant service extended without hope of material reward. The only forms of charitable service to which they were accustomed were those rendered by the laity on a volunteer basis and those rendered by religious communities whose members had dedicated their lives to service. The lay worker who dedicated his life to service but who was compelled to depend on his labor to secure the necessities of life for his own family was something new in their experience.

Central Office Established by Society in Baltimore

The question of full-time lay service in Catholic charities had to be faced sooner or later in the light of facts. It is rather common to note that the advisability of full-time paid service in connection with the special works of the Society of St. Vincent de Paul, like child-placing and fresh air work, had never been questioned. The debate was confined entirely to the advisability of service to families in their own homes.

The debate in regard to the advisability of paid service in family welfare work was brought to a focus by the establishment under the auspices of the Particular Council of the Society of St. Vincent de Paul in Baltimore of a central office with a salaried staff. Many Vincentian leaders began to regard the Baltimore plan as the only solution of their problems. They recognized that in certain work volunteers could not give adequate attention and that the services of paid workers were necessary. Other Vincentians taking a more conservative view of the situation were unwilling to recognize the limitations of volunteer service. The Baltimore program was tried in a mild form in Chicago. The Society of St. Vincent de Paul in that city established a central office in 1911 as a clearing house for the parish conferences and for emergency cases.[29]

Adjustment of Society to Central Agencies Under Diocesan Auspices

Before the Society of St. Vincent de Paul as a whole had made much progress in the development of full-time service in Catholic family welfare work the responsibility passed to other hands. The various dioceses had come to take an official interest in developing a full-time service program for families in need of special care. The question now confronting the members of the St. Vincent de Paul Society was how to adjust their activities to a full-time family service program under diocesan auspices. The period of adjustment was bound to be a transitional one in the work of the Society. Without attempting to analyze a situation that is still with us, the writer can not refrain from two observations. While it was not given to the Society of St. Vincent de Paul to work out a program for Catholic family welfare work, the society did excellent pioneer work in this as in other fields of Catholic charity. What would have happened to such pioneering had the work of developing a full-time program been left in the hands of the Vincentians? The tendency on the part of a number of dioceses to return to the St. Vincent de Paul Society in developing their family service program is also note-

[29] *The Archdiocese of Chicago*, p. 788.

worthy. The most far-reaching developments in this field have taken place in St. Louis, Buffalo and Milwaukee.

Society Has Aided Development of National Outlook in Catholic Charities

One of the most interesting contributions of the Society of St. Vincent de Paul is the development of a national outlook in charity work in the face of strong local, diocesan traditions in the American Catholic Church. Even after the Civil War whatever national unity was found among the Catholics was more of a racial than a religious character. Both the Irish and the German Catholics had their national societies with a national outlook. But the St. Vincent de Paul Society was the first Catholic lay organization to bring together Catholics of different nationalities on a local basis and later on a national platform.

Division of Organization of Society of St. Vincent de Paul in the United States

When the Superior Council of New York was instituted in January 1860, it was assumed that it would exercise jurisdiction over the whole Society in the United States. The Brooklyn organization however refused to accept the jurisdiction of New York and continued to deal directly with the Council General at Paris. In 1863 a Superior Council of the Society was instituted at St. Louis and, in 1869, the New Orleans Superior Council was instituted.

While the Superior Council of the New York Society of St. Vincent de Paul did not have actual jurisdiction over the Society in this country, it exercised a leadership that was rather far-reaching in its influence. It was responsible for the first National Assembly of the Society held in New York in 1865. It was responsible for the second National Assembly held in New York City in 1866, for the third in Philadelphia in 1876, and for the fourth in Washington in 1886. The

Superior Council of New York called a national meeting of the Society at the World's Fair in Chicago and an International Meeting of the Society in St. Louis in 1904.

The National Meetings of the Society of St. Vincent de Paul as a Stimulus to Catholic Charities in the United States

These national meetings were the first focal points for national planning in regard to Catholic charities. Each local group was striving as best it could to meet its own problems. It scarcely had any channels of communication with other communities. There was no means by which the experience of each might be made available to all. The leaders of the St. Vincent de Paul Society were the first to rise to the occasion. They envisioned the problems as national problems; they were anxious to develop a national outlook in regard to them. From reading the Proceedings of the first National Assemblies of the Society of St. Vincent de Paul, one is caught by the enthusiasm which was communicated from one group to another. The whole spirit of the meetings vibrated with glowing enthusiasm and apostolic zeal. The Vincentians from one city told how they succeeded in the face of great opposition in bringing the consolations of religion to Catholics in the penal institutions; they told of new Sunday schools set up; they told of institutions established for dependent and neglected children. The Vincentians from other cities were moved to do likewise. From the national meetings of the St. Vincent de Paul Society there radiated a spirit that did much towards the development of Catholic charities in the United States.

Agitation for the Reorganization of the Society of St. Vincent de Paul in the United States

The existence of four Superior Councils of the Society of St. Vincent de Paul in this country, namely, New York, Brooklyn, St. Louis and New Orleans, was regarded by Vincentian leaders as a handicap to unity of action. Beginning in 1886 serious thought was given to the possibility of bringing the four councils together under one Superior Council. In a paper on this topic delivered at the Fourth General Assembly of the Society held in the National Capital in that year, Mr. Joshua Huntington, formerly President of the Particular Council of Washington, said: "Under the present organization of the Society of St. Vincent de Paul in the United States there is little or no union of action. Even the existence of the western branches of the Society is unknown to many of its members in the east. That we should be obliged to go to Dublin or Paris to learn what they are doing in Louisiana or Missouri seems an unnatural arrangement, and one which should be changed if possible." [30]

The coördination of the activities of the Society of St. Vincent de Paul in the United States under one Superior Council was considered at the national meeting held in Chicago in 1893 and at the international meeting held in St. Louis in 1904, but without any definite decision. At the national meeting of the Society held in Richmond, in 1908, a resolution was adopted recommending a reorganization of the Society in the United States. The proposed reorganization called for one Superior Council and an Upper Council in each ecclesiastical province. The Superior Council would be known as the Superior Council of the United States and would be composed of the presidents of the Upper Councils and twelve members selected by the president of the Superior Council.[31]

At a meeting held in 1912 the problem of reorganizing the Society in the United States again came up for consideration. The matter had been placed before the Council General for decision but that body decided that the time was not ripe for placing all the branches of the Society in the United States under one central direction. It recommended the organiza-

[30] *Report of Proceedings of the Fourth General Assembly of the Society of St. Vincent de Paul in the United States and Canada*, 1886, p. 61.
[31] *St. Vincent de Paul Quarterly*, Vol. XIII, No. 3 (August, 1908), p. 265.

tion of additional superior councils similar to those already in existence. It was therefore decided to proceed immediately with the organization of Superior Councils in Boston and Philadelphia. This made in all seven separate jurisdictions of the Society of St. Vincent de Paul in the United States. It was the last straw. The process of decentralization had gone to the extreme. Vincentians everywhere saw the handwriting on the wall. They must have one supreme body for the entire United States.

The councils throughout the United States were willing finally to submerge their differences and work together under one common body by 1914.[32] A year later, the Superior Council of the Society of St. Vincent de Paul became an accomplished fact. The Catholic University at Washington was to be its headquarters and Thomas M. Mulry of New York was elected its first President.[33]

The Society of St. Vincent de Paul Takes Initiative in Organizing Catholic Charities

In its effort to develop a national outlook in Catholic charities, the Society of St. Vincent de Paul was anxious to include charities other than those under its immediate direction. Under the leadership and guidance of the officers of the Superior Council of New York what practically amounted to a National Conference of Catholic Charities was held at the Catholic Summer School, Cliff Haven, New York (August, 1898).[34] The development of its special works interested the Society in many charities outside of the parish. From the very beginning it had endeavored to foster special programs in Catholic charities. As many of the Catholic charitable institutions and organizations of the United States owed their origins either directly or indirectly to the St. Vincent de Paul

[32] *Ibid.*, Vol. XIX, No. 4 (November, 1914), pp. 270-271.
[33] *Ibid.*, Vol. XX, No. 3 (August, 1915), p. 169; *Catholic News*, October 23, 1915.
[34] *St. Vincent de Paul Quarterly*, Vol. III, No. 2 (May, 1898), pp. 131-132; Vol. III, No. 4 (November, 1898), pp. 315-316.

Society, it was quite natural that the Society should have assumed leadership in developing a more definite bond of union between the various Catholic charitable organizations. Dealing as they were with problems of family life the St. Vincent de Paul leaders recognized the limitations of the special charities.

Organization of Catholic Women's Charitable Societies

The National Conference of Catholic Charities held in Cliff Haven evidently was not continued. At the international meeting of the Society of St. Vincent de Paul held in St. Louis in 1904, many of the larger problems of Catholic charities were discussed. There was deep interest in the establishment of juvenile courts. Problems of child-placing were fully discussed. The Richmond convention showed a wider interest in problems of Catholic charities. A significant result of this meeting was the formation of a national association of isolated Catholic women's organizations in the United States to be known as St. Elizabeth's Union.

The St. Vincent de Paul Society had national meetings that aided in developing a national consciousness. Why could not Catholic women's organizations be banded together in the same way? Why could they not enjoy the advantages of a national clearing house of experience? Rev. Dr. D. J. McMahon, Supervisor of Catholic Charities in New York, was largely responsible for calling together the representatives of Catholic women's organizations in connection with the St. Vincent de Paul meeting in Richmond. He had witnessed the wholesome results of close cooperation between the St. Vincent de Paul Society and the Ladies of Charity. Would not an annual conference of Catholic women's organizations held at the same time and place with the annual meeting of the Society of St. Vincent de Paul tend to foster such cooperation on a national basis?[35] The meetings of the So-

---

[35] *Ibid.*, Vol. XIII, No. 3 (August, 1908), pp. 268–269.

ciety of St. Vincent de Paul and of Catholic women's organizations held in Richmond laid the foundation of a National Conference of Catholic Charities, although the participants did not realize that they were preparing the way for a National Conference of Catholic Charities.

National Conference of Catholic Charities

Brother Barnabas, a Christian brother, who had been very active in the Richmond meetings, addressed a letter to Bishop Thomas J. Shahan, rector of the Catholic University of America, in which he suggested the establishment of a National Conference of Catholic Charities (1909). Exactly what he had in mind is doubtful. For nearly twenty years he had been active in Catholic and civic work in New York City and State. Very probably he had found that social work was no longer merely a practical method of attending to the problems of the needy but that it was developing its own philosophy. This made it all the more necessary for Catholic workers to be guided by fundamental principles of Catholic philosophy.

The Literature of the Catholic Charities Movement

The literature of Catholic charities as late as 1910 consisted only of reports of institutions and organizations. Most of these were purely statistical. They give little insight into methods and results. Lost in the files of Catholic newspapers, there were a number of articles and sermons by Catholic priests and bishops in which the nature and motives of Catholic charities are restated. In a scientific way, there was little contribution. By far the most valuable literature that we find in 1910 were the papers and addresses of the meetings of the Society of St. Vincent de Paul. Between 1895 and 1916 the Superior Council of New York published what was known as the *St. Vincent de Paul Quarterly*. This is the best source book of Catholic charities. The Quarterly did not contain many original articles but rather papers and addresses delivered on various occasions by the members of the Society. From its pages one obtains a picture of the struggles of the Catholic laity to apply the traditional principles of the Church to the solution of modern problems of American life. *The Proceedings* of the various annual assemblies of the Society of St. Vincent de Paul present a picture of the growth and development of a Catholic leadership.

The Conference a Union of Catholic Viewpoints

Brother Barnabas hardly recognized all the possibilities of a National Conference of Catholic Charities. He was a practical man and he saw the practical results of a conference, but the men, Bishop Shahan and Rev. Dr. William J. Kerby, whom he urged to assume leadership, thought in terms of its largest social and philosophical implications. They were men of vision and scientifically trained minds. At any rate the Conference, when it was formed in 1910, represented a merger of two points of view in Catholic work, namely, the academic and the practical.

The Vincentians the Backbone of the National Conference

The Society of St. Vincent de Paul became the backbone of the National Conference of Catholic Charities. When Bishop Shahan and Dr. Kerby looked around the country for men whom they might call together for the preliminary meetings of the first Conference they were compelled to fall back on the leaders of the St. Vincent de Paul Society. Their cooperation in establishing the National Conference of Catholic Charities in 1910 was not intended to interfere with the autonomy of the Society of St. Vincent de Paul. It was decided that the Conference of Catholic Charities would meet biennially at the Catholic University and that the Society of St. Vincent de Paul would meet at the same place and time. In the off years the Society planned to hold its own annual meeting. Since 1920, the National Conference of Catholic

Charities has been meeting annually and the Society of St. Vincent de Paul has been holding its meetings simultaneously.

A Catholic Charities Monthly Advocated

In 1899 the editor of the *St. Vincent de Paul Quarterly* suggested that the magazine should be published monthly. In a paper read at the Richmond meeting, Dr. Kerby suggested the establishment of a Catholic Charities monthly magazine, which the delegates unanimously favored.[36] At its first meeting the National Conference of Catholic Charities went on record in favor of a monthly review. In 1914, a joint committee of the National Conference of Catholic Charities and the Society of St. Vincent de Paul was appointed to study the advisability of publishing a Catholic Charities Review. In 1915, the Superior Council of the Society of St. Vincent de Paul resolved that such a review should succeed the old *St. Vincent de Paul Quarterly* in the event that a section of the review should be reserved for the St. Vincent de Paul Society. In 1916 the National Conference of Catholic Charities went on record in favor of a Catholic Charities Review to be published monthly. In November 1916, the *St. Vincent de Paul Quarterly* which for twenty years had been a valuable storehouse of information on Catholic Charities published its last issue. It was succeeded by the *Catholic Charities Review* in January 1917.

The Vincentians' Part in Formulating Standards of American Philanthropy

The members of the Society of St. Vincent de Paul were the first Catholic laymen to participate actively in social and civic movements. This participation on their part was not the result of any organized action on the part of the Society. For years it was defensive. When the Charity Organization Society released itself from sectarian moorings, it offered a

[36] *Ibid.*, Vol. XXI, No. 4 (November, 1916), pp. 283–284.

welcoming hand to representatives of all denominations. Among Catholics invited, they naturally included members of the St. Vincent de Paul Society. Some with the past in mind spurned the invitation, but others recognized it as an opportunity of entering the old enemy's camp and gladly accepted. Yet, the first Vincentians entered into this communion with natural timidity and misgivings. They expected to find a thoroughly Protestant atmosphere, to find workers who were weaning Catholic children away from their faith. They were not disappointed. Their presence modified bigotry and tended to end old policies. They found the leaders of the Charity Organization movement willing to cooperate and even anxious for the guidance of St. Vincent de Paul men in their work. A number of them assumed positions of leadership in the general field of social work. Mr. Mulry and Mr. Butler became outstanding leaders in the New York State Conference of Social Work and also took an important part in the sessions of the National Conference of Social Work of which Mr. Mulry was elected president in 1907. Vincentians, therefore, deserve a share of the credit in terminating active proselytizing on the part of organized American philanthropy.

The Influence of the Vincentians Through the National Conference on Child Welfare

In the latter part of 1908 a group of persons representing various child-caring agencies and institutions requested President Roosevelt to call a national conference on child welfare. The President refused to consider their petition without the cooperation of Mr. Mulry as a representative of Catholic child-caring interests. On President Roosevelt's suggestion the group decided to confer with Mr. Mulry and his name was included in the hundred outstanding citizens petitioning for the conference. When President Roosevelt called the conference which has come to be known as the 1909 White House Conference on Child Welfare to meet in the East Room of the White House, both Mr. Mulry and Mr. Butler took a prominent part in its deliberations. Butler was a member of the committee on resolutions which brought together the best American experience in child welfare and paved the way for some of the most important developments of subsequent years. Thus the ideals of the Society of St. Vincent de Paul had an opportunity of permeating the program of American child welfare.

In 1919 the United States Children's Bureau called a conference on child welfare for the purpose of reviewing the ten years' progress since the first White House Conference and to chart the lines of a future program. Mr. Butler, as a representative of the St. Vincent de Paul Society and of Catholic interests, again took an active part in the conference as chairman of its committee on Standards for Children Requiring Special Care.

A True Evaluation of the Society of St. Vincent de Paul

It would be a mistake to evaluate the work of the St. Vincent de Paul Society in the United States solely as a relief-giving organization. Its best contributions have been its sensitiveness to the needs of the Church in each period of its history; its influence in the development of a high type of spiritual leadership; and the inspiration that it gave to a certain number of its members to assume a leadership in social and civic movements. In 1872 the various councils and isolated conferences of the Society of St. Vincent de Paul coming under the jurisdiction of the Superior Council of New York expended a total of $104,440 for the relief of 7,058 families.[37] In 1882 the same councils and conferences expended $127,227 for the relief of 9,936 families; in 1893 they expended $184,-

---

[37] *Report of Superior Council of New York to Council General at Paris,* 1872, pp. 18–19.

410 for the relief of 19,470 families; in 1905 they expended $235,205 for the care of 19,193 families.

During the two decades following the Civil War the Society of St. Vincent de Paul in its parish work gave as much attention to the religious instruction of neglected Catholic children as to material relief. It may be noted that up to 1893 special provision was made on the blanks on which the councils and conferences made their report to the Superior Council of New York for members assisting in Sunday school work. In 1894 this question was evidently eliminated from the information blank because there is no longer any reference to it in the reports made by the various councils to the Superior Council of New York.[38] Instead of the question in regard to Sunday schools, there is substituted one with regard to situations procured. In the nineties the various councils were giving more attention to their special works. Thereafter some of the very ablest Vincentians were developed by the special works committees.

The whole history of the Society of St. Vincent de Paul is the story of the rise of a great spiritual leadership from the ranks of the Catholic laity. Out of the immigrant settlements, here, there and everywhere, arose groups of men consumed with a noble enthusiasm for the faith of neglected Catholic children. They banded the children together in Sunday Schools. They kept up a constant bombardment at the door of public institutions until they were permitted to bring the message of faith to the Catholic inmates. They led in the building of institutions for neglected Catholic children. They played a large part in obliging American philanthrophy to respect the religion of Catholic families under its care. They pioneered in keeping Catholic charities abreast of the times and in bringing to it the best experience in American social work. Catholic child-placing, organized Catholic aid for handicapped fami-

---

[38] *Report of Superior Council of New York to Council General at Paris*, 1893, p. 106; *Ibid.*, 1894, pp. 122-123.

lies, summer fresh air work, day nurseries, Catholic work for delinquent children, owe their origin very largely to the pioneer efforts of the members of the St. Vincent de Paul Society. It is all a very striking evidence of what a group of consecrated Catholic laymen with proper incentives and encouragement can accomplish for religion and their fellowmen.

CHAPTER XIV

THE NEW IMMIGRATION AND ITS PROBLEMS

Industries Attract Immigrants After 1880

Before 1880 free land was a loadstone that attracted immigrants to this country. The new states of the middle west vied with one another in attracting European settlers within their borders. While there was considerable opposition to the newcomers in cities on the Atlantic seaboard the opposition did not have any far-reaching immediate effects. The desire for an increased adult population to develop the country's limitless natural resources still remained the dominant force in determining governmental policy towards immigration. Opponents of the older immigration emphasized the extent to which the immigrants became dependent on public charity. It was quite natural that a fairly large number of the immigrants should have been reduced to poverty. The whole spirit and institutions of the United States were exceedingly individualistic. America offered unlimited opportunities to the thrifty and enterprising, but little protection to the weak. The immigrants, dealing with new conditions, received little guidance in finding their places in a rapidly changing economic structure. Those who did not have the desire or the necessary capital to seek cheap and later free land were compelled to accept the menial occupations in the cities which natives were unwilling to undertake.

After 1880 good free land was nearly exhausted. The immigrant must look to the iron and steel mills, to the mines, the meat-packing establishments and the clothing industry for employment opportunities. In his testimony before the Federal Immigration Commission in 1908, Louis N. Hammerling, President of the American Association of Foreign

Language Newspapers, cited some very significant figures in regard to the extent to which American industries were manned by the new immigrants. Of the 890,000 coal miners, 630,000 had come from southern and eastern Europe. Of the 580,000 steel and iron workers, sixty-nine per cent belonged to the new immigration.[1]

Immigration from Southern and Eastern Europe

It was not until after 1880 that the people from southern and eastern Europe, in large numbers, turned to the United States. In that year only 8.3 per cent of the immigrants came from southern and eastern Europe as compared with 67.9 per cent from northern and western Europe. Immigration from the various countries of southern and eastern Europe, which was like a little rivulet in the seventies, assumed the proportions of a flood in the late eighties and nineties, and the flood continued gathering new force up to the outbreak of the World War. The immigrants from Italy, who had numbered 11,725 in the decade from 1861-1870 and 55,759 in the decade 1871-1880, jumped to 307,309 in 1881-1890, 651,893 in 1891-1900 and 2,045,877 in 1901-1910. The immigrants from the late Austro-Hungarian empire, who numbered 7,800 in the decade 1861-1870 and 72,969 in 1871-1880, increased to 353,719 in 1881-1890, 592,707 in 1891-1900, and 2,145,266 in 1901-1910.[2]

In 1896 for the first time immigration from southern and eastern Europe exceeded the immigration from northern and western Europe. In that year 57.0 per cent of the immigrants came from southern and eastern Europe as compared with 40.0 per cent from northern and western Europe. In 1907, 76.2 per cent of the immigrants to this country came from southern and eastern Europe as compared with 17.7 per cent from northern and western Europe.[3]

[1] Cited in Peter Roberts, *The New Immigration*, Part II, p. 51.
[2] *Annual Report of the Commissioner General of Immigration*, 1929, p. 186; *Reports of Immigration Commission*, Vol. I, p. 63.
[3] *Ibid.*

The basic reason for the increase in Italian and Slavic immigration to the United States after 1880 was the phenomenal development of American industry. The production of coal increased from 14,333,922 short tons in 1860 to 71,481,570 in 1880 and 629,684,120 in 1900. The production of iron and steel increased from 509,084 tons in 1860 to 3,263,585 tons in 1870, 6,484,773 tons in 1880 to 29,507,860 tons in 1900.[4]

The developments in the various industries called for a greatly increased supply of labor, and the rapidly expanding American industries were not slow in advertising the demand in southern and eastern Europe. In Italy and the Slavic countries they discovered a fruitful field from which they might secure a large supply of labor. In their quest they were aided very materially by the zealous agents of the transportation companies and by the favorable reports of immigrants who had found homes in America. To the Slavs living under German and Magyar domination in Austria-Hungary, the opportunities of America were a great source of relief and spelled relative prosperity, and the same was true of the Poles living under German, Russian and Austrian rule.[5]

The Italian immigrants before 1880 came largely from northern Italy. They represented a variety of occupations and scattered themselves rather evenly over the country. Since 1880 Italian immigrants for the most part have come from southern Italy and Sicily.[6] The southern Italian welcomed the opportunity presented by American industry as an escape from the exactions of feudal landlords and a means of improving his standard of life. The landowning nobility had forced rents to the highest notch and had given only short leases so that the tenants had no incentive to make improvements. In Italy wages were about forty per cent of English and French wages and from thirty to fifty per cent lower than

---
[4] E. L. Bogart, *op. cit.*, pp. 319, 402.
[5] Emily G. Balch, *Our Slavic Fellow-Citizens*, pp. 236–237.
[6] R. F. Foerster, *Italian Emigration of Our Times*, pp. 323–326.

in Germany. It was to be expected, therefore, that the high wages of America would prove very attractive to the Italian.[7]

The newer immigrants did not have the same bargaining power or the same standard of life as wage-earners who had been schooled in American industry. In many instances they entered into competition with native workers and with workers of the older immigration. This competition drove the older workers to a higher level or forced them out of certain industries. Many of them were given supervisory positions in the industries, while many were submerged and compelled to seek other opportunities. In some industries like bituminous and anthracite coal mining or like textile manufacturing and clothing, the native workers and the workers of the older immigration were successful in banding the new immigrants together into strong labor organizations that have since helped to secure an American standard for all the workers in these trades. However, the objectives of organized labor have not been so easily attained in large scale industries like steel and oil.

Racial Differences Retard Leadership Development

The economic conflict accentuated by racial differences created a wide chasm between the old and the new immigration groups. This conflict has created a serious problem for American labor organizations. It has made it very difficult to get the various racial groups to merge their differences in order to promote their common interests. It has made it very difficult for American labor to present a united front in dealing with American industry. The new immigrants have been loath to accept American leadership in the labor movement. It took them considerable time to develop a native leadership capable of appraising pressing problems in their true light.

Many times the leaders of the immigrant groups used their power to promote their own selfish aims and objectives. In

[7] Commons, *op. cit.*, p. 73.

the early period of Italian immigration, according to the Immigration Commission: "Ignorance of the English language and the conditions of labor in the United States compelled laborers of that race to depend entirely upon their employers, who were, as a rule, contractors of the same race and fairly familiar with the language and labor conditions here. Some of these employers boarded the laborers in their charge and paid them a certain stipulated amount of wages, with the understanding that anything received above the said amount on account of their labor should go to the padrone."[8] Similar conditions prevailed among the Austrians, Greeks, Bulgarians, Turks, Macedonians and Mexicans.[9] This situation has practically become a thing of the past. The new immigrants are rapidly coming into their own. Their native vigor and natural intelligence are asserting themselves. They are developing leaders who will compare favorably with those of other groups in American life.

Catholic Church Feels Strain of New Immigration Tides

The new immigration imposed a severe strain on the leadership and resources of the Catholic Church, which had only caught up with the religious needs of the older immigrants when it was called upon to solve even greater problems. It has been estimated that the Catholic growth through immigration between 1881 and 1910 was 4,791,000.[10] One has only to observe the conditions in the large cities in the east and middle west in order to understand the magnitude of the Church's problems. While the new immigrants shared a common faith with the older Catholic immigrants, they were widely separated by race and cultural traditions. Differences of language created a chasm that could not be bridged in the first generation. Many times the historic conflicts in Europe influenced the groups within the Church in the United States.

---

[8] *Reports of Immigration Commission*, Vol. II, p. 391.
[9] *Ibid.*, Vol. II, p. 392.
[10] Shaughnessy, *op. cit.*, pp. 165, 169, 175.

Old racial hatreds were imported. Racial differences and memories of European struggles were accentuated by economic conflict in the United States. The new immigrants were pitted against those of the older immigration. The latter felt that their positions and their standards of life were endangered by the competition of new immigration.

How often is it said that this organization or that institution is "Irish" or "German?" There is the "orphanage for the Irish children," or the "orphanage for the German children," or the "Italian orphanage." Each nationality wanted to carry on its own traditions of mutual aid and charity—a policy which in the beginning had much to commend it. The new immigrants were inclined to give more generously to their own institutions. The new immigrants at first did not take kindly to existing Catholic lay charitable organizations. The various Slavic peoples brought with them traditions of mutual insurance. For this reason insurance associations form a very essential part of their parish life. There is scarcely any Slavic parish without one or more societies of this character. These parish groups are frequently bound together in national associations like the Polish National Union and the Lithuanian Women's Alliance.

Immigrants Form Insurance Associations

The various mutual insurance associations among the new immigrant groups serve as an outlet for their national consciousness and ideals; they help to maintain the best traditions of the respective peoples. At a relatively small cost they provide some protection against the industrial hazards to which their membership is exposed. For the sum of twenty-five to thirty-five cents a week they pay a death benefit of about $150 and a sick benefit of $5 a week for a number of weeks.[11] The various national groups failed to realize that their mutual insurance associations were not able to give their

[11] Roberts, *op. cit.*, p. 209.

members all the protection which they needed. Their hazards were far greater than in their own countries. The cost of protection against these hazards of life was, therefore, far greater. In fact, it imposed a burden which ordinary laborers could ill afford.

Heretofore, one of the great obstacles in the way of the development of unified Catholic programs of social work has been the chasm separating the different nationalities. The German immigrants felt that it was their special duty to provide for the members of their own race. It appeared to them that the Irish had all they could do to care for their own. As the Germans and the Irish were coming closer together the new immigrants began to crowd American cities. New churches had to be built and priests trained to understand the traditions of the new nationalities. The only practical procedure for the Catholic bishops was to secure priests from the various countries from which the immigrants had come. In dealing with the social and charitable problems presented by the new immigration it might have been theoretically a better policy to develop the work of existing organizations and institutions, but, in practice, this plan was out of the question. The Church had to take a pragmatic point of view. It did not fail to reckon with the racial traditions of the different groups, and, thus, secured better results than if it had tried to impose something upon these peoples to which they were unaccustomed. Religion had always been identified with the struggles, sufferings and ideals of the various nationalities. It spiritualized and refined their culture. Those who would rob them of their national ideals were regarded as the arch-enemies of their religion.

The members of the second generation of the new immigrants are coming to fraternize more and more with the descendants of the older immigrants; intermarriages have become increasingly common. They work together harmoniously in organizations, like the Knights of Columbus, the St.

Vincent de Paul Society and the Holy Name Society. In many instances they have brought new life and enthusiasm to these organizations. If one wants to get a clear picture of the extent to which the children of the new immigrants have made common cause with the old, let him study the present class rolls of the different Catholic colleges, where the most noticeable trend is the increase in Latin and Slavic names. One finds representatives of many racial strains working together for the common objectives in the civic and religious life of the United States.

The Immigrant's Contribution to American Industry

The new immigrant was welcomed as an asset in the building of American industries. He bulked large not only as a producer but as a consumer of the products of industry. A job in a factory looked good to him even at comparatively low wages. In many industries he constituted the largest part of the labor force. He was naturally exposed to the hazards of unskilled wage-earners in all modern industries. His unacquaintance with the English language and the customs of the country made the industrial hazards all the more serious. American industry has profited greatly by the strength and the weaknesses of the immigrant; but when he became the victim of accident or industrial fatigue, it cast him aside as a burden on a grudging philanthropy. It is a curious paradox that immigrants of all decades, after they have given of their best, should be criticised because they become victims of the very conditions that American industry has created. This forced dependency has been used in favor of restricted immigration. Today a growing humanitarianism has compelled men to recognize that, if the immigrant becomes a dependent, the blame should be laid quite as much at the door of American industry as on his own weakness or shortcomings.

In order to test the oft-repeated assertions regarding the relationship between immigration and poverty, the Immigration Commission made a study of the families who were receiving assistance from social agencies in forty-three cities during the period from December 1, 1908, to May 31, 1909. The total number of families studied was 31,685. In 12,140 or 38.3 per cent of the cases the head of the family was foreign born, in 3,388 or 10.7 per cent the head of the family was native born of foreign parents, in 12,597 or 39.8 per cent the head of the family was a native white of native parents, and in 3,489 or 11 per cent the head of the family was a native Negro born of native Negro parents. In all, 61.7 per cent of the families assisted were native born and only 38.3 per cent were foreign born.[12]

More important still were the Commission's findings in a study of the causes of poverty. Unemployment or insufficient wages were the most important factors. They were the chief causes of the poverty of 58.6 per cent of the native born, of 62.1 per cent of the native born of foreign parents, and of 59.8 per cent of the foreign born. The next most important factor in the cases studied was the death or disability of the breadwinner of the family, which accounted for the dependency of 30.2 per cent of the foreign born, of 27.7 per cent of the native born, and of 27.2 per cent of the native born of foreign parents.[13]

There is nothing startling about these figures as far as the relative incidence of poverty among the native and foreign born is concerned. If anything the balance seems to favor the foreign born. Instead of being an economic liability to the United States the new immigrant really has contributed more than he has received. It is very doubtful if without his aid American industry could have made such rapid strides in the past fifty years. It required a tremendous amount of cheap labor, and this could be procured legally only in southern and eastern Europe.

[12] *Reports of Immigration Commission,* Vol. II, pp. 91, 92, 100.
[13] *Ibid.,* Vol. II, p. 118.

While the new immigrants did not have as great opportunities as those of the older immigration, they were not exposed to the same social, religious, or even economic privations. When the new immigrants came they found American social, charitable and educational institutions in a comparatively advanced state of development. When in need they could receive assistance without being pauperized. Those who were unable to pay the costs of medical and hospital care might avail themselves of the free medical and hospital resources of American cities. Epidemics which had been a scourge to the earlier immigrants had been brought under control. Immigrant aid under both public and private auspices had reached a rather advanced stage of development. Even labor in a machine age was less arduous than in the pick-shovel-and-wheelbarrow period of the older immigration.

Problems Facing the Immigrant

One of the problems of the new immigrant has been to distinguish between his actual friends and his enemies who may pose as friends and up-lifters. He is soon aware that large numbers of Americans are hostile to him, sometimes for no other reason than the fact that he differs in language, in dress and in customs. They regard him and make him feel that he is an inferior human being. Common labor, he finds in this democracy, is not held in such high repute. Besides this group of definitely hostile persons there is an Americanizing group that wants the immigrant to discard straightway the language and traditions of his homeland. These two groups do not represent the enlightened attitude of America towards the immigrant. A very large group of the American people are genuinely interested in his welfare. They contribute generously to the various immigrant aid societies and to social welfare agencies which aid in the care of the immigrant as a part of their programs. But the immigrant does not always avail himself of the things that are done for him, partly because of the spirit in which they are done and partly because of his lack of knowledge of American institutions. This condition, however, has been changing rapidly during the past few years, not so much through American philanthropy as through the development of capable leadership in the immigrant's own people. This is giving him an understanding of American opportunities.

The transfer from Europe to America imposed a severe strain on the family life of the immigrants. Most of them had been brought up in a simple rural civilization governed by customs and traditions. In their homeland the standards of family life handed down from one generation to the other and interpreted by parents were accepted without question by the rising generation; but in American city streets the child of the immigrant found a new and totally different attitude towards family life and discipline. He found that his associates on the streets, in the playground and in the school were given certain privileges which he was denied. The parents could not adjust themselves to the new ways and their children refused to accept the old. Hence it is that in the home life of the immigrant we have a conflict between two cultural patterns, that of the European village and that of American city life, which is hardly the best in America. Children will not look for guidance to parents whom they regard as old-fashioned. They look rather to their companions on the streets as behavior models. Since they are in rebellion against the authority of the home, they develop a rebellious attitude towards law and authority in general in the companionship of children with the same lawless spirit. One would, therefore, naturally expect to find a high rate of juvenile delinquency among the children of immigrants; but the percentage is no higher than among any group of families who have shifted from a rural to an urban civilization. The conflict that develops in the family life of the immigrant is not due entirely to immigration but also to the fact that the parents represent a rural and the children an urban environment.

It would be a mistake to assume that the delinquency of the immigrant child is due solely to conflict with parental standards. The immigrant family in the American city is compelled to settle in the slum section where rents are low and housing conditions poor. In these surroundings the children do not have a normal outlet for their leisure time interests. It is a well-known fact that the slum sections of American cities are quite neglected. As a general rule they are not reached by the programs of the boy scouts, the girl scouts, or boys' or girls' clubs.

While every immigrant family represents a conflict of cultures it is only in a comparatively small number of cases that the conflict rends the bonds of family union. The ordinary immigrant family shows a remarkable power of resisting disintegrating forces. Any differences that arise between the parents and children are compromised in the privacy of their homes. It is surprising how well immigrant families on the whole adjust themselves to the new and complicated situations of American life. They certainly would not have done so well had they followed the advice of those who desired to see them change their habits and customs almost overnight. The hostile attitude of many Americans towards the immigrants and the defensive consecration of the latter to their racial ideals and traditions have worked for the best. A gradual blending of the old and the new has resulted. The immigrant has been enabled to retain much that is best in his own culture without sacrificing any of the essentials of good American citizenship.

Growing Opposition to the Immigrant

With the phenomenal increase of immigration in the eighties and nineties opposition to the alien began to assume new forms and larger proportions. At this time as in every period of

American history the immigration question let loose some of the most intense nationalistic and religious prejudices. In the forties and fifties opposition to the German and Irish immigrants found its expression in the Know-Nothing movement. In the nineties opposition to the Italian and the Slav found its expression in the American Protective Association. But the apostles of bigotry in the guise of extreme nationalism were not the only persons who regarded the new immigrants with suspicion. Large numbers of men and women, who would not be classed as bigots or extreme nationalists, regarded the ever-increasing number of immigrants as a menace to American institutions and American culture. They felt that America was receiving more immigrants than it could possibly absorb. To this class might be added the labor organizations who considered the new immigrant as a threat to their economic standards. In a convention held at Washington (February 1898), the American Federation of Labor favored a literacy test as a means of restricting immigration. The Knights of Labor at its Louisville convention (November 1897), adopted a similar resolution.[14]

Until 1897 Congress in its efforts to regulate immigration confined itself to the exclusion of certain undesirable classes such as paupers, criminals, anarchists, and diseased and immoral persons; but in that year, it passed a bill which provided a literacy test with the specific purpose of limiting the number of immigrants. President Cleveland's veto did not discourage the advocates of restricted immigration. In fact they gathered new strength year by year. In 1906 the literacy test was again brought before Congress, but its friends compromised on a federal commission to investigate the whole question of immigration. Heartened by the favorable recommendations of the Immigration Commission the friends of the literacy test against sought the approval of Congress, which they secured without difficulty, only to be rebuffed by Presi-

[14] *Ibid.*, Vol. XXXIX, p. 49.

dent Taft's veto. In 1916 President Wilson returned the literacy bill to Congress with his veto; but in 1917, the bill secured sufficient votes to be passed over the presidential veto.

After the war, the movement for immigration restriction assumed new proportions. It was feared that the disturbed economic conditions of European countries would cause millions of Europeans to emigrate and thus create a serious unemployment crisis in the United States. This situation gave the restrictionists the long awaited opportunity of attaining their objective. In 1919 Congress passed a bill restricting the number of immigrants from any country in a particular year to three per cent of the natives of that country here already resident in the United States in 1910. President Wilson vetoed the bill as something out of harmony with our traditional policies. The bill was again passed by Congress in the fall of 1920 and signed by President Harding.

The immigration restrictionists were not yet satisfied. They wanted not only restriction but also selection. Under the influence of this attitude Congress passed a law in 1922 which restricted the number of immigrants coming from any country in the course of a year to two per cent of the natives of that country here in 1890. The law provided, moreover, that the total number of immigrants from Europe in any one year should not exceed 150,000. This law embodied a new immigration policy. In it the United States virtually announced to the world that, in so far as it desired any European emigration, it was prepared to give preference to the emigrants from northern and western Europe. The law of 1922 included the well-known national origins clause as a further step in selective immigration. It provided that after July 1, 1928, the number of immigrants from any country within the course of a year should be based on the number of inhabitants of the United States in 1920 who traced their origin to that country. The national origins plan for restricting immigration was finally put into effect July 1, 1929, despite presidential opposition.

Immigration restriction has come to be regarded as a permanent policy of the United States. Within a few years American social problems will no longer be the problems of the immigrant. American industry in the future will have to depend for its unskilled labor on the poor whites of the south, the Negro, and to representatives of all races and groups who by chance or weakness have fallen in the social scale. Its large social problems will be those of the "poor white" and the Negro, who have heretofore remained in the background. They and their problems are even now coming into the clear light of day.

CHAPTER XV *

THE FRINGES OF PARISH LIFE

New Emphasis on Poverty in Relation to Home Conditions

When the immigrants from southern and eastern Europe began to pour into the United States in the eighties and nineties of the last century they created problems for the Catholic Church that were just as serious as those of the older immigration. There was, however, this difference. The Church was much better prepared to deal with the new than with the old immigration. It was on a much firmer basis; its various institutions and agencies were much better developed. Certain changes, of course, had to be made and certain new points of approach developed in order to meet new situations. As has been pointed out, the Church had to struggle hard to save the faith of the children of the older immigrants. It was for this purpose that it fostered the establishment of schools, orphan asylums and industrial protectorates. Between 1850 and 1880 Protestant charities expended much energy in so-called "rescue work" which meant the removing of Catholic children from their homes and placing them in Protestant homes. Between 1880 and 1900 Protestant charities, under the leadership of the Charity Organization Society, took a new turn. It was no longer so easy to find western homes for children picked up on the New York City streets. The Charity Organization Society emphasized volunteer service on a neighborhood basis. It emphasized the study of poverty in relation to the conditions under which people lived. The emphasis placed by the Charity Organization Society on home and neighborhood work was further stressed by the settlement movement after 1890. In the

* This chapter appeared in the *Catholic Charities Review*, Vol. 15, May, 1931, under the title of "The Catholic Settlement Movement."

settlement many declining Protestant churches saw an opportunity of giving a new vitality to their work.

Settlement Movement Offers First-Hand Contact With Poor

In the settlement movement, many great humanitarian leaders found an opportunity of coming into closer contact with the poor and their problems. They believed that by living close to the poor they would get an understanding of social conditions that would be most important in reforming social conditions. For Catholics the settlement movement was a challenge. The settlements, as a rule, were located in districts peopled by the newer immigrants. Those that were organized in connection with Protestant churches were a distinct menace to the faith of Catholic children. Even the settlements that were organized on a non-sectarian basis were not regarded by Catholics with favor. It was feared that their non-sectarian character was used as a cloak for propaganda. Moreover, the non-sectarian agency was something wholly new in American social work; for then even the Charity Organization Society was regarded as a non-sectarian agency in only two cities in the United States.

Settlement Movement an Awakener for Catholics

The settlement movement had a far-reaching influence in reminding Catholics of the need of a better organized program for the religious care of the new immigrants. As in dealing with the older immigrants, its first task was to organize classes in Christian doctrine in sections that were not reached by any parish. In many instances the Christian doctrine centers paved the way for the establishment of new parishes.[1] Those who set out to organize Christian doctrine centers found it necessary to make them attractive. Protestant settlement houses were real educational and recreational centers. Catholics had to do likewise in order to hold

[2] Cf. Chapter XIII.

their own children. In other words, they had to copy as far as practicable the Protestant program.

First Catholic Settlement: Santa Maria Institute, Cincinnati

The first Catholic settlement in the United States was the Santa Maria Institute at Cincinnati which owed its origin to Sister Blandina of the Sisters of Charity of Mt. St. Joseph-on-the-Ohio. With the desire to give her life to the religious welfare of Italian immigrants, she begged her superior to assign her and her own natural sister, Sister Justina, also a Sister of Charity, for this work. The superiors gladly acquiesced in this matter. They were delighted to see these sisters dedicate themselves to the welfare of the people of their own race.[2]

In their new venture Sister Blandina and her companion were confronted with many difficulties. Protestant missionary activities had been well organized among the Italians. Many people were asking why it was necessary to make special provision for the Italians. Did they not have the same opportunities for attending Mass and practicing their religion as other Catholics? These critics failed to see as did Sister Blandina that the Italians had not yet developed their own leadership in this country. They were in somewhat the same position as the Irish and the Germans prior to 1860. They did not feel welcome in other groups even to practice their religion. Therefore, leaders like Sister Blandina were a blessing to the American Italians.

In developing the Santa Maria Institute, Sister Blandina began with a school, but she soon found that a school was not enough. The Italians needed some mission they could call their own to which they could go for advice and information. They required a sort of institute that would preserve their own traditions, that would maintain their own culture, and prepare them for intelligent participation in American

---

[2] Anna C. Minogue, *Santa Maria Institute*, p. 6.

life. The Santa Maria Institute, organized formally in September of 1897, began in a modest way. It has been said that the entire possessions of the two sisters consisted of five dollars, but they had courage and vision. In the face of numerous obstacles, they succeeded in making the Santa Maria Institute a center of Italian Catholic life in Cincinnati.

In addition to its catechetical work, its clubs for boys and girls and its educational classes, the Santa Maria Institute promoted the organization of a federation of Catholic women's societies for the purpose of assisting the parish conferences of the St. Vincent de Paul Society.[3] It organized a day nursery and a girls' protectory. In 1919 the institute established a branch center for religious, educational and recreational work in another large Italian district, and in 1921, it established still another branch.[4]

Catholic Settlement Movement Gains Through Leadership of Converts

In the settlement movement, as in others, the Catholic Church gained considerably by the inspiration of converts to the faith. In 1896 a Dominican father on East Sixty-ninth Street found a valuable opportunity of utilizing the services of a convert in Catholic settlement work. Miss Gurney, a recent convert from the Episcopalian Church, had placed herself at his disposal. He knew very well that her experience would be most valuable in developing a Catholic program for the Italians on the East Side. He, therefore, invited Miss Gurney to come to his parish and organize a settlement. She rented a house on East Sixty-ninth Street and with her parents became a resident of that quarter. The Third Order of Dominicans assumed the financial burden of the undertaking. Such were the beginnings of St. Rose's Settlement

[3] *Ibid.*, pp. 126–127.
[4] *Ibid.*, pp. 150–160.

which has exercised such a far-reaching influence in Catholic settlement work throughout the whole country.

St. Rose's Settlement, New York City

St. Rose's Settlement marked the entrance of the Catholic laity into an important religious and social movement. It provided the laity with a first-hand contact with the poor. Under the plan as outlined the lay workers were not merely to make periodical visits among the poor. They were actually to go and live among them; they were to serve the poor as neighbors and friends. There was to be one central residence to which all who were in trouble or difficulty might come for advice and assistance. The settlement workers made it their task to become acquainted with every person in the neighborhood. And they did not confine themselves to giving counsel. The original program of St. Rose's included a night school where reading and writing were taught on four evenings a week. Italian men and boys had an English class. Owing to lack of space, like advantages could not be given to the women and girls. Mothers met at the settlement to learn scientific methods of caring for their children; the children were gathered up from the streets and instructed in religion and the practical arts of life. When St. Rose's Settlement was founded on the East Side scarcely any of the adult Italians attended mass and there were very few Italian children in Sunday schools. Both the adults and the children in large numbers patronized a neighboring Protestant mission with a large relief and social program. Within a short time after the establishment of St. Rose's Settlement the whole situation was changed.[5]

Living Among Poor, the Basic Principle of Religious

As far as the religious orders were concerned there was nothing new about living among the poor whom they served.

[5] "The Italian in America: What He has Been, What He Shall Be," by Laurence Franklin, *Catholic World*, Vol. LXXI (April, 1900), p. 67.

This was a basic principle in the life of many religious communities. When Sister Blandina moved into one of the Italian districts of Cincinnati in order that she might bring to those living there the best ideals of their past and the best hopes for their future, she was doing nothing new for a religious. In fact she was just unfolding the plan of the founder and patron saint of her community, St. Vincent de Paul. For the Catholic laity, however, there was something new about a settlement in the last decade of the nineteenth century. The wealthy were getting more and more out of touch with the poor. They lived in a separate section of the city and did not come into close contact with them. They were acquiring the habit of doing their charity vicariously. A donation for some agency once a week freed them of further responsibility. It was the purpose of the settlement movement to bridge this gulf that had been developed between the rich and the poor in American cities. The settlement leaders proposed to give persons of means, of culture and of leisure, an opportunity of living among the poor and acquiring a first-hand knowledge of their problems. The movement made quite an appeal in Protestant circles and, therefore, gathered considerable strength in a short period of time. It did not, however, make an appeal to the wealthy Catholic laity. Miss Gurney made, as we have seen, a good start in St. Rose's Settlement in New York City. Her work received favorable comment in Catholic circles in New York City. In fact, it was the nucleus of a strong movement to organize Catholic settlements in New York City. The interest created by the Dominican project led to the calling of a city-wide conference of Catholics interested in settlement work in the early part of 1900. This conference was presided over by Archbishop John Farley. It was the general feeling of those in attendance that every effort should be made to develop settlements for the purpose of reaching the new immigrants.[6]

Settlements are Organized under Both Lay and Religious Auspices

Following the precedents established by the pioneer Catholic settlements in Cincinnati and New York, one finds that the Catholic settlement movement in the United States followed two important lines of development. In the first place there were a number of settlements organized under lay auspices with a lay personnel. Secondly, there were settlements organized and manned by religious communities. In the Brownson House in Los Angeles, the Christ Child Society in Washington, and the Angel Guardian Settlement in Chicago, there are examples of lay settlements organized by lay organizations with a lay personnel.

Brownson House, Los Angeles

As early as 1901 the spiritual care of Mexican immigrants had become a serious problem in Los Angeles. In March of that year, Rev. John J. Clifford, an assistant to the cathedral, appealed to the Catholic women of the city to do something for the Mexicans. There was one person who became especially interested in the situation and whose name was identified closely with the development of a settlement program in Los Angeles, namely, Miss Mary J. Workman, the founder of Brownson House in that city. From its foundation in March 1901, Brownson House brought to the Catholic settlement movement the best experience in settlement work as a whole. Miss Workman made her settlement an educational center. It was a place where the families of the poor might go for the things they needed, but which they could not secure in any other way. Parents might go there for advice and assistance in their own and the illnesses of their children.

[6] *St. Vincent de Paul Quarterly*, Vol. V, No. 3 (August, 1900), p. 240.

The young who were yearning for an opportunity to play might go there and satisfy themselves to their heart's content. The Brownson House extended a helping hand in acquainting the immigrant with the laws, customs and institutions of his adopted country. The whole program was distinctly Catholic. The people that it reached were Catholics. They looked to the Church for guidance not only in regard to the spiritual but also the material things of life.[7]

Settlement Program for Mexican Immigrants in Los Angeles Diocese

Brownson House became the center and nucleus of an extensive Catholic settlement movement in the diocese of Los Angeles. After its establishment in 1917 the Catholic Welfare Bureau made the extension of the Brownson House plan one of its basic objectives. The program of this settlement lent itself admirably to the problems of the Mexican immigrant. On its basis, the diocese of Los Angeles has been able to build a religious and a welfare program for Mexican immigrants that is unequaled in the United States. Five other settlements are now carrying on the work initiated by the Brownson House—the Santa Rita House, Santa Maria Community Center, El Santo Nino Community Center and Watts Community Center House in Los Angeles and the East Side Social Center in Santa Barbara.[8]

All these diocesan settlements, including Brownson House, are now operated by the Catholic Welfare Bureau. They are an integral part of a coordinated program of welfare work. One of the unique features of the Los Angeles settlements is the manner in which they combine the work of the sisters with professional lay workers. As a rule the religious program is in charge of sisters, assisted by a number of lay

---
[7] *Ibid.*, Vol. XX, No. 3 (August, 1915), pp. 175–177.
[8] *Report of the Catholic Welfare Bureau of Los Angeles and San Diego*, 1930, p. 37.

teachers, while the educational, recreational and health programs are in charge of lay workers.

Christ Child Society, Washington, D. C.

The same year in which Miss Workman was getting her work under way at the Brownson House, an important beginning was being made in settlement work in Washington. The Christ Child Society of the Capital City, under the leadership of its founderess, Miss Mary V. Merrick, decided to broaden its program of child welfare. In addition to providing clothing and shoes for handicapped children it organized Christian doctrine and recreational centers in various sections of the city which were not reached effectively by the organized parishes. A large number of Italians had been attracted to Washington by work on government buildings. They were scattered throughout the city. The Christ Child Society felt that there was a great opportunity for Catholic women to aid these newcomers by assuring their allegiance to the old faith and interpreting for them the institutions and ideals of their adopted country. At the present time, the settlement program of the Christ Child Society includes a boys' club, summer outings for boys and girls, a mothers' club, sewing classes for girls, dramatics, a dental clinic and classes in Christian doctrine.

The work of the Christ Child Society of Washington, which is the parent organization, naturally exercised considerable influence over the increasing number of branches of the society that have been formed throughout the United States. Outside of Washington the two cities in which the society has made the largest contribution to settlement work are Cleveland and Omaha.

Merrick House, Cleveland

In Cleveland, the society sponsored the establishment of Merrick House in 1919 as a part of a community program undertaken by the National Catholic War Council. The local leadership and support for the project were supplied by the Christ Child Society and the War Council agreed to finance the program for two years. Merrick House has endeavored to meet the needs of its neighborhood. It established a day nursery which was an acute need. It also has endeavored to provide necessary recreation and educational facilities. At the present writing it has thirteen junior clubs including a boy scout troop and a girl scout troop. It has twenty-one senior clubs, boys, girls and mixed. It has twenty-six senior gymnasium groups, including basketball and tumbling. Last spring it had sixteen junior teams and ten senior baseball teams. Merrick House also conducts dances, parties, plays, rallies, suppers, and girls' style shows. It has a very active mothers' club and a neighborhood council. The council has aided in a study of garbage disposal, playground, and housing conditions. The educational program includes classes in hand and machine sewing, knitting, cooking, dramatics, dancing, manual training and toymaking.

Weinman Club, Detroit

The Catholic settlement movement was inspired by the thought of bringing a religious message to Catholic immigrants who were not reached by the ordinary mechanism of the Church. There is no place where this moving principle of Catholic settlement work is illustrated more fully than in Detroit. In 1906 Miss Josephine Brownson organized a group of young women to conduct classes for Catholic boys and girls who were attending the public schools. These classes were held in the basement of the Jesuit parish school. The first thirty minutes of the classes were devoted to religious instruction, followed by recreational pursuits. The increase in class attendance soon made additional space necessary. A meeting was called and an association formed under the name of the Weinman Club in memory of the distinguished

Ferdinand Weinman, S.J., (d. 1906), who had been especially devoted to the welfare of the children of the neighborhood.[9]

When the Weinman Club was organized in a large stable (1908), it was practically without resources. In this improvised center clubs were formed for boys and girls and also for mothers. Classes in Christian doctrine, sewing and music were held daily after school hours for children attending the public schools. In 1911 the women who were associated with the Weinman Club decided to enter on a larger field of work and adopted the name of the Catholic Settlement Association. The basic purpose of the association was to extend to other sections of the city the pioneer program of the Weinman Club. In 1915 the Catholic Settlement Association changed its name to the League of Catholic Women, and under its direction the Weinman Club became the Weinman Settlement. Besides enlarging the program at the Weinman Settlement the League has opened three new centers: St. Ann's Community Center, near the Ford works in Hamtramck, Michigan (1919); and the St. Rita's Community Center (1921) and the Residence Club (1928) in Detroit.[10]

The Polish Activities League of Detroit has extended the pioneer work of the League of Catholic Women through St. Elizabeth's Community House opened in 1923. This is a very significant movement in that it indicates a development by Polish citizens of their own leadership in caring for their own people.

Margaret Barry Settlement, Minneapolis

In 1912 there were two significant developments in Catholic settlement work. The Educational Committee of the Minneapolis League of Catholic Women rented a room in an Italian district where classes in sewing and catechism were

[9] *Report of Catholic Settlement Association of Detroit*, 1911–1913, p. 5.
[10] *Annual Report of the League of Catholic Women of Detroit*, 1928.

held four times weekly. Picnics and parties were also given during the year. Thus did the members of the committee become acquainted with the people and their needs. They found that the members of six parishes were located in a community that was nearly two miles from the nearest church. For nearly three years the work in the Italian district was carried on through volunteers. In the meantime plans were being made for an extensive settlement program. In 1915 the Margaret Barry Settlement, to which the Catholic women of Minneapolis had looked forward so anxiously, opened its doors.

Madonna Center, Chicago

The second significant development in Catholic settlement work in 1912 was the organization of the Angel Guardian Center in one of the Italian districts of Chicago by Miss Mary Agnes Amberg, who has continued as its active leader and resident director. Since 1922 it has been known as the Madonna Center. The Madonna Center has been a real force in building up the religious life of the neighborhood. Its program and spirit can not be expressed more fully than in the words of Miss Amberg: "Our daily routine program is unspectacular. Just 'a house by the side of the road' that cheerily opens its doors each morning for the wee tots of its kindergarten and closes them in the evening with a friendly 'good night' only when its senior groups are leaving; nor is any call, day or night, left unanswered. It is a program that finds its incentive, its underlying propelling force in its spiritual significance. . . . It is a progressive program in the sense that there is no age, once a little tot wanders into our sunny kindergarten, but what there is a group into which it may enter. They graduate into play clubs, then the little girls into sewing, singing, dancing classes, girl scout activities, thence into the high school or two business girls' groups, supper clubs, gym groups, boy scouts, high school and working boys' groups, camping and hiking clubs, etc."[11]

Charles House, Rochester, New York

Settlement work became an important part of a diocesan program in Rochester, New York, when Charles House, the first Catholic settlement in the city, was opened in November 1917. In a short time Charles House became a religious center through which the diocese endeavored to reach spiritually neglected children and foreign-born adults. A worker was secured at diocesan expense, who was to devote herself to establishing contact with children who were not receiving any religious instruction. The classes in Christian doctrine for these children are now in charge of priests from the neighboring parishes who visit the settlement daily. Charles House endeavors to meet the recreational and cultural needs of its clients through a head resident assisted by a corps of volunteers.

In 1918 the Genesee Institute was established in Rochester as a recreational and religious center for its community. The recreational work is in charge of a lay director, while the religious work is in charge of the Missionary Sisters of the Most Blessed Trinity.

World War Gives Impetus to Settlement Work

The war gave a new impetus to all forms of social work but especially to settlement work. Its stresses and strains opened up anew the cracks and scars in our social structure. There was everywhere the conviction that success depended just as much on the soundness of our social structure as on our fighting men. Men and women were anxious to participate in some kind of patriotic service which came to include all forms of social service. The welfare work that was under-

[11] *The Madonna Center, Chicago. Fourteenth Year Book*, November, 1926, pp. 7–8; 29.

taken for the benefit of the soldiers in the camps reached out into the surrounding communities. Therefore, it was that the vast program of service developed under the direction of the war welfare organizations in cities and towns adjoining cantonments. While a large part of this work was of a purely temporary character, some of it took a permanent form. The war welfare agencies, as far as possible, endeavored to build their programs around local organizations and to get local organizations to assume part of the responsibility in the hope that the work might become a permanent part of the local program.

The National Catholic War Council

Among the organizations that participated in the development of recreational and educational programs in the communities adjacent to camps was the National Catholic War Council through its committee on special war activities. The Knights of Columbus represented Catholic interests in educational and recreational work within the camps, while the Committee on Special War Activities of the Catholic War Council had charge of Catholic activities outside the camps.

Settlements Aided by National Catholic War Council

While the National Catholic War Council was interested primarily in girls' welfare in war camp communities, in a number of places it aided in the development of general settlement programs. The writer has already referred to the program of Merrick House in Cleveland which was developed by a local group with the assistance of the National Catholic War Council. Other settlement projects aided by the War Council were the National Catholic Community House in Cincinnati, opened in 1919, and the Catholic Community House in Baltimore, opened the same year. The most unique contribution of the Cincinnati institution has been its citizenship work. For a number of years it conducted classes in English for the foreign-born several evenings a week. Classes in citizenship are now conducted several evenings a week; classes in English and citizenship are held also during the day for those who can not attend in the evening. "As a part of its recreational program, the Community House has fostered the development of as many self-governing clubs as possible. Among the clubs fostered by the organization are the Italian Young Men and Young Women's Clubs, Mothers' Club, McKinley Mothers' Club, Young Women's Community Club. With the aid of the workers in the House, each of these clubs develops its own program. The Community House also provides a meeting place for the various organizations of the neighborhood."[12]

The Catholic Community House in Baltimore has become a true neighborhood center. One of its basic objectives has been to provide leisure time activities for the under-privileged children of the district. Its staff has aided the pastors of the city in organizing parish leisure time programs.

Mexican Problems in Southwest

The Committee of Special War Activities of the National Catholic War Council exercised a wide influence on the outlook of Catholic women's organizations throughout the country. The Mexican problem began to loom large in the southwest and presented a challenge to Catholic lay leadership. The extensive settlement movement in the Los Angeles diocese represented an effort to deal with the religious aspects of the Mexican problem. The Amberg Club in Kansas City, Missouri, organized a settlement program for the Mexicans in that city. In the Guadalupe Neighborhood Center in the Mexican district the club carries on a religious, educational, recreational and health program. Its most important contribution, however, has been in health work. The health

[12] A Study of the National Catholic Community House, Cincinnati, made by the writer, 1926.

standards of the Mexicans were very low. The club found that through its health clinics it could make its best approach. It has, therefore, used health as a basis on which to build the other parts of its program. Encouraged by its success among the Mexicans, the Amberg Club has decided to organize child health centers in Italian, Polish and Belgian districts of Kansas City.

The Diocesan Council of Catholic Women has also developed a very successful neighborhood program for the Mexicans of Denver.

European Immigrant Problems in East and Middle West

While the Mexicans presented a serious religious problem in the southwest the European immigrant in the large industrial centers of the east and middle west still make a strong appeal to Catholic leadership, both lay and clerical. It was recognized on all sides that the religious needs of the latter were not met as fully as might be desired despite existing settlements. Two of the most recently organized settlements for this purpose are the Judge Gary-Bishop Alerding Settlement in Gary, Indiana, and the Catholic Neighborhood House at Newark, New Jersey.

For a number of years, Rev. John B. De Ville had been anxious to organize a welfare program for the Mexican, Spanish and Italian immigrants in Gary, Indiana. He made a small beginning in a temporary headquarters in 1918. In 1922 he secured a promise of financial support from the United States Steel Corporation provided that the diocese of Fort Wayne would pledge an equal amount. Bishop Alerding finally gave his approval to the joint program. In 1923 the new building was opened and a complete program of settlement work launched. Everything went along smoothly for a few years and then the leaders in the movement began to recognize that the diocese had taken over a rather heavy responsibility. There was nothing to do except limit the program in accord with available resources. At the present writing most of the recreational and educational work is being done by volunteers and the religious work is in charge of the Society of Missionary Catechists.

The Catholic Neighborhood House at Newark was a project of the Diocesan Council of Catholic Women (1926). It is still carried on under the auspices of the council, but it is financed in large part by the diocese of Newark. The Catholic Neighborhood House, according to a statement supplied by the director, aims "to supply a medium for Catholic training for Catholic children in the public schools and religiously neglected children and adults, to fill the leisure time of school children with healthful and improving recreational activities, to provide wholesome recreation and social opportunities for boys, girls and adults in industry, to train young girls and mothers in improved methods of child-care, nutrition, etc., to set high ideals of citizenship and develop the individual in his relationship to his community."

Work of Sisters of Charity in Cincinnati Marks New Epoch in Catholic Charity

The pioneer Catholic effort in settlement work in the United States was inspired by two religious members of the Sisters of Charity of Mount St. Joseph-on-the-Ohio. In the years that followed a number of lay leaders, inspired by the same ideals, took over a large share of the field. So much have the lay leaders in the movement impressed themselves on Catholic thinking that many have come to regard the Catholic settlement movement as an exclusively lay movement. The pioneer work of the Sisters of Charity in Cincinnati however was not without its influence upon other communities. It was a return to the basic objectives of St. Vincent de Paul in the establishment of the Sisters of Charity. By force of circumstances, American communities had been compelled to follow other paths. As has been emphasized so frequently throughout this volume, many of their traditions were developed by their efforts to save the children of the immigrant to the faith. They were, therefore, compelled to adopt the same methods that had been followed by Protestant organizations. They had to confine themselves very largely to institutional work because they found that it was the only practicable method of saving the faith of Catholic children.

Engaged in institutional work and education, it is easy to understand why communities have been unable to develop that program of neighborhood service which has been so characteristic of religious communities since the time of St. Vincent de Paul. It is not exaggerating to refer to the work of the Sisters of Charity in Cincinnati as beginning a new epoch in Catholic social work. With some exceptions, the older communities have not been able to return to neighborhood service on any large scale. However, the Daughters of Charity of St. Vincent de Paul, even when engaged in institutional programs, always endeavor to conduct a certain amount of friendly visiting among the poor.

Settlements of Servants of the Immaculate Heart of Mary and the Franciscan Sisters of the Atonement

The Servants of the Immaculate Heart of Mary, who may be classed among the older communities, have taken charge of the work of the Madonna and L'Assunta Houses in the Italian sections of Philadelphia, and the Catholic Settlement House of Norristown, Pennsylvania. The Madonna Settlement House (1904) may be regarded as one of the pioneer Catholic settlements. At the invitation of Cardinal Dougherty, the Franciscan Sisters of the Atonement opened St. Simon's Mission Settlement in one of the colored districts of Philadelphia in 1922.[13]

---

[13] *Catholic Charities and Social Welfare Activities of the Archdiocese of Philadelphia, Year Book,* 1926, pp. 124–126.

Settlements of Helpers of the Holy Souls

The Helpers of the Holy Souls, introduced into this country in 1892, have adhered closely to the original objective of active neighborhood service. This community opened settlements in St. Louis (1903), in San Francisco (1904), in New York (1913), and in Chicago (1925). Their neighborhood work grew out of home visitations of the sick and the poor. In visiting homes the sisters find that there are many things that point to the need of group programs, as the lack of religious instruction, of proper recreational outlets for the children, and of any cultural pursuit in the young girls of the neighborhood. The sisters naturally begin with the religious instruction. Afterwards come the recreational groups, including boy scout troops and girl scout troops, and then clubs for the older girls. This is how the work of the community has developed in St. Louis and it may be assumed that this is typical of their work elsewhere.

Newly Established Religious Communities Have Important Part in Settlement Work

Perhaps it is to the newly established religious communities, more than any other group, that we must look to bring the message of religion to Catholic children and adults who are not reached by the parish organizations. In a short space of time newly established religious communities have come to play an important part in Catholic settlement work. They have gone down into the congested districts in order to bring friendship and hope into cheerless lives. In describing the settlement program of the Los Angeles diocese, reference was made to the fact that a considerable part of the religious work in the Los Angeles settlements is in charge of the Sisters of the Holy Family, a new American religious community. The religious program of the Judge Gary-Bishop Alerding

Settlement in Gary, Indiana, is in charge of the Missionary Catechists, another new American religious community.

The new community however which has stood out most prominently in Catholic settlement work in the United States is the Missionary Sisters of the Most Blessed Trinity. The religious of this community have opened two centers: Trinity Community Center at Ensley, Alabama, and St. Elizabeth's Social Center, Rockford, Illinois. They have also organized centers in Philadelphia and Newark. They have charge of the religious work in the Genesee Institute, Rochester, New York. In addition, the sisters engage in parish visiting and census taking in Birmingham, Mobile, Rockford, Brooklyn, Lyons, N. Y., Rochester, East Pittsburgh, and in the mining districts around Uniontown, Pa. In 1918 The Missionary Sisters of the Most Blessed Trinity took over the Doctor White Memorial Settlement House in Brooklyn, originally established in 1903, and named after its founder, Rev. Dr. William J. White, later Supervisor of the Catholic Charities of Brooklyn and one of the pioneer leaders in American Catholic charities. The sisters have endeavored to make this settlement an active, religious and social center. The program includes kindergarten, summer camps, sewing clubs, mothers' clubs, folk dancing, boy and girl scout troops, boys' recreation clubs, working boys' clubs, and classes in industrial arts, Spanish, first aid, catechism, domestic science and home making. They have done their very best to carry out the charter framed by Dr. White that: "A settlement is not a kind of laboratory where human specimens are prepared for inspection and classification, nor is it a center from which alms are dispensed to the poor; but it is the bringing together in a spirit of kindliness by means of classes and various kinds of social assemblage those whose different environments have kept them heretofore too widely separated. It is the creation of an atmosphere of hope and friendly service, of restfulness, of harmony and happiness among sordid surroundings for over-tired and under-nourished lives. It is the protection and guidance of youthful energies, the opening of the door of opportunity to those to whom their Creator has given capacities for a fuller life and thus it is the expression of a truth we believe but do not always practice, the truth that all men are brothers, all are one in Jesus Christ.''

Reduced Immigration Has Influenced Settlement Movement

The conditions that gave birth to the Catholic settlement movement have changed in the past few years. European immigration has been reduced to a negligible quantity. The parish organization of the Church has adjusted itself increasingly to the needs of the newer immigrants. In a number of places enterprising priests have been able to make their parishes real social centers. The changes in the character of non-sectarian settlements has enabled priests to use their facilities without endangering the faith of the children. While the original objectives of the settlement has, in a measure, disappeared, there is other work to which it can pass on and in which it can satisfy its pioneering spirit. There are always those who live on the outer fringes of parish life. Their problems will be different from those of the immigrant. The settlement has a mission for such people; it will be a constant source of light and inspiration to the Church as well as to the human agencies dealing with them. There is every evidence, moreover, that the Church has taken into its own parish organization much of the experience that has been gathered by the settlement workers.

CHAPTER XVI
A SUPPORT FOR THE HOME
First Institutions a Safeguard of Religious Life of Children

The leaders of the immigrants at first regarded the institution as the great means of saving the faith of their children. A very large part of the efforts of religious communities that had been introduced from abroad or established in this country were devoted to institutions for dependent and neglected children. After the Civil War the slogan of Catholic leaders was "Give us institutions, and above all give us industrial schools and we will save the faith of the children." They said: "We will gather up all neglected children from the homes of careless parents and will bring them together in the sheltered atmosphere of the institution, where they will live under the care and guidance of the good sisters, will receive a practical education that will fit them for their tasks in life and will return to the world prepared to meet all the dangers that confront them."

Recognition of Need for Complete Child Welfare Program

Even before the movement for the building of children's institutions gathered its full force, many Catholics began to recognize the need of a more complete program of child welfare. An article in the *Catholic World* (July 1868) on "The Sanitary and Moral Condition of New York City," estimated that there were 40,000 vagrant children in the city. "Every year," the writer declared, "with the tide of emigration constantly increasing new material is added to develop this character at a more rapid rate. Such being the case self-protection demands that something be done to give these children homes and draw them away from the pollution surrounding them.

In the lower portions of the city, there are some institutions intended particularly to take care of these little vagrants, and they form a breakwater to this torrent of infantile depravity. The first of these is the Five Point Mission established under 'An Act' passed in March 1856 by the Senate and Assembly of the State of New York, 'to incorporate the Ladies' Home Missionary Society of the Methodist Episcopal Church.' . . . The 'Old Brewery,' a most notorious den of infamy, just at the Five Points, was selected by the association as headquarters for their missionary labors; and to gather round them here the little ones from the worst section of the city to be fed, clothed and instructed in the rudimentary English branches as well as the Methodist Episcopal faith, became a labor of love. This enterprise prospered and now in place of the 'Old Brewery' stands a large commodious mission building. A peculiar feature in the management is, that entire families are taken in and cared for and given work of some kind to do so that it forms a character of a tenant house. . . . It is well known that nearly one-half the population of this city profess to be members of the Roman Catholic religion; and to show the great excess of persons belonging to this Church among the lower classes in our city, we extract the following analysis of a block of buildings from the *Little Wanderer's Friend* for March 1868: '59 old buildings occupied by 382 families, in which are 2 Welch, 7 Portuguese, 9 English, 10 Americans, 12 French, 39 Negroes, 186 Italians, 189 Polanders, 218 Germans and 812 Irish. Of these 113 are Protestants, 287 Jews, and 1,062 Roman Catholics.' The Catholic Reformatory in Westchester County, established by the late Dr. Ives, is doing everything possible for the children under its control; but the little vagrants, unless arrested for some petty crime and thus committed to that institution, are not within reach of its benefits.'"[1]

[1] Page 553.

The First Catholic Day Nursery

A number of pastors in New York City concluded that the most effective method of dealing with the children of the immigrants was through a program of religious education. Hence, they organized what were known as "poor schools." Among the pioneer leaders in this movement was Rev. F. H. Farrelly, pastor of St. James' Church. In 1865 this zealous pastor established a "poor school" in the basement of his church in charge of the Sisters of Charity. In 1868 the school was moved to more spacious quarters at the corner of St. James and New Bowery Streets. Since his parish was very poor, made up entirely of immigrant workers and their families, Father Farrelly was compelled to appeal to the city as a whole in order to support his new project. Shortly after the opening of his school, Father Farrelly was faced with another problem. He found that many of the children in his school were the children of widows who had to go out to work in order to earn a livelihood. He had to provide for these children for the entire day. The children under school age also required attention. Father Farrelly was therefore compelled to open a day nursery as a supplement for the poor school. As far as we have been able to learn this was the first Catholic day nursery in the United States.[2]

As the opportunities for women working away from their own homes is increased, the need of the day nursery increased. Many parishes in large industrial centers came to regard the day nursery as a most appropriate method of caring for the children of working mothers. Until very recently the facilities at the disposal of family relief societies for the care of children in their own homes were wholly inadequate. Even in communities where relief programs are fairly adequate it is many times desirable for the mother to go to work in order to earn part of her sustenance. Many mothers, moreover,

[2] *Ibid.*

prefer to earn their own livelihood rather than depend on public or private relief.

Religious Apostolate and Day Nursery Development

The religious apostolate has occupied a most important place in the development of Catholic day nurseries. They have been a most effective instrument in reaching families and children who are not reached by the ordinary instrumentalities of the Church. The sisters in many nurseries carry on a regular program of parish visitation. They gather in large numbers of children who are not attending parochial schools and organize classes in Christian doctrine for them. In order to give their program a broader foundation many day nurseries also conduct mothers' clubs, and provide a leisure-time program for the children. Through these enlarged programs many day nurseries exercise a wide influence on the social and religious life of their neighborhoods.

Rapid Spread of Day Nurseries in Nineties

In all probability, there were many other early examples of day nursery care similar to that of St. James Parish in New York. Many parishes undoubtedly made provision for the infants of working mothers. It was only in the nineties, however, that the day nursery came to occupy any large place in the program of Catholic child-care. In 1888 Our Lady of Mercy Day Nursery, formerly known as St. Vincent de Paul Day Nursery, was organized in New York. A year later the Holy Family Day Nursery was also organized.

Between 1890 and 1900 the following day nurseries were organized: St. Joseph's Day Nursery, Brooklyn, N. Y. (1895); St. Joseph's Day Nursery, New York, N. Y. (1895); St. Agnes' Day Nursery, Brooklyn, N. Y. (1895); Sisters of Perpetual Adoration Day Nursery, New Orleans, La. (1896); Santa Maria Institute, Cincinnati, Ohio (1897); Cathedral Day

Nursery and Kindergarten, Philadelphia, Pa. (1897); St. Anthony's Kindergarten and Day Nursery for Boys and Girls, Philadelphia, Pa. (1900); and St. James' Day Nursery, Trenton, N. J. (1900).

St. Joseph's Day Nursery, New York City

A very good illustration of the circumstances leading to the establishment of day nurseries in the nineties is found in that of St. Joseph's Day Nursery in the Paulist Parish of New York. There had been a large increase in the number of Catholic working mothers on the west side. A number of day nurseries were organized under non-Catholic auspices to care for the children. The members of the St. Vincent de Paul Society began to urge the establishment of a Catholic day nursery. In their visitation of the poor they had occasion to come into contact with many working mothers whose children were endangered through contact with Protestant day nurseries.[3]

St. Elizabeth's Day Nursery, Chicago

St. Elizabeth's Day Nursery in Chicago, organized about the same time, adopted a broader program. In addition to its regular day nursery program it included a Sunday school, classes in sewing, a health clinic for children and a club for girls. In order to maintain the self-respect of the mothers, St. Elizabeth's decided to have a small charge for those who could afford to pay.[4] In St. Elizabeth's, one can see the Catholic day nursery branching out from its original, restricted objective of providing day-care for the children of working mothers to a larger community program. The day nurseries very soon realized that there was not only the question of caring for the children but also of assisting the mothers in the understanding and discharge of their responsibilities.

[3] "Little People and Great Ideas," by John J. O'Shea, *Catholic World*, Vol. LXI (April, 1895), p. 77.
[4] *Ibid.*

Many of the nurseries following the pattern of St. Elizabeth's became conscious of the recreational needs of the older children and therefore decided to develop clubs for them. The teaching of Sunday school also became an important part of the nursery program.

Mission Helpers, Servants of the Sacred Heart, Make Departure in Nursery Programs

The community known as Mission Helpers, Servants of the Sacred Heart, of Baltimore, illustrate an important departure in the work of Catholic day nurseries. The whole spirit and purpose of the Mission Helpers was to reach spiritually neglected persons in American parishes by continuous house-to-house visitations. The day nursery served as a sort of missionary outpost and a center for the religious instruction of children who were not reached by the parochial school. The Mission Helpers regard their catechetical work as a basic objective. The day nursery to them is simply a means to an end. They are not willing to accept day nurseries when they can not be made a means of attaining their larger objectives.

On the invitation of Bishop James A. McFaul of Trenton, the Mission Helpers, Servants of the Sacred Heart, made their first venture in day nursery work (1898). The chief purposes of St. James' Day Nursery of Trenton were parish visitation and catechetical work. In 1905 Monsignor D. J. McMahon, Director of Catholic Charities of New York, induced the Mission Helpers to open St. Pascal's Day Nursery in New York City. The community continued with the same program as in Trenton. St. Pascal's Day Nursery, like the Keating Day Nursery, which was taken over by these sisters (1916) at the request of Monsignor Lavelle, rector of St. Patrick's Cathedral, became a center for religious parish visitation and religious instruction. In connection with the Keating Day Nursery a summer home for children from the congested quarters of New York City was opened at Hawthorne (1921), from which it was transferred to Mt. Mongola, Ellenville, New York. In 1928 the Mission Helpers opened a day nursery in the Nativity Parish, New York City, with a program similar to those carried out in St. Pascal's and the Keating Day Nurseries. At the request of Bishop J. F. R. Canevin, the Mission Helpers took over St. Raphael's Home in Pittsburgh as a temporary shelter for children (1921). In St. Raphael's the sisters also did some day nursery work and made the institution a center for their regular work of home-visitation and religious instruction. From St. Raphael's Home the sisters conduct St. Ann's Day Nursery in another section of the city. In 1928 a day nursery for colored was begun in Baltimore on the site of the old novitate on Mc-Culloh Street. It is a model institution caring for three classes of children, babies, kindergarten, and school children. Visiting is also done from this center among the families of the children.[5]

Day Nurseries in Cincinnati and Cleveland

A number of Catholic day nurseries have become a part of a general Catholic community program. Of these one of the most conspicuous is the Santa Bambino Day Nursery in Cincinnati established by Sister Blandina to whom reference has already been made.[6] She successfully joined the material with the spiritual in her program. Before long her Santa Maria Institute was a veritable hive of activity with clubs, educational classes for boys and girls, athletics and, in fact, everything that enters into a real settlement program. From the beginning she found that one of the important problems of the district was the care of children whose mothers were compelled to go out to work. Hence it was that she decided to make the day nursery a part of her program. In similar

[5] *The Mission Helpers, Servants of the Sacred Heart*, manuscript report prepared for writer, 1930.
[6] Chapter XV.

A SUPPORT FOR THE HOME 315

fashion, the Merrick House in Cleveland added day nursery as an essential part of its program.

Place of Day Nursery in Social Work Program

Many persons have asked why should we have day nurseries when there are so many other forms of care available for mothers with children who have been deprived of their chief support. The aiding of mothers with dependent children is one of the basic purposes of family relief agencies. Most of the states provide public aid in their own homes for mothers with dependent children. If public and private relief were sufficiently large it could conceivably meet the needs of all mothers with dependent children, but there is scarcely any city in the United States in which public or private relief is sufficiently large to care adequately for all mothers of this type. In most jurisdictions relief, both public and private, is wholly inadequate. In many places agencies engaged in the administration of mothers' aid use day nurseries as a part of their program. If the children are older and are able to assist in the home work, these agencies permit the mother to work in order to earn partial support. When the children are very young, however, it is not considered a desirable social policy to have the mother go out to work and to place them in a day nursery.[7]

The day nursery can not plan for the children and the family without a careful study of individual cases. It should be in a position to know whether or not the plan that it offers is the best for the family. After the children have been received it should reckon not only with their needs but those of the family as a whole. In so far as may be necessary it should cultivate in the parents a sense of responsibility. It should acquaint mothers with the best principles of child-care. Some Catholic day nurseries, like the Merrick House Day Nursery in Cleveland, have their own facilities for the

[7] *Catholic Charities Review*, Vol. XI (November, 1927), pp. 328-330.

study of the cases that come to them. Other day nurseries, like the Holy Family Day Nursery in Washington, avail themselves of the services of the personnel of diocesan Catholic Charities.

The day nursery enters into a cooperative relationship with the parent in the care of the child. It supplements the efforts of the parent and works with the latter in an effort to overcome their handicaps. The children coming to the day nursery will present many problems. A large number of them will be under-nourished because of improper food. Others will suffer from physical handicaps pointing to the fact that they are not receiving proper medical attention. Some will not have developed habits of personal cleanliness. The day nursery that is in tune with the best experience in its field will work with parents in seeing that the children are given an opportunity of growing up in good health and with good health habits. In order that its health program may be built on a sure foundation the day nursery that is alive to its obligations and possibilities will insist that every child be given a medical examination on admission. It will have the children examined once a month while they are under its care. It will see that all the children are given proper food based on a standard dietary, that they are taught proper health habits, and that they are inspected by the superintendent each morning before admission.[8]

Parents frequently have difficulty in understanding their young children. They are at a loss to know how to deal with certain difficulties these children present. The day nursery should be able to interpret children to their parents. In order to do so, the directors must first understand the children. They must be persons who are capable of giving advice in regard to the behaviorism of children.

[8] "Horizon Lines in the Day Nursery Situation," by Alice Padgett, *Catholic Charities Review*, Vol. XI (November, 1927), pp. 332–333.

Diocesan Charities Lend Hand to Day Nurseries

In some dioceses, the diocesan charities have given special attention to the coordination and improvement of day nurseries. The most notable example of what Catholic Charities has done for day nurseries is to be found in New York, where (1922) the diocesan bureau was supplying clinical equipment for eleven day nurseries. It employed doctors for weekly visitation of the nurseries. It arranged for the organization of health classes in five nurseries. A nutrition worker was engaged to prepare dietaries. Visiting nurses were added to nursery staffs. Kindergarten teachers were secured through the cooperation of the Board of Education with Catholic Charities.[9]

A beginning, if only a beginning, has been made in regard to day nurseries as an essential part of a diocesan program of Catholic Charities. The day nurseries are here. In the past they were isolated parish institutions without necessary aid, advice and encouragement from a central source.

[9] *Report of the Catholic Charities of New York*, 1922, pp. 57–59.

CHAPTER XVII
THE CONTRIBUTION OF CATHOLIC WOMEN
Women the Pioneers in Parish Charitable Organizations

The first Catholic lay organizations for charity in this country were organizations of women. These organizations grew up like our Rosary Societies, our Altar Societies or our Sodalities. The Catholic parishes were like so many isolated colonies with only their own resources to care for their own needs. They were, therefore, fertile fields for the development of that mutual aid of which there is no record except in the book of life. It was that simple informal charity that the world passes by unnoticed. Such records as we have of organized parish charities before the Civil War, indicate that a large part of the work was done by women's organizations. There is a continuous record of the activities of the Charitable Society of St. Patrick's Church of Washington, a group of Catholic women, who divided the parish into districts to each of which a chairman was named who was responsible for the care of the poor within its confines. This society only disappeared with the organization of the Society of St. Vincent de Paul in the parish in 1861.[1]

Earliest Charitable Societies of Women

An organization of Catholic women known as St. Paul's Catholic Guild was established in Brooklyn in 1846: "Under patronage of Blessed Virgin Mary for the encouragement of the following duties: the practice of Christian charity . . . ; visitation of the sick and if in danger of death, procuring the services of a clergyman; prevention and discountenancing of scandal; religious instruction of youth."[2] It was intended

---
[1] *Archives* of St. Patrick's Church, Washington, D. C.
[2] *Catholic Directory*, 1852, p. 214.

that this society should become a national society with branches throughout the entire United States. Another illustration of a local parish charitable organization of women was the Dorcas Society established in the Cathedral Parish of Baltimore in 1850.[3]

Women's Organizations Local in Character

The early organizations of Catholic women established for parish charities did not adopt any uniform name. They were just as local and as isolated, one from the other, as the parishes out of which they grew. Through the Society of St. Vincent de Paul parish organizations of Catholic men have been given a community-wide and a national point of view. There has been no parallel movement in Catholic women's work. Various types of women's aid societies have been growing steadily out of the life of our parishes but there has been no bond of union between them. They have remained purely parochial. The impetus to the development of leadership in the work of Catholic women in the United States has not come from the parish.

The Ladies of Charity

In France the Ladies of Charity worked in close cooperation with the Society of St. Vincent de Paul in the various parishes. The Ladies of Charity there gave the women an opportunity not only for work but for leadership in charity. In the United States there has been no parallel development. The first confraternity of the Ladies of Charity was established in the City of St. Louis in 1857, twelve years after the first conference of the Society of St. Vincent de Paul was established in that city. For nearly twenty years the St. Louis Ladies of Charity was the only branch of the organization in the United States. In 1876 speaking before the Third General Assembly of the Society of St. Vincent de Paul, Rev.

[3] *Baltimore Catholic Mirror*, February 24, 1872; February 10, 1877.

J. A. Walter, pastor of St. Patrick's Church in Washington, told about the organization of the Ladies of Charity in Washington two years previously. He said it came about in this way: "A wardrobe kept by a member of the Society (Society of St. Vincent de Paul) had nearly always been empty. Then some ladies suggested to him that they should be organized into a society for the purpose of assisting the conferences in the work of procuring clothing for the poor. The idea so coincided with his own that the ladies of the parish of every social position being called together were organized into a society called the Ladies of Charity of St. Vincent de Paul.[4] Father Walter's program was so entirely new that many of the delegates expressed a desire to know more about it. From the accounts of the organization of the Ladies of Charity of Washington, published in the *Baltimore Catholic Mirror*, it is quite clear that it was to be city-wide rather than parochial in its scope. In the diocesan paper we find the following description of the Ladies of Charity of the Capital City: "A new association bearing the name Ladies of Charity has just been formed in this city to assist the St. Vincent de Paul Society in its works of charity. A preliminary meeting was held in Carroll Hall last Monday when about fifty ladies from the several parishes were present. . . . The object of this association is to collect clothing of every description and then place it in a wardrobe subject to the wants of the several Conferences of the St. Vincent de Paul Society."[5]

The Association of Catholic Charities of New York City

The organization of the Association of Catholic Charities of New York City marked an important stage in the development of the parish charitable activities of Catholic women's organizations in the United States. In 1902 Monsignor McMahon, local Director of Catholic Charities, called a meeting of the

[4] *Report of Proceedings of the Third General Assembly of the Society of St. Vincent de Paul in the United States*, 1876, p. 25.
[5] January 16, 1875.

women of the city for the purpose of developing St. Vincent de Paul auxiliaries in the different parishes. In addition to the parish work he felt that the women should develop auxiliary committees for the hospitals, children's institutions and day nurseries. It was decided that both the parish and institution auxiliaries should be joined together in one organization to be known as the Association of Catholic Charities. The first president of the association was Mrs. Joseph J. O'Donohue and its first secretary was Miss Teresa R. O'Donohue.[6]

The Broader Viewpoint of the Association of Catholic Charities of New York

The Association of Catholic Charities of New York envisaged its problems from a city-wide point of view. From the beginning its members acted as volunteer probation officers in the children's court and engaged in prison visitation and in conducting classes in English, civics, and Christian Doctrine for immigrants.[7] In 1912 the Association of Catholic Charities was affiliated with the Ladies of Charity in Paris and thus became a part of a world-wide organization of charity. Seven years later the council of the association, at the suggestion of Cardinal Hayes, decided to surrender its old name and to substitute the name Ladies of Charity of the Catholic Charities of the Archdiocese of New York, Inc. For a number of years the members sought a means to cherish the memory of their founder in some substantial way. Their objective was realized in 1920 with the opening of the McMahon Memorial Shelter for children.

Development of the Ladies of Charity

In 1907 the Ladies of Charity were organized by Rev. Hugh Monaghan in SS. Philip and James' Parish, Baltimore. It

[6] *St. Vincent de Paul Quarterly*, Vol. VIII, No. 1 (February, 1903), pp. 58, 65-66; *A Short History of the Ladies of Charity of New York, formerly the Association of Catholic Charities*, Taken from the Records of the Secretary.
[7] *Ibid.*

was his plan to have an active group of Catholic women work with the St. Vincent de Paul Conference.[8] During the past three years there has been an organized movement for the development of the Ladies of Charity in Baltimore. There are at present twelve branches of the society in that city. In addition, confraternities of the Ladies of Charity have been established in Huntsville, Alabama, and Keokuk, Iowa.

The Queen's Daughters

An association which for a number of years promised to become national in scope was the Queen's Daughters of St. Louis, organized for the same fundamental purpose as the Ladies of Charity, namely, the supplementing of the work of the parish conferences of the Society of St. Vincent de Paul. The first branch of the organization was established by Miss Mary I. Hoxsey in St. John's Parish, St. Louis, in December of 1889. It was approved by a conference of archbishops held in Philadelphia in 1894. Its growth was rapid between 1900 and 1910, with branches in Missouri, Illinois, New York, Texas, Minnesota, Massachusetts, Colorado, Connecticut, West Virginia, Rhode Island, Mississippi, Louisiana and Alabama.[9]

In addition to their parish activities the Queen's Daughters branched out into a number of special works. In St. Louis they operate a home for business women. In 1908 the Queen's Daughters of Providence assumed responsibility for financing the work of the White Sisters a religious community engaged in home nursing.[10]

St. Margaret's Daughters

Another organization, almost entirely local in character, which has aimed to provide an outlet for women in the parish charities of the Church is St. Margaret's Daughters of New

---

[8] *Proceedings of National Conference of Catholic Charities*, 1925, p. 243.
[9] *St. Vincent de Paul Quarterly*, Vol. XVII, No. 3 (August, 1912), pp. 251–252; "The Work and Aims of the Queen's Daughters," by Mary V. Toomey, *The Catholic World*, Vol. LXVII (August, 1898), p. 610.
[10] *Catholic Charities Review*, Vol. VII, May, 1923, p. 180.

Orleans. In 1889 Father James Meyers of that city was anxious to interest a number of women in providing clothing for poor children. He talked the matter over with Miss Evelyn A. Waldo and Miss Sidney Elder. The first thought was to establish a group of women in one parish. If, however, one group could be organized successfully, why not a number of parish groups; and so the idea was conceived of a city-wide organization with branches in the various parishes. At the present time St. Margaret's Daughters has circles throughout the city of New Orleans. The organization divides the field of Catholic family social work with the Society of St. Vincent de Paul. By mutual agreement with the parish conferences of the Society of St. Vincent de Paul the circles of St. Margaret's Daughters take over certain types of cases with which women volunteers are more fully qualified to deal.[11]

The groups of women whose work has been described in the foregoing paragraphs received their inspiration from the parish. They grew out of the need for women volunteers to supplement the parish conferences of the Society of St. Vincent de Paul. While some of them took up problems of a city-wide character, their basic interests remained in the parishes.

Catholic Women as a Factor in the Financing of Charitable Institutions

Catholic women from the very beginning have aided in the financing of charitable institutions in charge of religious communities. Catholic women aided Father John Hughes, later archbishop of New York, in establishing St. John's Orphan Asylum, Philadelphia. Catholic women aided the Sisters of Charity in establishing their first orphan asylum in Boston. A Catholic convert, Mrs. Peter, was responsible for bringing the Sisters of the Poor of St. Francis to Cincinnati in 1858. Another Catholic woman, Mrs. McTavish, was largely responsible for opening the first Good Shepherd Home in Baltimore.

[11] *Silver Jubilee Report of St. Margaret's Daughters*, 1889–1914, pp. 6–8.

It was only after 1890, however, that auxiliary boards of women for Catholic charitable institutions became popular. According to a study made by Miss Sara E. Laughlin, the first auxiliary of this type in Philadelphia was formed in 1897.[12]

The New Era of Women's Organizations

In the nineties of the last century there was a new development of Catholic women's organizations. It was becoming apparent that the Catholic problems growing out of the new immigration could not be met by parish organization alone. The Italian immigrants were not being reached by the existing parish mechanisms of the Church. A few leaders at first appeared, here and there, but they were crying in the wilderness, until gradually their number increased. Out of their efforts grew a chain of city-wide organizations of Catholic women. These organizations sponsored special agencies to reach the new immigrant. They were among the pioneers in establishing day nurseries and settlements. They did for the new immigrants what the St. Vincent de Paul Society did for the older immigrants. With the establishment of juvenile courts they interested themselves in supplying volunteer probation officers to care for Catholic children. Later they became interested in special protective programs for Catholic girls.

The Christ Child Society of Washington

The Christ Child Society of Washington was one of the pioneer Catholic women's organizations. The first thought of the foundress of the Christ Child Society, Miss Mary V. Merrick, was to bring the joys of Christmas to the children of the poor. She also wanted to interest women of more fortunate financial circumstances in providing clothing for the children of the poor on a year-round basis. Out of these two basic thoughts the whole program of the Christ Child Society

[12] *Proceedings of the National Conference of Catholic Charities*, 1922, p. 266.

grew. In carrying out their mission to children the volunteers of the Christ Child Society found that the little ones to whom they ministered needed more than food and clothing. Many were growing up without any religious instruction. Such a situation could not fail to appeal to a group of women genuinely concerned with the care and upbringing of children. Hand in hand with the classes in religious instruction went the settlement program of the Christ Child Society. At first the settlement program was not extensive, but it grew with the development of the Society's consciousness of the community problems. In the settlement program special attention has been given to the recreational needs of children.

In their contacts with poor children the visitors of the Christ Child Society found many who were anaemic and under-nourished. Taking the children from the slums into the country for a short period during the summer was becoming a popular idea. Why could not the Christ Child Society provide summer outings for some of the neglected children of Washington? The society did not have much means at its disposal and must, therefore, begin such a work on a small scale. The thought occurred to the president of the Society that they might begin by boarding a few children in a country home. Gradually the summer work grew. A home was acquired in nearby Maryland to take care of the children. Many of the members of the Society saw no reason why a home that was used for summer work should remain idle all winter. Hence, they conceived the idea of using the building for convalescent care during the winter months. After some experimenting the Christ Child Society found that it could not include two types of work in one building. It finally decided to concentrate on the convalescent care of children. The convalescent home accepts children who need special health upbuilding from the various hospitals and social agencies of the community.

Contact with children at Christmas led to an all-year-round program of children's aid. The Society assigned a volunteer visitor to each parish to visit the families of children needing special care. All the parish visitors were supervised by the executive secretary of the Society. In the course of their work the parish visitors of the Christ Child Society came into contact with the St. Vincent de Paul visitors and in time, they came to discharge the functions of auxiliaries to the St. Vincent de Paul conferences. The members of the Society of St. Vincent de Paul called on the Christ Child visitors for service in families with which they felt themselves unqualified to deal. With the increased cost of its settlement program and convalescent home, the Society found it necessary to ask the Catholic Charities to take over its relief work.

Branches of the Christ Child Society

Beginning in 1907 the branches of the Christ Child Society were established in a number of cities in the United States, as Chicago, Cleveland, Detroit. Omaha, Philadelphia and St. Paul. Reference has been made to the work of the Cleveland branch in sponsoring the Merrick House Settlement.[13] The Omaha unit entered a parallel field of activity in 1921. Here the new development has been associated with an increased activity in community affairs on the part of the members of the Society. Indeed, there is no city in the country in which the Catholic women have been more active in civic movements.

Beginning of a National Women's Organization

A meeting of representatives of women's organizations was held in connection with the World's Columbian Exposition in Chicago in 1893. A number of Catholic women who participated in this meeting decided on a general organization of Catholic women that would interest itself in problems of

[13] Chapter XV.

charity and education. These women banded themselves together in the Catholic Woman's National League. It was evidently their intention to make the organization national in scope. Subsequent events, however, compelled them to restrict their work to the city of Chicago, and the organization assumed the name, The Catholic Woman's League of Chicago.[14]

As Protestant organizations were exceedingly active in the development of day nurseries the league felt that it could not make a more effective contribution to the welfare of Catholic dependent children than by undertaking a similar program. Thereupon, the league organized St. Elizabeth's Day Nursery and St. Mary's Settlement and Day Nursery (1893), St. Anne's Day Nursery (1894), and St. Juliana's Day Nursery and Social Settlement (1912).[15]

Travelers' Aid Program of the Catholic Woman's League of Chicago

From 1893 to 1910 the Catholic Woman's League of Chicago limited itself definitely to its settlement program. A paper on the work of the International Catholic Association for the Protection of Young Girls, read by Monsignor Mueller-Simonis at the first meeting of the National Conference of Catholic Charities, held at the Catholic University in 1910, exercised a far-reaching influence on the program of the League of Chicago as well as of other Catholic women's organizations in the United States. It is sometimes erroneously said that this marked the beginning of Catholic protective work for girls in the United States. The first activity to which the Sisters of Mercy devoted themselves in the United States was the protection of young girls. Mueller-Simonis' address, however, did mark the beginning of a lively interest on the part of Catholic women in girls' protective programs.

[14] "The Catholic Life of Chicago," by Kathryn Prindiville, *Catholic World*, Vol. LXVII (July, 1898), p. 477; *The Archdiocese of Chicago*, p. 795.
[15] *Thirty-third Annual Announcement of the Catholic Woman's League of Chicago*, 1926–1927, pp. 26–31.

Just a year after the Washington meeting, the Catholic Woman's League of Chicago opened its protective department, known as the Protectorate. Guides were detailed to the various railroad stations to assist girls who were arriving in the city without friends. Plans were made for their temporary housing and employment. Later a home for transient girls was opened in which they could be housed temporarily. The Catholic Woman's League really developed a complete travelers' aid program which it has continued.[16]

Catholic Women's Leagues of Brooklyn and Pittsburgh

The Catholic Woman's League of Chicago was the forerunner of a number of similar organizations in different cities. They received their inspiration in large measure from the appeal of the newer immigrants. The Catholic Women's Association of Brooklyn was organized by Rev. Edward W. McCarty in 1894 for recreational and educational work among young girls.[17] The Catholic Women's League of Pittsburgh was organized in 1904 "to unite all our Catholic women, either as representing organized bodies or as individual members, into one Grand Federation or Union to aid in religious, educational and charitable work, assist the orphans, relieve the poor, provide homes for friendless Catholic children and engage in any other work of zeal or public charity."[18]

The first activity undertaken by the Catholic Women's League of Pittsburgh was mission work in the immigrant settlements particularly among the Italians. A sewing class for girls and a kindergarten for smaller children were established in St. Peter's Italian Parish. This work was carried on until the parish was able to open its own school. During the first year of its existence, the League appointed a committee to look after neglected and dependent children and see to it that they attended Mass and Sunday school. In 1905 branches of the

[16] *Catholic Charities Review*, Vol. 1, February, 1917, pp. 46-47.
[17] "The Catholic Women's Association," by Louise Girod, *Catholic World*, Vol. LXXII (January, 1901), p. 497.
[18] *Pittsburgh Catholic Social Study*, 1919, National Catholic War Council, p. 543.

League were established in the different parishes. In 1910 a full-time worker was employed to assist the Good Shepherd Sisters in planning for the girls under their care and a year later the organization developed a protective program for girls, including travelers' aid work.[19]

In the process of centralization after the war the Catholic Women's League of Pittsburgh lost much of its old enthusiasm. Social work was now entering a new age. Standards were changing and professional service was being stressed everywhere. The organization, however, still continues but under a new name, the Pittsburgh Council of Catholic Women. The program, also, is entirely different from what it used to be. The only institutional activity in which the Council is engaged is the conduct of a boarding home for business women. Some attention is being given to educational and industrial problems.

Guild of Catholic Women of St. Paul

In 1906 a group of Catholic women in St. Paul organized the Guild of Catholic Women. They felt that there were many problems in the city calling for the attention of an organization of Catholic women. There was a need of a boarding home for girls. Then there were the possibilities of a girls' protective program. There was also a place for Catholic women in the municipal relief program. Their services would supplement the work of the Society of St. Vincent de Paul. With the development of the diocesan program of Catholic Charities the St. Paul Guild naturally lost its zeal and enthusiasm. Many of the services in which it pioneered became a part of the work of the diocesan charities, and the guild has not found it easy to adjust itself to the new situation.[20]

The League of Catholic Women in Detroit

The League of Catholic Women of Detroit is one of the most interesting organizations of Catholic women in the

[19] *Ibid*, pp. 543–545.
[20] *Proceedings of the National Conference of Catholic Charities*, 1916, pp. 375-376.

United States. Its ground work was laid in the effort to reach the spiritually neglected children of the new immigration. Soon settlement work was added: The Weinman Settlement House, St. Ann's Community Center, and St. Rita's Community Center.[21] After the settlement work came the protective program. Plans were made for the care of delinquent and semi-delinquent girls referred by the Recorder's Court, the police department, and other local agencies. The organization deals with delinquent girls through its casework and offers a temporary shelter. In 1915 the League of Catholic Women of Detroit opened a boarding home for business women. After 1920 the members began to give serious thought to the possibility of expanding its educational and housing program for business women. Its other activities were now rather well developed so there was no reason why it should not extend into new and larger fields. In 1926 plans were perfected for a large hotel and club for business women. Instead of erecting the building with borrowed money, the League decided to organize a building fund campaign. The new hotel and club, with facilities for housing 250 women, an auditorium, club and recreational rooms, was opened in 1928. An extensive educational program is carried on among its own members through lecture courses and a monthly publication, *The Catholic Woman*. Recently it sponsored a conference on women in industry in cooperation with the Social Action Department of the National Catholic Welfare Conference (1930).

Further Expansion of Leagues of Catholic Women in the United States

Between 1906 and 1920 the idea of city-wide organizations of Catholic women spread rapidly in the United States. Among the organizations established in this period were: The Catholic Woman's League of Dallas (1910), the League of

---

[21] *Annual Report of the League of Catholic Women*, Detroit, 1928.

Catholic Women of Minneapolis (1911), the Catholic Women's League of St. Louis (1917), the Catholic Women's Association of St. Louis (1917), the Alliance of Catholic Women of Philadelphia (1918), the Catholic Women's Association of Cincinnati (1921).

Protective Work for Girls Adopted by Women's Organizations

As a result of the discussions at the first meeting of the National Conference of Catholic Charities in 1910, many organizations of Catholic women developed a new interest in girls' protective work. The juvenile court and the Good Shepherd Sisters had already aroused general interest in the plight of the delinquent girl. The Association of Catholic Charities of New York had supplied volunteer probation officers to the children's court since 1902, and the Catholic Women's League of Pittsburgh had been working with the Good Shepherd Sisters since 1907. Within a few years, Catholic women's organizations saw new horizons in protective work. They thought seriously about the girl away from home. Why could they not assist in the international work for the protection of young girls and provide guides at railroad stations and temporary housing accommodations for women away from home? It was the first time that any large group of Catholic women's organizations in the United States had been able to profit by inspiration from a national source. The results were far-reaching. During the following ten years there was scarcely any organization of Catholic women in this country which did not give some attention to girls' protective work.

The Big Sister Movement

The desire to help the delinquent and pre-delinquent girls was also responsible for the creation of a number of new organizations with protective care as their sole aim: The Big

Sisters of Chicago (1916), the Big Sisters of Cincinnati (1916), and the Big Sisters of Brooklyn (1918). The original purpose of the Chicago Big Sisters was to aid the Sisters of the Good Shepherd in their educational program and to provide after-care for the girls discharged from their institution. They naturally reached out to the juvenile court, which would call upon them for advice and assistance in planning for Catholic children. A number of the Big Sisters were inspired to provide clubs for the temporary housing of girls. The Brooklyn Big Sisters and the Cincinnati Big Sisters also endeavor to interest volunteers in work for delinquent and pre-delinquent Catholic girls. Another appealing feature of these organizations is the provision for scholarships in Catholic educational institutions for promising girls handicapped by a lack of home training.

The Catholic Daughters of America

In recent years, the Catholic Daughters of America, a fraternal order, has become interested in social work. They have financed a program of child-placing in the diocese of Pittsburgh. They have aided in the development of a program of Catholic child-care in Vermont. In a number of the smaller towns in the south and southwest they have organized a program of service and relief for Catholic families. In many cities, including Atlantic City, Baltimore, Washington and Scranton, they have opened boarding homes for business women. Their interest in social service is both noteworthy and promising. The Catholic Daughters represent a cross-section of the rank and file of Catholic business women, in striking contrast to the personnel of the Leagues of Catholic Women, which is largely from the upper classes. Their outlook on life and their approach to social problems are quite different.

Early German Benevolent Societies

Beginning about 1840 the German Catholic immigrants to the United States found expression for their charity through benevolent societies. These societies had been a part of German tradition for centuries, and when they came to America, they naturally brought their racial traditions of benevolence: "Wherever the stream of German Catholic immigration sent its waves from New York along the Hudson, the Erie Canal and the Great Lakes into the states of New York, northern Ohio, Michigan, northern Illinois and Wisconsin; from Baltimore along canals and railroads and the Ohio River into Pennsylvania, Ohio, northern Kentucky and Indiana; from New Orleans along the Mississippi River to the states of Missouri, Illinois, Iowa, Minnesota—everywhere benevolent societies sprang up, at once crystallizing in themselves what was best among the immigrants and radiating into their surroundings the spirit and the wholesomeness of their united action." [22]

The Central Verein of America

The German Catholic benevolent societies were brought together in the German Roman Catholic Central Verein of America (1855). Since that date the Central Verein has provided a national outlet and leadership for its various local units. In 1908 the Central Verein created a central bureau with offices in St. Louis to promote Catholic social studies and Catholic social action. Through its monthly publication, the *Central Blatt,* and numerous leaflets, the central bureau has maintained an active interest on the part of German Catholics in larger, philosophical questions of social reform, child labor laws, social insurance, minimum wage legislation, child and woman labor, employment bureaus and the problems of unemployment. The pioneer work of the Central Verein and its central bureau helped lay the foundations of a Catholic

---

[22] *Souvenir Volume, Diamond Jubilee Celebration and Seventy-fourth Annual Convention of the Catholic Central Verein of America and the Fourteenth Annual Convention of the National Catholic Women's Union,* 1930, p. 44.

social movement in America; for the Germans were not satisfied with palliatives but in thorough fashion have sought the fundamental causes and curatives of poverty and its resultant problems.

The Federation of German Catholic Women's Societies

One of the important contributions of the Central Verein, and the one with which this chapter is especially concerned, was the federation of the German Catholic women's societies into an organization known as The National Catholic Women's Union of the United States of America (1914). This union aims to "promote participation in charitable activities, to furnish to Catholic women opportunity to cooperate in Catholic Public Action to create wholesome public opinion according to christian principles, to arouse and encourage self-reliance and leadership amongst Catholic women." [23]

The National Catholic Women's Union has fostered a number of charity projects. In February, 1929, the Missouri branch of the federation opened the Mother of Good Counsel Home for Incurables in St. Louis. About the same time the New York branch opened St. Elizabeth's Home for Working Girls in New York City. The Wisconsin branch also opened a home for working girls, the Mother of Good Counsel Home in Milwaukee (1929).[24]

Post-War Developments in Catholic Social Work

After the war Catholic social work in the United States entered a new stage. The pioneer work of the Society of St. Vincent de Paul and the organizations of Catholic women opened a great many new fields of Catholic activity. There was a general feeling now that these fields needed more intensive cultivation such as could be carried on only by large organizations coming directly under episcopal leadership. Im-

[23] *Ibid.*, p. 66.
[24] *Ibid.*, pp. 66-67.

portant changes were taking place in the whole structure of American social work. On all sides there was a very pronounced drift towards central financing. It is important that Catholic agencies should be coordinated under a central authority in order to profit by the community chest or central finances. In cities in which Catholics for sufficient reasons decided that it would be unwise to participate in the community chest, a strong organization was needed in order to keep in step with the procession. Social agencies of all kinds were coming to rely more on professional service. Catholics, therefore, found it impossible to maintain these standards without full-time and well-trained workers. There was still a very large place for the volunteer but he was supposed to work as a part of a coordinated program. He had to submit to rigid standards; his work had to stand the test of objective analysis.

Catholic Women's Organizations in a Coordinated Program

For Catholic women's organizations the transition from the old order to the new was by no means easy. In the old order their leadership was unquestioned. In the new they had to share it with the professional worker. In the old order they could develop programs according to their own conception of the needs; they now found it necessary to relate their work to diocesan and city-wide programs. It was quite natural that this transition should have given rise to questions in the minds of many volunteers who had given years of consecrated service and that, furthermore, a number of them should fail to find their places in the new system. It was quite natural, moreover, that many of the new professional leaders, with a keen consciousness of their power and efficiency, should lose patience with those whose glory was in the past.

The Survival of the Fittest

If men were more far-sighted they could bring the experience of the past into the practical affairs of life to a much greater degree. If Catholic leaders had only been more foresighted in the transition from the old to the new in Catholic work they could have maintained the zeal and enthusiasm of the Society of St. Vincent de Paul and of Catholic women's organizations to a greater degree. Of the two organizations, the Catholic women's group suffered the more seriously in the transition. For a number of women's organizations it marked the end of their active participation in Catholic charities. Some, however, succeeded in weathering the storm and in adjusting themselves. Wherever a successful adjustment has been made, it has been due to wise leadership, to the ability of the organizations to develop projects for which they were especially fitted, or to the failure of processes of coordination and centralization to develop as rapidly in some cities.

New Interests Inspired by National Council of Catholic Women

While Catholic women in recent years have suffered reverses in the domain of charity work, they have gained in the wider fields of social action and education. The writer has been told by a woman whose knowledge of Catholic women's organizations after the war was unquestioned, that not one of them had an interest in industrial programs. The same might also be said of general educational programs. Today things are different. Many Catholic women's organizations are keenly interested in industrial programs; they are also more actively concerned with education. The new interests of Catholic women's organizations are due in great measure to the leadership of the National Council of Catholic Women. The fortunes of Catholic women's organizations in the United

States during the past ten years have been bound up closely with the National Council of Catholic Women. They have come to regard the council as a clearing house and guide. It opens the world of social and educational problems. One of the main tasks of the National Council has been to interpret its functions and its usefulness to the Catholic women of the country. Such a task demands patience and long-continued effort. It takes local organizations a long time to understand the work of national organizations, just as it does national organizations to sense the philosophy of their local constituents. The work of the National Council of Catholic Women is a part of a process that runs through all America. The Catholic body in this country grew up as separate and isolated units. Its localism was a source of strength. It has been a long, slow process to weld so many isolated units into a homogeneous national body.

The National Council of Catholic Women and the National Catholic Welfare Conference

One can not very well understand the National Council of Catholic Women except as a part of the National Catholic Welfare Conference, of whose mechanism the Women's Council is an integral part. It is through this organization that the Conference reaches the Catholic women of the United States.[25]

The origin of the National Catholic Welfare Conference was thus clearly expressed by the late Archbishop Dowling, one of its supporters and a member of its Administrative Committee: "In February, 1919, seventy-seven bishops of the United States met in Washington to celebrate the Golden Jubilee of Cardinal Gibbons. At that meeting the now Cardinal Cerretti appeared and expressed the wish of His Holiness, the then Pope, Benedict XV, that the bishops should make

---

[25] *The National Catholic Welfare Conference*, by Austin Dowling, D.D., Archbishop of St. Paul. Reprinted from *The Ecclesiastical Review*, October, 1928, pp. 10–11.

plans for an annual meeting whereat they would take common counsel on matters of general import and establish departments that would, under their supervision and direction, carry out the work assigned. The bishops immediately and unanimously decided to act in accordance with the Holy Father's request."[26]

According to the plans formulated and accepted by them, the bishops of the United States were to constitute the National Catholic Welfare Conference and were to meet once a year. Between the annual meetings of the bishops the work of the Conference was to be carried on by certain departments operating under the direction of an administrative committee composed of seven bishops. These departments were the Executive, Education, Social Action, Legal, Press and Publicity, and Lay Organizations. The National Council of Catholic Men and the National Council of Catholic Women were to form the department of Lay Organizations.[27]

Origin of National Council of Catholic Women

In March 1920, Bishop Schrembs, the episcopal chairman of the Department of Lay Organizations of the National Catholic Welfare Conference, called together some 200 women to organize the National Council of Catholic Women. It was not the intention of the meeting to form a new organization, but to devise ways and means of bringing existing organizations into one national body. The council, however, was not strictly a federation. It admitted to membership not only the existing organizations of Catholic women, national, state and local, but also individual Catholic women, whether or not they were members of existing organizations.

One who has followed the fortunes of the National Council of Catholic Women since 1920 can not fail to note in its work a decided tendency towards a loose federation. The question

[26] *Ibid.*, p. 6.
[27] *Ibid.*, pp. 9-10.

of individual membership has aroused discussion, particularly in the formation of diocesan councils of Catholic women. It is noteworthy in this connection that in the revision of the constitution (1928), distinction was made between active members and individual or associate members.[28]

The National Council Subdivides Into Diocesan Councils

With the permission of the bishop the National Council of Catholic Women endeavors to have established a diocesan council in each diocese in order to bring together the various organizations in the diocese, to assist them in developing their programs, and to act as a medium of communication between the national and the local organizations. In the development of its program the diocesan council is subject entirely to the will of the bishop. He can decide that the diocesan council should be merely a federation of existing agencies or that it should be for all practical purposes a separate organization with its individual membership and its own program.[29]

The Program of the Diocesan Councils of Catholic Women

In most dioceses the diocesan councils of Catholic women have confined themselves to purely educational movements. They have provided a medium of communication between the national and the various local organizations. Once a year they hold conventions that bring together representative women of the diocese. In a few places, notably Hartford, Denver and Houston, the diocesan councils of Catholic women have undertaken concrete pieces of social work. In Hartford, the council acts as a sort of auxiliary to the diocesan social service bureau; in Denver, the council operates a settlement in the Mexican district; and the Houston Council has opened a clinic for Mexican children.

[28] *Constitution and By-Laws of the National Council of Catholic Women*, Art. IV, Sections 2 and 3, p. 4.
[29] *Handbook for Diocesan Councils.* Published by the National Council of Catholic Women, pp. 3–4.

Problems of the Diocesan Councils

The relations between the diocesan council of Catholic Women and its constituent locals have created delicate problems. The various local women's groups have naturally been jealous of diocesan councils that were competing with them for individual members. The local groups have also been afraid of being over-shadowed by diocesan councils with appealing programs. The relations between the diocesan councils of Catholic women and the diocesan charities have also given rise to questions. The diocesan charities have assumed that it was their purpose to formulate social programs for the dioceses and to assist the organizations of men and women in formulating their individual programs. In some instances, the diocesan councils of women have tended to take over part of these functions claimed by the diocesan charities.

The National Catholic School of Social Service

The most far-reaching contribution of the National Council of Catholic Women has been the fostering of the National Catholic Service School for whose finances the Women's Council has held itself responsible from the beginning. The National Catholic School of Social Service was opened in Washington in November 1921, for the purpose of preparing Catholic women for social work. This school was not a new departure for Loyola University in Chicago and Fordham University in New York City had been engaged respectively in professional training for social work since 1912 and 1916. Yet, the opening of the national school in Washington was most significant as a recognition on the part of the American hierarchy of the importance of special training for social work. The bishops were well aware that social work was a recognized profession demanding special training just as much as other professions. People were coming to depend more and more on trained social workers for leadership in social movements. If the Church is going to bring to modern problems the influence of its philosophy and its centuries of experience in dealing with the poor and the afflicted, it must have trained leaders who have mastered its philosophy and drunk deep at the fountains of its experience.

The present National Catholic School of Social Service is a continuation of a training school for war workers opened in 1918 under the auspices of the women's division of the Committee on Special War Activities of the National Catholic War Council. It, therefore, may be regarded as a war product. Although the need for such a school had existed for many years, it was the war that gave the necessary impetus. The Service School is a war product in the same sense as the National Catholic Welfare Conference. The work of the National Catholic War Council in coordinating Catholic activities during the war called the attention of Catholics to the need of a permanent organization to give expression to our national Catholic life.[30]

The National Catholic School of Social Service is essentially a graduate school. It is open to women who hold a bachelor's degree from a recognized college or have its equivalent in training and experience. Its regular course extends over a period of two years. Students who have a bachelor's degree on admission may obtain the degree of master of arts from the Catholic University at the end of the regular two-year course on completion of all the requirements of the University. The Service School is affiliated with the Catholic University and is a member of the Association of Training Schools for Professional Social Work.

The Breadth of Interest of the National Council of Catholic Women

The National Council of Catholic Women has focused the attention of Catholic women on the social and educational problems of interest to them as Catholics and as American

[30] *The National Catholic School of Social Service, Prospectus,* 1930-1931, p. 7.

citizens. It is one of the basic assumptions of the Council that Catholic women of today must enter actively into social and educational movements. They must no longer be satisfied with immediate problems that arouse their attention; but they must concern themselves with the greater forces that make for the undermining or the upbuilding of our social structure. In order to appreciate the breadth of interests of the National Council, one has only to scan the resolutions passed in its annual conventions during the past ten years. For instance, the resolutions passed at the 1930 meeting in Denver dealt with a variety of topics as liturgy, annual retreats, family education, parent-teacher associations, Catholic schools, safeguarding purity, standards in dress, the theater and movies, the federalization of education, opposition to competition of women and girls in the Olympic Games, the youth movement, Catholic women of Mexico, immigration, industrial legislation, old age pensions, peace, eugenics, sterilization, historical records, narcotics, the Catholic Radio Hour, Catholic press, and the National Catholic School of Social Service. At so close a range, one can not appreciate or interpret the significance of the National Council of Catholic Women in American life. It is only in years to come that one will be able to trace its influence in a better and more enlightened leadership among the Catholic women of the United States.

CHAPTER XVIII
PRODUCTS OF THE SOIL
Early American Church Struggles to Meet Needs

From 1830 onwards Catholic leaders in the United States were compelled to give serious thought to the problems of the masses of immigrants who were arriving annually. Catholic bishops struggled to provide churches, hospitals for the sick, asylums for dependent children, and the innumerable charities which have already been noticed. The Church in the United States had few material resources at its disposal. Its only hope was the spirit of sacrifice of its own members and assistance from Europe.

There was a hope that the same spirit of sacrifice that gave birth to the Sisters of Charity of Emmitsburg, the Sisters of Charity of Nazareth, the Sisters of Loretto at the Foot of the Cross and the Dominican Sisters, would give birth to other communities. In this the Church was not disappointed. New religious communities did grow out of American soil all through the nineteenth century. Native communities, however, could not be expected to grow in sufficient proportions to provide for the current needs created by the immigration tide. After all, the care of the immigrant was more than an American problem. The Church in various European countries had definite responsibilities towards its people who had set out for the new land. It could not throw all these responsibilities on the infant Church in America. It was bound to aid in the missionary and charitable work among its nationals in America. It was quite natural that a number of European religious communities should look to the United States as a proper field for missionary labors and that American bishops should turn to Europe for aid. Another chapter[1]

[1] Chapter XIX.

deals with European communities that made important contributions to the development of American Catholic charities. This chapter will consider American communities established after 1830 which have been active in charity.

Communities of American Origin Arise

In discussing the work of American communities and those of European origin it should be remembered that it is not easy to draw a clear line of demarcation between them. Some American communities owe their inspiration to persons recently from Europe. Most communities of American origin, moreover, looked to Europe for subjects quite as much as those that had been founded in Europe.

Sisters of Charity of the Blessed Virgin Mary of Philadelphia

The American communities established between 1830 and 1860 continued the same traditions as the pioneer communities. They were interested primarily in education. During this period many pastors were striving to build schools to preserve the religious faith of the people. Looking around for sisters to teach in these schools they found that it was impossible to get any aid from existing American or European communities. As an expedient, a number employed lay teachers. A few of the more enterprising spirits with the aid of a number of consecrated women founded new religious communities. One of the most interesting of these spirits was Father Terence J. Donaghoe, pastor of St. Michael's Church, Philadelphia. For some time Father Donaghoe had been in quest of teachers for his parochial school. On a certain date his attention was called to a number of young women who were leading a common life and who had come recently from Ireland to engage in some work of service in the United States. The necessary arrangements were completed forthwith. On the Feast of All Saints, 1833, about two months after they had taken up their work of teaching, the members of this group pronounced their vows as members of a religious community and adopted a habit. The name given by Father Donaghoe to the new institute was the Sisters of Charity of the Blessed Virgin Mary. Such were the modest beginnings of one of the most active religious communities in the United States.

Sisters of Charity of the Blessed Virgin Mary of Dubuque

Ten years after beginning its work in Philadelphia, Father Donaghoe's infant community was transferred to the frontier diocese of Dubuque. Bishop Loras, like most bishops in new dioceses, had been searching for sisters to teach religion in his Sunday schools and to take charge of Catholic schools. Having learned about the new community in Philadelphia he immediately sought its assistance. On his return from the First Council of Baltimore (1843), he arranged to see Father Donaghoe in person and succeeded in obtaining five sisters for Dubuque. So successful were the sisters in their new field of labor that Bishop Loras decided to invite the entire community into his diocese.[2] During its first years in Iowa the community of Sisters of Charity of the Blessed Virgin Mary devoted itself not only to education, but to the visitation of the sick and the poor in their own homes. In the course of time, however, its educational work expanded and demanded all the energy of its membership.

Oblate Sisters and Holy Family Sisters Undertake Work for Colored

Even in pre-Civil War days, Catholic charities pressed as it was by a multitude of problems was not unmindful of the welfare of the Negro race. We find two notable instances of systematic welfare programs. Two religious communities of colored women were organized for work among their own people: The Oblate Sisters of Baltimore and the Holy Family

---

[2] *The American Catholic Historical Society*, Vol. XV (1905), pp. 46–48.

Sisters in New Orleans. It is interesting to note that both communities are a product of French missionary effort. The former, as has been noticed, was organized by a Sulpician émigré, Rev. J. H. Joubert, S.S., in 1829, and the latter by a French woman, Miss Alicot, who had decided to dedicate herself to Negro missions. The story of the Oblate Sisters has already been told.[3] Like other efforts in behalf of the Negro, the Sisters of the Holy Family encountered serious obstacles. It required unusual courage on the part of Miss Alicot to undertake the task of establishing her community in 1843. Where could she hope to find the subjects? The founder of the Oblates had been able to secure recruits from San Domingo. Fortunately, she was able to find able colored co-workers and with the assistance of Rev. Father Rousselon, then Vicar General of the diocese, and the approval of the Archbishop of New Orleans, she succeeded in laying the foundations. Its first work was the care of the aged and the religious instruction of children and adults. Miss Alicot devoted herself personally to the instruction of slaves on the different plantations. After the Civil War the activities of the congregation expanded rapidly. The catechism classes conducted in connection with the Lafon Home for old men and women led in time to the opening of the Lafon Boys' Asylum and the St. John Berchmans' Home for Girls.[4] These three institutions comprise the charitable activities of the order. The sisters are now engaged very largely in educational work. From the city of their foundation, New Orleans, they have spread to the archdiocese of San Antonio and the dioceses of Galveston, Lafayette and Mobile.[5]

Sisters, Servants of the Immaculate Heart of Mary

In 1845 the Redemptorist Fathers of Monroe, Michigan, decided to open a school for the religious training of children

[3] Chapter I.
[4] *The Congregation of Sisters of Holy Family of New Orleans*, manuscript report prepared for the writer, June, 1929.
[5] *The Official Catholic Directory*, 1931, p. 95.

if they could obtain teaching sisters. The superior of the community, Father Louis Florent Gilet, C. SS. R., talked over his plans with his neighboring pastor, Father Rappé of Toledo, afterwards bishop of Cleveland. He learned that Father Rappé had succeeded in securing for his school a colony of Ursuline Sisters from Bologne, France. Father Gilet, however, abandoned the idea of securing aid from any foreign religious community and decided to found a new community. He invited a young woman, Teresa Maxis of Baltimore, who had experienced a call to religion, to come to Monroe. She was soon joined by two other Baltimoreans, Charlotte Ann Schaaf and Theresa Renauld. The Redemptorist Fathers vacated their home and turned it over to these new co-workers. Father Gilet now decided that the recruits for his prospective community should have a rule. In preparing the rule he based it, as far as possible, on that of St. Alphonsus, under which his own community lived. On November 28, 1845, Father Gilet secured episcopal approval for his new community. In 1847 the community assumed the title of Sisters, Servants of the Immaculate Heart of Mary.[6]

The main purpose of the Sisters of the Immaculate Heart of Mary was the Christian education of the young, and so it remains. At the time of their foundation the religious training of children was the most important question confronting the Church. Two months after the community was approved by Bishop Lefevre of Detroit a boarding and day school for girls was opened in a little log cabin home in Monroe. The sisters, however, did not overlook the care of dependent and neglected children. Their spirit could not have been expressed more eloquently than in the words of their superior, Mother Teresa, to Rev. J. V. O'Reilly, who invited them to Pennsylvania in 1858: "I can not help expressing to you my satisfaction on hearing that it is among the poor that we

[6] *The Sisters of the Immaculate Heart of Mary*, by a Member of the Scranton Community, pp. 9–12, 37.

are to labor. It is exactly what we like."⁷ Their first foundation in Pennsylvania was an academy at St. Joseph's in Susquehanna County, not far from Scranton. A year later they opened an academy at Reading. These two institutions were destined to become the foundations of two separate communities. In 1859 the sisters in Pennsylvania became a diocesan community of Philadelphia. When Scranton was erected into a new diocese in 1871 the Sisters of the Immaculate Heart within its territory became a diocesan community.

Bishop William O'Hara, the first bishop of Scranton, looked to the Sisters of the Immaculate Heart as his main hope in maintaining the charities of his diocese. When he opened St. Patrick's Orphanage (1875), he asked the Sisters of the Immaculate Heart to take charge. They were given control of St. Joseph's Infant Asylum, Scranton (1890), and of St. Joseph's Shelter and Day Nursery (1920). The Philadelphia Community has been active in settlement work in the archdiocese.

American Religious Communities Become Localized

One of the most interesting facts in the history of American religious communities has been the tendency to break up into local units. When a community settled in a city and particularly, a city of any importance, it was influenced by the local attitudes and ideals. In many places the feeling grew that if a community was to be developed it must be essentially a part of the local diocese. This intense localism seemed a traditional part of America from the days of its earliest settlements. The very nature of ecclesiastical authority gave additional force to this general tendency. Every bishop was ruler of his own demesne. He considered it an inconvenient limitation to be compelled to consider outside superior-generals, who sometimes removed sisters who were the very backbone of his organization. Taking him as he was, engaged in

⁷ *Ibid*, p. 57.

a severe struggle, one can not be surprised if he was interested in having his own community, subject to his own authority, and in agreement with his own plans. This general tendency has been observable in the history of the Sisters of the Immaculate Heart of Mary. Reference has already been made to establishment of an independent community in Philadelphia within a year after the sisters established themselves in that diocese. Another illustration of the same tendency is found in the Sisters of Charity of Leavenworth, though such instances might be multiplied endlessly.

Sisters of Charity of Leavenworth

The story of the Sisters of Charity of Leavenworth is replete with interest for the student of Catholic charities. Historically the community represents a division in the ranks of the Sisters of Charity of Nazareth, Kentucky. In 1841 Bishop Richard P. Miles of Nashville secured the services of a number of sisters from Nazareth to open a boarding school, day school, and hospital in his diocese. In the course of a few years the bishop experienced the usual difficulties in dealing with the authorities at Nazareth. He ordered the sisters to undertake certain responsibilities to which their superiors objected. He was also disturbed by the frequent change of teachers. The bishop saw no solution except by forming a diocesan community. The sisters were finally given their choice. Those who desired to return to Nazareth might do so, and those who desired to become members of the new diocesan community might remain in Nashville.[8]

It seems, however, as if Nashville did not provide the proper soil for the growth of the new community. Before many years it found itself in serious financial difficulties and its property was sold. There was nothing left except to seek a new home. As a representative of the sisters, Mother Xavier

[8] *History of the Sisters of Charity of Leavenworth, Kans.*, by a member of the community, p. 23.

went to St. Louis in 1858 for the purpose of interviewing the bishops in attendance at a metropolitan council. Through Father Peter De Smet, S.J., the famed Indian missionary, Mother Xavier met Bishop Miege of Leavenworth, who was anxious to obtain a colony of sisters for his diocese. The lot of the sisters was cast. With Leavenworth as their center, they were to follow the trail of the missionary into the mountainous states of Colorado and Montana. They were to plant the foundations of Catholic education and Catholic charities in the Rockies.[9] While this community has expended its main effort on education, it has always assigned a part of its personnel to the care of the sick, and dependent and neglected children. Directed from the mother house at St. Mary's Academy, Leavenworth, the charitable activities of the community include: St. Joseph's Hospital, Denver, Colo.; St. Mary's Hospital, Grand Junction, Colo.; St. Vincent's Hospital, Leadville, Colo.; Providence Hospital, Kansas City, Kans.; St. John's Hospital, Leavenworth, Kans.; St. Francis Hospital, Topeka, Kans.; St. Ann's Hospital, Butte, Mont.; St. Vincent's Hospital, Billings, Mont.; St. James' Hospital, Anaconda, Mont.; St. Joseph's Hospital, Deer Lodge, Mont.; St. John's Hospital, Helena, Mont.; St. Vincent's School for Crippled Children, Billings, Mont.; Mt. St. Vincent's Home for Boys, Denver, Colo.; St. Vincent's Orphanage, Leavenworth, Kans.; St. Joseph's Orphans' Home, Helena, Mont., and St. Ann's Infant Home, Helena, Mont.[10]

Franciscan Sisters of Glen Riddle

There are a number of communities of Franciscan Sisters in the United States of both American and European origin. Of the American Franciscan Sisters the parent organization was that established by the saintly Bishop Neumann of Philadelphia in 1855. The bishop had considered the advisability

[9] Chapter XI.
[10] *The Official Catholic Directory*, 1931.

of introducing the Dominican Sisters into his diocese; but while attending the ceremonies in connection with the promulgation of the doctrine of the Immaculate Conception in Rome he was advised by Pope Pius IX to establish the Tertiaries of St. Francis. As the bishop was contemplating the establishment of a community, three young ladies approached him in regard to the same problem. The leader of the group, Barbara Boll, was a recent emigrant from Germany. Her companions were Marianne Bachman and Anna Dorn. The bishop had found the first recruits for his new community. On April 9, 1855, they were formally received; and during the following year they pronounced their religious vows. From its original convent near St. Peter's Church, Philadelphia, the Sisters of the Third Order of St. Francis went about visiting the sick and the poor in their own homes. They also took care of the parish school at St. Alphonsus' Church.[11]

In 1871 the novitiate was removed to Glen Riddle near Philadelphia, and since that time the sisters have come to be known as the Franciscan Sisters of Glen Riddle. There are three provinces under the jurisdiction of the motherhouse at Glen Riddle, the eastern, the southern and the western provinces.[12] At present the Franciscan Sisters of Glen Riddle conduct the following charitable institutions: St. Mary Hospital, Philadelphia, Pa. (1860); St. Joseph Hospital, Baltimore, Md. (1864); St. Francis Hospital, Trenton, N. J. (1872); St. Joseph Hospital, Reading, Pa. (1873); St. James Protectory, Delaware City, Del. (1879); St. Joseph Hospital, Lancaster, Pa. (1883); St. Agnes Hospital, Philadelphia, Pa. (1888); St. Joseph Home for Colored Boys, Wilmington, Del. (1890); St. Joseph Orphanage, Spokane, Wash. (1890); St. Joseph Hospital, Tacoma, Wash. (1891); St. Francis Home, Roxbury, Boston, Mass. (1891); St. Joseph Hospital, Providence, R. I.

---

[11] *The Order of Sisters of St. Francis.* Historical Sketch, prepared for the writer, 1929.
[12] Burns, *The Growth and Development of the Catholic School System in the United States,* p. 82.

(1892); St. Mary Home, New Brunswick, N. J. (1893); St. Mary Home, New Bedford, Mass. (1894); St. Joseph Industrial School for Colored Boys, Clayton, Del. (1895); St. Elizabeth Hospital, Baker City, Oreg. (1897); St. Michael Orphanage, Hopewell, N. J. (1898); Georgetown University Hospital, Washington, D. C. (1898); St. Anthony Hospital, Pendleton, Oreg. (1902); St. Joseph Sanatorium, Hills Grove, R. I. (1904); Morris Hall for the Aged, Lawrenceville, N. J. (1905); St. Ann Orphanage, Fern Hill, Tacoma, Wash. (1921); St. Francis Orphan Asylum, Orwigsburg, Pa. (1921); St. Joseph Day Nursery and Home for Working Girls, Philadelphia, Pa. (1922); St. Francis Hospital, Wilmington, Del. (1924); St. Michael Home for Aged, Tamaqua, Pa. (1927).[13]

Franciscan Sisters of Buffalo

In the latter part of 1861 four Franciscan Sisters from Philadelphia went to Buffalo at the invitation of Bishop Timon to open a home for the aged. Their first convent in Buffalo was a small rented house between William Street and Broadway. Besides caring for the aged the sisters visited the sick and the poor in their own homes.[14] In 1863 the Franciscan Sisters of Buffalo became independent of Philadelphia.[15] The following charitable institutions are now operated by the Franciscan Sisters of Buffalo: German Roman Catholic Orphan Asylum, Buffalo, N. Y. (1874); St. Francis' Home, Gardenville, N. Y.; Mt. St. Mary's Hospital, Niagara Falls, N. Y. (1907); Holy Family Home for the Aged and Infirm, Williamsville, N. Y. (1902); St. Mary's Hospital, Scranton, Pa. (1916).

---

[13] *Institute of the Sisters of the Third Order of St. Francis*, Glen Riddle, Pa., 1927, pp. 16–20.
[14] Thomas Donahue, *Catholic Church in Western New York*, p. 222.
[15] Burns, *op. cit.*, p. 83.

Franciscan Sisters of Syracuse

An important branch foundation of the Sisters of the Third Order of St. Francis is that of Syracuse, N. Y. This community was separated from the original foundation in 1860. The Franciscan Sister of Syracuse have been interested not only in education but in such charitable institutions as: Mercy Hospital, Auburn, N. Y.; St. Joseph Hospital, Syracuse, N. Y.; St. Elizabeth's Hospital, Utica, N. Y.; St. Francis Home for Orphans, Oswego, N. Y., and Loretto Rest Diocesan Home for Aged, Syracuse, N. Y. They have also taken over a hazardous mission for lepers in the Hawaiian Islands.[16]

Another Franciscan community of American origin is the Franciscan Sisters of Perpetual Adoration, organized in 1853 by Rev. Michael Heiss, later Archbishop of Milwaukee. In 1864 the motherhouse of the community was moved to La Crosse. The sisters have charge of St. Michael's Orphanage, St. Francis' Hospital and St. Joseph's Home for the Aged in La Crosse, Wisconsin.[17]

Sisters of St. Agnes

Fathers Donaghoe and Gilet and Bishop Neumann established religious communities because they needed the assistance of sisters in teaching religion. In the beginning these missionaries had to work alone, but they could not continue to do so indefinitely. They needed a teaching organization such as a religious community provided. To the name of the missionaries who established religious communities in pre-Civil War days should be added that of Rev. Caspar Rehrl, who had been sent to this country by the Leopoldine Society of Vienna to work among the German immigrants in Wisconsin. Father Rehrl taught school in addition to his other missionary labors. In order to extend his work he vainly en-

[16] *The Third Franciscan Order, O. M. C.*, report prepared for author, 1929; *The Official Catholic Directory*, 1931.
[17] Burns, *op. cit.*, p. 85; *The Official Catholic Directory*, 1931.

deavored to secure sisters from Europe; later, he decided to establish a community under the patronage of St. Agnes of Rome. In 1858 he brought together in a little stone convent at Barton, Wisconsin, the first candidates for membership in his prospective community. While the primary purpose of the institute was the religious education of the young, it did not overlook works of charity. One of its pioneer contributions in the field of charity has been in connection with the Leo House in New York City, which was opened for the care of German immigrants in 1889. It was at Archbishop Corrigan's request, that the Sisters of St. Agnes took over its management.

In 1896 the Sisters of St. Agnes opened St. Agnes' Hospital at Fond du Lac for the care of the sick in this region of Wisconsin. St. Anthony's Hospital, established at Hays, Ellis County, Kansas, in 1909, serves a large territory in western Kansas. Other charitable institutions in charge of the community are the Boyle Home for the Aged at Fond du Lac (1903), the Indian orphanage at the historic old Indian mission at Assinins, Michigan, and the Holy Family Orphanage at Marquette, Michigan.[18]

New Religious Communities Devoted to Catechetical Work

Since the Civil War education and the accepted forms of charity, such as the care of children away from their own homes, the care of the sick in hospitals and the care of the aged have, as a general rule, been cared for by the religious communities from Europe or the earlier religious establishments in America. Special objectives, however, have continued to inspire the foundation of new communities. It was quite natural that during this period of revolutionary changes special needs should have arisen which were not included in the programs of the established communities. There was

[18] *The Sisters of St. Agnes, of Fond du Lac,* manuscript report prepared for the writer, 1929.

the large group of children who were beyond the reach of parochial or Sunday schools. If these children were being reared without any religious instruction there was a strong probability that their parents were not zealous Christians. This opened up a large field of missionary work not only among children but also among their parents. Here was a strong appeal and a challenge to the faith. Since 1872 several religious communities have been founded in this country for this home missionary and catechetical work, as, Sisters of the Holy Family in San Francisco, the Parish Visitors of the Immaculate Heart of Mary in New York, the Mission Helpers of the Sacred Heart in Baltimore, and the Missionary Servants of the Most Blessed Trinity at Cottonton, Alabama.

Sisters of the Holy Family, San Francisco

In 1872 Rt. Rev. John J. Prendergast, Vicar-General of San Francisco, conceived the idea of a religious community whose members would go out and gather up the fragments of lost faith in his parish. Under his inspiration Miss Elizabeth Armer and a companion rented a house as a mission center for the purpose of reaching spiritually negligent individuals and families. In 1880 the little group whom Miss Armer had attracted to the work, took religious vows and formed the Sisters of the Holy Family. This was California's first native religious community. In addition to giving religious instruction, the members of the community planned to visit the sick and the poor in their own homes. Later the conduct of day homes was added to their original objectives.[19] From these humble beginnings, the Sisters of the Holy Family have extended their work over the greater part of California. They have been an important asset in providing religious instruction for the large numbers of Mexican immigrants who have entered the state since 1914. In Los Angeles they

[19] *Gleaners Along the King's Highway*, published by the Gilmartin Company, San Francisco, 1929.

are responsible for a large part of the catechetical work for Mexican children which centers around the various Catholic settlements. They conduct four day nurseries; the Holy Family Home and St. Francis Day Home in San Francisco, St. Vincent's Day Home in Oakland, and St. Elizabeth Day Home in San Jose, California.[20] Since 1914 three new communities with virtually the same purpose as the Sisters of the Holy Family have sprung into existence: The Missionary Servants of the Most Blessed Trinity, organized in 1914; the Society of Missionary Catechists, organized in 1917, and the Parish Visitors of the Immaculate Heart of Mary, organized in 1920.

Missionary Servants of the Blessed Trinity

The Missionary Servants of the Blessed Trinity owe their origin to Rev. Thomas A. Judge, C. M. As a member of the mission band of the Vincentian Fathers, he was impressed with the need to train mission workers to reach Catholics who had become indifferent to religion. In many places he had used volunteer committees to make a thorough canvass of the parishes in which he was giving missions. In the course of time some of the members of these committees expressed a desire to devote their lives to the work. In 1914 he found an excellent opening for them in Passaic, New Jersey. To those who had decided to become religious in mission work he gave the name "inside cenacle"; and to the volunteers he gave the name "outside cenacle." Both groups were to form a part of one program. The former would provide the leadership and the inspiration for the development of an active lay apostolate.

In the beginning the Missionary Servants of the Most Blessed Trinity concentrated their efforts in the sections of cities in which parish organization was undeveloped. In a short time, many pastors came to the conclusion that the community had a mission even in well organized parishes. Most

---

[20] *The Official Catholic Directory*, 1931.

parishes have large numbers of children in attendance at public schools. To provide religious training for these children is an important problem. The Trinitarians, as they are commonly known, pointed to the solution of the problem, hence pastors were glad to welcome them to their parishes. The community has had more invitations for parish missionary work than it can possibly satisfy. In one parish in which they have been engaged they increased the attendance at weekday religious instruction for public school children from 250 to 500. Their success in reaching religiously neglected children has opened another field of labor for the Missionary Servants of the Most Blessed Trinity, as many pastors use the sisters to make a continuous census of their parishes.

In the past four years the community has been engaged in missionary work in Porto Rico. The Missionary Servants have not confined themselves to purely religious work. In 1918 they took charge of the Doctor White Memorial Settlement in Brooklyn, New York, and, in 1922, they took charge of St. Elizabeth's Settlement in Rockford, Illinois. In 1921 the work of the Catholic Children's Bureau of Philadelphia, one of the largest Catholic child-placing agencies in the United States, was given over to the Missionary Servants. They have been given charge of the program of Catholic Charities in the diocese of Mobile.[21]

Parish Visitors of the Immaculate Heart of Mary

In 1920 a community with a program somewhat similar to that of the Missionary Servants of the Most Blessed Trinity was established in New York City. The foundress, Julia Teresa Tallon, with a few companions, had previously been engaged in parish visitation for a number of years. They had been endeavoring to reach those individuals and families not affected by the usual methods of the parish apostolate. With

[21] *Missionary Servants of the Most Blessed Trinity,* Booklet and Manuscript Reports, 1929.

the approval of Cardinal Hayes these parish visitors finally decided to band themselves together in a religious community, under the title, Parish Visitors of Mary Immaculate. At present they are active in fifteen parishes in New York City.[22]

Society of Missionary Catechists

The Society of Missionary Catechists, like the other missionary societies of Catholic women, has important implications for Catholic charities. In planning his new society (1917), Rev. J. J. Sigstein turned his thoughts principally to the lonely and neglected mission fields of the southwest. In this vast expanse were many small missions that were visited by a priest at infrequent intervals. What an advantage it would be to these missions to have a religious who would keep the doctrines and the ideals of faith ever before them! This was the ideal that Father Sigstein set out to attain and which he has kept steadily in view in the work at Victory Noll, Huntington, Indiana. Out of the work of the catechists many forms of social service have grown. They have opened a medical clinic at Las Vegas, New Mexico. A similar clinic is planned for Brawley in California. The catechists are in charge of the social service program at the Gary-Bishop Alerding Settlement at Gary, Indiana.[23]

Handmaids of the Most Pure Heart of Mary

Work among the colored population presents a serious challenge to the Catholic social and religious apostolate. Of a total of approximately 11,600,000 colored in the United States in 1926, only about 203,986 are members of the Catholic Church. While the colored population of the country has increased by 54.7 per cent during the past forty years, the Catholic colored population has increased by only 27.5 per

---

[22] *The Parish Visitor*, October, 1930, p. 4–5.
[23] *The Society of Missionary Catechists*, manuscript reports prepared for the writer, November, 1930.

cent.[24] The Church has, therefore, not been able to hold its own among the colored population. This is the type of challenge that naturally would inspire the creation of new communities and give renewed enthusiasm to the old. Thirty-three communities are doing some form of work among the colored in the United States.[25] Reference has been made to two colored communities organized for work among the members of their own race. In 1920 another colored community, the Handmaids of the Most Pure Heart of Mary, was organized in Savannah, Georgia. Since 1887 two communities of white women were organized within a period of two years for work among the members of the colored race: The Sisters of the Blessed Sacrament (1889), and the Mission Helpers of the Sacred Heart (1890).

Sisters of the Blessed Sacrament for Indian and Colored People

The Sisters of the Blessed Sacrament for Indian and Colored people were founded in 1889 by Miss Katharine Drexel of Philadelphia. For a number of years, Miss Drexel had been actively interested in missionary work among the Indians and colored. She had been financing several schools on Indian reservations. After the Third Plenary Council of Baltimore gave its special sanction to these neglected fields of Catholic work, Miss Drexel decided to devote her life and fortune to them. Under the direction of Bishop O'Connor of Omaha and with the approval of Archbishop Ryan of Philadelphia, the foundation of the new community was laid. A group of young women desirous of consecrating themselves to this apostolic work was gathered together by Miss Drexel and towards the close of the year, 1889, they began their community life. The old Drexel homestead near Philadelphia served as a motherhouse of the community, until 1892, when

[24] Gillard, *op. cit.*, pp. 1, 2, 49.
[25] *Ibid.*, p. 163.

the present motherhouse was built at Cornwells, Pennsylvania.[26] While the Sisters of the Blessed Sacrament are not engaged in purely charitable work their educational and missionary efforts serve to bring the races among which they labor to a higher plane, religious, social, cultural and economic. In this way, they stiffen the fiber of the people so that they will be better prepared to depend on their own resources.

Mission Helpers, Servants of the Sacred Heart

The Institute of Mission Helpers, Servants of the Sacred Heart, established in Baltimore was first intended exclusively for missionary work for the colored. Immediately after their foundation, the sisters organized sewing and catechetical classes for the children attending public schools. They also visited in the homes of their pupils in the colored parishes, almshouses, jails, and the colored wards in city hospitals. The work of the institute gradually spread beyond the city limits and catechism classes were begun in country districts. The experience of the sisters led to the conclusion that the white as well as the colored were in need of religious instruction. In 1894 the matter was laid before Cardinal Gibbons who decided that the sisters should serve all who needed them regardless of race or nationality.[27]

Care of spiritually neglected children is the work of primary interest to the Missionary Helpers. They want to bring religion to Catholic children in public schools. In many places they have organized religious vacation schools during the summer months in order to give children an intensive course of religious training. The Mission Helpers have always associated this work with the visitation of their homes. They have taken it for granted that one can not very well reckon with a child without reckoning with his parents. In

---

[26] *Ibid.*, p. 44; *Catholic Encyclopedia*, Vol. II, p. 599.
[27] *The Mission Helpers, Servants of the Sacred Heart.* Manuscript report prepared for the writer, 1930.

recent years the Mission Helpers of the Sacred Heart have become active in parish census-taking as a means of reaching the children who need religious instruction.

Besides their work of religious instruction and parish visitation, the Mission Helpers, Servants of the Sacred Heart, operate in Baltimore St. Peter Claver's Industrial School for Colored Girls (1893), St. Francis Xavier's School for the Deaf (1897), and a day nursery for colored children. They have been in charge of the St. Vincent de Paul Summer Home for Poor Children at Catonsville, Maryland, since 1927. In Trenton, they have St. James' Day Nursery (1898); and in New York St. Pascal's Day Nursery (1905), the Keating Day Nursery, and Mary Help of Christians Settlement (1916), and the Nativity Day Nursery (1928). St. Raphael's Temporary Home and Shelter in Pittsburgh with a day nursery was opened in 1921. In 1902 the Mission Helpers extended their missionary and catechetical work to the Island of Porto Rico.[28]

Home Nursing Communities are Formed

After the Civil War, the sisterhoods that had been engaged in home nursing shifted their emphasis to hospitals and other forms of institutional work. This was quite a natural development. The hospitals offered better facilities for the care of those acutely ill. They satisfied a most essential need in American city life. With the demands made on their personnel by the hospitals it was exceedingly difficult for religious communities to continue on any large scale their traditional work of home nursing. A service that has always formed such an essential part of Catholic charities, however, was bound to find new recruits. New communities were destined to spring up to take over activities surrendered by the old. To the extent that American communities were unable to take over these activities, European communities

[28] *Ibid.*

would be called to the rescue. At all events, the visitation of the sick and poor in their own homes by the sisterhoods could not be overlooked.

Two American communities have come into existence since the Civil War for the purpose of caring for the sick poor in their own homes, the Sisters of St. Mary of the Third Order of St. Francis, or the Sisters of St. Mary as they are popularly known, and the Dominican Sisters of the Sick Poor.

Sisters of St. Mary

While the foundress of the Sisters of St. Mary, Mother Odilia, with her first associates came directly from Germany, the community was actually organized and developed in St. Louis. Compelled by the Kulturkampf to leave her native land, Mother Odilia and five companions accepted the invitation of Vicar-General Muehlsiepen to come to St. Louis. After their arrival in November, 1872, the Ursuline Sisters offered them hospitality until they could secure a home of their own. Their first residence was in the upper part of a tenement opposite St. Mary's Church. A smallpox epidemic was raging at the time and the sisters gave their services so generously to the afflicted that they became known as the "Smallpox Sisters." New candidates were attracted to the community and by 1873, more accommodations were imperative. A new home had to be erected. The site chosen was a lot south of St. Mary's Church. On account of their close association with this church they came to be known as the Sisters of St. Mary's.[29]

During the first years of their existence the Sisters of St. Mary devoted themselves to the nursing of the sick and the relief of the poor in their own homes. The sisters gradually found the nursing of the sick, and especially the sick poor, in their own homes exceedingly difficult. Many times the homes did not offer proper facilities for the speedy recov-

---

[29] Rothensteiner, *op. cit.*. Vol. II, pp. 335–336.

ery of the patients. There was lack of proper diet, unsanitary living conditions and lack of medical care. The sisters thought that if they only had a hospital these conditions would be remedied. A plot of ground at Fifteenth and Papin Streets, St. Louis, was purchased and the fine old mansion thereon became the nucleus of St. Mary's Infirmary, the first hospital of the Sisters of St. Mary.[30] It was the beginning of an extensive hospital program for the community, but practically marked the end of its interest in home nursing. In St. Louis, besides St. Mary's Infirmary, the Sisters of St. Mary have St. Rose's Sanitarium for consumptive adults and children (1900) and St. Mary's Hospital (1928). The community has a number of other hospitals: St. Mary's Hospital, Jefferson City, Mo. (1905), St. Francis Hospital, Blue Island, Ill. (1905), St. Mary's Hospital, Kansas City, Mo. (1907), St. Mary's Hospital, Madison, Wis. (1908), and St. Mary's Ringling Hospital, Baraboo, Wis. (1922).[31]

The Sisters of St. Mary of the Third Order of St. Francis is one of the few communities in the United States that has adhered rigidly to hospital work. From 1876 to 1882 the community operated a home for children in St. Louis, but in the latter year this was given up. The Sisters of the Precious Blood later purchased the property.[32]

Dominican Sisters of the Sick Poor

The community of the Dominican Sisters of the Sick Poor was formed in New York in 1879 for the purpose of nursing the sick in their own homes. It was an outgrowth of the activities of the Paulist Parish. The sisters do not receive any remuneration for their services. They care only for those who are unable to pay the costs of nursing. Frequently, they take over household duties, such as the care of

[30] *Ibid.*, Vol. II, p. 337.
[31] *The Official Catholic Directory*, 1931.
[32] Rothensteiner, *op. cit.*, Vol. II, pp. 336–337.

children and the preparation of meals during the illness of the mother. They also give temporary relief in emergencies.[33] The Dominican Sisters of the Sick Poor are now engaged in home nursing in the archdioceses of New York and Cincinnati and in the dioceses of Columbus, Denver, and Detroit.[34]

Congregation of Dominican Sisters of St. Rose of Lima

There is no form of human suffering, no matter how abandoned, to which Catholic charities does not stoop. The galley slaves had their apostle and protector in St. Vincent de Paul, the lepers in Father Damien and Brother Dutton, and the victims of incurable cancer had a devotee in Rose Hawthorne Lathrop, daughter of Nathaniel Hawthorne. After the death of her husband, George Parsons Lathrop, Mrs. Lathrop felt herself called upon to do something for the glory of God and the salvation of human souls. With the thought of self-consecration in mind she appealed to a priest for guidance. It happened that the particular priest whom she approached had just returned from the bedside of a cancer patient, a woman of refinement and culture, but without sufficient means of support. A conference with the priest opened up to Mrs. Lathrop a great field of service. She would devote herself to those afflicted with incurable cancer. In order to prepare herself properly she entered a hospital in New York City for training in the nursing of cancer. After completing the course of training she accepted into her own home an elderly woman suffering from cancer who had been neglected by her family. In 1899 Mrs. Lathrop opened a free home for cancer cases in Cherry Street, New York City, but she was not satisfied to work alone. She needed other consecrated hands. Very soon her example of heroism attracted others. In 1899 Mrs. Lathrop, as Sister Alphonsa, and her first associate, Miss Alice Huber of Louisville, were banded

---

[33] *Annual Report of the Dominican Sisters of the Sick Poor*, 1915, p. 5.
[34] *The Official Catholic Directory*, 1931.

together in a new community known as the Congregation of Dominican Sisters of St. Rose of Lima. By 1901 the community had grown so that a new motherhouse and novitiate had to be established at Hawthorne, New York. Here the work of caring for destitute cancerous patients is also carried on.[35]

Foreign Mission Sisters of St. Dominic

In 1912 the appeal of the foreign missions gave birth to a new American religious community, the Foreign Mission Sisters of St. Dominic, commonly known as the Maryknoll Sisters. In the early part of that year the recently formed Catholic Foreign Mission Society of America welcomed to a little cottage at Hawthorne, New York, three young women who had decided to dedicate their lives to the foreign mission field. A few months later they were joined by two others and by the end of the year the nucleus of America's first sisterhood for foreign missions numbered seven. In the fall of 1912 the group moved to Maryknoll-on-the-Hudson. Their house at Maryknoll was named after St. Theresa and thus the members of the embryo community came to be known as Theresians. In 1916 they were enrolled as Dominican Tertiaries by Rev. John McNicholas, O. P., now archbishop of Cincinnati. Four years later the community was approved by Rome under the title, Foreign Mission Sisters of St. Dominic. In 1927 the "Maryknoll Sisters" numbered about 300. A number of them are already laboring in the Orient where they conduct schools for girls, homes for dependent children, and hospitals. In Los Angeles and Seattle they conduct schools and institutions for Japanese children. In the former city, they also conduct a sanitarium.[36]

[35] Dehey, *op. cit.*, pp. 165-168; see Sketch of Sister Alphonsa, by Dr. W. J. Kerby in the Dict. of Amer. Biography.
[36] *An American Sisterhood for Foreign Missions*, Brochure published by Foreign Mission Sisters of St. Dominic, Maryknoll, N. Y., 1927.

Franciscan Sisters of the Atonement

Very frequently throughout the course of its history the Church has gathered new inspiration from converts. They come with the zeal and enthusiasm of neophytes. They want to surrender unselfishly everything they have. In the Franciscan Sisters of the Atonement, there is an interesting illustration of the inspiration that converts bring to the Church. Here it is the inspiration of a group whose members had been leading a community life in the Episcopalian Church and had decided, as a group in 1909, to join the Catholic Church. No sooner had they entered the Church than they made plans to share their faith with others. They wanted to engage in mission work in the home and foreign field. The members of the community have been very active in the home mission field. They now conduct St. Cecilia's Mission Settlement in New York City and St. Simon's Settlement for Colored in Philadelphia. They have catechetical centers in the archdiocese of Baltimore and the dioceses of Amarillo, Galveston, Monterey-Fresno, Ogdensburg and Pittsburgh.[37]

Dominican Sisters of St. Catherine Di Ricci

Since the early forties of the last century a number of Catholic sisterhoods have been engaged in providing accommodations for working women away from their own homes. This was one of the original purposes of the Sisters of Mercy. Although homes for women wage-earners have come to be regarded as a lay activity a large number of them are still in the hands of religious communities. There is one sisterhood of American origin, established at Albany (1880), known as the Dominican Sisters of St. Catherine di Ricci, whose work centers entirely around such homes. It now conducts residences for employed women away from home in Albany, New York City, Philadelphia, Saratoga Springs, and Dayton. One

---

[37] *A Brief Sketch of the Society of the Atonement*, 1928, p. 29; *The Official Catholic Directory*, 1931.

of the special activities in connection with homes operated by the Dominican Sisters has been the organizing of retreats for women.[38]

Religious Communities with a Racial Appeal

It was scarcely to be expected that the peoples of the new immigration would be able to develop any new religious communities in the United States within the first generation. Like the peoples of the old immigration they had to lean on American communities or those that followed them from Europe. With the rise of the second generation of the new immigrants we look for the development of a leadership among them that will inspire them to develop their own charities. Part of this leadership will naturally find its way into the religious life and it will not always be satisfied with the established religious communities. It will want to develop new communities and the appeal of these communities will at first be racial.

Sisters of St. Casimir

In illustration of this general tendency there are two recent communities, the Sisters of St. Casimir and the Sisters of SS. Cyril and Methodius. The former were founded by Rev. Anthony Staniukynas, D.D., aided by Bishop J. W. Shanahan of Harrisburg, in Scranton in 1907 for the education of children of Lithuanian birth and descent. In accordance with the wish of Archbishop J. E. Quigley of Chicago, the motherhouse was transferred to Chicago in 1911.[39] The interests of the community are mainly educational, with schools in the archdioceses of Baltimore, Chicago and Philadelphia and the dioceses of Fort Wayne, Harrisburg, Rockford, Scranton and Springfield, Massachusetts.[40]

[38] *Report of the Dominican Sisters of the Congregation of St. Catherine Di Ricci* (1930).
[39] *The Archdiocese of Chicago*, pp. 719, 781.
[40] *The Official Catholic Directory*, 1931, p. 784.

Sisters of SS. Cyril and Methodius

The Sisters of SS. Cyril and Methodius were organized in Scranton in 1910. For a number of years the *Jednota* or Catholic Slovak Union of America had been endeavoring to form a religious community for the education of Slovak children and for the care of the dependent children and the aged members of the race. Rev. Matthew Jankola, director of the union and pastor of St. Joseph's Church in Hazleton, Pennsylvania, was especially interested in this project. He turned over to the Sisters of the Immaculate Heart of Mary, at Scranton, the first candidates for his new community. After three years of training under these sisters, they received their religious habit from Bishop Hoban of Scranton. In 1909 the community was approved by the Holy See. In the same year, Bishop Hoban received the vows of the three original sisters of the congregation. In 1919 the motherhouse was located in Danville, Pennsylvania. While the work of the Sisters of SS. Cyril and Methodius is primarily educational, they have a home for dependent and neglected children, the Immaculate Conception Slovak Home at Middletown, Pennsylvania.[41]

One might well ask do we not have a sufficient number of religious communities? Why can not all our religious consecration find expression in existing communities? But new leaders will be wont to express themselves in new ways. They will undertake types of work for which the old communities have neither the inclination nor the resources and the Church will always give them an opportunity of testing their metal.

[41] *The Sisters of the Immaculate Heart of Mary*, by a member of the Scranton Community, pp. 357–363.

CHAPTER XIX
THE CALL TO OTHER LANDS
The Immigrants and Early Religious Life of America

It was quite natural that until very recent years the Catholic Church in America should depend on Europe for the building up of her religious life. The Church here was an immigrant church made up mostly of peoples from Europe. It was like a child who must look to its parents for nurture and assistance for many years to come. The conditions under which the immigrants labored naturally retarded the growth of their religious life. They had come from countries whose whole spirit and tone of life helped to strengthen their religious faith. Here they were thrown into an atmosphere in which each person had to struggle for himself, without the aid of the old supports to which he had become accustomed. Many times the immigrant's lot was cast in isolated settlements where he was far removed from the influence and inspiration of religion. Everything, moreover, in the United States was in a state of constant change. The people were constantly moving from one place to another. There was always an *El Dorado* somewhere on the horizon. Material rewards were great. Material success became the all-inspiriting motive of life. It was to be expected that under such conditions the immigrants would find it difficult to develop the highest standards of religious life. An environment with material gain extolled does not develop vocations. Vocations come from homes of sacrifice; they grow out of a developed religious life in the community. The development of vocations is a good measure for the growth of religious life in parishes.

The Sulpicians Lay Foundations of American Catholic Charities

The French Revolution sent a number of able, cultured and zealous Sulpician Fathers to the United States. They had come primarily for the purpose of establishing a seminary at Baltimore, but they not only became directors of a seminary, but also active missionaries and founders of some of America's pioneer religious communities. In laying the foundations of American Catholic charities the Sulpicians could not expect much assistance in men or money from European countries which had been decimated by revolution and war.

The Fruits of the Catholic Revival in France and Germany

During the years following the French Revolution all Europe and especially France and Germany experienced a Catholic revival. There is scarcely a period in the history of the Church more fruitful in the foundation of new religious communities than that between 1800 and 1860. To this period one can trace the origin of some of the best known religious communities of women in the United States: The Religious of the Sacred Heart (1800), Sisters of Notre Dame de Namur (1803), Sisters of Providence of St. Mary-of-the-Woods (1806), Bon Secours (1824), Sisters of Mercy (1831), Sisters of the Precious Blood (1833), Franciscan Sisters of Penance and Christian Charity (1835), Little Sisters of the Poor (1839), Sisters of the Holy Cross (1841), Sisters of the Holy Names of Jesus and Mary (1843), Sisters of the Poor of St. Francis (1845), Poor Handmaids (1851), Felician Sisters (1855), The Helpers of the Holy Souls (1856), Sisters of St. Francis Seraph of the Perpetual Adoration (1860), Sisters of Charity of the Incarnate Word (1866), and the Sisters of the Third Order of St. Francis of the Holy Family (1868).

The American Church Welcomes European Assistance

This Catholic revival in Europe was indeed a godsend to the struggling Church in America. It could not possibly develop a sufficient number of native vocations to meet its needs. The two problems that stood out most prominently were the religious training of children and the care of the orphans. Priests, finding their parishes literally deluged by the immigration tide, were crying for assistance to care for orphans whose parents were carried away by the ever-recurring epidemics and children whose homes were a mere wreckage. Thousands of such children of various races and creeds were said to be wandering around the streets of American cities. In New York in 1860, it was estimated that there were not less than 40,000.[1]

The New York Children's Aid Society

The saving of the children of the immigrant became the inspiration of organized Protestant charities. The appeal of non-Catholic leaders bore the earmarks of a great revival, as they urged the churches and the Sunday schools to join the crusade to save the children, especially Irish Catholic children. The genius of this crusade was the Rev. Charles Loring Brace. While a theological student, he gave much thought to the problem of vagrant and delinquent children. He had done missionary work among the prisoners at Randall's Island. This he found to be a hopeless task. He concluded that the only hope for reform lay in the children who were just entering careers of crime. For this reason he organized the New York Children's Aid Society (1853) to improve the condition of the poor and destitute children of the City of New York.[2] The aims of the society are set forth in detail in its first circular issued March, 1853: "This Society

[1] *Nineteenth Report of New York Association for Improving the Conditions of the Poor*, pp. 45-46.
[2] Brace, *Dangerous Classes*, p. 84.

has taken its origin in the deeply settled feelings of our citizens, that something must be done to meet the increasing crime and poverty among the destitute children of New York. Its objects are to help this class by opening Sunday Meetings and Industrial Schools, and, gradually as means shall be furnished, by forming Lodging-houses and Reading-rooms for children, and by employing paid agents whose sole business shall be to care for them."[3]

Child-Placing Program of New York Children's Aid Society

The policy of placing children in country homes was the most important feature of the program. In Europe the labor market was overcrowded and there was nothing to do but herd the poor according to some congregate plan. In the United States the situation was different. A vast market in the western rural districts called for the labor of the army of immigrants that clogged the seaport towns. Mr. Brace advocated the placement of children in rural homes rather than in institutions. It saved the expense of institutions and as far as possible made the child pay for everything he received.[4] This was the old argument for indentureship. It was cheaper to place out children than to retain them in poor houses. The child-placing program of the New York Children's Aid Society was a return under another name to the discredited system of child indenture. Its founder probably assumed that its religious appeal would prevent the recurrence of (or disguise) the evils of indentureship.

Underlying the whole program was a materialistic philosophy covered by a religious garb. Brace, its leader, was steeped in English classical economics. He spoke with a dogmatic assurance of economic laws governing all human social relationships. He wanted to build individuals who would be able to take their place in the economic struggle, and he was con-

[3] *Ibid.*, pp. 90–91.
[4] *Ibid.*, pp. 440-442.

vinced that the best means of doing so was by throwing the influence of education and discipline and religion about the abandoned and destitute children of the large cities. He was fully convinced that charitable enterprises not "in harmony with natural economic laws . . . would eventually fail."[5] His whole aim was to get individuals to do things for themselves rather than to do things for them. The program outlined by Brace was avowedly religious. It endeavored to gather the neglected and vagrant children of New York City, many of whom were Catholics, into its Protestant Sunday schools. The district visitors of the society offered the children various inducements including material relief to attend the Sunday schools.[6]

The Children's Mission to Children

In 1849 an organization somewhat similar to the New York Children's Aid Society was organized in Boston. It was known as the Children's Mission to Children. The leaders of the Boston society claimed the credit for having inspired the foundation of the New York Children's Aid Society.[7] The purpose of the Children's Mission to Children, as stated in its constitution was "to foster in the minds of the young a spirit of Christian sympathy and active benevolence and to adopt such measures as shall rescue from vice and degradation the morally exposed children of the city."[8]

This organization grew out of the Unitarian Sunday schools of Boston. It sought the children of Irish immigrants; it gathered them into Sunday schools; it found work for and placed them in homes in Massachusetts and the neighboring states. Its first year's report gives a significant description of its Sunday school. Joseph E. Barry, whose name is significant, was appointed as the children's missionary. He claimed

[5] *Ibid.*, p. 441.
[6] *Third Report of New York Children's Aid Society*, p. 7.
[7] *Tenth Report of Children's Mission to Children*, Boston, p. 14.
[8] *First Annual Report of Children's Mission to Children*, Boston, p. 2.

to scour the wharves, rum shops and streets of the city for the little waifs and reported that many children were addicted to gambling and some were found drunk, even at the tender ages of eight, nine and ten years. These he gathered into a Sunday school and for this purpose was given a ward room of District Nine. At first the school was composed of 125 members, mostly Catholics. Suddenly the membership dropped, so that the first report counted fifty-four Protestants. This decline in numbers happened when a Catholic man and a Catholic woman stationed at the door of the Sunday school turned away Catholic children. The officers of the school were accused of using money for proselytizing. Emboldened by the action of their elders the children flung bricks and mud at the building and it had to be closed for seven weeks. The missionary protested against this treatment and stated that religious training consisted only in the simplest moral lessons and readings from the Bible. He complained, moreover, that Catholics were doing very little for the religious training of their children. For months they had talked about opening a school in the district but, as yet, had done nothing.[9] According to its reports, which may have been padded, the institution during its first year placed seventy boys in homes in Boston and elsewhere. In its first seventeen years, 1,596 children were associated with its sewing schools, 247 with the boys' meetings, 1,309 with the Sunday schools, and 2,410 children were placed out in seventeen states.[10]

The Association for Improving the Condition of the Poor

In the early forties private family relief in New York City was quite disorganized. There were some thirty or forty private organizations engaged in relief-giving. A strong reaction had developed against public relief. In 1843 the Association for Improving the Condition of the Poor was organ-

[9] *Ibid.*, p. 7.
[10] *Seventeenth Annual Report of the Children's Mission to Children,* Boston, pp. 5–13.

ized in protest against the extravagant methods of public relief and in an effort to coordinate and supplement the activities of private relief agencies. The basic objective of the Association, however, was the elevation of the moral and physical condition of the indigent.[11]

The Association for Improving the Condition of the Poor maintained that it endeavored to raise the moral tone of the poor by improving their environment and by the education of their children. It was, therefore, active in tenement house legislation and the promotion of school attendance. It was largely responsible for the Truant Act of 1858. Its leaders were fully convinced that if the children received a proper education in the public school that much could be done for the elimination of poverty.[12] In its program for moral education the association sought to make over the immigrants according to the so-called Protestant traditions of America. It withheld relief from parents who did not agree to send their children to the regular schools and to Sunday school.[13] It was a matter of serious regret to the association that Irish and German Catholic immigrants adhered so tenaciously to their faith. Changes of abode did not bring a change of spiritual allegiance to a power, "which may be called an ecclesiastical despotism to which no free mind will submit."[14] It regarded the advance of the Catholic Church as a menace to free institutions. Yet with all its nativist leanings, it preferred to see the immigrants adhere to the Catholic Church rather than give up all religion. Catholicism was better than no religion at least as policing power: "There are vast masses that will respect no other religious influence."[15] Therefore, it is to be tolerated because of its influence among those who can not be reached other ways. Evidently the association did not find its work among the immigrants so easy, especially as

[11] *First Report of the New York A. I. C. P.,* p. 8.
[12] *Eighth Report, New York, A. I. C. P.,* p. 66.
[13] *Seventeenth Annual Report, New York, A. I. C. P.,* p. 31.
[14] *Twenty-first Annual Report, New York, A. I. C. P.,* p. 57.
[15] *Ibid.,* p. 59.

it was regarded increasingly as a Protestant missionary society.[16]

While the New York Association for Improving the Condition of the Poor was interested primarily in the moral training of children in their own homes, it emphasized its concern with children whose parents had failed to provide for them. Year after year the annual reports of the association painted dark pictures for its patrons of the thousands of children roaming the streets of New York. The association had endeavored to place them in schools, but apparently without any great degree of success. The annual report for 1862 complained that three-fourths of this class were still unreached either by remedial or preventive agencies. The only hope that the Association held out for this large group of children was the enforcement of the school attendance laws. For the children who violated school law, the Association for Improving the Condition of the Poor had organized the Juvenile Asylum in 1851. Children were to be retained in the asylum only for a relatively brief period, after which they were to be indentured in homes in the west.

Protestantism Fights for Self-Preservation

The agencies whose work and philosophy have just been detailed represented pioneer efforts in a nation-wide movement on the part of Protestantism to deal with the immigrant. The work of these agencies was carried on with a religious fervor if not fanaticism. It was based on a definite philosophy of life. America was facing in immigration a new force that might revolutionize its life, for a growing majority of newcomers represented a different racial background and a different religion. They enkindled the zeal of American Protestantism for its own self-preservation and aroused a nativist hostility to Catholicism.

[16] *Twentieth Annual Report, New York, A. I. C. P.*, pp. 31-32.

Poverty of the Catholic Church in America

The activities of Protestant agencies were a serious challenge to the Catholic bishops. They had relatively few priests, churches, schools, hospitals, and orphanages. Writing to the Leopoldine Society of Vienna (1845) Bishop William Quarter of Chicago gave a first-hand description of conditions in Illinois: "The Catholics of the state are mostly immigrants. These are largely German. As a rule they settle on farms far from church and in a short time lose their love for church and priests and gradually become lax and indifferent. The children grow up without religion or, if they have been faithful in their youth, in growing up they abandon their religion and join the nearest Protestant church or none at all. There are no means to save such lost ones for the Church. There are no priests to prevent the loss. . . . We need priests, we need churches. . . . They can only be cheap log buildings. In Europe they would scarcely use them for stables."[17] However, it must be remembered that in seeking foreign aid, Catholic leaders exaggerated for the good of the cause.

Writing to the same society in September 1849, Bishop John Timon of Buffalo also referred to the great number of immigrants stranded in Buffalo because of lack of funds. Many of them were sick and worn out from their long journey and the bishop had to open a hospital in order to take care of them. He was also most solicitous for the orphans, whom a Protestant orphan asylum had been receiving for proselytizing as well as philanthropic reasons.[18]

The Catholic Church leaned heavily on European assistance. Every year the Propagation of the Faith at Lyons and the Leopoldine Society at Vienna sent over large sums of money to aid the mission Church of America. The American Church looked to Europe not only for priests and for funds to carry on its work, but also for religious brothers and nuns. It had

---
[17] *Letters of Leopoldine Society*, Vol. XX, 1845, pp. 47-51.
[18] *Ibid.*, Vol. XXII, 1850, p. 21.

constantly to be reenforced from Europe by men and women ready to sacrifice themselves in building its material structure and its traditions.

Both Schools and Institutions of America Protestant in Character

Only through the aid of European religious communities could the American Church hope to build an educational or charities program. The public schools were, for all practical purposes, Protestant institutions.[19] In a letter to the Society for the Propagation of the Faith in 1854 Bishop Timon refers to the great number of Catholic children lost to the faith in Buffalo through attendance at public schools before the building of the parochial schools. He also stated that before the opening of Catholic orphan asylums in Buffalo and Rochester large numbers of Catholic children died in the public poor houses or were raised in Protestantism.[20] Private associations for the care of children, as we have seen, were openly and avowedly Protestant in their character and objectives. It is interesting to note that beginning in 1848 Father Pax, the pastor of St. Louis' Church, Buffalo, made provision for the placement of orphans in private homes at the expense of his congregation.[21]

Religious Communities Active in Charitable Field Between 1830 and 1860

Between 1830 and 1860 fifteen religious communities of women that were destined to play a prominent part in the Catholic charities of the United States were introduced into this country from Europe: The Sisters of St. Joseph of Carondelet, the Sisters of Providence of St. Mary-of-the-Woods, the Sisters of Our Lady of Charity of the Good Shep-

[19] *Ibid.*, Vol. XXIV, pp. 7–15.
[20] *Annals of the Propagation of the Faith*, Vol. XXVII, p. 315.
[21] Joseph Salzbacher, *Meine Reise Nach Nord-Amerika in Jahre*, 1842, Vienna, 1845, p. 261.

CALL TO OTHER LANDS 379

herd, the Sisters of the Holy Cross, the Congregation of Sisters Marianites of the Holy Cross, the Sisters of Mercy, the Sisters of the Precious Blood, the Sisters of Charity of St. Augustine, the Benedictine Sisters, the Grey Nuns, the Sisters of Charity of Providence, Sisters of the Third Order Regular of St. Francis (Oldenburg), the Grey Nuns of the Cross, the Grey Nuns of the Sacred Heart, and the Sisters of the Poor of St. Francis.

Basic Principle of European Religious Communities of Women

When these European religious communities were introduced into this country they brought with them their own traditions. All these communities were established for charity work of some form or other. The design of their founders in most instances was that they should minister unto the poor in their own homes. The institutions they founded, and they were few in number, were merely incidental to their basic work of home care. In providing instruction for poor children, however, they had to bring them together in schools or institutions. Some religious institutes, like the Sisters of the Good Shepherd and the Little Sisters of the Poor, were exceptions to this general rule. They necessarily had institutional programs. The founders of European religious communities in the nineteenth century were as a rule active missionaries. Like St. Vincent de Paul, himself, they felt that their work was along the highways and byways, among the poor and the spiritually neglected. When they came to this country they endeavored to carry out the same program. Of the work of the Sisters of Mercy in Pittsburgh, in 1845, it was reported: "This is a branch of the order of this name founded in Ireland in 1827 by Mrs. McCauley. It is the only house of the order in the United States. The Sisters make perpetual vows; they are devoted to the spiritual and corporal works of mercy, especially the visitation of the sick, instruction of the ignorant and the protection of distressed females of good character."[22] Similar work was done by the community in New York: "There is in New York a convent of the Sisters of Mercy devoted to the visitation of the sick poor and the instruction of the ignorant."[23] On November 10, 1847, Bishop William Quarter of Chicago wrote to the Leopoldine Association that the Sisters of Mercy had started their convent and that they instructed children and cared for the sick.[24]

The Sisters of Mercy

The original purpose of Mrs. McCauley in founding the Sisters of Mercy in Dublin in 1827 was to bring together a group of women who would devote a few hours each day to instructing the poor. Their first institution was a home for destitute women and orphans.[25] Seven Sisters of Mercy came to the United States in 1843 in response to the earnest appeal of Bishop Michael O'Connor of Pittsburgh to assist him in carrying on both the corporal and spiritual works of mercy in his diocese.[26] Three years after the Pittsburgh foundation Bishop Hughes of New York brought a group of Sisters of Mercy to New York City for the purpose of establishing a house of protection for young girls. At the invitation of Bishop Quarter of Chicago, the Sisters of Mercy went to that city from Pittsburgh in 1846.[27]

The Evolution of the Work of the Sisters of Mercy in the United States

In all their original American foundations the Sisters of Mercy followed the same program, the visitation of the sick and the poor in their own homes, religious instruction of

[22] *Metropolitan Catholic Directory* (1845), p. 84.
[23] *Ibid.*, 1847, p. 150.
[24] *Letters of Leopoldine Society*, Vol. XXI, pp. 11-18.
[25] Helen M. Sweeney, *The Golden Milestone*.
[26] Herron, *op. cit.*, p. 1.
[27] *Ibid.*, pp. 7, 27-28.

children, protection of young girls, and the visitation of jails, poorhouses and other public institutions. Gradually the community took over the care of the orphan in cities in which no other organization was engaged in the work. Then the great need for hospitals demanded their services. Their active work among both the sick and the poor attracted the attention of pastors who were eager to secure religious teachers for their schools. The sisters could not resist the appeal and thus they embarked on their extensive educational program, which in late years has consumed the largest part of their energy. The evolution of the work of the Sisters of Mercy is fairly typical of that of most religious communities introduced from Europe.

From their beginning the Sisters of Mercy were essentially local in character. In each diocese they were subject directly to the bishop. In 1928 it was decided to give the sisters an opportunity to form a general community, subject directly to the Holy See. About 60 per cent of the members in the United States voted in favor of the proposed change. The other forty per cent decided to retain their local diocesan character. The motherhouse of the general community is now located near Washington, D. C.

European Religious Communities Follow Plan of Pioneer American Communities

Unlike the Sisters of Mercy, the other European religious communities had to adopt a specific program from the beginning. They had to be guided by the experience of America rather than their European background. The question of support was very real. In Europe it was possible to find patrons for special works of charity; but in a pioneer country the situation was quite different. The bishops who invited them did not have any surplus funds and the people among whom they were to work were mostly poor. They had, therefore, to learn from the pioneer American communities how to become partially self-supporting. Thus they had to combine education with charity.

The Sisters of St. Joseph of Carondelet

When the Sisters of St. Joseph of Carondelet came to St. Louis in 1836 they combined teaching with the care of the orphans. Later they added to the original institution at Carondelet a department for the instruction of deaf mutes for which they received aid from the Missouri State Legislature. The first two orphanages of which they took charge, namely, St. Joseph's Orphan Asylum in St. Louis (1846) and St. John's in Philadelphia (1847), had been in operation for some years under the Sisters of Charity and had developed fairly definite methods of support. When the community opened its first two hospitals, namely, St. Joseph's at St. Paul (1851) and the Wheeling Hospital in Wheeling, West Virginia (1853), it was taking over services that were at least partially self-supporting. When Bishop Timon introduced the Sisters of St. Joseph into Buffalo (1857) for the instruction of deaf mutes he had already secured land for the project from a generous benefactor, Louis Le Couteulx. Having no funds for the erection of buildings, he decided to move to the Le Couteulx property some cottages which had been used by the Sisters of Charity for the care of their orphans. He planned to operate a parochial school in connection with his deaf-mute institution.[28]

The Sisters of St. Joseph of Carondelet still operate many institutions for dependent and neglected children and many hospitals. As the community has developed, however, it has placed its main emphasis on education. Their institutions for the care of children include: St. Joseph's Orphanage, Tucson, Ariz., St. Joseph's Orphanage for Boys, Washington, Ga., Catholic Orphan Asylum for Boys, Minneapolis, Minn., Catholic Orphan Asylum for Girls, St. Paul, Minn., St.

---

[28] Savage, *op. cit.*, pp. 77–78.

Joseph's Orphan Home for Girls, Kansas City, Mo., St. Joseph's Male Orphan Asylum, St. Louis, Mo., St. Mary's Catholic Orphan Home, Binghamton, N. Y., St. Joseph's Infant Home, Troy, N. Y., Catholic Infant Home, St. Paul, Minn., and the Masterson Day Nursery, Albany, N. Y. Their institutions for the care of the sick include the following hospitals: St. Mary's Hospital and Sanitarium, Tucson, Ariz., St. Joseph's, Lewiston, Idaho, St. Joseph's, Hancock, Mich., St. Joseph's, St. Paul, Minn., St. Mary's, Minneapolis, Minn., St. Joseph's, Kansas City, Mo., St. Mary's, Amsterdam, N. Y., St. Joseph's Maternity, Troy, N. Y., St. John's, Fargo, N. D., St. Michael's, Grand Forks, N. D., Holy Trinity, Jamestown, N. D., and Our Lady of Lourdes, Pasco, Wash.[29]

The Brothers and Sisters of the Holy Cross

The Association of the Holy Cross brought to the United States an idea which was destined to exercise a profound influence on its charities. Shortly after their arrival the brothers of the association set up a manual labor school for boys at Notre Dame and the sisters set up a similar institution for girls over the line at Bertrand, Michigan. These manual labor schools were to supplement the local orphanages which could not retain children over fourteen years of age. It was not practicable, nor was it regarded as right to farm children out to strangers at this age. The Brothers and Sisters of the Holy Cross found the way out. They established institutions in which the dependent and neglected children would be retained throughout their minority and taught useful trades. The industrial school filled a need and was at the same time practically self-supporting. The *Catholic Directory of 1850* printed this interesting notice: "The 'Sisters of the Holy Cross,' consecrated to the Most Immaculate and Sorrowful Heart of Mary, like the Sisters of Charity, are devoted to the education of youth, to the service of orphan asylums

[29] *The Official Catholic Directory*, 1931.

and hospitals; they also discharge for the colleges of the institute, the various functions of infirmarians, sacristans, etc. Their novitiate is at Bertrand, Berrien Co., Mich., five miles from Notre-Dame-Du Lac. They have also there an academy and a female orphan asylum, nearly on the same plan as that of the Brothers."[30] Here again we note the combination of education and charity that was characteristic of all early American Catholic institutions. The brothers of the community followed the same plan at Notre Dame.

The coming of the Association of the Holy Cross to America was due to the initiative of Bishop de la Hailandiere of Vincennes, who appealed to Father Moreau, the founder, for Indian missionaries. In response to the appeal Rev. Edward Sorin and six brothers of the Association came to America. After teaching one year near Vincennes, Father Sorin and his brothers moved to the site of the present University of Notre Dame. In 1843 Father Sorin secured the services of a number of Sisters of the Holy Cross from France to aid the brothers in their work at Notre Dame. Since Bishop de la Hailandiere had already secured the services of the Sisters of Providence he objected to another community of women in his diocese.[31] The attitude of the bishop compelled Father Sorin to open an institution for the Sisters of Holy Cross at Bertrand, Michigan, five miles from Notre Dame.[32] In 1855 this community moved its headquarters to a large farm about a mile and a quarter from Notre Dame.

The industrial school program of the Brothers and Sisters of the Holy Cross gave them a wide appeal. If they had had the necessary personnel they could have opened industrial schools in all the large cities during the fifties and sixties. In 1855 the Sisters of the Holy Cross took charge of St. Joseph's Orphan Asylum in Washington, and a year later, they opened

[30] Page 110.
[31] *A Story of Fifty Years, from Annals of Congregation of Sisters of Holy Cross,* 1855–1905, p. 22.
[32] *Ibid.*

industrial schools in Chicago and Philadelphia.[33] They took charge of St. Joseph's Orphanage and Manual Training School, Rensselaer, Indiana (1867), and St. Joseph's Orphan Manual Training School at La Fayette, Indiana (1875).[34] The industrial school continued to be a part of the program of the Sisters of the Holy Cross until demands for the services of the sisters in other fields caused its curtailment. The Civil War brought the community into hospital work on a large scale. Since that time its educational activities and hospital program have consumed a large part of its energies.

The Brothers of the Holy Cross, like the sisters, have not found it possible to continue their industrial school program. All efforts of the brothers are now expended in educational work. In recent years the brothers have taken over St. Charles' Industrial School at Wauwatosa, Wisconsin, which they are operating according to the best standards. The Brothers of the Holy Cross, like other brotherhoods, contend that the failure to maintain a larger charities program is due in the last analysis to their inability to secure a larger number of vocations.

The Sisters Marianites of the Holy Cross

Another branch of the Holy Cross Sisters, the Marianites of the Holy Cross, came to New Orleans from France in 1851 and began their work of caring for the sick and the orphans and of educating children. Ten years later the sisters took charge of the orphan asylum of St. Vincent de Paul in New York City. They are now serving in the French Hospital in New York City, where they also conduct a day nursery in connection with the parish of Our Lady of Mercy. In New Orleans they now conduct St. Mary's Boys' Asylum. The Marianite Sisters of the Holy Cross still maintain their con-

[33] *Ibid.,* pp. 59–60.
[34] L. A. Scheetz, *A History of Catholic Child-Caring Institutions in the Diocese of Fort Wayne,* An Essay, Catholic University of America, Washington, D. C., 1931, pp. 33-44.

nection with France, although the Sisters of the Holy Cross became an independent community in 1869.[35]

The Sisters of Providence of St. Mary-of-the-Woods

Reference has already been made to the opposition of Bishop de la Hailandiere to the settlement of the Sisters of the Holy Cross in his diocese. His opposition was based on the fact that another community of nuns, the Sisters of Providence of St. Mary-of-the-Woods, whom he had brought from France in 1840, was already engaged in schools and orphanages in that territory. He felt that one community was sufficient to satisfy all the needs of the diocese. In 1841 the Sisters of Providence had opened a school and orphanage at Vincennes.[36] They continued to care for the Catholic orphan girls of southern Indiana until 1919, when this work was taken over by the Sisters of the Good Shepherd at Indianapolis. In 1922 the care of the orphan boys which was begun by the Sisters of Providence in 1851 was given over to the Sisters of St. Francis of Oldenburg.[37] The Sisters of Providence now devote themselves exclusively to education.

The Franciscan Sisters of Oldenburg

The Franciscan Sisters of Oldenburg who took over the care of the dependent and neglected boys of the Indianapolis diocese (1922) were introduced into this country from Vienna in 1850 by Father Joseph Rudolf, pastor of Oldenburg, Indiana, who sought the sisters for the education of children in the immigrant settlements around Oldenburg. Like other religious communities this group of sisters felt that they should do something for charity. Therefore, in opening their school for girls they advertised for orphans, girls, and boys, the latter not "over eight years."[38]

---
[35] *The Sisters, Marianites of the Holy Cross.* Manuscript report prepared for writer, 1929.
[36] Scheetz, *op. cit.*
[37] *Notes from the Convent Dairy,* Saint Mary-of-the-Woods.
[38] Alerding, *op. cit.*, p. 589.

The Sisters of the Precious Blood

Other communities introduced into this country from Europe in the period from 1840 to 1860 which have large educational interests, but which conduct a number of charitable institutions, are the Sisters of the Precious Blood, the Benedictines, and the Sisters of the Presentation of the Blessed Virgin Mary. The Sisters of the Precious Blood were introduced into Cincinnati from Switzerland in 1844. They opened their first orphanage at New Reigel, Ohio (1845).[39] They are now in charge of the following charitable institutions: St. Joseph Orphan Home and The Maria-Joseph Home for the Aged in Dayton, and Kneipp Sanitarium, Rome City, Indiana.[40]

The Benedictine Sisters

The Benedictine Sisters made their first foundation in this country in St. Mary's, Pennsylvania, in 1852. The second foundation was made at St. Joseph, Minnesota (1857). Other foundations were made later at Allegheny, Pa., Atchison, Kans., Chicago, Ill., Covington, Ky., Duluth, Minn., Erie, Pa., Ferdinand, Ind., Mount Angel, Ore., Newark, N. J., New Orleans, La., Shoal Creek, Ark., and Yankton, S. D.[41] Hospitals conducted by the Benedictine Sisters include: Our Lady of Lourdes, Hot Springs, Ark., St. Benedict's, Sterling, Colo., St. Valentine's Hospital and Home for the Aged, Wendell, Idaho, St. Joseph's, Brainerd, Minn., St. Vincent's, Crookston, Minn., St. Mary's Hospital, Duluth, Minn., St. Joseph's Hospital and Sanitarium, St. Cloud, Minn., St. Joseph's, Boonville, Mo., Sacred Heart, Lynch, Neb., Our Lady of Victory, Kingston, N. Y., St. Alexius, Bismark, N. D., St. Joseph's, Deadwood, S. D., St. Mary's, Pierre, S. D., and St. John's, Rapid City, S. D. They have also the following orphanages:

---

[39] Lamott, *op. cit.*, pp. 255–256.
[40] *The Official Catholic Directory*, 1931.
[41] *Catholic Encyclopedia*, Vol. II, p. 455.

Lisle Manual Training School for Boys and Girls, Lisle, Ill., St. John's, Covington, Ky., St. James', Duluth, Minn., St. Walburgh's, Roselle, N. J., and St. Joseph's, St. Paul, Minn. Homes for Aged: St. Anne's, Duluth, Minn., St. Joseph's, St. Cloud, Minn., and St. Raphael's, St. Cloud, Minn.[42]

Sisters of the Presentation of the Blessed Virgin Mary

The Sisters of the Presentation of the Blessed Virgin Mary from Cork, Ireland, opened a house in San Francisco in 1854. While these sisters were originally founded for the education and the care of the poor, their main service in this country has been in educational institutions. The community, however, conducts a number of charitable institutions: St. Michael's Home for Destitute Children, Mt. St. Michael, Green Ridge, Staten Island, N. Y., St. Colman's Industrial School and Orphan Asylum, Watervliet, N. Y., The McKennan Hospital, Sioux Falls, S. D., St. Luke's Hospital, Aberdeen, S. D., and St. Joseph's Hospital, Mitchell, S. D.[43]

The Sisters of Charity of St. Augustine

The Sisters of Charity of St. Augustine of Cleveland offer an unusual illustration of a community that has concentrated its efforts mainly in the building-up of the charities of one diocese. Their first undertaking on arrival from France (1852) was a hospital, the present St. Vincent's Charity Hospital of Cleveland. They opened St. Vincent's Orphan Asylum in the same city (1853) and St. Louis'. Orphanage in Louisville, Ohio (1871). These were combined in 1925 in a cottage plan institution known as Parmadale, or the Children's Village of St. Vincent de Paul. The sisters established a maternity hospital and infant asylum in Cleveland in 1873. Mercy Hospital, Canton, Ohio, St. John's Hospital, Cleveland, Ohio, and St. Thomas' Hospital, Akron, Ohio, are all under their direction.[44]

---

[42] *The Official Catholic Directory*, 1931.
[43] *Ibid.*
[44] *Archives* of Sisters of Charity of St. Augustine, Cleveland, Ohio.

Programs of Newly Arrived European Communities Shaped by American Needs

It was not easy for the incoming sisterhoods before the Civil War to adhere to any uniform objectives. They were really carried along by the needs of the hour. Their development was fashioned more by the leadership and conditions of the Church than in accordance with the purposes of their founders. They were drawn hither and thither by this bishop and that one who wanted the sisters to assist where their services would be most valuable. The communities, as a whole, saw more hope in attaching themselves to the parish than to the diocese. The pastor could do more for them than the bishop. He was closer to the people, and it was much easier for him to get support for the work of the parish than it was for the bishop to get support for the work of his diocese.

Some European Communities Adhere to Original Objectives

However, some communities as the Sisters of the Good Shepherd and the Sisters of the Poor of St. Francis have been able to adhere to their original objectives. The Good Shepherd Sisters now have two branches; the original branch known as the Sisters of Our Lady of Charity of Refuge and the Sisters of Our Lady of Charity of the Good Shepherd.[45] The Sisters of Our Lady of Charity of the Good Shepherd came to Louisville, Kentucky, at the invitation of Bishop Flaget (1842). They now have forty-five houses in the United States, divided into five provinces. The Sisters of Our Lady of Charity of Refuge were invited to Buffalo by Bishop Timon in 1853. This branch of the community has ten houses in the United States. There is no essential difference between the programs of the two branches of the Good Shepherd Sisters. Both have adhered rather steadfastly to the original purpose of the community in caring for delinquent girls.

[45] Cf. Chapter X.

Factors Making for Uniformity of Good Shepherd Sisters' Work

One of the factors that has aided the Good Shepherd Sisterhood in adhering to its original objective is that it is an independent institute subject directly to the Holy See. This characteristic, however, the community possesses in common with others. More important still is the fact that its work has been largely self-supporting. This same plan of self-support was tried in connection with the industrial schools for boys, but failed because they could not compete with outside industries and because schools on a productive basis could not develop an all-round program of training. In the Good Shepherd Homes, however, it has been possible to carry out the theory of self-support with much greater success. The Good Shepherd convents have specialized in a few simple industries because they found that the opportunities open to girls under their care are exceedingly limited. The sisters also have had great faith in the disciplinary and character-building value of their work. Today there is a gradual drifting away from the idea of self-support, which means that the sisters are looking more for support from the charitable public. Hence, there are marked changes in the program in the way of a broadening in the educational and social policies. It may be that this closer contact with the public will win for the Good Shepherd Sisters more friends and inspire a greater number of novices to take up this life of sacrifice.

The Sisters of the Poor of St. Francis

The Sisters of the Poor of St. Francis have adhered rather faithfully to the original purposes of their foundress, Mother Frances Schervier. When she gathered her little group of followers together for the first time in Aix-La-Chapelle in 1845 she conceived of them as a group dedicated to the sick poor in their own homes and hospitals.[46] Thirteen years after

---

[46] Ignatius Jeiler, *Mother Frances Schervier, A Sketch of Her Life and Character,* p. 107.

its foundation, Mother Schervier's community was introduced into Cincinnati by Mrs. Sarah Peter of that city. On the property donated by Mrs. Peter, the sisters built their first hospital, St. Mary's, on Betts Street, Cincinnati (1859).[47] From this beginning the Sisters of the Poor of St. Francis have spread until at the present time they have fifteen hospitals, one home for the aged and a home for women wage-earners. Hospitals: St. Mary's, Quincy, Ill., St. Margaret's, Kansas City, Kans., St. Elizabeth's, Covington, Ky., St. Mary's, Hoboken, N. J., St. Francis', Jersey City, N. J., St. Michael's, Newark, N. J., St. Peter's, Brooklyn, N. Y., St. Francis', New York City, St. Joseph's for Consumptives, New York City, St. Anthony's, Woodhaven, Long Island, N. Y., St. Francis, Cincinnati, Ohio, St. Mary's, Cincinnati, Ohio, St. Anthony's, Columbus, Ohio, St. Francis, Columbus, Ohio, St. Elizabeth's, Dayton, Ohio; St. Francis' Home for Aged and Incurables, New York City, and a home for working girls, St. Joseph's, Quincy, Ill.[48] Their hospitals have remained essentially institutions for poor persons and those of moderate means. They have resisted every inducement and pressure to develop expensive hospitals, which feature they leave to other communities. They have adhered to their original purpose of serving the sick poor. They not only serve the acutely ill but also chronics and incurables. In recent years some of their hospitals have been devoted exclusively to these two special types of patients. The sisters are always able to serve the poor free of charge and they are always able to give a patient a bed at a price he can afford to pay. And what is still more interesting they are never at a loss for the means, for they move around among the people and follow their original rule of begging.

[47] Lamott, *op. cit.*, pp. 264-266.
[48] *The Official Catholic Directory*, 1931.

French Communities Aid American Charities: The Grey Nuns

Between 1850 and 1860 the Church profited by the missionary spirit of French Canada in building up its charities, when three Canadian communities came to the United States. The Grey Nuns had a long record of missionary and charitable endeavors since their foundation by Madame d'Youville (1737). Through many years they had brought the messages of religion and of health to the primitive peoples of the far north. They had taken a large part in developing the Catholic charitable institutions of Quebec. They took special pride in the establishment of the first hospital for foundlings in North America in 1754. The daughters of Madame d'Youville, or the Sisters of Charity of Montreal as they are sometimes known, today number over 4,000 with over 200 houses in the United States and Canada.[49] From the original foundation at Montreal other branches of the Grey Nuns have been developed. There is one at St. Hyacinth, P. Q., and another at Quebec, P. Q. Sisters from these three motherhouses conduct the following charitable institutions in the United States: Healy Asylum, St. Mary's General Hospital and Girls' Orphanage, St. Joseph's Orphanage and Marcotte Home for Aged, all in Lewiston, Me, St. Joseph's Orphanage (French), Fall River, Mass., French-American Orphan Asylum, Lowell, Mass., Sacred Heart Home for Aged, New Bedford, Mass., St. Ann's Orphan Asylum, Worcester, Mass., St. Louis Hospital, Berlin, N. H., St. Peter's Orphanage for Boys, Notre Dame Orphanage for Girls, Hospital of Our Lady of Lourdes and Orphanage for Girls, all in Manchester, N. H., St. Charles Orphans' Home, Rochester, N. H., and L'Hospice St. Antoine (for aged), Woonsocket, R. I.[50]

The pioneer effort of the Grey Nuns in the United States

---

[49] *The Missionary Work of the Grey Nuns*, Pamphlet from Motherhouse, Montreal, P. Q.
[50] *The Official Catholic Directory*, 1931.

was in Toledo, Ohio (1855), then a city of only about 8,000. Because of stagnant pools and swamps the health conditions were poor. The Canadian Sisters of Charity were sheltered by the Ursulines until their house was completed. In this two-story frame building they opened the first Catholic hospital and the first Catholic orphanage in the city.[51]

The Grey Nuns of the Cross and the Grey Nuns of the Sacred Heart

A second group of Grey Nuns was introduced into Buffalo in 1857. These came from the Ottawa branch of the community and were known as the Grey Nuns of the Cross. From Buffalo, missions were established in other parts of New York, Pennsylvania, New Jersey and Massachusetts. Among them was a hospital at Plattsburg, New York, and two hospitals and an orphanage at Ogdensburg, New York. In 1921, a separate foundation of Grey Nuns was formed in Buffalo, whose purpose was to organize and increase the number of American educational and charitable institutions already established by the Grey Nuns of Ottawa. The following year, 1922, the new community known as the Grey Nuns of the Sacred Heart moved to Philadelphia. The charitable institutions under the direction of the Grey Nuns of the Sacred Heart include: A. Barton Hepburn Hospital, St. John's Hospital, and the Diocesan Orphanage and Home for Aged, all in the city of Ogdensburg, and the Champlain Valley Hospital at Plattsburg, New York.[52]

The Sisters of Charity of Providence

The Sisters of Charity of Providence were introduced from Montreal in 1856 by Rt. Rev. A. M. A. Blanchet, Bishop of Nesqually, now Seattle. After many struggles they finally succeeded with the assistance of the Society of St. Vincent

[51] *The Samaritan,* The Toledo Catholic Charities Corporation, Easter, 1928, p. 5.
[52] Dehey, *op. cit.,* pp. 557-558; 560-561; *The Official Catholic Directory,* 1931.

de Paul in establishing a hospital in Portland, Oregon, in 1875.[53]

A second group of Sisters of Charity of Providence was introduced into the diocese of Springfield, Massachusetts (1873), where its first mission was in Holyoke. The success of its efforts is attested by the fact that the sisters now conduct all of the charitable institutions in Holyoke. They are: Providence Hospital (1873), St. Vincent's Home for Girls (1880), Holy Family Institute, orphanage for boys (1893), Father Harkin's Home for Aged Women (1898), Bethlehem Infant Asylum (1900), Beaven-Kelly Home for Aged Men (1908), Holyoke Day Nursery (1916). Other institutions conducted by the Sisters of Charity of Providence in the diocese of Springfield are: St. Vincent's Hospital, Worcester, Mass. (1893), St. Vincent's Home for Aged Women, Worcester, Mass. (1893), Mercy Hospital, Springfield, Mass., (1896), Farren Memorial Hospital, Montague City, Mass. (1900), Greylock Rest Sanitarium, Adams, Mass. (1903), St. Mary's Maternity Hospital, Springfield, Mass. (1907), St. Agnes' Home, day nursery and working girls' home, Worcester, Mass. (1914), St. Luke's Home for Working Girls, Springfield, Mass. (1915), and St. Luke's Hospital, Pittsfield, Mass. (1918).[54]

Advantages and Disadvantages of a Diocesan Community

In 1892 the Sisters of Charity of Providence in Springfield, Massachusetts, became a diocesan community.[55] Their activities have been confined entirely to the Springfield diocese. Their growth is fairly typical of the growth of many diocesan communities in the United States. They have become an essential part of the mechanism of the diocese. They are always subject to the call of the bishop and their works are as varied as the charities of the diocese. The plan works well

---

[53] Sister Miriam Theresa, *History of Social Work done by Religious Communities in the Archdiocese of Portland in Oregon;* manuscript prepared for writer, August, 1929. See sketch of Blanchet by R. J. Purcell in *Dict. of Amer. Biography.*
[54] *The Official Catholic Directory,* 1931.
[55] *Catholic Encyclopedia,* Vol. XII, p. 508.

in a diocese with a large Catholic population and a great variety of institutions. Its most serious limitation is found in smaller dioceses in which the sisters have not sufficient opportunity for specialization. They are required frequently to take over institutions for which they have no special preparation.

The Sisters of the Holy Names of Jesus and Mary

In 1859 a third Canadian religious community, the Sisters of the Holy Names of Jesus and Mary, were introduced into this country. These sisters came to Portland, Oregon, at the invitation of Archbishop Blanchet and opened a home for destitute and orphaned children. This institution is now known as the Christie Home for Children.[56]

The Problem of Caring for Male Orphans Intensified by Withdrawal of Sisters of Charity

Nearly all the early Catholic institutions for dependent and neglected children in this country confined themselves exclusively to the care of girls. It was a part of the tradition of religious communities of women that their work should be confined to the care of children of their own sex. The pioneer leaders of the Church in this country hoped to secure brothers from Europe to take charge of boys or failing in this to institute new communities of men. Early efforts, however, to secure European brotherhoods or to develop new communities of men in this country were unsuccessful.[57] In the meantime the bishops had to provide ways and means of caring for boys as well as girls who had been bereft of their own parents. Their only alternative was to press the sisters into service. This plan seemed to meet the situation until the Sisters of Charity were withdrawn from the boys' orphan asylums in 1846.

[56] Sister Miriam Theresa, *op. cit.*, pp. 2–7.
[57] Burns, *op. cit.*, pp. 97–98

The Brotherhoods Partially Solve the Problem of Boys' Asylums

In New York and Cincinnati where the Sisters of Charity decided to become diocesan organizations they continued in charge of the boys. In Philadelphia and St. Louis the Sisters of St. Joseph filled the gap. Other dioceses again considered the possibility of securing brothers. They looked to the Brothers of the Holy Cross, who had just opened a manual labor school for boys at Notre Dame. Then there were the Brothers of the Christian Schools who had been introduced from France into Baltimore (1846) and into New York (1848) and the Brothers of the Sacred Heart who had come to Mobile, Alabama (1847).[58] Why could not they take care of boys' asylums? The principal objective that Père André Coindré, founder of the Brothers of the Sacred Heart, had in mind in his institute was the care of homeless and neglected boys. In point of fact the brothers did answer the call to the boys' asylums in many places. For a number of years the Brothers of the Holy Cross took charge of the boys' asylum in New Orleans, the Brothers of the Christian Schools took charge of boys' asylums in Washington and in Baltimore; and the Brother of the Sacred Heart took charge of the boys' asylums in Mobile and later in Natchez. The demands made on the brothers in the field of education and their limited membership soon compelled them to surrender the orphan asylums they had taken over and the bishops again had to call upon the sisters.

The Industrial School Movement Impeded by Limited Membership of the Brotherhoods

The industrial school movement of the sixties and seventies again turned the attention of the bishops to the brotherhoods. The sisters could not be expected to take care of the older boys. In many instances the Brothers of the Christian Schools

---

[58] *Ibid.*, pp. 102–104, 113.

came to the rescue. They took charge of the New York and Philadelphia Catholic Protectories. Archbishop Spalding induced the Xaverian Brothers to take St. Mary's Industrial School in Baltimore in 1866. As bishop of Louisville he had originally introduced the community from Bruges into his diocese.[59] The Brothers of the Poor of St. Francis Seraph came to Cincinnati in 1868 and opened a protectory for boys.[60] In the work of the industrial schools, as in the orphan asylums, the brotherhoods were handicapped by the demands made upon them by education and their limited membership. Most of the orders of brothers found it exceedingly difficult to secure vocations in the United States.

Religious Communities of Women from Germany Concentrate on Hospital Organization

Since 1860 a total of forty-nine religious communities of women engaging in various forms of charitable work have been introduced into this country from Europe and three from Canada. Like their predecessors in the United States practically all of these communities had been instituted for the care of the sick poor and the training of dependent and neglected children. When they came to the United States, they had to adjust themselves to conditions as they found them. As the writer has emphasized, the Civil War gave a great impetus to Catholic hospitals. In every city there was a demand for more hospitals. In the centers populated by German immigrants this demand was particularly insistent. The clamor for hospitals gave the European communities a new outlet. The German communities seemed to have a special penchant for hospitals. Five of the German communities coming to this country after the Civil War have become almost exclusively hospital communities: The Franciscan Sisters of St. Louis, the Sisters of the Third Order of St. Francis

[59] J. L. Spalding, op. cit., p. 160.
[60] Lamott, op. cit., p. 242.

of the Holy Family, the Hospital Sisters of St. Francis of Springfield, Illinois, the Poor Sisters of St. Francis Seraph of Perpetual Adoration, and the Franciscan Sisters of the Sacred Heart. Another German community, the Poor Handmaids of Jesus Christ, has also devoted the major part of its energies to hospital work.

The Poor Handmaids of Jesus Christ

Of these German hospital communities the first to come to the United States was the Poor Handmaids of Jesus Christ. The community was instituted at Dernbach, Germany, to minister to the sick and needy and especially orphans (1851). In the course of time the sisters took up teaching, but they were compelled to abandon this by the Kulturkampf.[61] At the invitation of Bishop Luers of Fort Wayne the community of Poor Handmaids came to the United States in 1863. In 1868 they took charge of Angel Guardian Orphan Asylum, Chicago, which had been established by the board of administrators of St. Boniface Cemetery in 1865.[62] In 1887 the Poor Handmaids took over the management of St. Vincent's Orphan Asylum, Fort Wayne.[63] Since that time the community has been placed in charge of the following: Hospitals— Sacred Heart, Aviston, Ill., St. Mary's, Centralia, Ill., St. Anne's, Chicago, Ill., St. Elizabeth's, Chicago, Ill., Municipal Isolation, Chicago, Ill., St. Mary's, East St. Louis, Ill., St. Catherine's, East Chicago, Ill., St. Joseph's, Fort Wayne, Ind., St. Mary's Mercy, Gary, Ind., Holy Family, Laporte, Ind., St. Joseph's, Mishawaka, Ind., Loretto, New Ulm, Minn., St. Joseph's, Ashland, Wis., St. Francis, Superior, Wis., St. Mary's, Superior, Wis.; Homes for Aged, St. Vincent's, Belleville, Ill., St. Mary's, Carlyle, Ill., St. Vincent's, Quincy, Ill., St. Alexander's, New Ulm, Minn.; and an orphanage, St. John's Catholic Orphanage, Belleville, Ill.[64]

[61] Alerding, *op. cit.*, p. 456.
[62] *The Archdiocese of Chicago*, pp. 747-749.
[63] Scheetz, *op. cit.*
[64] *The Official Catholic Directory*, 1931.

The Franciscan Sisters, Daughters of the Sacred Hearts of Jesus and Mary

The Franciscan Sisters, Daughters of the Sacred Hearts of Jesus and Mary, now known as the Franciscan Sisters of St. Louis, came to St. Louis (1873) from the motherhouse of the community at Salzkotten, Germany, at the invitation of Father Schindel to take charge of a hospital which he had built for the sick poor of his parish and vicinity. The institution known as the St. Boniface Hospital was destroyed by fire four years later. In 1900 they opened the present St. Anthony's Hospital, St. Louis, Missouri. Besides St. Anthony's Hospital the Franciscan Sisters of St. Louis now operate the following hospitals: St. Francis', Cape Girardeau, Mo., St. Joseph's, Milwaukee, Wis. (1879), St. Mary's, Racine, Wis. (1882), St. Andrew's, Murphysboro, Ill. (1897), St. Elizabeth's, Appleton, Wis. (1899), St. Francis', Waterloo, Iowa (1909). The sisters also have two orphanages, St. Clara's, Denver, Colo. (1890), and the Sacred Heart Orphanage, Pueblo, Colo. (1902), and two homes for girls, The House of Providence, Chicago, Ill. (1882), and St. Rosa's Home, Denver, Colo. (1909).[65]

Sisters of the Third Order of St. Francis of the Holy Family

The circumstances leading to the foundation of the Sisters of the Third Order of St. Francis of the Holy Family center around the historic town of Herford in Westphalia. The pastor of this town, Rev. Bernard Heising, was interested in making systematic provision for the dependent and neglected children of his parish. After numerous efforts, he finally succeeded in founding a community for the purpose in 1864. This was the nucleus of the present Sisters of the Third Order of St. Francis of the Holy Family.[66] Everything went

---

[65] Rothensteiner, *op. cit.*, Vol. II, pp. 343-346; *The Official Catholic Directory*, 1931.
[66] Sister M. Cortona Gloden, *Sisters of St. Francis of the Holy Family*, pp. 10-14.

well with the new community until the enactment of the May Laws in 1875 compelled them to leave their native land. In Father Emonds, pastor of St. Mary's Church, Iowa City, Iowa, they found a friend who gave them an opportunity to carry out the purposes of their mission. Shortly after their arrival in Iowa City, Father Emonds suggested that they open an orphanage. A building was acquired and the institution known as St. Mary's opened (May 1876).[67] The same year Rev. B. Baak of Peoria, Illinois, invited the sisters to open a hospital in his parish.[68] After Bishop John L. Spalding's appointment as first bishop of Peoria (1877), he suggested a separate motherhouse in his episcopal city. The resultant branch of the community is now known as Hospital Sisters of St. Francis of Peoria. They are now in charge of the following hospitals: St. Joseph's, Bloomington, Ill. (1880), St. Francis', Escanaba, Mich. (1884), St. Joseph's, Keokuk, Iowa (1887), St. Joseph's, Menominee, Mich. (1887), St. Mary's, Marquette, Mich. (1891), St. Francis', Burlington, Iowa (1893), St. Anthony's, Rockford, Ill. (1899), and St. James', Pontiac, Ill. (1906).[69]

In 1878 the original group of the Sisters of the Third Order of St. Francis of the Holy Family moved from Iowa City to Dubuque, where Bishop John Hennessy wanted them to take charge of an orphanage. In 1878 the sisters came with nine orphans and took up their abode in a remodeled church. In 1880 ground was broken for a new motherhouse at Dubuque.[70] These sisters have not adopted hospital work to the same extent as the Peoria community, only controlling the single hospital, the Sacred Heart Hospital at Le Mars, Iowa (1923). They have two orphan asylums, St. Mary's Orphan Home, Dubuque (1879), and St. Anthony's Home, Sioux City (1910), and two homes for women wage-earners,

[67] *Ibid.*, p. 47.
[68] *Ibid.*, p. 49.
[69] *The Official Catholic Directory*, 1931.
[70] Gloden, *op. cit.*, pp. 57-61.

Mary of the Angels Home (1892), and Our Lady of Lourdes and a home for the aged, St. Francis Home, all in Dubuque.[71]

Hospital Sisters of St. Francis of Springfield

The Hospital Sisters of St. Francis of Springfield, Illinois, as their name indicates, are exclusively a hospital community. They were forced by the Kulturkampf to leave Westphalia in 1875. On their arrival at Alton, Illinois, they placed themselves at the disposal of Bishop Peter J. Baltes. At first they devoted themselves to nursing the sick in their own homes in Springfield; but in a few months they secured a residence which they transformed into a hospital, the nucleus of the present St. John's Hospital, Springfield.[72] St. John's is now the motherhouse and the principal link in a chain of fourteen hospitals operated by the community: St. Elizabeth's, Belleville, Ill., St. Anthony's, Effingham, Ill., St. Francis', Litchfield, Ill., St. Mary's, Decatur, Ill., St. Joseph's, Highland, Ill., St. Joseph's, Chippewa Falls, Wis., St. Clara's, Lincoln, Ill., St. Vincent's, Green Bay, Wis., St. Mary's, Streator, Ill., Sacred Heart, Eau Claire, Wis., St. Nicholas', Sheboygan, Wis., St. John's Sanitarium for Tuberculosis, Springfield, and St. Francis', Washington, Mo. In connection with St. Nicholas' Hospital, Sheboygan, Wisconsin, they have a home for aged. They also conduct the St. John's Girls' Home at Springfield, Illinois, which was begun in 1928 by Bishop James A. Griffin.[73]

Poor Sisters of St. Francis Seraph of the Perpetual Adoration

Towards the end of 1875 six Poor Sisters of St. Francis Seraph of the Perpetual Adoration arrived at La Fayette, Indiana. They had neither friends nor money. They had been compelled by persecution to leave their native Westphalia,

---
[71] *The Official Catholic Directory,* 1931.
[72] J. A. Griffin (ed.), *The Diocese of Springfield in Illinois,* 1928, p. 555.
[73] *Ibid.,* p. 585; *The Official Catholic Directory,* 1931.

where for fifteen years they had been engaged in nursing the sick poor in their own homes and in caring for neglected children. Some charitably disposed persons in La Fayette placed a small house at their disposal. Eight months later a benefactor gave them two lots on which they erected St. Elizabeth's Hospital, their first hospital in the United States.[74] The community is now in charge of the following hospitals: St. Margaret's, Hammond, Ind., St. Joseph's, Logansport, Ind., St. Edward's, New Albany, Ind., St. Anthony's, Terre Haute, Ind., St. Francis', Beech Grove, Ind., St. Anthony's, Michigan City, Ind., St. Francis', Evanston, Ill., St. James', Chicago Heights, Ill., St. Alexis', Cleveland, Ohio, St. Joseph's, Memphis, Tenn., St. Anthony's, Louisville, Ky., St. Anthony's, Denver, Colo., St. Francis', Colorado Springs, Colo., St. Joseph's Creighton Memorial, Omaha, Neb., St. Mary's, Columbus, Neb., St. Francis', Grand Island, Neb., Good Samaritan, Kearney, Neb., St. Elizabeth's, Lincoln, Neb., St. Mary's, Emporia, Kans., and St. Mary's, Gallup, N. Mex. They also conduct St. Joseph's Orphan Asylum and Manual Labor School, Lafayette, Ind., St. Thomas' Orphanage, Lincoln, Neb., St. Anthony's Orphanage, Albuquerque, N. Mex., St. Joseph's Orphanage, Torrington, Wyo., and the St. Anthony Home for Aged, Lafayette, Ind.[75]

The Franciscan Sisters of the Sacred Heart

The last group of Franciscan Sisters coming from Germany during the period of the Kulturkampf were the Franciscan Sisters of the Sacred Heart, who first settled in Avilla, Indiana, but, in a short time, moved to Joliet, Illinois. The sisters opened their first hospital, St. Joseph's Hospital, Joliet, in 1882. In addition to this hospital they now conduct the following charitable institutions: Hospitals—St. Anthony of Padua, Chicago, Ill., St. Joseph's Home and Hospital, San

[74] Alerding, *The Diocese of Fort Wayne*, p. 460.
[75] *The Official Catholic Directory* (1931).

Francisco, Calif., Sacred Heart, Garrett, Ind., Queen of Angels, Los Angeles, Calif., St. Francis', Santa Barbara, Calif., St. Elizabeth's, Danville, Ill., St. Mary's, La Salle, Ill., St. Charles', Aurora, Ill., St. Joseph's, Elgin, Ill., St. Francis', Freeport, Ill.; the Home for the Aged, Avilla, Ind., St. Joseph's Home for Aged, Freeport, Ill., and St. Vincent's Orphan Asylum, Freeport, Ill.[76]

The Sisters of Misericorde

A Canadian community coming to the United States in the eighties, namely, the Sisters of Misericorde, might be classed as a specialized hospital community. Their first institution was the Misericordia Hospital in New York City (1887). In 1900 they went to Green Bay, Wisconsin, where they began the St. Mary's Mothers' and Infants' Home. Two years later, 1902, they opened St. Mary's Hospital in the same city.[77] In 1907 they opened a hospital in Oak Park, Illinois. The following year they began the Misericordia Hospital in Milwaukee and in 1914 the Huber Memorial Hospital in Pana, Illinois.[78] The fundamental objective of the Sisters of Misericorde is the care of unmarried mothers. In their hospitals, however, they carry out a general maternity program. As in other hospitals, they assume that the earnings on pay patients will aid in meeting the losses in the care of unmarried mothers, as well as others who are unable to pay in full.

The Little Sisters of the Poor

Of the communities of European origin in the United States that have adhered rigidly to their original objectives there is none so unique as the Little Sisters of the Poor. Since the program of the Little Sisters has been discussed fully

[76] *The Official Catholic Directory*, 1931.
[77] *Catholic Charities of Green Bay*, manuscript report, 1929.
[78] *Report of St. Mary's Mothers' and Infants' Home and St. Mary's Hospital*, Green Bay, Wis., 1900-1925, pp. 11-12.

in the chapter on the care of the aged,[79] there is little to be added in this chapter. In discussing the general development of religious communities this much should be said in regard to the Little Sisters. They have been able to adhere to their original objectives because they have thrown themselves directly on the charity of the public and because they have been independent of diocesan control. It remains to be seen whether they can resist the processes of change as firmly in the future as in the past. They will have to look, more and more, for American subjects. The inevitable change of personnel is bound to influence their whole program, as it has influenced the programs of other communities.

Diocesan Responsibility for Child-Care After the Civil War

After the Civil War Catholic child-caring work was placed on a new basis. It was no longer possible for the sisters to depend on their own unaided efforts. They had to look to the dioceses and in many instances to the public authorities for support. During the years following the war there was an increased recognition of diocesan responsibility for child-caring work. One diocese after another imposed an annual orphans' collection. Some dioceses in order to secure larger funds took over the Christmas or the Easter collection. In New York, in 1866, we find both the Christmas and Easter collections going to the orphans. The Christmas collection amounted to $25,333.26 and the Easter collection to $21,166.41.[80] In Fort Wayne, Indiana, the bishop, after depending on itinerant clerical collectors for a number of years, decided to take the Christmas collection for the orphans of the diocese.[81]

[79] Chap. XII.
[80] *New York Freeman's Journal*, Vol. XXIV, Jan. 9, 1864.
[81] Scheetz, *op. cit.*

Religious Communities Entering the Charitable Field in the United States After the Civil War

Most of the new developments in Catholic child-caring work after the war were in charge of religious communities already on the ground. Some dioceses, however, received religious communities that really became an integral part of the mechanism of those dioceses and played an important part in the development of their charities. This has been true of the Sisters of Charity of Providence, in Springfield, Massachusetts, the Poor Handmaids of Jesus Christ in Fort Wayne, and of the Sisters of Charity of the Incarnate Word in Texas.

The Sisters of Charity of the Incarnate Word

In 1866 the first group of Sisters of Charity of the Incarnate Word came to Galveston, Texas, from Lyons, France. A building which was to serve both as their convent and hospital was completed in the following year. An epidemic of yellow fever broke out and their "Charity Hospital" was crowded immediately. As a result of their heroic work during the epidemic, the city of Galveston decided to turn over the management of the city hospital to them, May 7, 1868. In 1869 the Sisters of the Incarnate Word opened Santa Rosa Infirmary in San Antonio, Texas. Five years later they had ready for occupancy a new home for the orphans, St. Joseph's Orphanage in the same city.[82]

Since 1880 the Sisters of Charity of the Incarnate Word have developed an extensive hospital and child-caring program. At the present time they have the following additional hospitals: Michael Meagher Memorial Hospital, Texarkana, Ark., St. Mary's Long Beach Hospital, Long Beach, Calif., St. Patrick's Sanitarium, Lake Charles, La., Schumpert Memorial Sanitarium, Shreveport, La., St. Mary's Infirmary, McAlester, Okla., St. Anthony's Hospital, Amarillo, Tex., Hotel Dieu,

---

[82] Sr. M. Helena Finck, *The Congregation of the Sisters of Charity of the Incarnate Word of San Antonio, Texas.* Catholic University of America, 1925, pp. 35-36, 43, 51, 56.

Beaumont, Tex., Spohn Sanitarium, Corpus Christi, Tex., St. Joseph's Infirmary, Fort Worth, Tex., St. Mary's Infirmary, Galveston, Tex., St. Joseph's Infirmary, Houston, Tex., Texas Pacific Hospital, Marshall, Tex., St. Joseph's Infirmary, Paris, Tex., St. Mary's Hospital, Port Arthur, Tex., St. John's Sanitarium, San Angelo, Tex., Santa Rosa Infirmary, San Antonio, and Santa Fe Hospital, Temple, Tex. They also have the following orphanages: St. Mary's Orphan Home, Lafayette, La., St. Joseph's Home, Pineville, La., St. Joseph's Home for Girls, Dallas, Tex., Dunne Memorial Home for Boys, Dallas, Tex., St. Margaret's Orphan Home, El Paso, Tex., St. Mary's Home, Galveston, Tex., St. Joseph's Institute for Boys, Marshall, Tex., St. Peter's Diocesan Orphanage, San Antonio, Tex. The sisters also conduct two homes for the aged, St. Anthony's Home, Houston, Tex., and St. Francis' Home, San Antonio, Texas.[83]

European Religious Communities Devoted to the Welfare of Their Own People

The desire to work among the members of their own race in the United States has always made a strong appeal to European religious communities. Again the immigrants in this country were anxious to have leaders and teachers of their own races. The appeal of the Irish immigrant played a prominent part in the pioneer work of the Sisters of Mercy in the United States just as the German immigrant was a strong factor in the work of the German communities. The same tendency is marked in the religious life of the Polish and Italian immigrants.

The Felician Sisters

The desire to help their own people in America appealed to the best ideals of the Polish people in their home land. Their priests and their religious in great numbers followed the immigrants. The Felician Sisters made their first founda-

[83] *The Official Catholic Directory*, 1931.

tion in this country in Polonia, Wisconsin, in 1874. In 1882 the community began a new province in Detroit. A third foundation was made in Buffalo (1896), when the Immaculate Heart of Mary Orphanage was begun. The Community now conducts the Felician Sisters' Orphan Home, Detroit, Mich., St. Joseph's Orphan Home, Jackson, Mich., Polish Manual Training School for Boys, Niles, Ill., St. Hedwig's Industrial School for Girls, Niles, Ill., St. Joseph's Orphan Asylum, Milwaukee, Wis. St. Mary's Orphan Asylum and Home for the Aged, Manitowoc, Wis., St. Clara's Orphanage, Polonia, Wis., St. Joseph's Patronage for Working Girls, New York City, Immaculate Conception Orphan Asylum, Lodi, N. J., Infant Jesus Day Nursery and Mt. Carmel Day Nursery, Buffalo, N. Y., and the St. Felix Home for Working Girls, Buffalo, N. Y.[84]

The Sisters of the Holy Family of Nazareth

At the beginning of the Polish immigration tide, there followed the Sisters of the Holy Family of Nazareth, founded in 1874 by Frances Siedliska, a Polish noblewoman, in Rome. In 1885 twelve sisters of the community answered the call of Archbishop Feehan of Chicago to work among their own people in this country.[85] From Chicago they have extended their activities to the various Polish centers in the United States. While their interests are primarily educational, they conduct four hospitals and a day nursery: St. Mary of Nazareth Hospital, Chicago, Ill., St. Joseph of Nazareth Hospital, Clayton, Tex., Loretto Hospital, Dalhart, Tex., Holy Family Hospital Mineral Wells, Tex., and St. Adalbert's Day Nursery, Chicago, Ill.[86]

---

[84] *Archives* of Felician Sisters, Buffalo, N. Y.
[85] *Catholic Encyclopedia*, Vol. VII, p. 408; see sketch of Feehan by R. J. Purcell in *Dict. of American Biography*.
[86] *The Official Catholic Directory*, 1931.

The Missionary Sisters of the Sacred Heart

The same desire to work among their own people in other lands is found among the Italian communities. It was this thought that inspired Mother Cabrini to organize her Missionary Sisters of the Sacred Heart in Codogno, Italy (1880). At the suggestion of Pope Leo XIII she decided to give special attention to the American Italians. The first band of Missionary Sisters arrived in New York in 1890. Since that time the community has become an important factor in developing Catholic leadership among the Italians. At the present time, it is in charge of the following institutions: Columbus Hospital, New York City, Columbus Hospital Extension, New York City, Sacred Heart Orphan Asylum, West Park, N. Y., St. Anthony's Orphan Asylum, West Arlington, N. J.; Sacred Heart Orphan Asylum, Philadelphia, Pa., Columbus Hospital, Philadelphia, Pa., Columbus Hospital, Chicago, Ill., Mother Cabrini Memorial Hospital, Chicago, Ill., Sacred Heart Orphan Asylum, New Orleans, La., Cabrini Day Home, New Orleans, La., Sacred Heart Orphanage, Seattle, Wash., St. Paul's School, Seattle, Wash., Sacred Heart Orphan Asylum, Burbank, Calif., Mother Cabrini Preventorium, Burbank, Calif., Mother Cabrini Day Nursery, Burbank, Calif., and Mother Cabrini Orphan Asylum, Denver, Colo.[87]

The Missionary Sisters of the Third Order of St. Francis

Another Italian community, the Missionary Sisters of the Third Order of St. Francis, known as the Franciscan Sisters of Peekskill, also came to New York in 1890. They now conduct St. Joseph's Home for Children, Peekskill, New York, the following day nurseries, All Saints' and St. Margaret's of New York City, St. Anthony's and St. Mary Magdalen de Pazzi of Philadelphia, a convalescent home for women, Lo-

---

[87] *The Missionary Sisters of the Sacred Heart of Jesus*, manuscript report prepared for the writer, September, 1929.

retto Rest at Cold Springs, New York, and a residence for self-supporting girls, St. Margaret's in New York City.[88]

The Home Missionary Service Attracts New Communities

In the early part of this chapter it has been emphasized that the basic objective that gave birth to most of the religious communities in Europe after the French Revolution was the visiting of the sick and the poor in their own homes. When these communities came to America they were carried along by the tide of the times. They did not have any choice except to adapt themselves to needs and conditions as they found them. Education and the care of the orphan were their first interests. Hospitals came next in development. With the demands made upon the communities in these important fields of labor there was no energy left to prosecute their original objective. Yet, the reaching out into the homes of the sick and the poor and the neglected occupied such an important place in the historic mission of the Church, that it could not be disregarded permanently. The home missionary appeal was bound to give birth to new communities. Service to the poor and neglected in their own homes was also bound to attract new communities from Europe.

The Sisters of Bon Secours

Beginning in 1881 the appeal went out to Europe for assistance in home service. In that year, the Sisters of Bon Secours came to Baltimore at the invitation of Archbishop James Gibbons. The community had originally been established in Paris for the purpose of nursing the sick in their own homes (1824). In 1882 they opened their first convent in Baltimore.[89] From Baltimore the sisters extended their activities to Washington in 1905. In 1909 another house was opened in Detroit. In 1916 Archbishop Prendergast invited the Sis-

---

[88] *The Official Catholic Directory*, 1931.
[89] *The Sisters of Bon Secours*, published by Burnes and Oates, London, 1912, p. 229.

ters of Bon Secours to Philadelphia to take charge of St. Edmond's Home for Crippled Children. After his appointment to Philadelphia Cardinal Dougherty placed the Sisters of Bon Secours in charge of the Home for Convalescents and Incurables, Darby, Pennsylvania. The sisters extended their program to a new field in 1907, when they took over St. Martin's Day Nursery in Baltimore. From the date of the foundation in America the Sisters of Bon Secours were handicapped very greatly by the lack of a hospital for training their own members. They recognized that they could not satisfy all the demands of modern nursing without scientific training. In 1919 Mr. and Mrs. George W. Jenkins of Baltimore came to their rescue by supplying them with a completely equipped hospital. This has provided the community with a training center for all its sister nurses.[90] The Sisters of Bon Secours in their program of home nursing do not confine themselves to any social group or class. They serve the middle and upper classes as well as the poor.

The Little Sisters of the Assumption

Just at the opening of the last decade of the nineteenth century two French communities whose efforts have been devoted exclusively to the care of the poor were introduced into this country. They were the Little Sisters of the Assumption and the Helpers of the Holy Souls. The Little Sisters of the Assumption were founded in Paris in 1865 to nurse the sick poor in their own homes. Their first American foundation was in New York City in 1891. The Little Sisters of the Assumption now have two convents in New York City and one in Philadelphia.[91]

[90] *Congregation of Sisters of Bon Secours*, Brochure, Baltimore, May, 1928, pp. 11-12.
[91] *Catholic Encyclopedia*, Vol. II, p. 51; *The Official Catholic Directory*, 1931.

The Society of the Helpers of the Holy Souls

The Society of the Helpers of the Holy Souls traces its origin to the year 1853 when Eugénie Smet, a French girl of deep religious convictions, was inspired to establish an association of prayer and good works for the dead. After three years of consideration and preparation, she was given permission by the Archbishop of Paris to establish her institute.[92] Her final plans called for a community that would practice the corporal as well as the spiritual works of mercy. Its members would not only pray for the dead but they would bring the message of service and consolation to the sick in their own homes. Their home nursing gradually broadened out into a large religious program. They organized classes in religious instruction. They gathered the children together in recreational centers. They tried in every way to get the laity to participate in their work. The first American foundation of the Helpers of the Holy Souls dates from 1892 when seven of the sisters arrived in New York City. They now operate a large settlement on Eighty-sixth Street in New York City. From New York they extended their work to St. Louis in 1903, to San Francisco in 1905 and to Chicago in 1925.

The Sisters of the Little Company of Mary and the Sisters of the Divine Saviour

In the year 1893, a nursing community from England, the Sisters of the Little Company of Mary, began its work in Chicago. In addition to home nursing, these sisters now operate a large general hospital in Chicago.[93] At the invitation of Archbishop Frederick X. Katzer, the Sisters of the Divine Saviour came to Milwaukee from Rome in 1894 to develop a program of home nursing.[94]

[92] *Reverend Mother Mary of Providence*, published by Sands & Co., London, 1928, pp. 9, 14–15.
[93] Dehey, *op. cit.*, pp. 713–714.
[94] *Ibid.*, p. 726.

The Missionary Sisters, Servants of the Holy Ghost

Another religious community of close resemblance is the Missionary Sisters, Servants of the Holy Ghost, from Holland. The community was established in 1881, and introduced into the United States in 1901. The first American foundation was at Techny, Illinois. Within two years a home for the aged was opened in this city. Three hospitals were later established: St. Mary's at Watertown, Wis., St. Joseph's at New Hampton, Iowa, and St. Theresa's at Waukeegan, Ill. The congregation also conducts a home for destitute girls in Milwaukee and a home for the aged at Hyattsville, Maryland. In addition to these institutions the sisters are actively engaged in missionary work among the colored of the south.[95] Like so many other communities these sisters have drifted more and more from home to institutional work.

French Anti-Clericalism of Present Century Aids Catholic Charities of the United States

Some of the most flourishing religious communities in the United States owe their beginnings in this country to religious persecution in Europe. In the first years of the present century, anti-clericalism in France drove three communities to the United States that have made important contributions to Catholic charities: The Daughters of Wisdom, the Daughters of the Holy Ghost, and the Sisters of the Infant Jesus. The Daughters of Wisdom have filled a great need in the diocese of Brooklyn. About the time of their arrival the diocese was planning a home for blind, defective and crippled children at Port Jefferson, Long Island. The Daughters of Wisdom were placed in charge and have made the St. Charles Home one of the best institutions in the country. It includes an up-to-date hospital for crippled children, an institution for the training of mentally handicapped children and instruc-

---

[95] *Missionary Sisters, Servants of the Holy Ghost.* Pamphlet published by the Sacred Heart Home, Hyattsville, Md., 1931.

tion for the training of the blind. The members of this community are also engaged in charitable work in the diocese of Portland, where they conduct a hospital and an orphan asylum at St. Agatha, Maine.[96]

The Daughters of the Holy Ghost came to this country from France in 1902. While their primary work is the visitation of the sick poor they also conduct the following institutions: The Bishop Stang Day Nursery and the St. John's Day Nursery, Fall River, Mass., the Nazareth Home and Day Nursery, Providence, R. I., the St. Clare Home, Newport, R. I.; Stella Maris Home for Convalescents, Newport, R. I., St. Elizabeth's Home. Hartford, Conn., and St. Clare Home, Newport, R. I.[97]

The Sisters of the Infant Jesus came to the Brooklyn diocese from France in 1906. They began by cooperating with the St. Vincent de Paul Society in that city.[98] Their work is exclusively the nursing of the sick poor in their own homes with the exception of one hospital, the Mercy Hospital which they opened at Hempstead, Long Island, New York, in 1913.

Latest European Communities Coming to the United States For Social Service

Among the latest additions to the long line of European religious communities coming to the United States are the Carmelites of the Divine Heart of Jesus, the Dominican Tertiaries from England and the Sisters of the Social Mission from Hungary.

The first of these, the Carmelites of the Divine Heart of Jesus, a German community, after many difficulties obtained their original foothold in this country in Milwaukee (1912). Here they opened St. Joseph's Home of the Sacred Heart, an

---
[96] *Catholic Charities Review*, Vol. XI, (Sept., 1927), 264-266; *The Official Catholic Directory*, 1931.
[97] *The Official Catholic Directory*, 1931.
[98] *St. Vincent de Paul Quarterly*, Vol. XIII, No. 4 (Nov., 1908), p. 402.

institution for aged men and women. In 1913 they began work in the diocese of Fort Wayne. At first they engaged in home visitation but later established two orphanages, St. Joseph's Home for Homeless Children, East Chicago, Indiana, and St. Joseph's Home of the Divine Child, Hammond, Indiana. In 1914 they began work among the Mexicans in San Antonio, Texas, and in the course of time established a day nursery and institution for children. They also conduct a day nursery in Corpus Christi, Texas.[99] The following homes for the aged are in charge of these sisters: St. Joseph's Home of the Sacred Heart, Detroit, Mich., St. Joseph's Home, St. Charles, Mo., St. Joseph's Home of the Sacred Heart, Kenosha, Wis. and St. Joseph's Home, South Kenosha, Wis.[100]

The second of this group, a community of Dominican Tertiaries from England, was introduced into Duluth, Minnesota, in 1920. It was their purpose to reach out to adults and children who had become careless in their religious duties. This was combined with a girls' protective program. Within the past few years the community has adopted a modified Carmelite rule. It is now known as the Carmelite Sisters of Corpus Christi. The best known work of these sisters in America is their Corpus Christi House in Duluth, Minnesota, a home for delinquents mentioned in the chapter on protective care of girls.[101] At Scott's Bluff in the diocese of Grand Island, Nebraska, they are laboring among the Mexican population. They are also conducting a home for aged at Kearney, Nebraska.

The Social Mission Sisters were introduced into the United States in 1922 by Bishop Schrembs of Cleveland. They came from Budapest and began work in a section of the city of Cleveland populated by a foreign element. The Social Mission Sisters as their name implies engage in all forms of social

---
[99] *Life and Work of the Carmelite Sisters of the Divine Heart of Jesus*, published by Motherhouse, Wauwatosa, Wis.
[100] *The Official Catholic Directory*, 1931.
[101] Chapter X.

work, family visiting, religious instruction to both children and adults and settlement work. They aim to cooperate with all the existing social agencies in Cleveland.[102]

The Church in America Becomes of Age

In the past the Catholic Church in the United States was forced to lean heavily on European religious communities [103] for teachers and for the personnel of its various charitable institutions. The Church here has now come of age. From the fullness of its own life there should grow that spirit of sacrifice which will inspire a sufficient number of its own sons and daughters to dedicate themselves to lives of religious service.

[102] *The Social Mission. A Solution for Present Day Problems*, published by the Social Mission Sisters, Cleveland, Ohio.
[103] The work of the religious communities of men engaged in the charitable ield in the United States has been treated rather completely in the chapter dealing with protectories and industrial schools, Chapter VII.

CHAPTER XX

TOWARDS A COORDINATED PROGRAM

The Orphanage as a Diocesan Responsibility

The orphanage, or children's home, was the first city-wide work of Catholic Charities. While a parish many times took the initiative in establishing an orphanage, the institution usually outgrew the resources of the particular parish and became diocesan in character. Soon all the parishes in the diocese looked to the orphanage to assist in caring for their children; but they were not as willing to join in supporting the institution as they were in sharing its benefits. They assumed that from a financial standpoint the orphanage was the bishop's responsibility or the responsibility of some religious community. There was little that the bishop could do for the orphans, because he did not have any funds save donations from the Propagation of the Faith at Lyons or the Leopoldine Society at Vienna. The burden of caring for the diocesan orphans, therefore, rested very largely with the religious communities in charge. By means of benefits, fairs, lectures, and individual begging, the religious managed to provide for their charges. As the number of children needing care increased after the Civil War, the problem proved too large for the sisters. Accordingly, one diocese after another made special provision for the financing of their orphanages. Some dioceses, like Baltimore, decided to have special collections in the churches; others like Hartford and Brooklyn decided to set aside the traditional Christmas collection for this purpose. Even with the adoption of a special collection or the setting aside of one of the regular collections, the growth of diocesan responsibility was an exceedingly slow process. For the most part, the parishes were poor and diocesan responsibility seemed remote. When the bishop had the courage to set aside one of the regular collections for the care of the orphans, his action at first provoked violent opposition; but in time there was a large orphans' fund. The special collection was not so successful.

A Broader Horizon for Charitable Organizations

After the dioceses had placed their orphanages on a firm financial footing, they were inclined to assume that they had discharged their full responsibility. The parishes were providing for families in need and diocesan institutions were caring for the children. What more was there to do? About 1890 the members of the Society of St. Vincent de Paul and a few organizations of Catholic women found that there were plenty of other things to do. Children of working mothers had to be provided for in day nurseries. Large numbers of the new immigrants who were not being reached by the existing parish organizations, must be given religious instruction. To religious instruction, educational and recreational features were added; and there were the beginnings of a Catholic settlement movement. Even for the care of children away from their own homes, the institutional program was not complete. Without contact with the courts, the institutions could not be sure that they were receiving all the children who should be committed to their care. Then there was the important matter of after-care of the children discharged from the institutions. In 1887 the Particular Council of the Society of St. Vincent de Paul of Boston decided: "To employ an agent to attend the courts, police stations and jails or wherever else he might be called upon, to look after such children as it might be proper for the Society to take charge of. . . . The conferences promptly donated five per cent of their gross receipts for the payment of the agent's salary and necessary expenses. . . . Whenever a report of a child destitute or neglected is sent to the agent his duty is to visit and ascertain the facts and to wait on the parish priest and president of the local conference and advise what is best to be done in the matter. . . . If it is deemed best to remove the child to a Catholic institution the expense, if any, is assumed by the conference of the parish where the child had a residence when taken by the agent.''[1] In 1897 the Particular Council of the Society of St. Vincent de Paul in Providence, Rhode Island, employed a full-time man who acted as an agent of the various Catholic institutions in the juvenile court.[2] In the same year the Providence Society began the systematic placing out of children from the Rhode Island Catholic Orphan Asylum and St. Vincent's Infant Asylum.[3]

The Catholic Home Bureau of New York Marks New Era in Catholic Child-Care

In another chapter[4] the writer has made extended reference to the establishment of the Catholic Home Bureau of New York by the St. Vincent de Paul Society in 1898. This was a most significant step in the evolution of our present programs of Catholic Charities. It marked the beginning of systematic child-placing under Catholic auspices. In the course of the years, it exercised an important influence in Catholic child-care. Considering the newness of its program, one should not be disappointed at the failure of other cities to take up the idea immediately. Their problem was not so acute. They were still discussing child-care in terms of expanding institutional programs. The seed planted by the Home Bureau did take root gradually. The first city outside New York to set up a similar agency was Newark with its New Jersey Catholic Children's Aid Society under the leadership of Rev. Francis Foy (1903). Then came the Little Chil-

---

[1] *Society of St. Vincent de Paul, Report of the Superior Council of New York to the Council General at Paris*, 1888, pp. 16-17.
[2] *St. Vincent de Paul Quarterly*, Vol. IV, No. 2 (May, 1899), pp. 155-156.
[3] *Society of St. Vincent de Paul, Report of Superior Council of New York to Council General at Paris*, 1900, p. 30.
[4] Chapter XIII.

dren's Aid Society of San Francisco, in 1907. Washington Vincentians began to take note of the work of the Catholic Home Bureau of New York and set up their own Home Bureau in 1909. In 1912 the Catholic child-caring situation in Detroit had reached an acute stage. The city had been growing by leaps and bounds; but there had been no increase in the Catholic child-caring facilities. The members of the St. Vincent de Paul Society began to take cognizance of the situation. It was a question of finding homes for children or of building more institutions. The local Vincentians conferred with Mr. William J. Doharty, Superintendent of the New York Catholic Home Bureau, and Mr. Edmond J. Butler, Secretary of the Superior Council of New York. With the encouragement they received from Messrs. Doharty and Butler and with the approval of their bishop, they decided to establish a child-caring department for the purpose of taking Catholic children from the juvenile court and institutions and placing them in good Catholic homes.[5] Thus, the Society of St. Vincent de Paul saved the diocese of Detroit untold sums in institutional construction. Since 1913 the population of Detroit has increased almost a million and yet the Catholic children's institutions have increased very little. There are many dioceses with a quarter of the Catholic population of Detroit that have twice the capacity in their Catholic children's institutions. It is likely that the Church in Detroit would be compelled to increase its children's institutions fourfold were it not for the work of the St. Vincent de Paul child-caring department. The department has also rendered a very important public service, as the courts look to it for the care of Catholic children. Most of the children under its supervision are public wards of Wayne County and are paid for by the county on a per capita basis.

The child-caring department of the Society of St. Vincent

[5] *Report of the Society of St. Vincent de Paul of Detroit and Its Child-Caring Department*, 1913, pp. 6–7.

de Paul of Detroit has not remained at a standstill; it has kept pace with the best developments. By arrangement with the Ford Hospital it has been able to maintain the highest standards of medical care. It has its own mental clinic. It has been especially diligent in the training of its foster mothers in child-care.

The Pioneers Recognize Trend Towards Home-Placing of Children

The pioneers in the organized Catholic child-placing work had a very clear understanding of the general trends in child-care. They knew very well that the foster home and especially the boarding home, year by year, would come to occupy a more prominent place in child-care. They wanted to see Catholic work grow and expand. Especially did they want to see the work of the Church develop in its cherished field of child-care. They were afraid that if the Church failed to develop a program of foster-care in the near future, its activities in the whole field of child-care would be limited greatly. A large part of the work would be taken over by non-sectarian and public agencies.

As was noted in another chapter,[6] the State of Massachusetts began to place out children in homes in 1866 because it was an inexpensive method of caring for them. Most of the children were Irish Catholics. There were very few Catholic homes available which pleased those in charge of the destinies of the commonwealth; for the ideal was to place the children of the Irish in transplanted Yankee homes in the middle west. And Catholic leaders permitted the nefarious traffic!

The Catholic Charitable Bureau of Massachusetts

No organized protest against this practice is noted until 1901, when Archbishop John J. Williams at one of the regular semi-annual conferences of the clergy of the archdiocese of Boston held during that year called attention to the need of

[6] Chapter VI.

cooperating with the state authorities in finding Catholic homes for Catholic children. Complaints had been made that large numbers of Catholic children were being placed in Protestant homes. In December of the same year a committee of priests, appointed by the vicar-general, met to devise plans to safeguard the faith of Catholic children who were wards of the state. From the discussion it was apparent that Catholics had no contact with the child-caring agencies of the state. Most of the Catholic children were being cared for by the public authorities of the state without any provision for their religious upbringing. It was a well recognized fact that a very large percentage of them were under the care of Protestant foster-parents. All present agreed that it was high time to do something about this deplorable situation. Since it was something of state-wide concern, calling for a state program, it was resolved to seek the cooperation of the other dioceses within the state. A central bureau, known as the Catholic Charitable Bureau of Massachusetts was finally set up in 1903, under the direction of Rev. Joseph G. Anderson, later auxiliary bishop of Boston.[7]

Arrangements were made with the State Board of Minor Wards to have the names of all Catholic children sent to the bureau for follow-up care of their religious training. At first the organization was state-wide in its scope. Later, however, its work was confined to Boston, when the dioceses of Springfield and Fall River had made special provision for the Catholic wards in their respective jurisdictions.

The Program of the Catholic Charitable Bureau of Boston

Since its opening in 1903 the Catholic Charitable Bureau of Boston has broadened its program very considerably. In addition to holding itself responsible for the spiritual welfare of the Catholic wards of the State Board of Minor Wards, the bureau has developed its own child-placing program. It

[7] "The Catholic Charitable Bureau of Massachusetts," by Rev. Maurice J. O'Connor, *St. Vincent de Paul Quarterly*, Vol. X, No. 1 (Feb., 1905), pp. 71–80.

has taken up family welfare work on a limited scale. Since 1921 it has developed a large program of immigrant welfare. The Boston bureau has not become a clearing house for childcare to the same extent as similar agencies in some other dioceses. The individual institutions still make their own plans for receiving and discharging children.

The Diocesan Commission of Hartford

When Bishop John Nilan was appointed to Hartford in 1910 he found the same conditions in Connecticut that had prevailed in Massachusetts before 1903. A law passed by the state legislature of Connecticut in 1904 provided for the placement of children in homes of the same religious faith as their parents; but the law was violated with impunity by the county children's homes. Accordingly, the bishop set up a diocesan commission to provide for the religious welfare of Catholic children in the county homes. This commission immediately appointed an agent to work with the county homes in an effort to have Catholic children placed in Catholic homes or Catholic institutions.

Juvenile Courts

For a long number of years the various Catholic dioceses depended on their industrial schools in caring for delinquent children. The development of these schools has been described in another chapter.[8] During the nineties of the last century, persons dealing with juvenile delinquents came to recognize that something more was needed. Their first thought was to provide special courts or special divisions in existing courts to deal with children's cases. The new juvenile court laws proposed during this period provided not only separate hearings but also separate treatment for juvenile delinquents. Once these laws were passed, it was unlawful to deal with children in the same court rooms and according

[8] Chapter VII.

to the same form as adults. It was illegal to house them in the same institution with adults.

It is interesting to note that the first juvenile court bill introduced in the legislature of Illinois in 1891, and probably the first to be introduced in any legislature, was prepared by Judge Timothy D. Hurley, President of the Catholic Visitation and Aid Society of Chicago. As a result of his contact with children in Cook County jail and the Chicago criminal courts, Judge Hurley became the pioneer crusader in Illinois for the humane treatment of juvenile offenders.[9]

The Society of St. Vincent de Paul Sponsors Juvenile Courts

The Society of St. Vincent de Paul cooperated with other organizations in the movement for special courts to deal with children's cases: "The St. Vincent de Paul Society assisted other local organizations in securing for Baltimore city the passage by the General Assembly of Maryland of what is known as the 'Juvenile Court Bill'. . . . In this connection the St. Vincent de Paul Society has reason to feel especially gratified inasmuch as the secretary of the Particular Council of Baltimore city was appointed by the Governor of the State.'"[10]

The Personnel of the Juvenile Court

The juvenile court means more than separate treatment for juvenile offenders. The state looks to the child as one who needs not so much punishment as correction and guidance. When the court, as representing supreme guardianship of the state, has reasonable ground for believing that the child's welfare is in danger, it can take cognizance of the case and see that proper steps are taken for the child's protection. All this calls for a personnel which the court did not have in the beginning. The different communities

---
[9] *Catholic Charities Review*, Vol. IX (February, 1925), p. 63.
[10] *Report of the Superior Council of New York to the Council-General at Paris*, 1902, p. 40.

thought that their whole duty had been done when the machinery was set up. They forgot that it needed fuel and oil. As in all public projects the taxpayers' money had to be extracted by slow and painful processes. Under the circumstances, there was nothing for the court to do except to appeal to private agencies, and the Society of St. Vincent de Paul was prompt in response. Like other agencies the Vincentians first depended on volunteer probation officers, but very soon learned that something more was needed. The report of the Pittsburgh Particular Council for 1903 tells the whole story: "They have performed excellent work and deserve thanks of their brothers. However we found it impossible to conduct this work properly without paid assistants as the non-Catholics were so represented and it required the utmost vigilance to protect out children in their faith. We spent much time in endeavoring to get our Catholic societies to help us in this work by money contributions. In this we are pleased to report that we have been fairly successful. A number of branches of the C. M. B. A. and Advisory Council contributing and since the close of the year the Young Men's Institute, Catholic Temperance Association and Duquesne Council, Knights of Columbus.... We have thus been able to employ a Catholic lawyer to attend all the sessions of the court and also have had some assistance from one of the probation officers."[11] The Brooklyn Society had the same experience. At first it depended on volunteers but soon found it necessary to employ a full-time woman probation officer.[12] In 1905 the Particular Council of the Society of St. Vincent de Paul of Cincinnati decided to have each parish conference select one of its members to act as a voluntary probation officer in the court.[13] Eight years later it was found necessary to add a full-time person to guide the volunteers in Cincinnati.

[11] *Ibid.*, p. 50.
[12] "Juvenile Court Work," by Patrick F. Mallon, *St. Vincent de Paul Quarterly*, Vol. X, No. 3 (August, 1905), pp. 268–273.
[13] *Report of the Superior Council of New York to Council-General at Paris*, 1905, p. 57.

The St. Vincent de Paul Society and its Relation to the Charity Organization Society

After 1900 a number of members of the St. Vincent de Paul Society became dissatisfied with the purely parochial outlook in charity work. As men of affairs, some of them were insistent that business methods should be carried over in their service of the poor. A number of them had seen service on committees of the Charity Organization Society and had profited thereby. In 1900 the Charity Organization Society of New York City assumed the leadership in organizing a city-wide committee to work with the Department of Charities in maintaining the home life of dependent children. Among the personnel of the committee was a member of the Society of St. Vincent de Paul. The report of the St. Vincent de Paul member at the end of the first six months' period is significant: "After a service of six months as a member of that committee," he says, "it gives me much pleasure to state from my experience in this new field that what appeared six months ago to be an evil was but a blessing in disguise. Our representation on this committee has resulted in creating a better and more intimate relationship between the two societies . . . and the poor families have been correspondingly benefited. . . . In caring for the large number of families assigned to us we have been aided in keeping many of them from breaking up by the cooperation of the Charity Organization Society, by means of its Provident Fund and public appeals and by the Association for Improving the Condition of the Poor." [14]

At the end of his second year on the committee, the St. Vincent de Paul representative was very much discouraged by the lack of cooperation on the part of the parish conference of the Society. He had referred a number of families to them in behalf of the city-wide committee. He had written

[14] *Ibid.*, 1900, pp. 14-15.

several letters to conference presidents, but had failed to receive any reply regarding their programs for the families concerned. The committee and the Department of Public Charities were pressing for a reply. Finally, in order to save the reputation of the Society and make sure that the families received what they needed, he had to turn the cases over to the committee on special works.[15]

Baltimore Takes Initiative in City-Wide Catholic Family Welfare Program

The members of the Society of St. Vincent de Paul, the pioneers in parish charities, were the first to see the need of a city-wide program, and they were the first to take steps to develop such a program. The report of the representative of the St. Vincent de Paul Society on the children's committee of the Charity Organization Society (1901), pointed to the beginnings of a city-wide Catholic family welfare program in New York City; but it remained for Baltimore to make the first real contribution in this field. In 1907 the Society of St. Vincent de Paul of Baltimore did for family social work programs in the United States what the New York Society had done for Catholic child-placing in 1898. The Central Bureau of the Society of St. Vincent de Paul in Baltimore was the pioneer city-wide family social work agency just as the Catholic Home Bureau of New York was the pioneer city-wide child-placing agency. While family work was its main point of emphasis, the Baltimore central office did not confine itself to this field. In 1909, two years after its opening, it was found that "the demands upon the Society, from time to time, to find suitable homes for children became so insistent that in the latter part of the year a committee was organized to take up the work of finding homes for Catholic children in Catholic families. The method adopted in handling this work is modeled closely after the methods of

[15] *Ibid.*, 1901, pp. 14-15.

the Home Bureau in New York.'' The report for the same year shows "that the work in the juvenile court is steadily growing . . . the court almost invariably communicates with us in reference to any permanent disposition of Catholic children.''[16]

Baltimore Central Office Develops First Coordinated Program

The central office of the Society of St. Vincent de Paul of Baltimore was more than a clearing house for the different parish conferences of the Society in the city. It aimed to supplement their work by the experience and skill of full-time trained workers. It had at its disposal a relief fund to be used in parishes in which there was no organization or in which the local relief fund was insufficient. The central office also made a beginning in carrying out a city-wide Catholic child-placing and protective program. It may be said in truth that the Baltimore organization was the first Catholic organization in the United States to develop a coordinated program of Catholic social work. In its children's and protective program it builded on the accumulated Catholic experience of the previous ten years, but in its family work it launched out into a new and unchartered field. It marked a most important step towards a coordinated program of Catholic Charities in the United States.

Leaders in the Movement for a Coordinated Program

No analysis of the processes leading to a coordinated program of Catholic Charities would be complete without reference to the work of two priests, who may be regarded as pioneers in the movement: Monsignor William J. White of Brooklyn and Monsignor Denis J. McMahon of New York. Monsignor White was appointed Supervisor of the Catholic Charities of Brooklyn in 1899. During the period between his appointment and his death (1911), he became an outstand-

[16] *Ibid.*, 1909, pp. 49, 51.

ing figure not only in the Catholic but also in the civic work of his native city. He had a keen appreciation of the dangers that imperiled the faith of the Italian immigrants and for the purpose of saving their faith he organized the Catholic Settlement Association in 1903. The Doctor White Memorial Settlement opened in 1918 was founded to perpetuate his memory.[17]

He founded the women's auxiliary of the Society of St. Vincent de Paul of Brooklyn (1903). The Fresh Air Home at Freeport, Long Island, which affords a two weeks' outing to over 2,000 poor children each year, was the result of a suggestion made by Dr. White at the meeting on the Feast of St. Vincent de Paul in 1905.[18] He was most active in promoting the Society of St. Vincent de Paul; he took a deep interest in all movements making for better standards in welfare work of the community; he was one of the leaders in the work of the Brooklyn Juvenile Protective Association; he participated whole-heartedly in city, state and national conference of social work; as an interpreter of Christian teaching, he always linked charity with justice; he had a vital interest in all movements having for their purpose the improvements of the economic conditions of the wage-earner. "More completely than any other man," says Dr. Devine, "he embodied for us the approachment between the eternal religious tradition and the new social spirit of our age." One of the central figures in the First National Conference of Catholic Charities in 1910, he helped pave the way for a wider interest in and a larger program of Catholic Charities.

Another priest who stands high among pioneers in organized Catholic Charities in the United States is Rt. Rev. D. J. McMahon, Supervisor of the Catholic Charities of the archdiocese of New York from 1901 until his death in 1915. In

---

[17] "The White Memorial Settlement," *Catholic Charities Review*, Vol. II (September, 1918), pp. 216-217.
[18] Patrick F. Mallon, *Very Rev. Msgr. Wm. J. White, D.D., a Tribute*, p. 21.

the chapter on the social work of Catholic women,[19] the writer has discussed Monsignor McMahon's work in the organization of the Association of Catholic Charities. This association really expressed the beginnings of organized interest in social work on the part of the Catholic women of New York. This pioneer leader wanted to see the Catholic women of the country acquire the same national outlook as the Society of St. Vincent de Paul. He assumed the leadership in calling together the representatives of Catholic women's organizations in connection with the national convention of the Society of St. Vincent de Paul in Richmond in 1908. At this meeting, he organized a national union of Catholic women known as St. Elizabeth's Union. It is interesting to note that the Richmond meeting brought together the same elements and the same leadership that entered into the first National Conference of Catholic Charities in 1910. The representatives of the women's organizations that met in Richmond in 1908 continued their meetings in connection with the National Conference of Catholic Charities in 1910, 1912 and 1914. The name of the association, however, was changed from St. Elizabeth's Union to that of the Women's National Federation of Catholic Charities.

Monsignor McMahon was one of the prime movers in the First National Conference of Catholic Charities in 1910. He regarded the conference as a powerful means of spreading the gospel of Catholic Charities and of giving the Catholic people of the country a more intelligent interest in its problems.[20]

Steps Leading to the National Conference of Catholic Charities

The bringing together of the representatives of the Society of St. Vincent de Paul and of Catholic women's organizations in Richmond in 1908, was a long step forward in fostering a national orientation among Catholics in regard to works of

[19] Chapter XVII.
[20] *St. Vincent de Paul Quarterly*, Vol. XX, No. 3 (August, 1915), pp. 194-200.

charity. It was further extension of a plan fostered by the Vincentians at the Catholic Summer School at Cliff Haven, New York, in 1898, when they brought together a number of Catholic leaders for a conference on charity problems. The plans laid in 1898 and 1908 were brought to maturity in 1910 when the First National Conference of Catholic Charities was held at the Catholic University, Washington. D. C. The immediate impetus to the 1910 conference came from a letter addressed by Brother Barnabas to Bishop Shahan, the rector of Catholic University. Brother Barnabas, like a number of other Catholic leaders, had been active in the National Conference of Social Work for many years. The Catholics in attendance at the Conference had been accustomed to holding an informal meeting of their own during the sessions. At the 1909 meeting a number of the Catholic members of the National Conference of Social Work suggested the desirability of a National Conference of Catholic Charities and Brother Barnabas was asked to write to Bishop Shahan, urging that the Catholic University foster such a conference. The bishop recognized immediately the possibilities of a charities conference in bringing the influence of the university to bear on the Catholic charities and the Catholic life of the country.

For a number of years the university had very close and sympathetic relationship with the Society of St. Vincent de Paul. Two of its professors, Doctors Kerby and Neill had organized a Catholic Charities exhibit in connection with the international meeting of the society held at the World's Fair in St. Louis in 1904. Dr. Kerby had been made the national director of St. Elizabeth's Union, formed in connection with the national meeting of the Society of St. Vincent de Paul at Richmond in 1908. When the Catholic University decided to sponsor the National Conference of Catholic Charities it was not taking over a work that was entirely new to it. It was merely extending its service in a field with which it was already familiar. With the aid of Dr. Kerby, Bishop

Shahan arranged a preliminary meeting of the leaders in Catholic Charities from different sections of the country, and at this meeting, the organization of the National Conference of Catholic Charities was given permanent form. The Conference held its first meeting in September 1910. After that time it met every two years until 1920, when it decided to meet annually. Bishop Shahan was president of the Conference from 1910 to 1928 with Dr. Kerby, the executive secretary, from 1910 to 1920.

Charter Members of Original National Conference of Catholic Charities

When the National Conference of Catholic Charities was established, its constituents were the members of the Society of St. Vincent de Paul and of Catholic women's organizations engaged in social work and a few priests who had assumed positions of leadership in the work of various local organizations and institutions. There were not as yet any directors of Catholic Charities in the present sense. Monsignor McMahon was Supervisor of Catholic Charities of New York; Monsignor White the Supervisor of Catholic Charities of Brooklyn, and Rev. Maurice O'Connor, Director of the Catholic Charitable Bureau of Boston. These pioneer directors were more inspirational leaders than executives of large organizations. The religious communities, the largest element in Catholic Charities in this country, were noticeable by their absence from the first meeting. In fact this was true for the first five meetings of the Conference. It was only in 1920 that they identified themselves with the movement. One of the most immediate results of the organization of the National Conference of Catholic Charities was the feeling of unity it created among Catholic organizations. There was a desire on the part of individual organizations to become better acquainted with other Catholic organizations and with social work as a whole. In a number of places there were concerted movements for the organization of city conferences of Catholic Charities. St. Louis had begun holding city conferences in 1909. In November 1910 Pittsburgh organized a city-wide conference of Catholic Charities.

Original Objective of the First National Conference of Catholic Charities

Those who participated in the First National Conference of Catholic Charities, as well as those who planned the first city conferences of Catholic Charities, assumed that one of the fundamental weaknesses of Catholic charitable agencies was their isolation. One of their principal needs was therefore to get together a common fund of experience in which they might all share. If only they could achieve this objective most of their difficulties would disappear. Later experience taught the leaders in the movement that they should not only confer and exchange viewpoints, but that they should do very definite planning and building. They found that the whole structure of Catholic Charities had to be changed in many particulars.

An Indication of Change in Catholic Charities Programs

The city conference of Pittsburgh in 1910 was an indication of the approaching change in Catholic Charity programs. Here the representatives of the St. Vincent de Paul Society, the Diocesan Unions of the Holy Name, Total Abstinence and Catholic Mutual Benevolent Societies, the Knights of Columbus, the Senate of the Ladies' Catholic Benevolent Association, the Catholic Women's League, the governing body of the Ancient Order of Hibernians, Ladies' Auxiliary of the Ancient Order of Hibernians, and Knights of St. George came together for a conference, but before they separated they had decided to form a permanent organization.[21] In 1911 Rev.

[21] "The Aims and Organization of the Pittsburgh Diocesan Conference," by Thomas J. Devlin. *Proceedings of the National Conference of Catholic Charities*, 1914, p. 88.

Thomas Devlin was appointed to take charge of the work of the Conference. Describing the work of the Pittsburgh Conference at the 1914 meeting of the National Conference of Catholic Charities, he said: "The Conference was hardly established when its importance and necessity were demonstrated. It was immediately recognized as the chief charitable agency of the diocese. As intended, it became at once the official medium of communication between the pastors and relief societies and the institutions, and between the institutions themselves. It holds the same relation with the city, county, state, and private non-Catholic institutions and philanthropic agencies. The sphere of its operations increasing day by day, it soon developed into a bureau of information and statistics, an emergency relief bureau, an employment bureau, and a child-placing agency, as well as the directive office of the charitable activities of the diocese."[22] To many, at the time, this might have looked like a strange doctrine, but there was nothing very unusual about it. The Pittsburgh Conference did not even go as far as the St. Vincent de Paul Society of Baltimore had four years earlier.

The Mission of the National Conference

From the very beginning the leaders of the National Conference of Catholic Charities stressed the wider implications of Catholic Charities. They saw that Catholic Charities could not isolate themselves, that they must join with other community agencies in meeting common community problems. The relations between charity and social justice were never lost sight of in the Conference program. Such problems as the relationship of wages to poverty, workmen's compensation, minimum wage legislation, regulation of child labor, social insurance, prevention and relief of unemployment occupied a prominent place in the discussions at all the meetings. The pioneer leaders of the conference were insistent

[22] *Ibid.*

that Catholic Charities should do more than relieve suffering, that they should strike out for a social order in which the principles of Christian justice should receive due recognition. These leaders did not regard the Conference merely as an assembly of experts or of those actively engaged in charity work. They stressed its educational mission. They regarded it as a means of bringing to the Catholic laity the aims and ideals of Catholic Charities. They assumed that Catholic Charities were the concern of all the people and not simply the preserve of a few.

Training Courses for Social Workers

About the time the Conference was organized there was a widespread interest in training resources for both volunteer and full-time workers. Catholic organizations were bound to be influenced by this discussion and the Conference could not overlook it in its deliberations. Accordingly, one finds that in the program of the 1914 meeting training courses for social workers were given an important place on the program. Reports made at the meeting showed that special courses of instruction in social work were begun at Loyola University in Chicago in September of 1912 and that a department of sociology with major emphasis on social work was opened at the same university in 1914. The reports at the meeting also indicate that active courses in social work were being given at Boston, Washington and Pittsburgh.[23]

Programs Based on Surveys

Their contact with the Catholic University through the National Conference of Catholic Charities tended to develop in Catholic organizations a more objective point of view. A serious effort was made to have the Conference papers based, as far as possible, on factual studies. It was hoped that this would develop in Catholic workers a more wholesome respect

[23] *Proceedings of the National Conference of Catholic Charities*, 1914, pp. 55-72.

for facts in dealing with their programs. It is very interesting to note the spread and the ramifications of this point of view during the past twenty years. It has made us somewhat more willing to avail ourselves of the general fund of experience in our work. It has brought about an increasing tendency to base our programs on careful surveys of needs. There is still room for more emphasis on this point of view, but like any point of view it can be carried to an extreme. Rigid analysis carried to an extreme may be just as bad as emotionalism run riot.

The Trend from Institutional Care to Home Care for Children

The first thought of the leaders of the immigrants after the Civil War was to build institutions in order to save their children to the faith. The institution offered a panacea for all their ills. Their attitude was fundamentally a defensive attitude. If they did not remove the orphans of the immigrants into a sheltered atmosphere Protestant organizations would lay hold of them. As a result of the great stress that had been placed on the institution as a means of saving the faith of children, Catholic Charities continued to multiply the number of institutions during the seventies and eighties. Then, after 1890, the ways and means of taking care of children in their own homes were discussed more and more. The Charity Organization Society made its contribution in this direction. Working side by side with it and helping very materially to broaden its point of view was the Society of St. Vincent de Paul. The settlement movement also contributed its part. Catholics could not go on thinking exclusively of institutions while the Protestants were stressing home care for the child. In self-defense they had to shift their emphasis. As the existing parish organization was not reaching the children of the newer immigrants, it was necessary to develop special ways and means of reaching them. This was the opportunity that inspired the organization of Leagues of Catholic Women, Catholic day nurseries, and Catholic settlements.

The Need of Systematic Programs of Child-Placing

Since 1880 the children's institutions in a number of states had been subjected to a running fire of criticism. While much of this criticism was not inspired by the highest motives, while it came from organizations that were jealous of the advancement of the immigrant and the increasing facilities which he had developed for the care of his children, it gradually forced Catholics to recognize that the institutions could not supply a complete program of care for children away from their own homes. It was easy to ward off criticism of institutions in the seventies and eighties by pointing out the "iniquities" of the rival system of care, namely, the foster-home. But the standards of foster-home work were improving, and it was becoming more apparent that it was to have a permanent place in American child-care. The Catholic institutions were overcrowded, and some provision had to be made for the overflow. Institutional methods of farming out children indiscriminately had been criticized very severely in the early nineties. It was increasingly evident that systematic after-care was needed for the children discharged from institutions. The Home Bureau, organized by the Society of St. Vincent de Paul in New York in 1898, was intended to satisfy the limitations of the institution in the field of child-care. This agency under the leadership of Thomas M. Mulry and Edmond J. Butler, pointed the way to a new development in Catholic Charities in the United States. It carried a warning that still needs to be repeated, namely, that if Catholics are to continue their traditional interests in child-care they must develop systematic programs of child-placing.

Beginnings of City-Wide Service in Catholic Relief

The Vincentians who served on the children's committee of the Charity Organization Society of New York City used to tell in plaintive tones of the difficulties they experienced in getting parish conferences to work with them. After the committee had decided that a certain Catholic family should be kept together the St. Vincent de Paul representatives would hold themselves responsible for the necessary relief. When they failed to secure any response from the parish conference, they appealed to the Particular Council. Here we have the beginnings of a city-wide service. A Particular Council of the Society of St. Vincent de Paul can always supplement the relief resources of a parish conference, or it can take over families in parishes in which there are no conferences. Their contact with city-wide organizations and growing appreciation of the necessity of higher standards made them recognize more and more the importance of enlarging the work of the Particular Council in family relief. There was no city in which the work of the Particular Council attained such a high degree of development in the field of relief as in Baltimore. And there were other elements in the Baltimore program that later became foundation stones. In other cities it has been the custom for the Particular Councils of the St. Vincent de Paul Society to develop city-wide services, one at a time. The Baltimore Council decided to develop three services, namely, family relief, child-placing and protective care. Here we have coordinated the three basic elements of the later programs of Catholic Charities.

The St. Vincent de Paul Society the First Step in Coordinated Program

The writer would not convey an impression that the growth of our diocesan programs of Catholic Charities represents a single stream of development. There are many little streams representative of all shades of opinion, traditions, viewpoints and antagonisms arising out of the experiences of the Catholic Church in the United States. However, the main source of development in the coordination and unification of Catholic Charities came from the Society of St. Vincent de Paul. It was the members of the Society that gave Catholic Charities a position of leadership in American communities.

Their contact with city-wide organizations convinced the leaders of the Society of St. Vincent de Paul of the necessity of city-wide programs of Catholic Charities. They took the initiative in developing these programs, but they appreciated their own handicaps in carrying them through. One of the pioneer Vincentians expressed the matter as follows: "We have done everything within reason in developing a program of family relief. We have made a beginning in child-care, but take all the children's institutions in this diocese—we have no influence with them. We can never have a complete program until their work is coordinated with ours and this coordination can be affected only through diocesan leadership."

Diocesan Directors Appointed

In some places the Vincentians found it necessary to have active diocesan leadership in order to insure active participation of lay organizations of Catholic women. The student of Catholic Charities cannot fail to note the important developments in the work of Catholic women's organizations in New York and Brooklyn after the appointment of Monsignors McMahon and White, respectively, as Diocesan Supervisors of Catholic Charities.

Financial Support for the Coordinated Program

As the special work of the Society of St. Vincent de Paul and the programs of Catholic women's organizations grew the problems of financial support loomed larger. With the growth of objective analysis the standards of social workers became more and more exacting. It soon became apparent that the old methods of securing funds, by bazaars, entertainments and individual personal appeals were no longer suitable. It was clear that if social agencies were to maintain proper standards of work they must have recourse to organized methods of fund-raising. The first thought in Catholic work was to look to a diocesan-wide appeal under the leadership of the bishop.

Rev. C. Hubert LeBlond was appointed Director of Catholic Charities of Cleveland in 1911 for the purpose of developing a financial program for the Catholic institutions of the diocese under the leadership of the bishop. As its program developed the Society of St. Vincent de Paul of Baltimore found it necessary to look to the diocese for support. In 1915 Cardinal Gibbons appointed Rev. Edwin L. Leonard, the present Diocesan Director of Catholic Charities, to assist in securing the necessary support. When the Catholic Children's Bureau of Philadelphia was established (1915), an assessment was levied by the archbishop on the various parishes to secure the funds necessary for the work. In 1918 Cardinal Mundelein organized the Associated Catholic Charities of Chicago as the official agency of the archdiocese to raise funds by an annual appeal for all Catholic charitable institutions. At the same time he set up a Central Charity Bureau for the purpose of coordinating and supplementing the work of the various charities of the archdiocese. The Central Charity Bureau took over and enlarged the program of the Central Bureau of St. Vincent de Paul, opened in 1911.[24]

The Influence of the Community Chest Movement on the Development of Diocesan Organizations of Charity

It was only after the period of the World War that diocesan organizations of Catholic Charities increased at a rapid rate. Before that time there were only five such organizations. At the present writing (1931), there are thirty diocesan organi-

[24] *The Associated Catholic Charities of Chicago,* 1918, pp. ix-xiii.

zations and if branch organizations are included, we have fifty-eight agencies, with more or less extensive city-wide programs. This growth of diocesan agencies since the war is not surprising in view of the general development in American social work. The important lessons of organization in fund-raising learned through war-time experience were helpful in social work. If organized methods of fund-raising had proved successful during a crisis, why should they not be successful in times of peace? This was the basic thought of the community chest movement. During the war the various agencies in a number of American cities had banded together for the purpose of making united appeals. After the Armistice, the United States War Work Fund Campaign represented one joint campaign on the part of all the war welfare agencies. The alignments formed during the period of the war for the purposes of fund-raising were carried into peace times. Cities like Cleveland, Rochester and Cincinnati, which had tried joint appeals determined to give up the old methods of raising money. Other cities gradually copied their example, until today there are about 350 cities in which all or at least a considerable proportion of the agencies join in an annual campaign for funds.

The community chest movement with all its ramifications was bound to have a far-reaching influence on Catholic Charities in the United States. The chest meant more funds, better organization and higher standards. These were cold facts to be reckoned with by those who were alive to the needs of Catholic Charities. The first question that confronted Catholic Charities was whether they should cast their lot with the chest or continue their own methods of finance. In some cities it seemed to Catholic leaders there was no choice. The chest made a wide appeal to business men, including Catholic business men.

Catholics had not developed up-to-date methods of supporting their own work; Catholic institutions were hard pressed in raising the necessary funds; there was no hope of a Catholic federation that could rally all Catholics in an annual financial campaign. Leaders in the chest movement, moreover, were willing to hold out important inducements to secure Catholic support. They felt that the success of the chest depended in large measure on its inclusiveness. The unwillingness on the part of any large group to participate would militate against its success. Catholic leaders in a number of cities such as Rochester, Cincinnati, St. Paul, and Omaha took advantage of the chest movement to aid them in developing their diocesan organizations of Catholic Charities. They had caught the fever of diocesan organization from other dioceses. With chest organization impending, they believed that the opportune time for diocesan programs had come. It was apparent that a central coordinating agency that was in position to provide leadership for the other Catholic agencies would aid them materially in dealing with the directors of the chest.

In a few cities like Baltimore and St. Louis, in which Catholic agencies were on a rather firm financial footing, the diocesan authorities believed that they had more to lose than gain from participation. They have continued successfully with their own methods of fund-raising.

Diocesan Financial Federations

The archdioceses of New York and Chicago and the dioceses of Buffalo and Providence have organized their own financial federations. In New York and Buffalo the diocesan federations have developed extensive programs for social work. The New York federation aims to meet such financial needs of the agencies as can not be met by their own methods of fundraising. It also provides for needed developments in Catholic work. The Chicago federation has the same objective. Both the Buffalo and Providence federations raise sufficient funds to provide for all the needs of the charitable agencies of the respective dioceses. Buffalo has also developed an extensive diocesan-wide family service and child-caring program.

Dioceses Without Coordinated Programs

A number of dioceses with large problems have not developed any coordinated program of Catholic Charities. These dioceses usually have two or more children's homes, a home for the aged, two or more hospitals, and sometimes a day nursery. There may be a few parish Vincentian conferences doing relief work in the parishes, if they have not been swept away in the wave of centralization. Generally speaking, these dioceses do not make any pretense of doing systematic work for needy families. If Catholic families are in need, they must look to the non-sectarian or public organizations. Children are received into the institutions without any investigation and there is no after-care when they have been discharged.

Obstacles in the Way of Further Development of Diocesan Organizations

It is more difficult at present to organize diocesan-wide programs of Catholic Charities than it was ten years ago. The raising of funds is not so easy. A number of the dioceses with undeveloped charity programs have serious commitments in other fields and are not, therefore, ready to assume large obligations in charity work. Another point to be kept in mind in regard to these dioceses, and in fact in regard to future developments in Catholic Charities, is the psychology that the community chest has spread abroad. Year by year, the people have it dinned into their ears by community chest speakers and publicity writers, "We take care of everything." When a new development is proposed the question arises, why can not the work be done by the chest? Under the chest existing arrangements tend to become stereotyped. If expansion is needed it will be in the field of non-sectarian work. In a number of cities in which Catholics have not been participating, or have been participating only partially, the chests have made concessions in order to secure complete Catholic support.

Post-War Programs of Catholic Charities

After the war programs for Catholic Charities, like other programs, took on something of an Utopian character. All institutions were in a state of upheaval. Many people were inclined to assume that all the impurities of life had been worn away by the heat of battle and that men were ready for a new social order. Some of the Catholic Charity programs shared this spirit: they touched every sphere of human activity; they would leave nothing undone; they would build a machine of nicely adjusted parts and delicate precision. This period of enthusiasm disappeared and people began to reckon with the hard realities of life. It became apparent that the fundamental purpose of a diocesan program of Catholic Charities was to build on the foundation that had been laid by the St. Vincent de Paul Society in New York and Baltimore. The Catholic Home Bureau of New York had blazed the way in Catholic child-placing. The same type of program was undertaken by the Catholic Children's Aid Society of New Jersey in 1903, the St. Vincent de Paul Society of Washington in 1909, the St. Vincent de Paul Society of Detroit in 1913 and the Catholic Children's Bureau of Philadelphia in 1915. The more radical departure of the Society of St. Vincent de Paul of Baltimore in its city-wide program of relief and professional service, did not make the same immediate appeal in Catholic work as the New York plan. Since about 1890 there had been a vigorous discussion of ways and means of supplementing the institution in child-care. For one thing, the institution could not take care of all the children who needed care away from their homes. Systematic child-placing must supplement the institution. From the very nature of their work, institutions had to engage in child-placing. No matter how long the child was retained he had to be placed in a home eventually. Lack of proper facilities for home-placing brought a considerable amount of criticism on the institutions. Hence, institutional authorities welcomed systematic diocesan programs of child-care as a means of supplementing their work.

The Institution as a Basis of a Diocesan Program of Child-Care

Dioceses like New York, Baltimore, Buffalo, Cincinnati, Los Angeles and Hartford that have endeavored to develop systematic and coordinated programs of child-care have begun with the institution as the basis of their program. They felt that their first task was to aid the institutions by placing at their disposal the best experience in child-care. This means the improvement of social policies governing the admission and discharge of children, better standards of medical care, access to child guidance clinics, and gradual improvement in personnel.

As the diocesan organizations have learned during the past ten years, these standards are not attained easily. Catholic children's institutions in many places had developed individualistic traditions. In the past they had to struggle ahead without definite assistance from the dioceses. Their individualistic traditions were strengthened in many instances by their canonical independence of the diocesan authorities and by racial consciousness. In many instances the diocesan agencies took over a much larger program than they could expect to carry out. They were, therefore, unable to give the service that the institutions expected of them.

The Drift Towards Boarding Home Care

All students of Catholic child-care recognize that the institution can not meet all our needs and that it must be supplemented by the foster home. They realize that Catholic agencies can not depend entirely on free homes but that they must be ready to meet the cost of boarding children. This brings us to a basic issue in Catholic child-care. It is very clear that the boarding home is becoming increasingly popular as a substitute for the children's own homes. If Catholic agencies are not willing to develop such care, they will have a diminishing role in the field of child welfare. A number of Catholic agencies are well aware of this and are making every effort to develop boarding homes. In cities like New York, Chicago, Baltimore, Philadelphia, Detroit, Los Angeles, and San Francisco, the task is not so difficult. In these cities, as well as in a number of others, public authorities pay the board of children placed with the private agencies. In cities in which public funds are not available for the payment of board, the problem is not so easy. In some places boarding homes have been developed by Catholic agencies exclusively through the use of private funds. By reason of the drift towards non-sectarian and public child-care, it is becoming increasingly difficult to develop boarding home care under religious auspices in cities in which public funds are not available for private agencies.

Problems of a City-Wide Program of Family Relief

The development of city-wide programs for Catholic families in need of relief has proven still more difficult than the development of city-wide programs of child-care. The tradition of parish responsibility had to be faced. It was not easy to convince pastors and parish volunteers of the value of a city-wide agency in supplementing their work. It was not easy to induce them to devise ways of raising large sums of money for the care of the poor. Before the advent of central Catholic agencies, parish relief was of a purely emergency character. Catholic families requiring assistance over long periods of time had to look to other agencies. As soon as the diocesan agencies opened their doors many pastors concluded that they were absolved from further responsibility in the care of the poor. Had they not contributed their quota to the diocesan campaign or the community chest? Why should they be asked to tax their people a secónd time? These were the questions that workers in Catholic Charities were compelled to face every day. This attitude created a powerful tendency towards centralization in Catholic, as well as in other forms of relief, and has also been a great force in divorcing the laity from active participation in charities. Large numbers of parishes that in times past boasted of active St. Vincent de Paul Conferences have practically disbanded their conferences and shouldered their responsibility on central organizations.

Diocesan Agencies as a Guide for Parish Organizations

Catholic Charities with clearly thought-out programs have assumed that their basic purpose was to provide leadership and inspiration for parish organizations. They are well aware that there is no hope of being able to supply professional service for all Catholic families in need and that they must depend on volunteers to carry a large volume of the work. They know, moreover, that participation of the laity in works of charity has a value far more important than the immediate results secured. It is an obligation of Christian life. It gives the laity an opportunity of entering more fully into the life and spirit of the Church.

Protective Care in the Programs of Diocesan Organizations

Reference has already been made to the activities of the Society of St. Vincent de Paul and of Catholic women's organizations in the beginnings of the juvenile court movement. In many instances they supplied paid and volunteer probation officers for the courts. Reference has also been made [25] to the general awakening of interest in protective work on the part of Catholic women as a result of the first meeting of the National Conference of Catholic Charities in 1910. The diocesan organizations of Catholic Charities have fallen heir to these pioneer contributions in Catholic work. They have taken it upon themselves to develop constructive programs for the care of pre-delinquent and delinquent children. Outside of four or five cities, the results have not measured up to expectations. The demands on Catholic agencies in family service and child-care have been so great that they have been unable to release a sufficient number of trained workers for protective care. The plan followed in many cities has been to depend on volunteers assisted by one full-time worker. This worker has been expected to deal with a fairly large number of cases personally, and, at the same time, provide training and leadership for volunteers. The relations between the diocesan organizations of Catholic Charities and Catholic institutions for delinquents still remain to be worked out effectively.

Recreational and Character-Building Efforts of Diocesan Organizations

A few diocesan organizations as the Catholic Charities of the Archdiocese of New York, the Catholic Charities of Cincinnati, and the Catholic Welfare Bureau of Los Angeles have given special attention to recreational and character-building programs. They have endeavored to coordinate and improve the work of existing Catholic recreational agencies as community centers and clubs. They have fostered the development of boy scouts, Catholic boys' brigade, and the girl scouts in their respective jurisdictions, and they have cooperated in promoting community-wide recreational programs.

[24] Chapter XVII.

The Place of the Catholic Hospital in the Diocesan Program

Traditionally the hospital has been an essential part of the Catholic program. There is no work in which the Catholic religious have entered with more enthusiasm. In view of its long association with the charity of the Church, it is curious to note the practically complete separation of Catholic hospitals in the United States from diocesan charities. There are some good reasons for this separation. The hospital presents many technical problems with which the diocesan organization is not qualified to deal. By reason of its heavy financial commitments the Catholic hospital in the United States has not been able to go as far as desirable in expanding its social service program. One can not, however, fail to notice a gradual tendency on the part of hospitals to identify themselves more closely with the diocesan charities to the mutual benefit of both.

The Mission of the Diocesan Organization of Catholic Charities to the Laity

Under the stress of its daily routine the diocesan organization of Catholic Charities is liable to overlook its mission to the Catholic laity. If it is doing its work efficiently according to the traditions of the Church, it must recruit a large number of active volunteers. It must encourage volunteer effort in all departments. It must remember that this is the only means of making the laity a part of the ministry of charity. But its mission to the laity does not end with the cultivation of volunteer effort—it must reach out past the volunteers and bring the message of charity to the thousands who never participate actively in its services. The diocesan organization of Catholic Charities is accumulating a vast storehouse of knowledge in regard to the failure of family life, child dependency, insufficient wages, ill-health, unemployment, and old age dependency. This should be made the common property of all Catholics and, for that matter, of all citizens. The institutions of a democracy can be changed only by the people. How can the people bring about the changes that public interest demands if they are not informed in regard to the limitations of present institutions? What agency is better prepared to bring to the people firsthand information on existing conditions and needed changes than an agency dealing with poverty and dependency?

BIBLIOGRAPHY
I. PRINCIPAL MANUSCRIPT SOURCES

ARCHIVES OF:
  The Daughters of Charity of St. Vincent de Paul, Mt. St. Joseph's College, Emmitsburg, Md.
  The Daughters of Charity of St. Vincent de Paul, St. Mary's Infant Asylum and Maternity Hospital, Buffalo, N. Y.
  The Daughters of Charity of St. Vincent de Paul, St. Vincent de Paul Orphan Asylum, Buffalo, N. Y.
  The Daughters of Charity of St. Vincent de Paul, St. Mary's Hospital, Detroit, Mich.
  The Daughters of Charity of St. Vincent de Paul, Providence Hospital, Washington, D. C.
  The Sisters of Charity of St. Augustine, Cleveland, Ohio.
  The Felician Sisters, Buffalo, N. Y.
  The Little Sisters of the Poor, Washington, D. C.
  St. Patrick's Church, Washington, D. C.

REPORTS PREPARED BY THE FOLLOWING COMMUNITIES:
  The Sisters of St. Agnes of Fond du Lac, Wis.
  The Sisters of St. Francis, Williamsville, N. Y.
  The Franciscan Sisters of Baltimore City, Baltimore, Md.
  Third Franciscan Order, O.M.C., Syracuse, N. Y.
  The Sisters of the Holy Family of New Orleans, La.
  Society of Missionary Catechists, Victory Knoll, Huntington, Ind.
  Mission Helpers, Servants of the Sacred Heart, Towson, Md.
  Missionary Sisters of the Sacred Heart of Jesus, Dobbs Ferry, N. Y.
  History of Social Work Done by Religious Communities in the Archdiocese of Portland in Oregon, by Sister Miriam Theresa, Ph.D. (Sisters of the Holy Names of Jesus and Mary.)
  Notes from the Convent Diary, The Sisters of Providence, St. Mary-of-the-Woods, Ind.
  A *History of Catholic Child-Caring Institutions in the Diocese of Fort Wayne*, Rev. Leo A. Scheetz. An Essay, Catholic University of America, Washington, D. C., 1931.
  Reports of various Religious Communities, Institutions and Organizations received through cooperation of Diocesan Bureaus of Catholic Charities.

BIBLIOGRAPHY
II. PRINCIPAL PUBLISHED SOURCES

ALERDING, RT. REV. H. J., *A History of the Catholic Church in the Diocese of Vincennes*, Carlon and Hollenbeck, Indianapolis, 1883.

AVERY, ELROY MCK., *History of Cleveland and Its Environs*, 3 vols., The Lewis Publishing Co., Chicago and New York, 1918.

BIBLIOGRAPHY 451

BAART, REV. P. A., S.T.L., *Orphans and Orphan Asylums*, Catholic Publication Co., Buffalo, N. Y., 1885.
BALCH, EMILY G., *Our Slavic Fellow-Citizens*, Charities Publication Committee, New York, 1910.
BAYLEY, REV. JAMES R., *A Brief Sketch of the History of the Catholic Church on the Island of New York*, Dunigan and Bro., New York, 1853.
BOGART, E. L., *An Economic History of the United States*, Longmanns, Green, and Co., New York, 1925.
BONN, MORITZ J., *Modern Ireland and Her Agrarian Problem*, translated from the German by T. W. Rolleston, Hodges, Figgis and Co., Ltd., Dublin, 1906.
BRACE, CHARLES L., *The Dangerous Classes of New York and Twenty Years Work Among Them*, Wynkoop and Hollenbeck, New York, 1872.
BRANN, REV. H. A., *Most Reverend John Hughes*, Dodd, Mead and Co., New York, 1892.
BURNS, REV. JAMES A., *The Catholic School System in the United States*, Benziger Bros., New York and Cincinnati, 1908; *The Growth and Development of the Catholic School System in the United States*, Benziger Bros., New York and Cincinnati, 1912.
COMMONS, JOHN R., *Races and Immigrants in America*, The Macmillan Co., New York, 1907.
COSTELLO, SISTER M. LORETTO, *The Sisters of Mercy of Maryland*, B. Herder Book Co., St. Louis, 1931.
CULLEN, JAMES B., *The Story of the Irish in Boston*, J. B. Cullen & Co., Boston, 1889.
DE BARBEREY, MADAME, *Elizabeth Seton*, The Macmillan Co., New York, 1927.
DEHEY, ELINOR TONG, *Religious Orders of Women in the United States*, Revised, W. B. Conkey Co., Hammond, Ind., 1930.
DEUTHER, CHARLES G., *The Life and Times of the Rt. Rev. John Timon, D.D.*, published by the author, Buffalo, N. Y., 1870.
DONOHUE, REV. THOMAS, *The Catholic Church in Western New York*.
FAUST, ALBERT B., *The German Element in the United States*, 2 vols., Houghton, Mifflin Co., Boston and New York, 1909.
FINCK, SISTER M. HELENA, M.A., *The Congregation of the Sisters of Charity of the Incarnate Word of San Antonio, Texas*. A Dissertation, Catholic University of America, Washington, D. C., 1925.
FITTON, REV. JAMES, *Sketches of the Establishment of the Church in New England*, Patrick Donohoe, Boston, 1872.
FOERSTER, ROBERT F., *The Italian Emigration of Our Times*, Harvard University Press, Cambridge, Mass., 1919.
FOLKS, HOMER, *The Care of Destitute, Neglected, and Delinquent Children*, The Macmillan Co., New York, 1902.
GALVIN, REV. THOMAS A., C.SS.R., *A Modern Apostle of Charity, Father Baker and His Lady of Victory Charities*, The Buffalo Catholic Publication Co., Inc., Buffalo, 1925.

GILLARD, JOHN T., S.S.J., *The Catholic Church and the American Negro*, St. Joseph's Society Press, Baltimore, 1929.
GLODEN, SISTER M. CORTONA, *The Sisters of St. Francis of the Holy Family*, B. Herder Book Co., St. Louis, 1928.
GUILDAY, PETER K., *The Life and Times of John Carroll*, 2 vols., The Encyclopedia Press, New York, 1922. *The Life and Times of John England*, 2 vols., The America Press, New York, 1927.
HARLOW, ALVIN F., *Old Towpaths; The Story of the American Canal Era*, D. Appleton & Co., New York and London, 1926.
HASSARD, JOHN R. G., *Life of the Most Reverend John Hughes, D.D.*, D. Appleton and Co., New York, 1866.
HERBERMANN, CHARLES G., LL.D., *The Sulpicians in the United States*, The Encyclopedia Press, New York, 1916.
HERRON, SISTER M. EULALIA, Ph.D., *The Sisters of Mercy in the United States, 1843-1928*. The Macmillan Co., New York, 1929.
JEILER, REV. IGNATIUS, O.S.F., *The Venerable Mother Frances Schervier, Foundress of the Congregation of the Sisters of the Poor of St. Francis*, B. Herder Co., St. Louis, 1895.
JOLLY, ELLEN RYAN, LL.D., *Nuns of the Battlefield*, The Providence Visitor Press, Providence, R. I., 1927.
JULIAN, BROTHER, *Men and Deeds*, Macmillan Co., New York, 1931.
KELSO, ROBERT W., *The Science of Public Welfare*, H. Holt and Co., New York, 1928.
KENNEY, WILLIAM F., *Centenary of the See of Boston*, J. K. Waters Co., Boston, 1909.
LAMBING, REV. A. A., *A History of the Catholic Church in the Diocese of Pittsburgh and Alleghany*, Benziger Bros., New York and Cincinnati, 1880.
LAMOTT, REV. JOHN H., *History of the Archdiocese of Cincinnati, 1821-1921*, Frederick Pustet Co., Inc., New York and Cincinnati, 1921.
LANSDEN, JOHN M., *A History of the City of Cairo, Illinois*, R. R. Donnelley and Sons Co., Chicago, 1910.
LEROY, REV. A., *History of the Little Sisters of the Poor*, translated from the French under the direction of the author, R. & T. Washbourne, Ltd., London. Benziger Bros., New York and Cincinnati, 1906.
LETCHWORTH, WILLIAM P., *Homes of Homeless Children*, transmitted to the Legislature with the Annual Reports of the New York State Board of Charities, January, 1876.
MCCANN, SISTER M. AGNES, *The History of Mother Seton's Daughters*, 2 vols., Longmans, Green and Co., New York, 1917.
MCGILL, ANNA BLANCHE, *The Sisters of Charity of Nazareth, Kentucky*, The Encyclopedia Press, New York, 1917.
MCGUIRE, JOHN F., M.P., *The Irish in America*, D. and J. Sadlier and Co., New York, 1876.
MAES, CAMILLUS P., *Life of Rev. Charles Nerinckx*, Robert Clarke and Co., Cincinnati, 1880.

BIBLIOGRAPHY

MINOGUE, ANNA C., *Pages from a Hundred Years of Dominican History*, Frederick Pustet and Co., Inc., New York and Cincinnati, 1921. *The Story of the Santa Maria Institute*, Santa Maria Institute, Cincinnati, 1922.

NUTTING, M. ADELAIDE, R.N., and DOCK, LAVINIA L., R.N., *A History of Nursing*, 2 vols., G. P. Putnam's Sons, New York, 1907.

O'BRIEN, GEORGE A. T., *The Economic History of Ireland in the Eighteenth Century*, Maunsel and Co., Ltd., Dublin and London, 1918.

O'BRIEN, M. J., *A Hidden Phase of American History*, The Devin-Adair Co., New York, 1919.

O'DANIEL, VICTOR F., *The Father of the Church in Tennessee or The Life, Times, and Character of the Rt. Rev. Richard P. Miles, O.P.*, The Dominicana, Washington, D. C., 1926.

O'DONNELL, REV. JAMES H., *History of the Diocese of Hartford*, The D. H. Hurd Co., Boston, 1900.

PALLADINO, L. B., S.J., *Indian and White in the Northwest; A History of Catholicity in Montana, 1831-1891*, Wickersham Publishing Co., Lancaster, Pa., 1922.

PURCELL, RICHARD J., *The American Nation*, Ginn and Co., Boston and New York, 1929.

ROBERTS, PETER, *The New Immigration; A Study of the Industrial and Social Life of Southeastern Europeans in America*, The Macmillan Co., New York, 1912.

ROTHENSTEINER, REV. JOHN, *History of the Archdiocese of St. Louis*, 2 vols., St. Louis, 1928.

RUSSELL, MATTHEW, S.J., *The Life of Mother Mary Baptist Russell*, The Apostleship of Prayer, New York, 1901.

SAVAGE, SISTER M. LUCIDA, Ph.D., *The Congregation of Saint Joseph of Carondelet*, B. Herder Book Co., St. Louis, 1923.

SHAUGHNESSY, GERALD, S.M., A.B., S.T.D., *Has the Immigrant Kept the Faith?* The Macmillan Co., New York, 1925.

SHEA, JOHN G., *The History of the Catholic Church in the United States*, 4 vols., New York, 1888.

SKELTON, ISABEL M., *The Life of Thomas D'Arcy McGee*, Garden City Press, Gardenvale, Can., 1925.

SPALDING, JOHN L., S.T.L., *The Life of the Most Rev. M. J. Spalding, D.D.*, Christian Press Association Publishing Co., New York and San Francisco, Calif.

SPALDING, MARTIN J., D.D., *Sketches of the Life, Times and Character of the Rt. Rev. Benedict Joseph Flaget*, Webb and Levering, Louisville, Ky., 1852.

SWEENEY, HELEN M., *The Golden Milestone, 1846-1896*. Benziger Bros., New York and Cincinnati, 1896.

WEBB, HON. BEN. J., *The Centenary of Catholicity in Kentucky*, Charles A. Rogers, Louisville, 1884.

THE SISTERS OF BON SECOURS, *The Sisters of Bon Secours*, by The Author of "Allons au Ciel," translated from the French, Burnes and Oates, London, 1912.

THE SISTERS OF CHARITY OF LEAVENWORTH, *History of the Sisters of Charity of Leavenworth, Kansas*, by a Member of the Community, Hudson-Kimberly Publishing Co., Kansas City, Mo., 1898.
THE HELPERS OF THE HOLY SOULS, *Reverend Mother Mary of Providence*, Sands and Co., London, 1928.
THE SISTERS OF THE HOLY CROSS, *The Story of Fifty Years from Annals of the Congregation of Sisters of the Holy Cross, 1855-1905*, The Ave Maria, Notre Dame, Ind.
THE SISTERS OF THE IMMACULATE HEART OF MARY, *The Sisters of the I. H. M.*, by a Member of the Scranton Community, P. J. Kenedy and Sons, New York, 1921.
CHICAGO, *The Archdiocese of Chicago—Its Antecedents and Developments*, published by St. Mary's Training School Press, Des Plaines, Ill., 1920.
MILWAUKEE, *History of Milwaukee, Wisconsin*, published by The Western Historical Co., Chicago, 1881.
MONTANA, *History of Montana*, 1739-1885, Michael A. Leeson, editor, Warner, Beers and Co., Chicago, 1885.
SPRINGFIELD, *Diocese of Springfield in Illinois, Diamond Jubilee History*. Prepared and published under the direction of Rt. Rev. James A. Griffin, D.D., 1927.

III. OTHER PUBLISHED SOURCES

L'ASSOCIATION DE LA PROPAGATION DE LA FOI, *Annales*, Lyons, France, 1822.
LEOPOLDINE SOCIETY OF AUSTRIA, *Letters*, 1831.
CONCILII PLENARII BALTIMORENSIS SECUNDI, *Acta et Decreta*, A.D., 1866.
THE CATHOLIC ALMANAC OR LAITY'S DIRECTORY, 1822, later the METROPOLITAN CATHOLIC ALMANAC AND DIRECTORY, SADLIER'S CATHOLIC DIRECTORY, HOFFMANN'S CATHOLIC DIRECTORY, now THE OFFICIAL CATHOLIC DIRECTORY, P. J. Kenedy and Sons, New York.
THE CATHOLIC ENCYCLOPEDIA, 17 vols., The Encyclopedia Press Inc., New York, 1913.
NATIONAL CONFERENCE OF CATHOLIC CHARITIES, *Proceedings*, Washington, D. C.
SOCIETY OF ST. VINCENT DE PAUL, *Report of the Proceedings of the General Assemblies of the Society of St. Vincent de Paul in the United States*, New York, 1866; Philadelphia, 1876; Washington, D. C., 1886.
SOCIETY OF ST. VINCENT DE PAUL, *Reports of the Superior Council of the Society of St. Vincent de Paul of New York to the Council General at Paris.*
IMMIGRATION COMMISSION, *Reports of the Immigration Commission*, Washington, D. C., 1911.
COMMISSIONER GENERAL OF IMMIGRATION, *Annual Reports*, Washington, D. C.
NEW YORK STATE COMMISSIONERS OF IMMIGRATION, *Report*, New York, 1847.

BIBLIOGRAPHY 455

STATE BOARDS OF CHARITIES, *Annual Reports*, Massachusetts, 1864, 1866, 1869; New York, 1881; Ohio, 1867, 1869.
SELECT COMMITTEE OF THE SENATE OF THE UNITED STATES, *Report on the Sickness and Mortality on Board Emigrant Ships*, Washington, D. C., 1854.
ASSOCIATION FOR IMPROVING THE CONDITION OF THE POOR, *Reports*, New York City.
CHILDREN'S AID SOCIETY, *Reports*, New York City.
CHILDREN'S MISSION TO CHILDREN, *Reports*, Boston, Mass.
DICTIONARY OF AMERICAN BIOGRAPHY, Charles Scribner's Sons, New York.

IV. BROCHURES, PAMPHLETS AND OTHER PUBLICATIONS

RELIGIOUS ORDERS

The Sisters of the Atonement, *A Brief Sketch of the Sisters of the Atonement*, Peekskill, N. Y., 1928.
The Sisters of Bon Secours, *Brochure*, Baltimore, May, 1928.
The Sisters of Charity of Quebec, *The Missionary Work of the Grey Nuns*, Montreal, P. Q.
The Dominican Sisters of the Sick Poor, *Report*, New York, 1915.
The Sisters of the Holy Family of San Francisco, *Gleaners Along the King's Highway*, Gilmartin Co., San Francisco, 1929.
The Foreign Mission Sisters of St. Dominic, *An American Sisterhood of Foreign Missions*, Maryknoll, N. Y., 1927.
Missionary Sisters, Servants of the Holy Ghost, *Brochure*, Sacred Heart Home, Hyattsville, Md., 1931.
Missionary Sisters, Servants of the Most Blessed Trinity, *Brochure*, Holy Trinity, Ala.
The Parish Visitors of Mary Immaculate, *The Parish Visitor*, New York, October, 1930.
The Sisters of the Precious Blood, *Brochure*, St. Teresa's Home, Cincinnati, Ohio.

INSTITUTIONS

Bliss, Arthur Ames, A.M., M.D., *Impressions of a Resident Physician* (Blockley, Philadelphia), Springfield, Mass., 1916.
New York Foundling Hospital, *Report*, 1890-1891.
New York Catholic Protectory, *Annual Reports*, May 1863-September 30, 1875.
Annual Reports and Other Publications of Various Orphanages, Homes, Hospitals, etc.

ORGANIZATIONS

The Catholic Colonization Bureau of St. Paul, Minn., *An Invitation to the Land. Reasons and Figures.* The Pioneer Press, 1877.
The Ladies of Charity of New York, formerly the Association of Catholic Charities. *A Short History taken from the Records of the Secretary*, Miss Teresa O'Donohue.

The Catholic Women's Leagues, *Reports and Other Publications of Leagues in Various Cities.*
The National Council of Catholic Women, Washington, D. C., *Handbook and Other Publications.*
St. Margaret's Daughters, *Silver Jubilee Report, 1889-1914,* New Orleans, 1914.
The Catholic Central Verein of America and the National Catholic Women's Union, *Diamond Jubilee Celebration,* Baltimore, 1930.
The Society of St. Vincent de Paul, *Report of the Society of St. Vincent de Paul of Detroit and Its Child-Placing Department,* Detroit, 1913.
Catholic Charities Bureaus and Agencies, *Annual Reports and Other Publications.*

V. REVIEWS, PERIODICALS AND PAPERS

HISTORICAL REVIEWS AND MAGAZINES

Records of the American Catholic Historical Society, Philadelphia, Pa.
Illinois Catholic Historical Review, published by the Illinois Catholic Historical Society, Chicago, Ill.
Minnesota Historical Society Collections, published by the Minnesota Historical Society, St. Paul, Minn.
Historical Records and Studies, published by the United States Catholic Historical Society, New York.
The United States Catholic Magazine, published by J. Murphy, Baltimore, Md.

PERIODICALS

The Catholic Charities Review, Washington, D. C.
Donahue's Magazine, Boston, Mass.
The Ecclesiastical Review, Philadelphia, Pa.
The National Catholic Welfare Conference Review, Washington, D. C.
The New England Quarterly, Boston, Mass.
Hospital Progress, St. Louis, Mo.
The St. Vincent de Paul Quarterly, New York City, N. Y.
The Catholic World, New York City, N. Y.

PAPERS

The Baltimore Catholic Mirror, Baltimore, Md.
The New York Freeman's Journal, New York City.
The Connecticut Catholic, Hartford, Conn.
The Catholic Herald, Philadelphia, Pa.
The Catholic News, New York City, N. Y.
The Lake Shore Visitor, Erie, Pa.

INDEX

Aged (see Home for Aged)
Aid, Irish Immigrant, Conference of Buffalo, 54, 55
Aid, public for immigrants, 47, 48
Alemany, Bishop Joseph S., 186
Alfred, Mother, 199
Alicot, Miss, 346
Almshouses, in early 19th century, 213, 214; after 1870, 215
Alphonsa, Mother, 364
Amberg, Club, 301, 302
Amberg, Miss Mary Agnes, 298
American Federation of Labor, 284
American Protective Association, 35
Anderson, Rev. Joseph G., 421
Angel Guardian Orphan Asylum, Chicago, 398
Armer, Miss Elizabeth, 355
Association, American Medical, 193
Association, American Protective, 35, 284
Association for Befriending Children and Young Girls, N. Y. C., 181
Association for Improving Condition of the Poor, 189, 374-376, 425
Association of Catholic Charities of N. Y. C., 320, 321
Association, Ozanam, 255
Association for Protection of Destitute Catholic Children, 250
Associations, German Catholic Orphan, 79

Associations, Immigrant Insurance, 277, 278
Asylum, Orphan, a unit of parish, 72; a city-wide responsibility, 77
Asylums (see Institutions)

Baak, Rev. B., 400
Bachman, Marianne, 351
Baker, Father, 121
Balais, Marie Frances, 17
Baltes, Bishop Peter J., 401
Baltimore, first central office of St. Vincent de Paul Society, 258, 259
Baltimore, Lord, 2
Baltimore, Second Plenary Council of, 121
Barbelin, Father, 187
Bardstown, 10, 12
Barnabas, Brother, 116, 265, 266, 430
Barry, Joseph E., 373
Barry, Margaret, Settlement, Minneapolis, 297
Bellevue Hospital, 189
Bertrand, Mich., 108, 383, 384
Biddle, Mrs. Ann, 131
Bienville, Governor, 18
Big Sister Movement, 331
Blanchet, Rt. Rev. A. M. A., 393, 395
Blandina, Sister, 289, 292, 314
Blockley, Philadelphia, 189-191, 207, 213
Board of Charities, first State, in Massachusetts, 92, 94; New York State, 102-104, 133
Boarding Home Care, drift towards, 435, 436, 444, 445
Boards of Charities, meeting of, Detroit, 95, 96
Boegue, Marie Rosine, 17

457

Bohemian, children's institutions, 159
Boll, Barbara, 351
Boston, first charitable institution, 30, 87; House of Industry, 213
Boys, care of dependent, 33, 84, 85, 395, 396
Brace, Rev. Charles L., 371, 372
Brooks, Joseph, 249
Brotherhoods, in industrial school movement, 395-397
Brothers of Charity, 110; Christian, 75, 112, 122, 243, 396; Franciscan, 76, 397; Holy Cross, 383-385, 396; Presentation, 76; Sacred Heart, 396; St. Joseph, 108; St. Patrick, 109; Xaverian, 109, 118, 397
Brownson House, Los Angeles, 293, 294
Brownson, Miss Josephine, 296
Brute, Dr. Simon G., 25, 183
Buckey, Msgr. Edward L., 231
Buffalo, Society for Protection of R. C. Children of City of, 120
Bull Run, battle of, 194
Bureau, Catholic Charitable of Boston, 152, 420-422, 431; Catholic Children's of Philadelphia, 357, 439, 443; Catholic Home of New York, 251-253, 418, 419, 426, 436, 443; Central Charity of Chicago, 439; U. S. Children's, 269
Busch, Adolphus, 170
Butler, Edmond J., 248, 252, 419, 436
Butler, Mary Ann, 9

Cabrini, Mother, 160, 408
Caldwell, Shakespeare, 224
Calvary, Women of, 211
Camillian Fathers, 211
Canal building, contribution of early Irish immigrants to, 43, 44, 51
Canevin, Bishop J. F. R., 314

Carmelites, 6, 7, 8
Carondelet, Sisters of St. Joseph of, 382, 383; in Philadelphia, 187; St. Paul, 188; Wheeling, 188
Carroll, Daniel, 194; Bishop John, 4-6, 8-10, 25, 83
Cassilly, Mr. of Cincinnati, 28
Castle Garden, 48, 68, 69
Catholic Charitable Bureau, Boston, 152, 420-422, 431
Catholic Charities, Association of N. Y. C., 320, 321, 331; of the Archdiocese of N. Y., 321; city conference, Pittsburgh, 432, 433; diocesan agencies, a guide for parish organizations, 446; diocesan organizations with protective care programs, 446, 447; diocesan organizations in recreational and character-building work, 447; National Conference of, 263-266, 331, 428-433, 447; literature of, 265-267; mission of, 448, 449
Catholic Charities Review, 267
Catholic Children's Bureau, Philadelphia, 357, 439, 443
Catholic Community House, Baltimore, 300, 301; Cincinnati, 300, 301
Catholic Daughters of America, 332
Catholic Home Bureau, N. Y., 251-253, 418, 419, 426, 436, 443; Washington, D. C., 253
Catholic Neighborhood House, Newark, 302, 303
Catholic population in time of Bishop Carroll, 4; after Revolution, 4; after 1860, 89
Catholic, early settlements, 5; of Maryland and Kentucky, 58, 88
Catholic Summer School, Cliff Haven, N. Y., 263, 430
Catholic University, 341, 430 434
Catholic Welfare Bureau, Los Angeles, 294

Catholic Woman's National League, 327
Catholic Women's Leagues (see Organizations of Women)
Catholicism, opposition of American colonists to, 2
Cellini, Father, 170
Central Verein of America, 333
Charities (see Catholic Charities)
Charity, Brothers of, 110
Charity, Daughters of, of St. Vincent de Paul, 10, 11, 15, 19, 83, 84
Charity Hospital, Galveston, 405
Charity, Ladies of, 23, 264, 319, 321, 322
Charity, public before Civil War, 188, 189
Charity, Sisters of, in Albany, 31, 72, 73; in Alton, 194; in Baltimore, 24, 108, 208 in Boston, 29; in Brooklyn, 24; in Buffalo, 73, 74, 86, 208; in Cincinnati, 27, 80; in Detroit, 184; in Harrisburg, 31; in New Orleans, 31, 208; in New York, 23, 112, 218, 310; in Philadelphia, 20; in Pittsburgh, 31, 76; in Richmond, 31; in Rochester, 71, 184, 185; in St. Louis, 24, 26; in Utica, 31; in Washington, D. C., 24, 193, 194; in Wilmington, 31 (see also Sisters of Charity)
Charles House, Rochester, N. Y., 299
Cheverus, Bishop, 9
Child-Care, 71-88, 147-162; agencies Protestant in character, 150; American philosophy of, 96, 97; diocesan responsibility after Civil War, 404; early state policies, 98; new era in 1915, 156; the institution as basis of program of, 444; drift from institutional to home care, 435, 436; drift towards public, 104, 105; programs of, in various states, 98; interest of St. Vincent de Paul Society in, 243, 24 ; 253, 254
Child-Placing, first agency in New York, 419, 426; in free western homes, 98, 99, 106, 250, 251, 372, 373; department of Society of St. Vincent de Paul of Detroit, 253, 419, 420, 443
Child Welfare, recognition of need of program of, 308, 309; influence of Vincentians on, 268, 269
Children's Aid Society, Brooklyn, 99; New Jersey Catholic, 418, 443; of New York, 99, 371, 372; of San Francisco, 419; Protestant Societies, 150, 251
Children's Bureau, U. S., 269
Children's Mission to Children, 373
Children, provision for dependent, in Colo., 97; Conn., 96; Ind., 96; Kans., 97; Mass., 94, 97; Mich., 95, 97; Minn., 97; Mont., 97; Neb., 97; Nev., 97; N. J., 96, 97; N. Y., 95; Ohio, 95; Pa., 96; R. I., 96, 97; Tex., 97; Wis., 96, 97
Children's Institutions (see Institutions, Children's)
Cholera epidemics, 73, 74, 82, 87
Christ Child Society, 295, 296, 324, 326
Christian Brothers, 75, 112, 122, 243, 396
Cleveland, President, 284
Clifford, Rev. John J., 293
Clossy, Susan, 9
Coindre, Pere Andre, 396
Colonization, Catholic, 69; in Kans., 65; Md. and Ky., 58; Neb. and Minn., 60-63, 65; Pa., 59; Va., 65
Colonization, Catholic Bureau of St. Paul, 65, 66

Colonization, Irish Catholic Association of the U. S., 67, 68
Colored, institutions for children, 161, 162; sisterhoods, 16, 17, 161; (see Sisters, Oblates of Providence, Holy Family of New Orleans, Handmaids of Most Pure Heart of Mary)
Colton, Joseph, 247
Community Chest, 227, 335, 439-442
Communities, American religious become localized, 348; advantages and disadvantages of diocesan, 394, 395; European adhering to original objectives, 389, 390, 391; basic principle of European religious, 379; European influenced by American communities and American needs, 381, 382, 389; devoted to catechetical work, 354, 355; engaged in home nursing, 409-413; German in hospital work, 397; European engaged in social service work in U. S., 413, 414
Compensation, methods of, in institutions caring for state wards, 97, 98
Conception, Sr. Marie de la, 218, 224
Conference, Irish Immigrant Aid, Buffalo, 54, 55
Conference of Catholic Charities (see National Conference)
Conference of Social Work (see National Conference)
Conference, Welfare (see National Catholic Welfare Conference)
Connolly, Bishop John, 23
Convalescent Homes (see Homes, Convalescent)
Cooper, Samuel, 8, 9
Corpus Christi House, Duluth, Minn., 141, 182
Corrigan, Archbishop, 354

Council, National Catholic War, 296, 300, 301, 341
Councils of Catholic Women (see Organizations of Women)
Cretin, Bishop Joseph, 87, 188
Cromwell, 1
Curley, Bishop Daniel J., 232

David, Father, 10, 12, 14, 15,
Day Nursery, first Catholic, 310; rapid expansion in nineties, 311; place in social work program, 315, 316; as a part of diocesan charities, 317; Holy Family Day Nursery, Washington, D. C., 316; Keating Day Nursery, N. Y. C., 313; Merrick House, Cleveland, 315, 316; St. Ann's Day Nursery, Pittsburgh, 314; St. Elizabeth's Day Nursery, Chicago, 312; St. James' Day Nursery, Trenton, 313; St. Joseph's Day Nursery, N. Y. C., 312; St. Pascal's Day Nursery, N. Y. C., 313; St. Raphael's Home, Pittsburgh, 314; Santa Bambino Day Nursery, Cincinnati, 314; Day Nurseries of Mission Helpers, Servants of the Sacred Heart, 313; Day Nurseries of Catholic Woman's League, Chicago, 327
Delinquency, among immigrants' children, 283; a preventive program for juvenile, 127, 422
Delinquents, institutions for, 165, 166, 168, 170-174, 176, 177, 181, 182 (see also Good Shepherd Sisters and Mercy, Sisters of); Corpus Christi House, Duluth, Minn., 141, 182; Good Shepherd Home, Louisville, 165, 166; Philadelphia, 170; St. Louis, 170, 171; Cleveland, 176; House of the Holy Family, N. Y. C., 181, 182; House of

INDEX 461

Mercy, San Francisco, 181; Mt. St. Mary's Training School, Cincinnati, 176, 177
De Paul Hospital, St. Louis, 184
De Smet, Rev. Peter, S.J., 350
De Ville, Rev. John B., 302
Devlin, Rev. Thomas, 433
Diocesan Commission of Hartford, 422
Diocesan Directors of Catholic Charities, 438
Diocesan responsibility for orphanages, 416
Doharty, Wm. J., 419
Dolan Aid, 109
Dolan. Rev. James, 108, 109
Dominican Fathers, 15, 16, 290
Donaghoe. Rev. Terence J., 344, 345, 353
Donohue. Rev. F., 107
Dorcas Society. Baltimore, 319
Dorn, Anna, 351
Dougherty, Cardinal, 304, 410
Douglas Military Hospital, Washington. D. C., 194
Dowling, Archbishop Austin, 337
Downey, Wm. F.. 247
Drexel. Mother Catharine, 161, 359
Drumgoole, Rev. John C., 123, 124, 243
Du Bois, Rev. John, later Bishop, 23, 72
Du Bourg. Father, 8-10, 24, 25
Duggan. Bishop James, 171, 172
Dunne, Fr., Newsboys Home, St. Louis, 128
Dutch, population in the United States in 1790, 3
D'Youville, Madame, 392

Elder, Miss Sidney, 323
Emmitsburg, Md., 9-11, 14, 20, 23
Emonds. Father, 400
England, Bishop John, 32
England. Church of, 2
Epidemics, in Albany, 73; Buffalo. 74, 82; St. Louis, 80; St. Paul, 87
Eudes, Blessed John, 164

Family welfare program, first city-wide in Baltimore, 426, 427
Farley, Archbishop John, 292
Farrelly, Rev. F. H., 310
Fathers, Camillian, 211; Dominican, 15, 16, 290; Jesuit. 9, 18, 26; Lazarist, 25, 130; Paulist, 218, 312; Redemptorist, 346, 347; Sulpician 6, 17, 25, 83, 249, 370
Federation of German Catholic Women's Societies, 334
Feehan. Archbishop, 407
Fell's Point, Balitmore, 108
Fenwick. Bishop Benedict J., 29, 30
Fenwick, Bishop Edward, 27, 28
Filicchi Brothers, 8
Financial Federations, diocesan, 441
Financing of institutions, 22, 30. 33. 81, 82, 113, 119, 179, 227, 230, 323, 324, 335, 390, 404, 416, 438-441; of coordinated programs, 438
Fitzgerald, Mother Angela, 229
Five Points House of Industry, 108
Five Point Mission, 309
Flaget, Bishop Benedict J., 10. 12-14, 165, 389
Flanagan, Father, 125
Foley. Bishop Thomas, 225
Fordham University, training for social work, 340
Forty-Eight Movement of Ireland, 57
Foy, Rev. Francis, 418
Franciscan, Brothers, 76, 397; Sisters (see Sisters)
French, anti-clericalism aids charities of U. S., 412; children's institutions, 137, 158· population in the U. S. in 1790, 3; Revolution, 5, 14, 409
Fresh-Air Homes (see Homes, Fresh-Air)

Gallitzin, Rev. Demetrius, 59
Garry - Alerding Settlement, Gary, Ind., 302, 303
Genesee Institute, Rochester, N. Y., 299
Georgetown, D. C., 6, 7; College, 7
German, care of orphans, 78-82; Catholics of Cincinnati first in organized care of orphans, 80; Central Verein, 91, 333; population in U. S. at time of Revolution, 3
Gibbons, Archbishop, later Cardinal, 67, 360, 409, 439
Gilet, Rev. Louis F., 347, 353
Good Shepherd Sisters, 164-167, 169-181, 217, 379, 386, 389, 390 (see Sisters of Our Lady of Refuge and Sisters of Our Lady of Charity of the Good Shepherd)
Grey Nuns, 158, 211, 392, 393
Guild of Catholic Women, St. Paul, 329
Gurney, Miss, 290, 292

Hailandiere, Bishop de la, 384, 386
Hammerling, Louis N., 272
Harding, President, 285
Haskins, Father, 109, 110
Havermans, Rev. Peter, 75
Hayes, Cardinal, 321, 358
Hecker, Rev. Isaac, 218
Heising, Rev. Bernard, 399
Heiss, Rev. Michael, later Archbishop, 353
Helmproecht, Rev. Joseph, C. SS.R., 82
Hennessy, Rt. Rev. John, 196, 197, 400
Henni, Rev. John M., 80, 86
Hevern, Ann, 13
Hickey, Rev. John F., 191
Hickey, Rev. Maurice, 124
Hines, Rev. Thomas, 121
Hoban, Bishop Michael J., 159, 368
Hogan, Bishop John J., 53
Holy Cross, Brothers, 383-385, 396; Sisters (see Sisters)

Holy Family Day Nursery, Washington, D. C., 316
Holy Family Orphan Asylum, Pittsburgh, 158
Holy Name Society, 279
Home, convalescent as complement to modern hospital, 206-208; county for children, 97; county children's, New Haven, 148
Home Nursing, 211, 212, 361-363, 409-413
Home Placing of Children, trend towards, 420, 435, 436, 444, 445
Homes, early child-caring, 71; development of children's, 100 (see Institutions, Catholic Children's)
Homes for Aged, 213-234 (see Little Sisters of Poor); Catholic Home for Aged Ladies, Washington, D. C., 231; Boston House of Industry, 213; House of Divine Providence, N. Y. C., 229; Loretto Rest, Syracuse, 232, 233; McCormick Memorial Home, Green Bay, 233; St. Ann's Widows' Asylum, Philadelphia, 217, 229; St. Francis Asylum, Buffalo, 217, 229; St. Joseph's Home for Aged, N. Y. C., 229; St. Mary's Home for Aged, Erie, Pa., 232; St. Teresa's Home for Aged, Cincinnati, 231; Diocesan Homes for Aged, 232; Homes for Aged of Various Nationalities, 229
Homes, Convalescent and Fresh-Air, 206-208, 247-249; Brice Home, Philadelphia, 248; Greylock, Adams, Mass., 207; St. Elizabeth Convalescent Home, Spring Valley, N. Y., 207, 247; St. Francis Country Home for Convalescents, Darby, Pa., 207
Homestead Act, 43, 63

Hope Haven, 125
Hospitals, Catholic, after Civil War, 195; evolution of, 204; rapid rise of since 1870, 201, 202; social service programs, 204, 205; place in diocesan programs of Catholic Charities, 448; conducted by German sisterhoods, 200; industrial, 198, 199; for Italians, 200, 201; Bellevue, N. Y. C., 189; Charity Hospital, Galveston, 405; De Paul Hospital, St. Louis, 184; Douglas Military Hospital, Washington, D. C., 194; Mercy Hospital, Davenport, 196; Mercy Hospital, Pittsburgh, 185, 186; Mullanphy Hospital, St. Louis, 183; Providence Hospital, Washington, D. C., 194; St. Elizabeth Hospital, La Fayette, Ind., 402; St. Francis Hospital, N. Y. C., 195; St. John's Hospital, Helena, Mont., 198; St. John's Hospital, Springfield, Ill., 401; St. Joseph's Hospital, Philadelphia, 187; St. Joseph's Hospital, St. Paul, 87, 382; St. Mary's Infirmary, Cairo, Ill., 195; St. Mary's Hospital, Cincinnati, 391; St. Mary's Hospital, Detroit, 184; St. Mary's Hospital, Philadelphia, 192; St. Mary's Hospital, Rochester, Minn., 199; St. Mary's Hospital, Rochester, N. Y., 184, 185; St. Mary's Infirmary, St. Louis, 363; St. Vincent's Charity Hospital, Cleveland, 195; Santa Rosa Infirmary, San Antonio, 405; Wheeling Hospital, Wheeling, W. Va., 382
Hospitals for Incurables, 210, 211; for insane, mental and nervous cases, 208, 209; for tubercular cases, 209, 210

House of the Angel Guardian, Boston, 110
House of Divine Providence, N. Y. C., 229
House of the Holy Angels, N. Y. C., 112
House of the Holy Family, N. Y. C., 181, 182
House of Industry, Boston, 213
House of Mercy, San Francisco, 181
House of Refuge, N. Y. C., 108
Hoxsey, Miss Mary I., 322
Huber, Miss Alice, 364
Hughes, Archbishop John, 22, 57, 61, 63, 164, 171, 323, 380
Hunt, Mrs. Anne Lucas, 170
Huntington, Joshua, 262
Hurley, Rev. Michael, 21
Hurley, Judge Timothy D., 253, 423
Hussey, E. J., 241, 246
Hynes, Thomas, 65, 244

Immigrant, Irish Aid Conference, Buffalo, 54, 55; Bureau, Castle Garden, 68; Insurance Association, 277, 278
Immigrants, contribution of, to American industry, 279; Irish as industrial workers, 52; opposition to, 283-286; problems of, 281, 282; public aid for, 47, 48
Immigration, old, 34-49; new, 272-286; Board of Commissioners of N. Y., 46; effect of new, on Catholic Church, 276, 277; German, 2, 42, 46; Irish, 2, 37-40, 44, 45; issues of old and new, 34; regulation of, 48, 49; restriction of, 284-286; from southern and eastern Europe, 273-275
Incurables (see Hospitals for Incurables)
Indenture, 93, 372
Industrial Hospitals, 198, 199
Industrial Institutions, 106-128, 396; of Brothers and Sis-

ters of the Holy Cross, 384, 385; Fr. Dunne's Newsboys Home, St. Louis, 128; Hope Haven, 125; House of the Angel Guardian, Boston, 110; House of the Holy Angels, 112; House of Refuge, N. Y. C., 108; Industrial School for Boys, Indiaapolis, 125; Industrial School for Boys, Milwaukee, 125; Lincolndale Agricultural School for Boys, 116; Mission of the Immaculate Virgin, 123, 244; New York Catholic Protectory, 78, 112-117; St. Anthony's Home for Boys, Cleveland, 128; St. Charles Industrial School, Wauwatosa, Wis., 385; St. Hedwig's Industrial School, Niles, Ill., 158; St. James' Home, Baltimore, 120; St. John's Protectory. Buffalo, 120, 121; St. Mary's Industrial School, Baltimore, 118-120; St. Michael's Industrial School, Hoban Heights, Pa., 125; St. Vincent's Home for Newsboys, Brooklyn, 124; St. Vincent's Home for Boys, Newark, 124; St. Vincent's Home for Destitute Boys, New Orleans, 243; St. Vincent's Newsboys Lodging Home, N. Y. C., 123; Working Boys' Home, Boston, 124

Infant and Maternity Homes, 132, 139, 140, 141; New York Foundling, N. Y. C., 132-138; St. Ann's Widows' Home, Lying-in Hospital and Foundling Asylum, St. Louis, 131 132, 135; St. Joseph's Maternity Hospital, Infant Asylum and Home for Little Children Cincinnati, 135; St. Mary's Infant Asylum and Maternity Hospital, Buffalo, 130, 131, 135

Insane, hospitals for (see Hospitals for Insane, Mental and Nervous Cases)

Institutions, American Protestant in character, 378; basis of program of child-care. 444; combination of aged and other types, 230, 231; a preventative against Protestantism, 99, 100, 308; founded on racial basis, 156-162; as safeguard of religious life of children, 308

Institutions, Catholic Children's. for Bohemians, 159; for French, 158; for Italians, 160; for Negroes, 161, 162; for Poles, 158, 159

Institutions, Catholic Children's. 71-88, 100, 150-155; Angel Guardian Orphan Asylum, Chicago, 398; German R. C. Orphan Asylum, Buffalo. 82; Holy Family Orphan Asylum, Pittsburgh, 158; McMahon Memorial Shelter for Children, N. Y. C., 321; Mission of the Immaculate Virgin, S. I., 123, 244; Our Lady of Victory Institute, Lackawanna, N. Y., 74, 121; Parmadale, Cleveland, 388; Roman Catholic Orphan Asylum, N. Y. C., 23, 24, 156; Roman Catholic Orphan Asylum, San Francisco, 75; St. Aemilian's Orphan Asylum, Milwaukee, 86; St. Aloysius Orphan Asylum, Cincinnati, 80; St. Anthony's German Catholic Orphanage, Baltimore, 82; St. Charles Home. Port Jefferson, L. I., 412; St. James' Orphanage, Omaha, 90; St. John's Orphan Asylum, N. Y. C., 323; St. John's Orphanage, Philadelphia, 22, 382; St. Joseph's Asylum, Buffalo,

74, 121; St. Joseph's Asylum, Chicago, 86; St. Joseph's Bohemian Orphanage, Lisle, Ill., 159; St. Joseph's Orphanage, Louisville, 81; St. Joseph's Orphan Asylum, Milwaukee, 86; St. Joseph's German Orphan Asylum, N. Y. C., 82; St. Joseph's Orphanage, Philadelphia, 21, 22; St. Joseph's German Orphan Asylum, Pittsburgh, 82; St. Joseph's Orphan Asylum, St. Louis, 382; St. Joseph's Orphanage, San Antonio, 405; St. Joseph's Orphan Asylum, Washington, D. C., 75; St. Mary's Orphan Asylum, Baltimore, 24; St. Mary's Asylum, Chicago, 85; St. Mary's Orphan Asylum, Cleveland, 86; St. Matthew's Orphan Asylum, Washington, D. C., 75; St. Joseph's Bohemian Orphanage, Lisle, Ill., 159; St. Patrick's Orphanage, Baltimore, 109; St. Patrick's Orphan Asylum, Rochester, N. Y., 87; St. Patrick's Orphanage, Scranton, 90; St. Paul's Orphan Asylum, Pittsburgh, 76, 77; St. Peter's Orphan Asylum and Free School, Cincinnati, 28, 80; St. Rose's Orphan Asylum, Milwaukee, 86; St. Stanislaus' Orphanage, Nanticoke, Pa., 159; St. Vincent's Orphan Asylum, Boston, 30, 87; St. Vincent's Orphan Asylum, Buffalo, 74; St. Vincent's Orphan Asylum, Cleveland, 86; St. Vincent's Orphanage, Columbus, 90; St. Vincent's Orphan Asylum, Louisville, 32; St. Vincent's Orphan Asylum, Philadelphia, 82; St. Vincent's Orphan Asylum, St. Louis, 81; St. Vincent's Home for Boys, San Francisco, 75; St. Vincent's School and Orphan Asylum, Washington, D. C., 24, 75; St. Vincent's Orphanage, Toledo, 158

Insurance, Immigrant, Association, 277, 278
Ireland, Archbishop John, 64-6, 199
Irish, care of orphans, 77, 78; as industrial workers, 52; in canal building, 43, 44, 51 (see also Immigrants and Immigration)
Irish Catholic Benevolent Union, 91
Irish Immigration Society, Minnesota, 63-65
Italian, children's institutions, 159, 160; hospitals, 200, 201
Ives, Dr. Levi S., 111, 112, 114, 116, 120, 250

Jankola, Rev. Matthew, 368
Jenkins, Mr. and Mrs. Geo. W., 410
Jesuits, in Louisiana, 18; in Maryland, 9; in St. Louis, 26
Jolly, Ellen Ryan, 193
Joubert, Rev. J. H., 17, 346
Judge, Rev. Thomas A., 356
Justina, Sr., 289
Juvenile Courts, 253, 254, 422, 423, 427
Juvenile Delinquency, among immigrants' children, 283; a preventive program for, 127 (see also Delinquents, institutions for)

Katzer, Archbishop Frederick X., 411
Keating Day Nursery, N. Y. C., 313
Kelly, Miss Elizabeth, 229
Kenrick, Archbishop Peter R., 81, 131, 170, 171, 220
Kenrick, Rt. Rev. Francis P., 170, 191
Kentucky, early Catholic settlements, 58, 88

Kerby, Rev. Dr. Wm. J., 266, 430, 431
Knights of Columbus, 125, 278, 300
Knights of Labor, 284
Know-Nothing Movement, 35, 56, 241, 284
Kulturkampf, 200, 362, 398, 401, 402

Ladies of Charity, 23, 264, 319, 321, 322
Lafon Asylum, New Orleans, 216
Land, free in the U. S., 50, 58, 69, 272
Lange, Elizabeth, 17
Lathrop, Rose Hawthorne, 364
Lavelle, Msgr., 313
Lawler, John, 67
Lawler, Miss, 7
Lay activities, 91, 235-271, 290-303, 318-342, 417 (see also Organizations)
Lazarists, 25, 130
Leagues of Catholic Women (see Organizations of Women)
LeBlond, Rev. C. Hubert, 439
Le Couteulx Institution for Deaf, 382
Le Couteulx, Louis, 130, 382
Lefevre, Bishop, 347
Lelievre, Abbe Ernest, 218, 219, 224
Leo House, N. Y. C., 354
Leonard, Rev. Edwin L., 439
Leopoldine Society, 353, 377, 416
Le Petit, Father, 18, 19
Letchworth, Commissioner Wm. P., 98, 99, 133
Lincolndale Agricultural School for Boys, 116
Little Sisters of the Poor, 216-228, 379, 403, 404
Logan, Lieutenant Governor, 2
Loras, Bishop Mathias, 61, 345
Loretto Rest, Syracuse, 232, 233
Loretto, Sisters of, 12-14, 16, 166
Loughlin, Bishop John, 218

Loyola University, training for social work, 340, 434
Luers, Bishop, 398
Lynch, James, 244, 246

McCarty, Rev. Ed. W., 328
McCauley, Mother Catherine, 164, 379, 380
McCloskey, Archbishop and later Cardinal, 69, 113, 123, 124
McCormick Memorial Home, Green Bay, Wis., 233
McFaul, Bishop James A., 313
McGee, D'Arcy, 54, 55, 57, 58
McGuire, Captain, 59
McGuire, Rev. Joseph L., 247
McMahon, Rev. Dr. D. J., 264, 313, 320, 427-429
McMahon Memorial Shelter for Children, N. Y. C., 321
McNicholas, Rev. John, O.P., 365
McTavish, Mrs. Emily, 119, 172, 323

Madonna Center, Chicago, 298
Magdalens, 171, 172, 174, 178
Marechal, Archbishop, 24
Marillac, Mo., 11
Maryknoll, 365 (see Sisters, Foreign Mission of St. Dominic)
Maryland, early Catholic settlements, 58, 88
Maryland Hospital for Insane, 208
Massachusetts, beginnings of state system of child-placing, 94; State Board of Minor Wards, 421
Matthews, Rev. William, 24, 75
Maxis, Teresa, 347
Mayo, Dr. Charles H., 199
Mayo, Dr. Wm. J., 199
Mayo, Dr. W. W., 199
Mental and Nervous Cases, institutions for (see Hospitals for)
Mercy Hospital, Davenport, 196
Mercy Hospital, Pittsburgh, 185, 186

INDEX

Mercy, Sisters of, in Baltimore, 194; Chicago, 86, 186; Davenport, 196; Dubuque, 197; New York, 168; Pittsburgh, 76, 168, 169, 185, 186; San Francisco, 186, 187, Washington, D. C., 193 (see also Sisters of Mercy)
Mercy, Sisters of Our Lady of, 32, 192
Merrick House, Cleveland, 315, 316
Merrick, Miss Mary V., 295, 324
Mexican, settlements for, 301
Meyers, Rev. James, 323
Miege, Bishop, 350
Miles, Bishop Richard P., 349
Minnesota Irish Immigration Society, 63-65
Mission of the Immaculate Virgin, 123, 244
Mitchel, Mrs. Judy, 196
Mitchell, Doctor, Hospital, 197
Monaghan, Rev. Hugh, 321
Monson Almshouse, 93, 94
Montreal, the Ursulines in, 8
Moreau, Father, 384
Mt. Hope Retreat, Baltimore, 208
Mt. St. Mary's Training School, Cincinnati, 176, 177
Muehlsiepen, Vicar-General, 362
Mueller-Simonis, Msgr., 327
Mullanphy, Bryan, 239
Mullanphy Fund, 239
Mullanphy Hospital, St. Louis, 183
Mullanphy, John, 26, 30, 131, 239, 240
Mullen, Catherine, 9
Mullen, John K., 226
Mulry, Thomas M., 248, 252, 255, 256, 436
Mundelein, Cardinal, 439
Murphy, Maria, 9

National Catholic School of Social Service, 340-342
National Catholic War Council, 296, 300, 301, 341
National Catholic Welfare Conference, 330, 337, 338, 341
National Catholic Woman's League, 327
National Catholic Women's Union, 334
National Conference of Catholic Charities, 263-266, 331, 428-433, 447
National Conference of Social Work, 430
National Council of Catholic Women, 336-341
Native-American movement, 35, 36
Neale, Rev. Leonard, 7
Neill, Dr. Charles P., 430
Nerinckx, Father, 12, 13, 14, 16
Nervous and Mental Cases, hospitals for (see Hospitals for)
Neumann, Bishop, 78, 350, 353
New York Catholic Benevolent Society, 23, 24, 156
New York Catholic Protectory, 78, 112-117
New York Children's Aid Society, 99, 371, 372
New York Foundling Hospital, 132-138
New York, Society for the Protection of Destitute Catholic Children, 112
Nightingale, Florence, 190
Nilan, Bishop John, 422
Notre Dame University, 108
Nugent, Father, 68
Nursing, schools of, 202; standards of, 203; value of, done by Catholic sisterhoods, 193; home, 211, 212, 409-413; home, communities, 361-363; wet, 134, 135

O'Connor, Bishop James, 65, 67, 359
O'Connor, Rev. Maurice, 431
O'Connor, Bishop Michael, 164, 223, 380
O'Conway, Cecilia, 9
Odilia, Mother, 362
O'Donohue, Mrs. Joseph J., 321
O'Donohue, Miss Teresa R., 321
O'Gorman, Vicar-Apostolic, 197

O'Hara, Rt. Rev. Wm., 90, 348
Old age, problems of, 233, 234
Olier, Abbe, 6
Onahan, W. J., 67, 68
O'Neil, Gen. John, 65
O'Reilly, Rev. Bernard, 71
O'Reilly, Rev. John, 76
O'Reilly, Rev. J. V., 347
Organizations, beginnings of lay, 91; parish charitable begun by women, 318
Organizations of men: Central Verein of America, 91, 333; Holy Name Society, 279; Knights of Columbus, 125, 278, 300; Society of St. Vincent de Paul, 110, 111, 123-125, 130, 134, 207, 214, 222, 224, 225, 235, 271, 279, 290, 312, 319, 320, 322-324, 326, 329, 334, 336, 393, 413, 417-419, 423-426, 428, 429, 431, 435-438, 442, 443, 446 (see also St. Vincent de Paul Society)
Organizations of women, earliest, 318, 319; first association of, 264; in coordinated program, 335; Association of Catholic Charities, N. Y. C., 320, 321; Big Sisters, 331; Catholic Daughters of America, 332; Catholic Woman's National League, 327; Catholic Women's Association, Brooklyn, 328; Catholic Woman's League, Chicago, 327, 328; Catholic Women's League, Pittsburgh, 328, 329, 331; Christ Child Society, 295, 296, 324-326; Council of Catholic Women, Denver, 302; Council of Catholic Women, Newark, 303; Council of Catholic Women, Pittsburgh, 329; Federation of German Catholic Women's Societies, 334; Guild of Catholic Women, St. Paul, 329; Ladies of Charity, 319, 321, 322; League of Catholic Women of Detroit, 329, 330; League of Catholic Women, Minneapolis, 297; National Catholic Women's Union, 334; National Council of Catholic Women, 336-341; Polish Activities League, Detroit, 297; Queen's Daughters, 322; St. Elizabeth's Union, 264, 429, 430; St. Margaret's Daughters, 322, 323; St. Paul's Catholic Guild, Brooklyn, 318; Weinman Club, Detroit, 296, 297, 330
Origins, National in 1920, 34
Orphan Asylum, a unit of parish, 72; a city-wide responsibility, 77
Orphan Asylums, development of, 72-75; German, 78-82; Irish, 77, 78 (see Institutions, Catholic Children's)
O'Toole, Rev. T., 75
Our Lady of Victory Institute, Lackawanna, N. Y., 74, 121
Ozanam Association, 255
Ozanam, Frederick, 236, 237

Palmourgnes, Father, 196
Parmadale, Cleveland, 388
Patterson, Mrs. Winifred, 170
Paulist Fathers, 218, 312
Pax, Father, 378
Payments, per capita, 103, 104
Pelletier, Mother Euphrasia, 164, 165
Penn, William, 2
Personnel, problem of in institutions for older boys, 126
Peter, Mrs. Sarah, 323, 391
Polish Activities League, Detroit, 297.
Polish, Catholic children's institutions, 158, 159
Poor Clares, 7
Population, Catholic, after the Revolution, 4; after Civil War, 89· French at time of Revolution, 3; Dutch, 3; German, 3

INDEX 469

Port Tobacco, Md., 6, 8
Poydras Orphan Asylum, New Orleans, 19
Preemption, right of, given settlers, 42
Prendergast, Rt. Rev. John J., 355, 409
Presentation Brothers, 76
Prevost, Father, 158
Program, coordinated, first in Baltimore, 427; first steps in, 437; based on surveys, 434, 435
Programs, educational in Good Shepherd Homes, 177, 178; health in Good Shepherd Homes, 175-177; recreational undertaken by St. Vincent de Paul Society, 254, 255
Propagation of the Faith, 377, 416
Protective work for girls, 327-331, 446, 447 (see also Good Shepherd Sisters and Mercy, Sisters of);
Protectory, Catholic, Bristol, Pa., 122; Clontarf, Minn., 122; Glencoe, Mo., 122; San Francisco, 122
Protectory, New York Catholic, 78, 112-117
Protectory, St. John's, Buffalo, 120, 121
Providence Hospital, Washington, D. C., 194

Quakers, 2
Quarter, Bishop William, 186, 377, 380
Quarterly, St. Vincent de Paul, 265, 267
Queen's Daughters, 322
Quigley, Archbishop J. E., 367

Rappe, Bishop Amadeus, 86, 195, 222, 347
Redemptorist Fathers, 346, 347
Reformation, effects of, on English Catholic beneficence, 1
Rehrl, Rev. Caspar, 353

Religion, recognition of, in child-care programs, 148, 149, 152, 153; as a reformative influence, 175
Renauld, Theresa, 347
Rese, Bishop Frederick, 28
Review, Catholic Charities, 267
Revival, Catholic in France and Germany, fruits of, 370
Revolution, French, 5, 14, 409
Rhodes, Mary, 12, 13
Riordan, Rev. J. J., 69
Roman Catholic Orphan Asylum, N. Y. C., 23, 24, 156
Roman Catholic Orphan Asylum, San Francisco, 75
Roosevelt, President, 268
Rosati, Rev. Joseph, later Bishop, 25, 26, 183
Rousselon, Father, 346
Rudolf, Rev. Joseph, 386
Ryan, Archbishop Patrick J., 122, 359
Ryan, Bishop Stephen V., 67

Sacred Heart, Brothers of, 396
Sacred Heart, Religious of the, St. Louis, 26
St. Aemilian's Orphan Asylum, Milwaukee, 86
St. Aloysius' Orphan Society, Cincinnati, 80
St. Ann's Day Nursery, Pittsburgh, 314
St. Ann's Widows' Home, Lying-in Hospital and Foundling Asylum, St. Louis, 131, 132, 135
St. Anthony's Home, Cleveland, 128
St. Anthony's German Catholic Orphanage, Baltimore, 82
St. Boniface's Beneficial Society, 236
St. Charles' Home, Point Jefferson, L. I., 412
St. Charles' Industrial School, Wauwatosa, Wis., 385
St. Elizabeth's Community House, Detroit, 297
St. Elizabeth's Day Nursery, Chicago, 312

St. Elizabeth's Hospital, La Fayette, Ind., 402
St. Elizabeth's Union, 264, 429, 430
St. Francis' Hospital, N. Y. C., 195
St. Hedwig's Industrial School, Niles, Ill., 158
St. James' Home, Baltimore, 120
St. James' Day Nursery, Trenton, 313
St. James' Orphanage, Omaha, 90
St. John's Female Benevolent School, Frederick, Md., 24
St. John's Hospital, Helena, Mont., 198
St. John's Hospital, Springfield, Ill., 401
St. John's Orphan Asylum, N. Y., 323
St. John's Orphanage, Philadelphia, 22, 382
St. John's Protectory, Buffalo, 120
St. Joseph's Asylum, Buffalo, 74, 121
St. Joseph's Asylum, Chicago, 86
St. Joseph, Brothers of, 108
St. Joseph's Day Nursery, N. Y. C., 312
St. Joseph's Hospital, Philadelphia, 187
St. Joseph Hospital, St. Paul, 87, 382
St. Joseph's Maternity Hospital, Infant Asylum and Home for Little Children, Cincinnati, 135
St. Joseph's Orphanage, Louisville, 81
St. Joseph's Orphan Asylum, Milwaukee, 86
St. Joseph's German Orphan Asylum, N. Y. C., 82
St. Joseph's Orphanage, Philadelphia, 21, 22
St. Joseph's German Orphan Asylum, Pittsburgh, 82
St. Joseph's Orphan Asylum, St. Louis, 382

St. Joseph's Orphanage, San Antonio, 405
St. Joseph's Orphan Asylum, Washington, D. C., 75
St. Joseph's Society, Philadelphia, 21
St. Joseph's German R. C. Orphan Society, Louisville, 81
St. Margaret's Daughters, 322, 323
St. Mary's Hospital, Cincinnati 391
St. Mary's Hospital, Detroit, 184
St. Mary's Hospital, Philadelphia, 192
St. Mary's Hospital, Rochester, Minn., 199
St. Mary's Hospital, Rochester, N. Y., 184, 185
St. Mary's Infirmary, Cairo, Ill., 195
St. Mary's Infirmary, St. Louis, 363
St. Mary's Industrial School, Baltimore, 118-120
St. Mary's Infant Asylum and Maternity Hospital, Buffalo, 130, 131, 135
St. Mary's Orphan Asylum, Baltimore, 24
St. Mary's Asylum, Chicago, 85
St. Mary's Orphan Asylum, Cleveland, 86
St. Mary's Seminary, Baltimore, 9, 220
St. Matthew's Orphan Asylum, Washington, D. C., 75
St. Michael's Industrial School, Hoban Heights, Pa., 125
St. Pascal's Day Nursery, N. Y. C., 313
St. Patrick, Brothers of, 109
St. Patrick's Church, Washington, D. C., 75, 222, 318
St. Patrick's Orphanage, Baltimore, 109
St. Patrick's Orphan Asylum, Rochester, N. Y., 87
St. Patrick's Orphanage, Scranton, 90

INDEX 471

St. Patrick's Society, Chicago, 67, 236
St. Paul's Catholic Guild, Brooklyn, 318
St. Paul's Orphan Asylum, Pittsburgh, 76, 77
St. Paul's R. C. Orphan Society, Pittsburgh, 76
St. Peter's Benevolent Society, Cincinnati, 28
St. Peter's Orphan Asylum and Free School, Cincinnati, 28, 80
St. Raphael's Home, Pittsburgh, 314
St. Rose's Convent, Springfield, Ky., 16
St. Rose's Orphan Asylum, Milwaukee, 86
St. Rose's Settlement, N. Y. C., 290-292
St. Stanislaus' Orphanage, Nanticoke, Pa., 159
St. Thomas' Seminary, 15
St. Vincent's Charity Hospital, Cleveland, 195
St. Vincent's German Orphan Society, St. Louis, 81
St. Vincent's Home for Boys, Newark, 124
St. Vincent's Home for Destitute Boys, New Orleans, 243
St. Vincent's Home for Newsboys, Brooklyn, 124
St. Vincent's Newsboys' Lodging Home, N. Y. C., 123
St. Vincent's Orphan Asylum, Boston, 30, 87
St. Vincent's Orphan Asylum, Buffalo, 74
St. Vincent's Orphan Asylum, Cleveland, 86
St. Vincent's Orphanage, Columbus, 90
St. Vincent's Orphan Asylum, Louisville, 32
St. Vincent's Orphan Asylum, Philadelphia, 82
St. Vincent's Orphan Asylum, St. Louis, 81
St. Vincent's Home for Boys, San Francisco, 75
St. Vincent's Orphanage, Toledo, 158
St. Vincent's School and Orphan Asylum, Washington, D. C., 24, 75
St. Vincent's Sanitarium, Santa Fe, 209
St. Vincent de Paul Quarterly, 265, 267
St. Vincent de Paul Society, 235-271; adjustment to central diocesan agencies, 259; central office in Baltimore, 258, 259; child-caring department of Detroit, 253, 419, 420, 443; relation to Charity Organization Society, 255-257; first conference, St. Louis, 239; an evaluation of, 269-271; in fresh-air work, 247-249; interest in destitute Catholic immigrant children, 243, 244; interest in Juvenile Courts, 253, 254; organization of, in U. S., 260-263; adverse to paid service, 258; in public institutions, 244-246; recreational programs, 254, 255; interest in seamen, 249; industrial schools, 243; progress in U. S., 240, 241; first projects, 241, 242
San Marino, Brotherhood of, 32
Sansbury, Sr. Angela, 16
Santa Bambino Day Nursery, Cincinnati, 314
Santa Maria Institute, Cincinnati, 289, 290, 314
Santa Rosa Infirmary, San Antonio, 405
Schaaf, Charlotte Ann, 347
Schervier, Mother Frances, 390
Schindel, Father, 399
Schools, Poor, 310
Schools, state for children, 97; of social service, 340, 341
Schrembs, Bishop, 338, 414
Scutari, 190
Seton, Mother, 8-12

Settlements, 287-307; first Catholic, 289, 290; movement, 287, 288, 292, 293, 296, 299, 303, 307; Amberg Club, Kansas City, 301, 302; Margaret Barry Settlement, Minneapolis, 297; Brownson House, Los Angeles, 293, 294; Catholic Community House, Baltimore, 300, 301; Catholic Community House, Cincinnati, 300, 301; Catholic Neighborhood House, Newark, 302, 303; Charles House, Rochester, N. Y., 299; Christ Child Society Settlements, 295, 296; Council of Catholic Women, Denver, 302; Council of Catholic Women, Newark, 303; Diocesan Settlements of Los Angeles, 294; Gary-Alerding Settlement, Gary, Ind., 302, 303; Genesee Institute, Rochester, N. Y., 299; Helpers of the Holy Souls, 305, 411; League of Catholic Women, Detroit, 297, 330; League of Catholic Women, Minneapolis, 297; Madonna Center, Chicago, 298; Merrick House, Cleveland, 295, 296; Polish Activities League, Detroit, 297; St. Elizabeth's Community House, Detroit, 297; St. Rose's Settlement, N. Y. C., 290-292; Santa Maria Institute, Cincinnati, 289-290, 314; Servants of the Immaculate Heart of Mary, 304; Sisters, Missionary of the Most Blessed Trinity, 299, 306; Weinman Settlement, Detroit, 296, 297, 330; Dr. White Memorial Settlement, Brooklyn, 306, 357, 428

Shahan, Bishop Thomas J., 265, 266, 430, 431

Shanahan, Bishop J. W., 367
Shields, General, 63
Siedliska, Frances, 407
Sigstein, Rev. J. J., 358
Sisterhoods, Catholic, in Civil War, 190, 193; in epidemics, 190-192; colored, 16, 17, 161; German in hospital field, 200; of American origin, 343-368; of European origin, 369-415; Sisters of St. Agnes, 353, 354; Benedictine Sisters, 210, 387, 388; Sisters of the Blessed Sacrament, 161, 359, 360; Sisters of Bon Secours, 211, 409, 410; Carmelites, 6, 7, 8; Carmelites of Corpus Christi, 414; Carmelites of the Divine Heart of Jesus, 413, 414; Sisters of St. Casimir, 367; Sisters of SS. Cyril and Methodius, 367, 368; Sisters of Charity of Convent Station, N. J., 11; Sisters of Charity of Emmitsburg, 8, 11, 14, 19-22, 25, 30, 31, 83, 84, 183, 185, 188, 191, 198, 208, 304, 382, 395 (see also Charity, Sisters of); Sisters of Charity of Greensburg, Pa., 12; Sisters of Charity of Halifax, Nova Scotia, 12; Sisters of Charity of Leavenworth, 11, 197, 198; Sisters of Charity of Mt. St. Joseph-on-the-Ohio, 11, 192, 209, 289, 303, 304; Sisters of Charity of Mt. St. Vincent-on-the-Hudson, 11, 192, 210, 229; Sisters of Charity of the Blessed Virgin Mary, 344, 345; Sisters of Charity of the Incarnate Word, 198, 405, 406; Sisters of Charity of Leavenworth, 349, 350; Sisters of Charity of Nazareth, 14-16, 31, 32, 192, 349; Sisters of Charity of

Providence, 393, 394; Sisters of Charity of St. Augustine, 195, 388; Daughters of the Holy Ghost, 413; Daughters of Wisdom, 249, 412; Sisters of Divine Compassion, 181; Sisters of the Divine Saviour, 411; Sisters of St. Dominic, 15, 16, 192, 211; Dominican Sisters of St. Catherine Di Ricci, 366; Dominican Sisters of St. Rose of Lima, 211, 364, 365; Dominican Sisters of the Sick Poor, 363, 364; Foreign Mission Sisters of St. Dominic, 365; Felician Sisters, 406, 407; Sisters of St. Francis, 82, 199, 210; Franciscan Sisters of Buffalo, 352; Franciscan Sisters of Glen Riddle, 350-352; Franciscan Sisters of Syracuse, 353; Franciscan Sisters of the Atonement, 304, 366; Sisters of the Third Order of St. Francis, 192, 217; Missionary Sisters of the Third Order of St. Francis, 408; Sisters of the Third Order of St. Francis of the Holy Family, 399-401; Hospital Sisters of St. Francis of Peoria, 210, 400; Hospital Sisters of St. Francis of Springfield, 210, 401; Franciscan Sisters of St. Kunegunda, 299; Franciscan Sisters of Baltimore City, 161; Franciscan Sisters of Oldenburg, 386; Franciscan Sisters of Perpetual Adoration, 353; Sisters of the Poor of St. Francis, 192, 193, 195, 210, 211, 323, 389-391; Poor Sisters of St. Francis Seraph of Perpetual Adoration, 401, 402; Franciscan Sisters of the Sacred Heart, 402; Franciscan Sisters, Daughters of the Sacred Hearts of Jesus and Mary, 399; Grey Nuns, 158, 211, 392, 393; Grey Nuns of the Cross, 393; Grey Nuns of the Sacred Heart, 393; Handmaids of the Most Pure Heart of Mary, 358, 359; Helpers of the Holy Souls, 305, 411; Sisters of the Holy Cross, 108, 192, 193, 195, 210, 383-385; Sisters, Marianites of the Holy Cross, 19, 383 3,86; Sisters of the Holy Family of Nazareth, 407; Sisters of the Holy Family, New Orleans, 161, 216, 345; Sisters of the Holy Family, San Francisco, 305, 355, 356; Sisters of the Holy Names of Jesus and Mary, 395; Sisters, Servants of the Immaculate Heart of Mary, 346, 347; Sisters of the Infant Jesus, 413; Sisters of St. Joseph, 121, 210, 382, 383 (see also Carondelet, Sisters of St. Joseph of,); Sisters of the Little Company of Mary, 411; Little Sisters of the Assumption, 410; Little Sisters of the Poor, 216-228, 379, 403, 404; Sisters of Loretto, 12-14, 16, 166; Sisters of St. Mary, 210, 362, 363; Sisters of Mercy, 164, 167, 168, 169, 181, 185, 186, 210, 229, 328, 366, 380, 381 (see also Mercy, Sisters of); Sisters of Our Lady of Mercy, 32, 192; Sisters of Misericorde, 403; Mission Helpers, Servants of the Sacred Heart, 313, 360, 361; Missionary Servants of the Blessed Trinity, 299, 306, 356; Missionary Sisters, Servants of the Holy Ghost,

412; Missionary Sisters of the Sacred Heart, 159, 200, 408; Sisters of Notre Dame, 82; Sisters of Notre Dame of Cleveland, 80; School Sisters of Notre Dame, 82; Oblate Sisters of Providence, 17, 161, 345; Sisters of Our Lady of Charity of the Good Shepherd, 164, 165, 389, 390 (see also Good Shepherd Sisters); Sisters of Our Lady of Charity of Refuge, 164, 173, 174, 389 (see also Good Shepherd Sisters); Sisters of Our Lady of Mt. Carmel, 192; Parish Visitors of Immaculate Heart of Mary, 357, 358; Poor Clares, 7; Poor Handmaids of Jesus Christ, 398; Sisters of Precious Blood, 387; Sisters of the Presentation of the Blessed Virgin Mary, 388; Sisters of Providence, 193, 386; Servants of the Holy Ghost, 161; Ladies of the Sacred Heart, 26, 220; Social Mission Sisters, 414, 415; Society of Missionary Catechists, 303, 306, 358; Sisters of the Sorrowful Mother, 210; Sisters of St. Ursula, 193, 347; Visitandines, 7, 8; White Sisters, 322

Smet, Eugenie, 411
Smith, Rev. Anthony, C.SS.R., 82
Society, of the Angel Guardian, Boston, 110; Boys' Lodging House and Children's Aid, Newark, 124; Catholic Visitation and Aid, Chicago, 253; Charity Organization, N. Y., 255-257, 287, 288, 425, 426, 435, 437; early German Benevolent, 333; German R. C. School, Philadelphia, 82; German St. Vincent's Orphan, St. Louis, 81; Holy Name, 279; Irish Immigrant, N. Y., 59; Minnesota Irish Immigration, 63, 64, 65; New York Catholic Benevolent, 23, 24, 156; New York Children's Aid, 99, 371, 372; for Protection of Destitute R. C. Children of City of Buffalo, 120; for Protection of Destitute Catholic Children of N. Y., 112; St. Aloysius' Orphan, Cincinnati, 80; St. Boniface's Beneficial, 236; St. Joseph's German R. C. Orphan, Louisville, 81; St. Joseph's, Philadelphia, 21; St. Patrick's, Chicago, 67, 236; St. Paul's R. C. Orphan, Pittsburgh, 76; St. Peter's Benevolent, Cincinnati, 28; St. Vincent's German Orphan, St. Louis, 81
Sorbonne, 236
Sorin, Rev. Edward, 384
Spalding, Mother Catherine, 31
Spalding, Bishop J. L., 66, 67, 400
Spalding, Archbishop M. J., 77, 111, 117, 118, 397
Spring Valley, N. Y., Fresh-Air Home, 207, 247
Staniukynas, Rev. Anthony, 367
Starrs, Rev. Wm., 242
State Board of Minor Wards, Mass., 421
Stuart, Christine, 13
Sulpicians, 6, 17, 25, 83, 249, 370
Sweetman, John, 66

Taft, President, 285
Tallon, Julia Teresa, 357
Teresa, Mother, 347
Tiers, Cornelius, 21
Timon, Bishop John 73, 74, 86, 120, 129, 130, 352, 377, 378, 382, 389

INDEX 475

Training for social work, 340, 341, 434
Travelers' Aid, 239, 327
Trecy, Father, 60-62
Truant Act, 375
Tuberculosis, hospitals for, (see Hospitals for,)

Union, Catholic Slovak of America, 368
Union, St. Elizabeth's, 264, 429, 430
Union, St. Joseph's, N. Y. C., 123
United States, Children's Bureau, 269
University, Catholic, 341, 430, 434
University, Fordham, N. Y., 340
University, Loyola, Chicago, 340, 434
University, Notre Dame, 108
Ursulines, 8, 18, 19, 183, 347, 191

Vincentians, the backbone of National Conference of Catholic Charities, 266; part in formulating standards of American philanthropy, 267, 268 (see also St. Vincent de Paul Society and Organizations of Men)
Victory, Lady of, Charities, 121
Visitation Convent, Georgetown, 6-8

Visiting agency, created by State Board of Charities, Mass., 94

Wadhams, Bishop, 242
Waggaman, Thomas E., 246
Wahrheitsfreund, 80
Waldo, Miss Evelyn A., 323
Walter, Rev. J. A., 222, 320
Ward's Island, 47
Wardner, Dr. Horace, 195
Wastl, Msgr. Francis X., 207
Weinman, Ferdinand, S.J., 297
Weinman Settlement, Detroit, 296, 297, 330
Westchester, the N. Y. Catholic Protectory at, 113, 117
Wheeling Hospital, 382
White, Mrs. Rose, 9
White, Rev. Dr. Wm. J., 306, 427
White Memorial Settlement, Brooklyn, 306, 357, 428
Williams, Archbishop John J., 67, 172, 420
Wilson, Rev. Thomas, O. P., 16
Wilson, President, 285
Women, (see Organizations of Women)
Working Boys' Home, Boston, 124 (see Industrial Institutions)
Workman, Miss Mary J., 293
Wynhoven, Rev. Peter, 125

Xaverian Brothers, 109, 118, 397
Xavier, Mother, 349, 350

POVERTY, U. S. A.

THE HISTORICAL RECORD

An Arno Press/New York Times Collection

Adams, Grace. **Workers on Relief.** 1939.

The Almshouse Experience: Collected Reports. 1821-1827.

Armstrong, Louise V. **We Too Are The People.** 1938.

Bloodworth, Jessie A. and Elizabeth J. Greenwood.
The Personal Side. 1939.

Brunner, Edmund de S. and Irving Lorge.
Rural Trends in Depression Years: A Survey of Village-Centered Agricultural Communities, 1930-1936. 1937.

Calkins, Raymond.
Substitutes for the Saloon: An Investigation Originally made for The Committee of Fifty. 1919.

Cavan, Ruth Shonle and Katherine Howland Ranck.
The Family and the Depression: A Study of One Hundred Chicago Families. 1938.

Chapin, Robert Coit.
The Standard of Living Among Workingmen's Families in New York City. 1909.

The Charitable Impulse in Eighteenth Century America: Collected Papers. 1711-1797.

Children's Aid Society.
Children's Aid Society Annual Reports, 1-10.
February 1854-February 1863.

Conference on the Care of Dependent Children.
Proceedings of the Conference on the Care of Dependent Children. 1909.

Conyngton, Mary.
How to Help: A Manual of Practical Charity. 1909.

Devine, Edward T. **Misery and its Causes.** 1909.

Devine, Edward T. **Principles of Relief.** 1904.

Dix, Dorothea L.
On Behalf of the Insane Poor: Selected Reports. 1843-1852.

Douglas, Paul H.
Social Security in the United States: An Analysis and Appraisal of the Federal Social Security Act. 1936.

Farm Tenancy: Black and White. Two Reports. 1935, 1937.

Feder, Leah Hannah.
Unemployment Relief in Periods of Depression: A Study of Measures Adopted in Certain American Cities, 1857 through 1922. 1936.

Folks, Homer.
The Care of Destitute, Neglected, and Delinquent Children. 1900.

Guardians of the Poor.
A Compilation of the Poor Laws of the State of Pennsylvania from the Year 1700 to 1788, Inclusive. 1788.

Hart, Hastings, H.
Preventive Treatment of Neglected Children.
(Correction and Prevention, Vol. 4) 1910.

Herring, Harriet L.
Welfare Work in Mill Villages: The Story of Extra-Mill Activities in North Carolina. 1929.

The Jacksonians on the Poor: Collected Pamphlets. 1822-1844.

Karpf, Maurice J.
Jewish Community Organization in the United States. 1938.

Kellor, Frances A.
Out of Work: A Study of Unemployment. 1915.

Kirkpatrick, Ellis Lore.
The Farmer's Standard of Living. 1929.

Komarovsky, Mirra.
The Unemployed Man and His Family: The Effect of Unemployment Upon the Status of the Man in Fifty-Nine Families. 1940.

Leupp, Francis E. **The Indian and His Problem.** 1910.

Lowell, Josephine Shaw.
Public Relief and Private Charity. 1884.

More, Louise Bolard.
Wage Earners' Budgets: A Study of Standards and Cost of Living in New York City. 1907.

New York Association for Improving the Condition of the Poor.
AICP First Annual Reports Investigating Poverty. 1845-1853.

O'Grady, John.
Catholic Charities in the United States: History and Problems. 1930.

Raper, Arthur F.
Preface to Peasantry: A Tale of Two Black Belt Counties. 1936.

Raper, Arthur F. **Tenants of The Almighty.** 1943.

Richmond, Mary E.
What is Social Case Work? An Introductory Description. 1922.

Riis, Jacob A. **The Children of the Poor.** 1892.

Rural Poor in the Great Depression: Three Studies. 1938.

Sedgwick, Theodore.
Public and Private Economy: Part I. 1836.

Smith, Reginald Heber. **Justice and the Poor.** 1919.

Sutherland, Edwin H. and Harvey J. Locke.
Twenty Thousand Homeless Men: A Study of Unemployed Men in the Chicago Shelters. 1936.

Tuckerman, Joseph.
On the Elevation of the Poor: A Selection From His Reports as Minister at Large in Boston. 1874.

Warner, Amos G. **American Charities.** 1894.

Watson, Frank Dekker.
The Charity Organization Movement in the United States: A Study in American Philanthropy. 1922.

Woods, Robert A., et al. **The Poor in Great Cities.** 1895.

HV91.043 1971
Catholic charities in the United States

CIRCULATING BOOK
NOT WITHDRAWN

063330   O'GRAD'

CATHOLIC CHARITIES

**Library
Auburn Community
College**
Auburn, N. Y.